Studies in Development Strategy and Systemic Transformation

*Also by Keith Griffin*

ALTERNATIVE STRATEGIES FOR ECONOMIC DEVELOPMENT

ECONOMIC REFORM IN VIETNAM (*editor*)

FINANCING DEVELOPMENT IN LATIN AMERICA (*editor*)

GLOBALIZATION AND THE DEVELOPING WORLD (*with Azizur Rahman Khan*)

GROWTH AND EQUALITY IN RURAL CHINA (*with Ashwani Saith*)

GROWTH AND INEQUALITY IN PAKISTAN (*editor with Azizur Rahman Khan*)

HUMAN DEVELOPMENT AND THE INTERNATIONAL DEVELOPMENT
STRATEGY FOR THE 1990s (*editor with John Knight*)

IMPLEMENTING A HUMAN DEVELOPMENT STRATEGY (*with Terry McKinley*)

INSTITUTIONAL REFORM AND ECONOMIC DEVELOPMENT IN THE
CHINESE COUNTRYSIDE (*editor*)

INTERNATIONAL INEQUALITY AND NATIONAL POVERTY

LAND CONCENTRATION AND RURAL POVERTY

PLANNING DEVELOPMENT (*with John Enos*)

POLITICAL ECONOMY OF AGRARIAN CHANGE

POVERTY AND LANDLESSNESS IN RURAL ASIA (*editor with Azizur Rahman
Khan*)

POVERTY AND THE TRANSITION TO A MARKET ECONOMY IN MONGOLIA
(*editor*)

SOCIAL POLICY AND ECONOMIC TRANSFORMATION IN UZBEKISTAN
(*editor*)

STUDIES IN GLOBALIZATION AND ECONOMIC TRANSITIONS

THE DISTRIBUTION OF INCOME IN CHINA (*editor with Zhao Renwei*)

THE ECONOMIC DEVELOPMENT OF BANGLADESH (*editor with E. A. G.
Robinson*)

THE ECONOMY OF ETHIOPIA (*editor*)

THE TRANSITION TO EGALITARIAN DEVELOPMENT (*with Jeffrey James*)

UNDERDEVELOPMENT IN SPANISH AMERICA

WORLD HUNGER AND THE WORLD ECONOMY

# Studies in Development Strategy and Systemic Transformation

Keith Griffin
*Distinguished Professor of Economics*
*University of California, Riverside*
*USA*

First published in Great Britain 2000 by
**MACMILLAN PRESS LTD**
Houndmills, Basingstoke, Hampshire RG21 6XS and London
Companies and representatives throughout the world

A catalogue record for this book is available from the British Library.

ISBN 0–333–80436–8

First published in the United States of America 2000 by
**ST. MARTIN'S PRESS, INC.,**
Scholarly and Reference Division,
175 Fifth Avenue, New York, N.Y. 10010

ISBN 0–312–23257–8

Library of Congress Cataloging-in-Publication Data
Griffin, Keith B.
Studies in development strategy and systemic transformation / Keith Griffin.
p.   cm.
Includes index.
ISBN 0–312–23257–8 (cloth)
1. Economic development. I. Title.

HD75 .G74   2000
338.9—dc21

99–087198

This book is printed on paper suitable for recycling and made from fully managed and sustained
forest sources.

10   9   8   7   6   5   4   3   2   1
09   08   07   06   05   04   03   02   01   00

Printed and bound in Great Britain by
Antony Rowe Ltd, Chippenham, Wiltshire

*To   Benjamin, Chelsea and Isabel*

# Contents

List of Tables and Figure     x

Preface     xii

1   **Introduction**     1

**Part I: Strategic Visions**

2   **Culture, Human Development and Economic Growth**     15
     The sources of economic growth     16
     Does growth promote human development?     18
     Does human development promote growth?     20
     Inequality and growth revisited     22
     Culture and the state     24
     Globalization and cultural interchange     27
     The intrinsic and instrumental values of culture     30

3   **Globalization and the Shape of Things to Come**     33
     Is globalization a new phenomenon?     34
     Asymmetrical liberalization     36
     Globalization and economic space     39
     The squeeze on the state     42
     Global governance     46
     Globalization, culture and development: the long view     51

4   **Human Development: Origins, Evolution and Impact**     53
     Origins     53
     Evolution     55
     Measurement     56
     Institutionalization     61
     Impact     63

5   **The Distribution of Wealth and the**
    **Pace of Development (*with Amy Ickowitz*)**     66
     Empirical evidence     67
     Theoretical explanations     75
     Evidence from country studies     84
     Policy implications     88

**Part II: Systemic Transformation and
Macroeconomic Reform**

6   **Economic Policy during the Transition to
    a Market-Oriented Economy**                          95
    Economic performance during the transition           97
    Alternative reform strategies                        116
    The role of the state                                127

7   **Macroeconomic Reform and Employment:
    an Investment-Led Strategy of Structural
    Adjustment in Sub-Saharan Africa**                    139
    Stabilization                                        144
    Structural adjustment                                151
    Structural adjustment in the external sector         159
    Investment: the neglected path to adjustment         161
    Labour and adjustment through contraction            163
    The structure of incentives                          167
    Investment and the role of the state                 170

8   **Domestic Resource Mobilization and
    Enterprise Development in Sub-Saharan
    Africa
    (with Mark D. Brenner)**                              179
    Stabilization, structural adjustment and
     an investment-led strategy                          180
    Financing investment-led adjustment: external sources 183
    Domestic financing for investment-led adjustment:
     the private sector                                  192
    Domestic financing for investment-led adjustment:
     the public sector                                   195
    The informal sector                                  200
    Investment-led structural adjustment:
     programmatic elements                               208
    Conclusions                                          230

**Part III: Case Studies**

9   **Structural Adjustment and Macroeconomic
    Reform in Vietnam**                                   237
    Structural change                                    240
    The accumulation of capital                          241

Are the data credible?                                                244
The nature and sequence of policy reforms                             246

10  **Employment, Poverty and Social Protection
    in Kazakhstan**                                                   251
    Objectives of development                                         251
    Systemic reform in Kazakhstan                                     255
    The outcome of the reform process                                 259
    Elements of a revised strategy                                    263
    Appendix: a note on poverty concepts and
    poverty lines in Kazakhstan                                       277

11  **Poverty Reduction in China
    (*with Azizur Rahman Khan*)**                                     281
    The nature and causes of China's poverty problem                  281
    China's poverty reduction strategy                                286
    Restructuring China's poverty reduction strategy                  288
    Conclusion                                                        295

*Notes*                                                               297

*Index*                                                               321

# List of Tables and Figure

*Tables*
1.1  Mechanization, employment and the productivity
     of capital by size of firm in Ghana, Kenya and Mexico          10
6.1  Population and per capita gross national
     product in 26 transition economies, 1995                       96
6.2  Percentage annual rates of inflation, 1990–95                  99
6.3  Year when growth rate first became positive                   102
6.4  Cumulative change in real GDP, 1990–97                        103
6.5  Gross domestic investment, 1990 and 1995                      105
6.6  Income inequality and poverty                                 106
6.7  Life expectancy at birth, 1980 and 1995                       110
6.8  Death and birth rates, 1980 and 1995                          112
6.9  Missing men                                                   113
6.10 Number of suicides, 1989–93                                   115
6.11 Central government revenue and expenditure, 1994              128
6.12 Privatization of medium and large state
     enterprises, 1995                                             134
6.13 Relative ranking of human development and
     real GDP per capita in 28 transition economies, 1994          137
7.1  Classification of countries in sub-Saharan Africa             140
7.2  Growth rates in sub-Saharan Africa, 1980–94                   141
7.3  Indicators of stabilization                                   146
7.4  Indicators of restructuring in sub-Saharan Africa             152
7.5  Export performance in 31 countries of
     sub-Saharan Africa, 1980–94                                   160
7.6  Investment performance in 31 countries of
     sub-Saharan africa, 1980–94                                   162
7.7  The labour force                                              164
7.8  Changes in the capital–labour ratio and
     the productivity of labour, 1980–94                           165
8.1  Manufacturing capacity utilization in Kano,
     Nigeria, July 1992                                            182
8.2  Overseas development assistance per person                    184
8.3  ODA as a percentage of GNP                                    186
8.4  Foreign direct investment per person                          188
8.5  Foreign direct investment as a percentage of GNP              190

8.6  Tax revenue and total central government
     expenditure                                         196
8.7  Tax revenue and total central government
     expenditure                                         198
8.8  Regional averages for tax revenue and total
     central government expenditure                      199
8.9  Bolivian informal businesses registered in the
     RUC and number of taxpayers by city                202
8.10 Market locations for home-based manufacturing,
     retail trade and food service, Lima, Peru, 1983    203
8.11 'Modern' small-scale manufacturing establishments,
     Kenya, 1983–87                                      207
8.12 Enterprise types among home-based enterprises,
     Lima, Peru, 1983                                    218
9.1  Vietnam, China and Russia compared                 239
9.2  The composition of output, 1991 and 1995           240
9.3  Gross capital formation, 1991–95                   242
9.4  Changes in consumer prices, 1990–95                249
10.1 Inflation and economic growth in
     Kazakhstan, 1971–96                                 260
10.2 The distribution of personal income in
     Kazakhstan, 1989–94                                 261
10.3 The change in real personal income in
     Kazakhstan between 1989 and 1994                    261
11.1 The proportion of the population in poverty,
     1988 and 1995                                       282

*Figure*
7.1  Alternative paths of structural adjustment         156

# Preface

These *Studies in Development Strategy and Systemic Transformation* reflect my work in recent years. In 1994 I was invited to become a Member of the World Commission on Culture and Development and to help prepare a report, under the leadership of Javier Perez de Cuellar, that was published under the title of *Our Creative Diversity* (1995). I then advised the United Nations Educational, Scientific and Cultural Organization (UNESCO) on the preparation of its first *World Culture Report* (1998) and as part of that effort wrote a background paper that is published here as Chapter 2. In 1998 Macalester College in St Paul, Minnesota gave me an opportunity to assemble my thoughts on globalization when they invited me to present the keynote address at their International Round Table. The address is reprinted as Chapter 3.

The human development approach has been a major interest for many years. I have worked with the United Nations Development Programme (UNDP) on several occasions to help in the preparation of their annual *Human Development Report* and I have been sent to a number of countries by UNDP to help in applying the human development concept to practical policy issues. In 1999 Bob Sutcliffe invited me to present the keynote address at the tenth anniversary conference of the Institute for the Study of Development and the International Economy in Bilbao, Spain. The address is printed as Chapter 4. Chapter 5 contains a paper written with Amy Ickowitz which explores the relationship between the distribution of productive wealth and the pace of development. This was written originally at the request of Terry McKinley, then of UNDP, to stimulate thinking within UNDP about the relationships between human development, distributive issues and the elimination of poverty in low-income countries.

The collapse of communism and the attempts by ex-socialist countries to transform their economies by introducing a more market-oriented system are events of signal importance. I was fortunate, thanks to UNDP and the International Labour Organization (ILO), to have an opportunity to work on these issues. In Chapter 6 I discuss transition strategies at a general level, presenting a point of view that at first was controversial but is now more widely accepted. The paper originally was written as a background study for UNDP's *Regional Human Development Report for Central and Eastern Europe and the CIS Countries* (1999); it was also presented at a UNDP-sponsored conference, 'Central Asia, 2010' in Almaty, Kazakhstan in July 1998.

The three case studies are of transition economies. Chapter 9, on Vietnam, is based on work originally done for UNDP. The issue I was asked to explore was the link between macroeconomic and structural adjustment policies and the reduction of poverty. My paper on Kazakhstan, presented here as Chapter 10, was written for UNDP and the ILO. The issue there was how to design policies to provide social protection to the poor in a context of falling average incomes and severe transition difficulties. Chapter 11, on China, was written with Aziz Khan. This is a background paper written for UNDP as part of a joint World Bank/UNDP study of the effectiveness of China's poverty reduction strategy.

The hardships and disappointments experienced by sub-Saharan Africa, and the development strategies intended to remedy them, are the subject of two chapters. The first, Chapter 7, contains a critique of conventional stabilization and structural adjustment programmes as well as a proposal for an investment-led strategy of structural adjustment. It was writtten for the ILO in 1996. Chapter 8, with Mark Brenner, also written for the ILO, is primarily concerned with mobilizing domestic resources to finance an investment-led strategy in Africa. That is, it addresses the savings issue which confronts not only much of Africa but many of the ex-socialist transition economies as well.

I am very grateful to my co-authors for their splendid collaboration, to UNESCO, UNDP and ILO for giving me an opportunity to travel and study widely, to government officials and ordinary citizens in China, Vietnam and Kazakhstan for sharing their knowledge with me, and to Macalester College and the Institute for the Study of Development and the International Economy for inviting me to present some of my ideas to them.

KEITH GRIFFIN

# 1
# Introduction

The leading issues in economic development are very different today from what they were even a short time ago.[1] This is due in part to conceptual changes, in particular to the rise of 'human development' as a focus of attention and to an attempt to incorporate 'culture' into the analysis of economic processes. The debate has also been influenced by increased international integration and the 'globalization' of culture, politics, the economy and technology.[2] Equally important have been the failures of 'structural adjustment' in sub-Saharan Africa and of systemic transformation in the former Soviet Union and Central and Eastern Europe. Indeed, apart from China and Vietnam, the 'transition economies' have encountered severe difficulty in effecting a smooth transition from central planning to a more market-oriented economic system.

These five leading issues – culture, human development, globalization, sub-Saharan Africa and the transition economies – are the subject of this book. Economic growth, at least since the time of Adam Smith, has been a central objective of policy and the accumulation of capital has been thought to be the means to achieve growth. At first, natural capital was emphasized, or the 'original and indestructible properties of the soil', but as industrialization proceeded, initially in the United Kingdom and later in Europe and North America, physical capital, or the 'produced means of production', occupied centre stage. Most theories of economic growth give pride of place to investment in plant and equipment. In the second half of the twentieth century, however, there was a shift in favour of human capital, i.e. expenditure on education and training, basic health and nutrition, research and applied science. In Chapter 2 I attempt to extend the analysis by introducing culture into the debate.

The essence of the argument is, first, that new knowledge, new technology and new institutions are the ultimate sources of development and, second, that cultural diversity stimulates innovation of all sorts and thereby makes a major contribution to growth and development. A friend of mine, Jan Pieterse, in a caricature of the argument, quipped that 'Multiculturalism is good for business'. In the long run, I think it is, but in the short run ethnic diversity and cultural pluralism can lead to violence, civil war and political disintegration, as we have seen in the former Yugoslavia and elsewhere.

Globalization, the subject of Chapter 3, increases the significance of the debate about culture and pluralism. In contrast to many progressive critics, I argue that global integration is increasing and that on balance globalization is desirable economically, politically and culturally. If anything, globalization has not gone far enough and a strong case can be made for greatly liberalizing global labour markets. The asymmetry between relatively free trade and liberal capital markets, on the one hand, and illiberal labour markets, on the other, is hard to defend, either on grounds of efficiency or equity.

Politically, globalization is exerting a slow but powerful squeeze on the state as we know it. Ever since the Treaty of Westphalia of 1648, the 'model' for international relations has been a society of territorial states, each enjoying full sovereignty and non-intervention in its internal affairs. Each state is presumed to enjoy full equality with other states and there is no supreme external authority. Disputes between states in this 'model' were to be settled privately, by force if necessary. While the Westphalian model never fully reflected actual practice, it approximated reality until the end of the Second World War.

The war crimes tribunals in Germany and Japan, the special courts to try crimes against humanity committed in Rwanda and the former Yugoslavia, the establishment of a permanent international court of criminal justice, the military intervention in Kosovo (a province of Serbia) all attest to the erosion of political sovereignty and the incremental and painfully slow spread of a system of international law. Economic forces, too, are weakening the ability of the state to control its own economy. Free trade and, in its absence, the ease of smuggling make it difficult for states to control the flow of goods (and bads) across their borders. Liberal capital markets make it difficult for states to determine the location of production, to impose high taxes on finance capital or to regulate the exchange rate. Low-cost transport, even with restrictive immigration controls, makes it difficult for states to prevent illegal migration. Sovereignty is indeed at bay.

The state is also being squeezed from below. Globalization neutralizes the advantages of large states in exploiting economies of scale and makes small states economically viable. The spread of international law reduces the need for large standing armies and increases the security of small states. And the quest for greater self-determination, the spread of sub-nationalist movements, weakens the legitimacy of existing states. We are entering an era in which fragmentation of existing states and the creation of looser federations are becoming commonplace.

In many cases these developments can be welcomed. Few now regret that Malaysia and Singapore went their separate ways, that Bangladesh split off from Pakistan, that the USSR disintegrated or that Scotland and Wales achieved greater autonomy within the United Kingdom. The problem is that in a world consisting of a large and growing number of states, our institutions of global governance are weak, undemocratic and poorly financed. The Westphalian model is on the verge of collapse, some sort of a supreme external authority is needed, and yet we cling to the outmoded concept of sovereignty. International governance is bound to be high on the agenda of the twenty-first century.

Self-determination and a more liberal economy can contribute to what has come to be called human development. In Chapter 4 I trace the origins and impact of human development to two central ideas. The first is that the overriding objective of policy should be the enhancement of people's capabilities, i.e. their ability to live a life of their choice. The expansion of output and incomes, i.e. economic growth as conventionally defined, can contribute to the enhancement of human capabilities, but economic growth is merely a means to a higher end, and not an end in itself. The ultimate objective is human development.

The second central idea is the importance of human capital. As mentioned above, human capital formation is a major source of economic growth; the return on investment in human beings can be quite high. Within a human development context, moreover, human capital becomes doubly important since expenditure on human capital contributes directly to increased capabilities (and hence is an end in itself) while simultaneously contributing to increased output and incomes (and hence is an important means for increasing human development). The human development approach also has implications for the role of equality in encouraging development. The return on education and health diminishes as one moves from primary to secondary and tertiary education and from basic health services and preventive medicine to curative health services in large urban hospitals. Thus a more equal expenditure on human capital actually raises the rate of growth of output and the pace of human development. There need be no conflict between equity and growth.

This theme is explored in detail in Chapter 5 in an essay written with Amy Ickowitz. Most economists who have addressed this issue have been concerned with the effects of a more equal distribution of income on efficiency in resource allocation and the rate of growth. Our concern, in contrast, is with the distribution of wealth. The general argument is that in many countries a redistribution of productive assets can stimulate growth, whether growth is defined as an increase in gross domestic product or the attainment of higher levels of human development. A more equal distribution of land, for instance, is likely to result in an increase in employment, a rise in yields (output per hectare) and in higher investment (and savings). A more equal distribution of housing assets will increase human development directly and it will also stimulate investment in home-based enterprises such as restaurants and shops, thereby increasing the rate of growth.

Microeconomic evidence from a large number of countries indicates that private and social returns to investment in education are high. This is supported by the macroeconomic evidence, which indicates that high enrolment rates in schools are associated with higher growth rates. Similarly, widespread malnutrition in sub-Saharan Africa and South Asia impair the life chances of millions of young people and help to explain why human development in those two regions is well below the average for developing countries as a whole.[3] A more equal distribution of all forms of human capital would almost certainly accelerate development.

Access to finance capital is very uneven in developing countries and in the ex-socialist transition economies. Indeed credit rationing is a normal feature of the loanable funds market. Most people are unable to borrow capital unless they possess an asset that can be used as collateral. The implication of this is that the more widely are assets distributed, the larger the number of people who are potential borrowers and hence the larger the number of high return investments in human, physical and natural capital that can be financed. That is, for any given level of investment, the wider the access to finance capital, the higher is likely to be the average rate of return on investment.

A more even distribution of wealth, however, is likely to result in a higher level of investment as well as in a higher return on investment. The reason for this is that in societies in which capital markets are shallow and poorly developed, savings largely depend on investment opportunities. That is, people 'save' (by consuming less or working longer) in order to undertake investment projects. Indeed the saving and investment decisions coincide; they are identical. The question then becomes how to increase investment opportunities, how to create a productive outlet for savings. One answer is to ensure that land, buildings and other forms of productive wealth are widely distributed so that people own assets which create opportunities for further capital accumulation. There is a virtuous circle here: assets give rise to investment opportunities; these opportunities increase the incentive to save; higher savings permit the accumulation of yet more productive assets, which create more investment opportunities.

Chapter 6, on the transition economies, is a study of a vicious circle. The poor economic performance of the former Soviet Union and most of Central and Eastern Europe contrasts sharply with the success enjoyed in China and Vietnam. The countries of the former Soviet bloc have encountered a multitude of difficulties in attempting to transform their economic system from one based on central planning to a more market-oriented regime. Inflation has been rapid, growth rates have been negative, inequalities in the distributions of income and wealth have increased dramatically and there has consequently been an alarming rise in poverty. Evidence of social pathology has become abundant: crime, alcoholism, drug abuse and suicides have reached unprecedented levels. In many countries there has also been a demographic collapse. Life expectancy has declined, the birth rate has plummeted and the death rate has risen. In a number of countries the natural rate of growth of the population has become negative. The triumphalism that greeted the fall of communism a decade ago has been followed, for millions of people, by a social and economic disaster.

Two alternative reform strategies are analysed. The Soviet bloc countries attempted to follow a strategy of simultaneous reform across a broad front, emphasizing instantaneous price liberalization and rapid privatization of state-owned enterprises. This approach is popularly known as shock therapy or the big bang. Nowhere did it prove possible to implement the strategy fully – Poland perhaps came closest – and in many countries – Russia is the prime example – the attempt to do too much at once meant that nothing was done well. Simultaneous reform, I argue, is not feasible even in principle and attempts to apply such a wrong-headed strategy only slow down the reform movement and create much misery in the process. Shock therapy, contrary to the belief of its advocates, is a recipe for a delayed transition to a well functioning market economy.

China, which began its transition to a market economy ten years before the Soviet bloc, adopted a strategy of sequential reform. The

Soviet bloc countries ignored China's experience; only Vietnam emulated it. In China and Vietnam growth was rapid, poverty declined and market relations were quickly established. The rise in living standards was unprecedented. What accounts for the difference in performance?

First, the transition strategy adopted in China and Vietnam was primarily concerned with maintaining and preferably accelerating the rate of growth. Increasing allocative efficiency was not the primary objective. This meant, second, that sustaining and increasing the rate of investment was given much higher priority than price liberalization. Prices were liberalized in stages; initial emphasis was placed on liberalizing certain 'key' prices rather than instantaneously freeing all prices; and these 'key' prices often were only partially liberalized initially, with above-quota output being allowed to be sold on the free market. The result was a system of 'dual prices' and a set of relative prices which provided strong incentives on the margin to increase output but which were not market clearing 'equilibrium' prices. This sequential approach worked well during the transition and gave both countries the time needed to create the institutions necessary to support a market economy.

Third, effort was concentrated in those sectors where output could respond quickly, i.e. in sectors where supply elasticities were high and investment lags were short. In China this occurred initially in agriculture and services aimed at the domestic economy; in Vietnam, in agriculture, fisheries and exports. This approach encouraged investment, helped to generate employment and ensured that average incomes rose even in the beginning stages of the transition. Restructuring of production occurred within a context of growth, not through a reallocation of the stock of primary inputs, and efficiency increased because resources on the margin were channelled into sectors where returns were high. There was no contraction of output in the relatively inefficient sectors; all sectors expanded, but some grew more slowly than others.

Fourth, the Chinese and Vietnamese gave very low priority to privatizing state-owned enterprises. The creation of a private sector through the transfer of property rights played virtually no role in the transition strategy in either country. Instead emphasis was placed on creating an environment in which new, small-scale, labour intensive private enterprises could emerge and flourish. This approach was intended to stimulate private investment, create employment and raise incomes. It worked extremely well. The growth of the private sector was explosive and particularly in China, the private sector quickly overtook the public sector, although output of public sector enterprises continued to expand.

Rather than privatize state-owned enterprises, the Chinese have subjected them to competition – from imports, from non-state domestic enterprises and from joint ventures with foreign enterprises – and have attempted to make them commercially viable through a series of enterprise reforms. Commercialization rather than privatization has been the thrust of policy. Although this approach has been strongly criticized by the advocates of shock therapy,[4] the policy has been reasonably successful. The state economic enterprises have continued to grow and factor productivity has increased.

Sustained investment is a key to success not only in the transition economies but also in the countries of sub-Saharan Africa where 'structural adjustment' has been the primary policy objective. In Chapter 7 I examine the economic dilemmas facing Africa in some detail.

Sub-Saharan Africa has experienced a combination of slow growth of output and rapid growth of population. The outcome has been a negative rate of growth of income per head. Indeed many countries, alas, are poorer than at the time of independence. Economic policy undoubtedly has been misguided and the case for major reform is indisputable, but the policies that have been pressed upon the countries of sub-Saharan Africa by the World Bank, the International Monetary Fund and bilateral aid donors leave much to be desired. These policies are highly orthodox and come under the label of 'stabilization' and 'structural adjustment'.

Curiously, the policies are quite similar to those advocated under the 'shock therapy' label in the transition economies and include tight monetary policies to prevent rapid inflation, liberalization of prices and removal of controls – particularly as they apply to the foreign trade sector, devaluation of the exchange rate, a reduction of public expenditure and of the role of the state in general, and privatization of state-owned enterprises. These policies seldom have been of much help and they usually have made matters worse. They have failed to stabilize the economy or bring about structural adjustment, let alone stimulate growth of average incomes or reduce poverty and inequality.

The problem in Africa, as elsewhere, arises from a misunderstanding of how economies bring about structural change, i.e. how they alter the composition of output. The mainstream theory assumes that a change in relative prices (say, a rise in the price of tradable goods relative to the price of non-traded goods) will lead to a reallocation of the stock of productive assets (land and other natural resources, physical capital and human capital) away from the now unprofitable activities and towards the newly profitable economic activities. This will occur smoothly and both capital and labour will remain fully employed. Output will decline in the unprofitable activities and expand in the profitable ones simply as a result of reshuffling the stock of factors of production. The magic of the market will result in allocative efficiency.

The difficulty with this view is that it ignores the fact that factors of production – whether natural, physical or human capital – are specific to certain uses and cannot easily be reallocated to alternative uses. A wheat field cannot be transformed into a gold mine; a forest cannot be transformed into an offshore fishery; smelting equipment cannot be converted into a textile loom; a diesel locomotive cannot be transformed into a tractor; a peasant farmer cannot be converted into a secondary school teacher; an accountant cannot be converted into a civil engineer. The specificity of factors of production means that resources cannot easily be reallocated in response to changes in relative prices.

Output can shrink in those industries where prices have fallen but it cannot readily expand in those industries where prices have risen. The orthodox policies listed above can indeed lead to a change in the composition of output, but the structural adjustment occurs through some activities contracting more severely than others. Neither capital nor labour remains fully employed and as a result incomes fall and poverty increases. Broadly speaking, this is what has happened in much of Africa.

Structural change normally occurs through a process of investment. Changes in relative prices do not lead to a reallocation of the stock of natural, physical and human capital, rather the change in prices provides a signal to investors as to where they are likely to get the highest returns on their capital. If the level of investment is high, and the response of investors to price signals is rapid, output in the profitable sectors will expand quickly and this will bring about the desired change in the composition of production. In other words, a successful policy of structural adjustment should pay as much attention to the rate of investment as to 'getting prices right'.

The failure in Africa arises from the neglect of investment in the design of reform programmes. In the majority of countries the growth of investment was slower than the growth of GDP and as a result the share of investment in total output tended to fall. In most countries, in fact, investment grew less rapidly than the population, implying that average capital–labour ratios and the productivity of labour tended to decline. In many sub-Saharan countries the growth of investment was negative and consequently the stock of capital tended to shrink. It is too much to expect that in such a context a reform which focuses on changing relative prices would have much beneficial effect.

In Chapter 8, Mark Brenner and I confront head on the issue of increasing investment in sub-Saharan Africa. We argue that external resources cannot be relied upon, whether in the form of private foreign investment or foreign aid, and hence emphasis must be placed on mobilizing domestic resources to implement an investment-led development strategy. In the private sector the objective of policy should be to encourage savings by creating investment opportunities and to create conditions in which 'surplus' household labour can be directly applied to productive, small-scale investment projects. In addition, the state should implement a guaranteed employment scheme which would create employment opportunities on larger-scale investment projects in both urban and rural areas. In other words, investment would be financed partly by reducing average consumption and partly by increasing the volume of employment.

There are particular advantages in shifting priorities in favour of micro, small and medium-sized enterprises and away from large enterprises, whether in the private or public sectors. Data from Ghana, Kenya and Mexico, summarized in Table 1.1, indicate that the degree of mechanization, as measured by the capital–labour ratio, rises quite rapidly as the size of firm increases. That is, large firms are intensive in the use of physical capital, a factor of production which is particularly scarce in Africa. Employment intensity, in contrast, is much lower in the large enterprises than in micro, small and medium-sized enterprises. In Ghana and Kenya small firms appear to create more employment per unit of output than microenterprises, but both of these are much more labour intensive than medium-sized and large enterprises. Perhaps even more important, the average productivity of capital declines steeply as the size of firm increases, particularly in Ghana and Kenya. This suggests that the profitability of new investment is likely to be higher the smaller is the size of the firm. All of these indicators thus suggest that equality and growth would be well served by concentrating investment in relatively small enterprises.

Much public sector investment is complementary to private investment and where complementarities exist, they should be incorporated into the investment-led strategy. We challenge the view that public investment 'crowds out' private investment; if the strategy is properly designed, public investment should 'crowd in' private sector investment. For example, government expenditures on primary and secondary education, occupational training, nutrition and basic health programmes, rural and urban physical infrastructure (power, transport, communications) and applied agricultural research are likely to raise

*Table 1.1*   Mechanization, employment and the productivity of capital by size of firm in Ghana, Kenya and Mexico (index: microenterprise = 100)

| | Size of enterprise | | | |
| --- | --- | --- | --- | --- |
| | *Micro* | *Small* | *Medium* | *Large* |
| Ghana | | | | |
| Capital–labour ratio | 100 | 560 | 1772 | 2108 |
| Employment per unit of output | 100 | 192 | 56 | 45 |
| Average productivity of capital | 100 | 20 | 15 | 8 |
| Kenya | | | | |
| Capital–labour ratio | 100 | 348 | 565 | 634 |
| Employment per unit of output | 100 | 122 | 59 | 41 |
| Average productivity of capital | 100 | 19 | 11 | 8 |
| Mexico | | | | |
| Capital–labour ratio | 100 | 153 | 166 | 243 |
| Employment per unit of output | 100 | 74 | 61 | 47 |
| Average productivity of capital | 100 | 89 | 99 | 87 |

*Notes*: Microenterprises are defined as those employing 1–4 workers in Ghana and Kenya and 1–15 workers in Mexico. Small enterprises are those defined as employing 5–28 workers in Ghana and Kenya and 16–100 workers in Mexico. Medium enterprises employ 30–97 workers in Ghana and Kenya and 101–250 workers in Mexico. Large enterprises employ 100 or more workers in Ghana and Kenya and 251 or more workers in Mexico. The sample size was 164 establishments in Ghana, 185 in Kenya and 138, 774 in Mexico.
*Source*: Data kindly supplied by Diana Alarcon of the Inter-American Development Bank.

the profitability of private investment and contribute to a rise in aggregate investment and the rate of growth.

Poorly functioning capital markets reduce opportunities for private sector entrepreneurs. Lack of access to credit, not a high price of credit, prevents many small projects from being undertaken. Access is particularly difficult in rural areas, for small businesses in the urban informal sector and for women in general. Measures to improve access to credit and, where necessary, targeted credit programmes could go some way to increase investment while improving the distribution of income. In addition, the creation of financial institutions specializing in mortgage lending to low-income households could stimulate investment in housing and in the home-based enterprises the poor often create. This, too, would increase investment and improve the distribution of income and wealth. Sub-Saharan Africa is not a hopeless case. There is much that can usefully be done, but the first thing that must be done is to change from a price-centred to an investment-centred approach to development policy.

Some of the themes in the first two parts of the book are illustrated in case studies of Vietnam (Chapter 9), Kazakhstan (Chapter 10) and China (Chapter 11). Vietnam is a success story. Macroeconomic policy managed to contain inflation within tolerable limits and to avoid unsustainable imbalances. During the early years of the transition to a more market-oriented economy, Vietnam concentrated on sectors where supply elasticities were high and on maintaining a high and rising rate of investment. By 1997, gross investment accounted for 29 per cent of GDP, well above the average for other developing and transition economies. The result was a rate of growth of GDP of 8.6 per cent a year during the period 1990–97, again well above the average for other developing countries and, of course, vastly superior to the negative growth experienced in most transition economies.

Kazakhstan is a story of failure. The fall in the level of investment was so steep that net investment became negative and the economy was unable to maintain intact the stock of capital inherited at the time of independence in 1991. The transition to a market economy was accompanied by a fall in output and in average income. The distribution of income became more unequal and as a result, the incomes of the poor declined more than the incomes of the rich.

The transition strategy in Kazakhstan contained an element of wishful thinking, namely, that the economy could be refloated on a pool of oil from the Caspian Sea. Foreign direct investment by oil companies, it was hoped, would initiate a period of rapid growth that would lead to prosperity. Some even thought that Kazakhstan could become another Kuwait. These dreams almost certainly will be shattered by a combination of low world prices for oil and the high cost of extraction and transportation of oil from Kazakhstan's oil fields. The natural resource rents which the government can appropriate are therefore likely to be exceedingly modest. It would be foolish for the government to rely on foreign capital to finance development; it will have to mobilize domestic resources, build on the country's valuable stock of human capital and seek a much more employment intensive pattern of growth. Between 1990 and 1997 the annual rate of growth of GDP was minus 7.9 per cent. The time evidently has come to change the transition strategy.

The chapter on poverty reduction in China, written jointly with Aziz Khan, shows that problems can arise even in countries which have adopted a well conceived strategy of sequential reform. Growth rates in China have been high from the beginning of the reform process and in the first few years of the transition there was a rapid decline in the incidence of poverty. In the mid-1980s, however, China switched from an agriculture-led to an export-led pattern of growth, and this change in priorities had serious implications for the struggle against poverty.

Growth continued to be rapid, but this growth was accompanied by a dramatic increase in inequality in the distribution of income. China began the transition process with a rather egalitarian distribution of income, although rural–urban inequality was high, but by the mid-1990s the distribution of income in China was considerably more unequal than in the other large countries of Asia, viz. Bangladesh, India, Indonesia and Pakistan. Inequality increased sharply in both rural and urban areas. As a result, the beneficial effects on poverty of the swift increase in average income was largely offset by the negative effects of increased income inequality. Poverty continued to decline in the rural areas, although at a slower pace than previously, but in the urban areas there probably was a slight increase in the incidence of poverty. Thus despite rapid growth, poverty failed to decline as quickly as policy makers expected.

The response of government was to identify 592 counties as 'poor counties' and to implement special regional development programmes in those counties. The problems with this approach are that it ignores urban poverty entirely, it excludes the large number of rural poor who live outside the 'poor counties' from the benefits of the programme, and it confers potentially substantial benefits on the non-poor who do live in the 'poor counties'. It is thus quite likely that the anti-poverty programme will be at best only a modest success. We present an alternative programme which attempts to do two things: first, to incorporate the reduction of poverty into a redesigned overall transition strategy rather than treat poverty as an afterthought, and second, to identify specific anti-poverty policies which are better targeted on the poor. Slight adjustments are all that are necessary to enable China to combine continued rapid growth with accelerated poverty reduction and human development.

# Part I
# Strategic Visions

# 2
# Culture, Human Development and Economic Growth*

Economic growth, the traditional objective of development policy, is concerned with increasing the output of goods and services, in the expectation that this will increase human well being and reduce poverty. More recently, there has been a shift in favour of human development, where emphasis is placed on increasing an individual's capabilities, widening choice and expanding freedom.[1] There is much discussion, even controversy, about the relationship between economic growth and human development:[2] are they in opposition? do they have different policy implications? or do they come down to much the same thing in the end?

More recent still is the incorporation of culture into the debate.[3] Human development focuses on the individual and pays relatively little attention to the social or communal aspects of life.[4] Yet individual human beings do not live and work in isolation. They band together in groups of various sorts extending from the nuclear family to transnational institutions. Human beings, individually and collectively, interact in many ways. They cooperate and compete with one another, engage in conflict, build harmonious relationships, borrow and lend and adapt attributes of others. This communal or communitarian or collective aspect of life we call culture and it is culture, in all its diversity and complexity, that constitutes a people's way of life. The old question, now before us once again, is what does culture have to do with economic growth and human development?

In this essay we do not propose to answer this question fully – indeed we are not capable of doing so – but rather we propose to explore some of the important connections among economic growth, human development and culture and to suggest, at least implicitly, where the argument is likely to lead in future.

## The sources of economic growth

The early tradition in economics was to emphasize the importance of *natural capital* in sustaining high levels of income per head and permitting steady growth, at least until diminishing returns set it. The French physiocrats and the early English political economists fall into this category. Growth based on natural capital, or on the exploitation of natural resources, could not continue indefinitely, it was thought, because as production expanded it was necessary to bring into use resources of lesser yield: land of lesser fertility, mineral deposits with lower ore content, etc. Eventually diminishing returns would result in a 'stationary state', i.e. constant real income and zero growth.

There are numerous examples today of countries which have based their growth on the exploitation of natural capital: oil and gas, timber, fisheries, minerals, surface and underground water supplies and so on. Many countries indeed have 'mined' the resource base with little regard for the future. The original insights of the classical economists, however, have been rediscovered and it is increasingly recognized that growth has occurred in part by consuming the stock of natural capital beyond the rate of natural replenishment (in the case of renewable resources) and without compensating investments in other sectors (in the case of non-renewable resources).

This has two profound implications. First, the level of net income and its rate of growth as estimated from standard national income accounts are likely to be overstated because the depreciation of natural capital is ignored. All countries' national accounts have exaggerated the level of net income and most countries probably have been growing less rapidly than they thought. Second, whatever the true rate of growth of net income, the growth process is not sustainable indefinitely. If the harvest rate of renewable resources exceeds natural regeneration, relative prices will rise and if the process continues we will eventually run out of fish, timber, even clean air and water.[5] If the extraction of non-renewable resources is not offset by the creation of an equivalent value of capital elsewhere, the capital base of the economy eventually will become insufficient to sustain current standards of living.

Modern theories of growth, both mainstream and Marxian, have placed little emphasis on the stock of natural capital but have instead concentrated on the accumulation of *physical capital*.[6] Ever since the first industrial revolution in Britain, analysts and policy makers concerned with growth have emphasized the 'produced means of production', i.e. investment in plant and equipment, as the key to progress.

The focus has been on savings and investment, domestic and external sources of finance for capital accumulation, and to a lesser extent, on technology as embodied in new vintages of physical capital.

Again, there are numerous examples of countries which based their growth on the accumulation of physical capital. And in general the statistical evidence shows that countries with above average rates of investment tended to experience faster rates of growth than average.[7] There are exceptions, which tend to be associated with countries which failed to incorporate new technology into investments in plant and equipment,[8] but on the whole modern theories of growth have turned out to be correct – up to a point.

The great weakness of modern growth theory is that the contribution of physical capital to economic expansion is surprisingly modest. The most important source of growth lies elsewhere. Indeed it is estimated that between them, natural and physical capital can account for less than half of the observed rate of growth; more than half of growth arises from human sources.[9] Indeed it is findings such as these which led to the most recent shift of emphasis in favour of *human capital*. It is now thought that investment in human capital – expansion of labour power, expenditures on health and nutrition, investments in education, training and research – is the single most important source of economic growth.

This has very deep implications for theory and policy. It alters the very categories we use for analysing economic phenomena. For example, the division of expenditure between consumption and investment loses much of its significance because many items classified as 'consumption', such as current outlays on health and education, really should be understood as a form of human capital expenditure. Similarly, it forces us to rethink all growth-promoting strategies of development. 'Capital' may still be the 'engine of growth', but the lead locomotive is human rather than physical capital. In addition, as we shall see below, it requires us to re-examine the relationship between the rate of growth of output and income and the distribution of income. It compels us to reconsider the link between employment policies (and short-term macroeconomic policies in general) and growth policies. Unemployment, for example, may well result in loss of skills through disuse and hence in a decline in the stock of human capital. The loss of human capital, in turn, could result in a lower long-term average rate of growth. And above all, the importance of human capital forces us to put people in the centre of the stage.

This transformation of thought is one of the things – but only one of the things – that has led to the conceptualization of *human development* and the advocacy and formulation of human development strategies and policies. At both the intellectual and practical levels we are going through an exciting period of reconsideration of much that was thought to be settled doctrine.

## Does growth promote human development?

The participants in the debate on human development agreed from the beginning that an expansion of the production of goods and services (growth) increases capabilities and choices as well as many freedoms (and thus makes a vital contribution to human development).[10] Two additional points, however, also were made. First, growth was seen as merely a means to the end of human development. Gross national product (GNP) was 'dethroned' as an objective of policy. This does not mean that the growth of GNP is unimportant but only that growth as such is an intermediate objective rather than a final objective. Growth is to be valued only in so far as it contributes to human development and not in its own right.

Second, the contribution of growth to increased human development was seen to diminish with the level of output and income per capita. That is, growth is characterized by diminishing returns on the margin. The higher is the level of a country's per capita GNP, the less any increment of GNP adds to that country's level of human development. The contribution, if any, of growth to utility, welfare, well being or satisfaction, or any other shorthand expression used by economists for happiness, is another matter. The argument does not depend on an assumption about diminishing marginal utility.

These propositions are straightforward even if still controversial. In addition, there are more subtle points to be made.

If growth is based on human capital formation as opposed to investment in physical capital and the exploitation of natural capital, the contribution of growth to human development is likely to be larger. The reason for this is that marginal increments of income are likely to be distributed more evenly under a human capital-based growth strategy than under alternative strategies, for the simple reason that human capital almost always is embodied in human beings and hence the returns to human capital usually can be captured directly by the individuals who possess that capital. Assuming that the principle of diminishing returns of growth to human development applies across individuals as well as across countries, a growth strategy centred on human capital will be more successful in raising a country's average level of human development, for any given rate of growth of GNP.

A corollary of this is that employment intensive growth patterns are likely to contribute more to human development than growth patterns characterized by high rates of unemployment and slack labour markets. It is high returns to labour that facilitate a transformation of income into human development. Growth, in other words, is a permissive factor; there is no mechanism that automatically translates growth into greater human development.

A further implication of this line of reasoning is that a growth process that results in a more equal distribution of income will have a more favourable impact on human development than a growth process that is accompanied by increased inequality. This is true whether the diminished inequality arises directly from the growth process itself or is a product of government policy regarding, say, public expenditure and taxation. The more evenly are the increments of growth spread, the larger will be the increase in human development. Egalitarian growth has a substantial pay-off.

The conclusion, thus, is that growth contributes to human development but at a diminishing rate. The tendency for returns to diminish can be attenuated by adopting policies which (a) encourage employment, (b) emphasize human capital as the engine of growth and (c) promote a more equal distribution of income. At the other extreme, 'jobless growth' based on natural and physical capital that results in a highly unequal distribution of income is likely to contribute relatively little to human development.

So far we have concentrated on the direct linkages between growth and human development, between higher incomes and a broader range of choices, capabilities and freedoms. There are also indirect linkages that should be considered.

These indirect linkages arise from the fact that growth generates additional resources and these additional resources can in principle be allocated in such a way that human development is increased. The allocation mechanism may be either public action by governmental institutions or private decisions taken by individuals, households, business enterprises and other institutions of civil society. Once again, there is nothing automatic about the process; growth is merely permissive.

It is not difficult to imagine a number of indirect linkages. For example, growth leads to higher government revenues; part of these additional revenues might be used to improve the public health service, which results in an increase in life expectancy of, say, those over 60 years of age; the higher life expectancy enlarges the capabilities of the elderly, i.e. contributes directly to human development. Similarly, growth leads to greater business profits; part of the additional profits might be used by firms to finance on-the-job training programmes for workers which by a similar chain of reasoning results in a higher level of human development. An analogous sequence can occur within the household: growth leads to higher incomes, which leads to expenditures on music lessons for the children, which increase their capabilities. How additional incomes are spent may be as important for human development as the amount of additional income generated by economic growth.

## Does human development promote growth?

The direction of causality considered so far runs from growth to human development. Let us now examine the reverse causality, from human development to growth. It should be clear from what has been said above that human development does indeed promote growth and hence we have a system of mutual interaction or two-way causation. This raises the interesting possibility of a virtuous circle in which growth leads to human development and human development leads to a further acceleration of growth.

Human development, above all, is the purpose of development, but it is also an instrument of development and a contributor to economic growth. Investing in people is desirable for its own sake, but there is also considerable evidence that investing in people is highly profitable.[11] Indeed it is now widely believed that the returns on human capital are as high if not higher than the returns on physical and natural capital. It is this which makes human development such an attractive strategy for development and extends the debate beyond a discussion of the appropriate goals for economic policy.

A well nourished and healthy population, a well educated and well trained labour force are simultaneously human development objectives and components of the stock of human capital. Seen in this latter incarnation, human capital is a major input into the growth process. That is, human development promotes growth. This is by now rather obvious.

Less obvious is the proposition that other aspects of human development, which do not fit readily under the label of human capital, also contribute to economic growth. Consider participation. It is widely agreed that people should participate in the decisions that affect their lives and that local participation in public affairs is one aspect of the goal of human development. Participation, however, also has instrumental value. Participation implies cooperation and a willingness to make sacrifices to achieve commonly agreed objectives.[12] Cooperation and sacrifice help promote growth. For example, the sacrifice of present consumption (savings) raises the level of investment and rate of growth, and individuals may be more willing to make this sacrifice if they know that others are cooperating by doing likewise. In addition, there is an informational dimension to participation. That is, the active involvement of the people in local decision making can help to improve the quality of decisions. Participatory institutions can help to identify local projects with high rates of return, they can help to anticipate problems before they arise, they can help to devise solutions to problems and they can help to decide how best to implement projects and programmes. All of this helps to promote growth by providing more complete and accurate information. The voice of the people, i.e. local participation in the public arena, plays a similar role to market signals in the private arena: both voice and prices convey valuable information which improves economic performance.

The same is true by extension of freedom, democracy and human rights at the national level. These things are of course highly desirable in themselves and are part of what is meant by human development: they increase choice and enhance capabilities. But it is also possible that they encourage growth. A dissenting individual, a collective protest or demonstration, a democratic election in which all voices are heard may convey information to policy makers that leads, for example, to greater public investment in primary and secondary education, or to the removal of barriers against the employment of women or to the expansion of transport and power facilities in the rural areas – all of which would be likely to accelerate the pace of economic growth.[13]

Jean Drèze and Amartya Sen have frequently called to our attention the fact that there has never been a famine in a democratic country with a free press.[14] This penetrating insight may have wider applicability. A respect for freedom, democracy and human rights may have instrumental value not only in avoiding catastrophe, such as a famine, but also in promoting the good things in life.[15] One must not push the argument too hard and discredit it by overstatement. Certainly democratic countries have done horrible things, or stood by while horrible things were done by others. Moreover, in the economic sphere, it is easy to list democratic countries which have experienced slow growth

(UK, USA) and countries with authoritarian features which have enjoyed rapid growth (China, South Korea, Singapore). If there is a positive relationship between this aspect of human development and economic performance, it is a subtle and indirect connection which is unlikely ever to be revealed in a statistical correlation. Cultural variables, as we shall see below, may be relevant in this connection.

## Inequality and growth revisited

There is a long tradition in economic thought that postulates a conflict between efficiency and equity, growth and equality. Indeed this conflict sometimes is described as the 'great trade-off'.[16] The conflict has its origins, depending on the author, in the historical role of the capitalist class, in the importance for investment of a high share of profits in national income[17] or in the propensity of the rich to save a higher proportion of their income than the poor.[18] Whatever the precise formulation, the conclusion inevitably reached is that any attempt by the government to reduce inequality in the distribution of income is highly likely to impair efficiency in the allocation of resources or lower the rate of growth, and probably both.

The human development perspective, however, casts a different light on these issues. It was argued above that the more equal is the distribution of income, the easier it is for the fruits of growth to be transformed into human development. Now it will be suggested that under some circumstances, the greater is the degree of equality, the faster is likely to be the rate of growth. Why might this be the case?

First, the perpetuation of inequality can be costly. Severe inequality produces resentment, discontent and unruliness, even rebellion. Containment of unruliness, and suppression of discontent require resources in the form of expenditure on the police and armed forces, the judiciary, prisons and the penal system – resources that could otherwise be used to promote economic expansion. In extreme cases inequality can make a society ungovernable and cause serious disruption of the economy.

Second, even in less extreme cases, inequality can undermine the legitimacy of the political regime. Inequality, and the avarice and ruthlessness that often are required to sustain it, weakens the rule of law, severs the bonds of trust that enable a society to function properly and destroys the social solidarity necessary for an 'imagined community' to operate as an effective state.[19] Moreover modern technology has destroyed the monopoly of the state over the means of violence.

Crime, terrorism and insurgent movements have become banal; violence has become democratized; the victims of injustice have explosive means to vent their anger. And all of this can lower the rate of economic growth. One need look no further than Africa, the Middle East or American ghettos for evidence.

The other side of this coin is that measures to reduce inequality can simultaneously contribute to faster growth. For example, third, there is much evidence that small farms are more efficient than either large collective farms of the Soviet type or the capitalist latifundia one finds in Latin America and elsewhere.[20] A redistributive land reform and the creation of a small peasant farming system can produce performances as good as if not better than those of other agricultural systems. The experience of such places as China and South Korea is instructive.

Fourth, what is true of small farms is equally true of small and medium industrial and commercial enterprises. An egalitarian industrial structure, as Taiwan vividly demonstrates, can conquer world markets.[21] Large enterprises do not in general enjoy competitive superiority – the importance of economies of scale is much exaggerated – and often in developing countries large enterprises depend on the state for protection from foreign producers, for subsidized bank credit, for tax favours and for guaranteed sales to the public sector under state procurement policies. Industrial policy thus often encourages both inequality and inefficiency. Small enterprises in contrast often face numerous official barriers, the removal of which would reduce inequality while encouraging faster growth.

Fifth, investment in education, particularly at the primary and secondary levels, is a highly effective way to reduce inequality in the distribution of income. It is also, as we have seen, an effective way to stimulate growth. Even if one remains an unreconstructed advocate of growth and is unpersuaded by arguments that human development is the ultimate objective, there is a strong case for supporting large public and private expenditure on education. There probably is no easier way to combine equality and rapid growth. The whole of East Asia is testimony to the veracity of this proposition.[22]

A final example of the falsity of the great trade-off is the liberation of women. Equal treatment of women would release the talent, energy, creativity and imagination of half the population. As it is, women already do more than half the world's work, but they have little control over resources (and often over their own bodies); they have restricted opportunities for education, employment and participation in political life; they are engaged in sectors such as the household economy which are severely undercapitalized compared to other sectors, and which therefore condemn them to low-productivity labour and low returns on their effort; and they are denied opportunities for advancement.[23] The subjugation of women produces inequality, inefficiency and a slower rate of growth than would otherwise be possible. The removal of discrimination, in contrast, would reduce inequality and promote growth, while of course raising the level of human development.

The old conflict between equality and growth thus turns out to be a shibboleth. Under some circumstances greater equality actually can accelerate economic growth and greater equality almost certainly would contribute to human development. Thus intervention by the state to reduce inequalities in opportunities, income and wealth, if properly designed and implemented, can have very beneficial consequences.

## Culture and the state

Although in principle the state can introduce policies to reduce inequality, increase the pace of economic growth and enhance human development, in practice states often are weak or use such power as they have to benefit particular classes, groups or factions in society rather than the population as a whole. This can occur in both democratic and authoritarian states as the experiences, respectively, of Brazil and the Sudan attest. There are many possible reasons for this, but one neglected explanation – and possibly an important one – has to do with the role of culture.

Defining culture broadly, as we have done, as 'ways of life' helps to highlight several notable features of the contemporary world. First, there are of course a great many ways of life that one can observe. Some ways of life are geographically restricted whereas some cultures cover a large terrain. Indeed there are more ways of life, i.e. more cultures, than there are states. One obvious implication of this is that cultures and states do not coincide; the jurisdiction of territorial states does not 'map' the space occupied by distinct cultures. There is a disunity of coverage and this lack of coincidence creates a possibility of conflicting allegiances, divided loyalties and contested claims for primacy of affection.

Second, the cultures that one observes today are almost always older than any existing state. In fact the contemporary state is a relatively recent institutional innovation, dating roughly from eighteenth-century Europe, and the majority of actual states were created in the twentieth century after the disintegration of the worldwide imperial system. Most cultures antedate the emergence of the state system and the nationalism and patriotism associated with it. This does not imply that cultures are necessarily ancient, traditional or static, much less that they are timeless. On the contrary, cultures should be seen as changing, dynamic, fluid, in a constant state of flux. Thus cultures, paradoxically, are simultaneously young and old; they represent distinctive ways of life yet they are influenced by other cultures with which they come into contact.

Third, cultures often are transnational phenomena. Geographically, cultures frequently transcend the boundaries of territorial states. This obviously is true of Arab culture in the Middle East, of many African cultures divided by arbitrary boundaries during the colonial period, of 'Western' culture, of Kurdish culture in Turkey, Syria, Iraq and Iran, of Chinese culture in East and South-east Asia, and so on. Cultures thus pose, or are perceived to pose, both an external challenge to some states and a risk, perhaps only a latent risk, of internal subversion. States often respond to these threats, real or imaginary, either by suppressing transnational cultural minorities (e.g. the suppression of the Kurdish minority by the Turkish state) or by half-hearted obeisance to ideals of transnational economic and political union (as in the various, and unsuccessful, pan-Arab, pan-African and pan-Latin American movements). Only in Western Europe, with the formation of the European Union, have strong supranational institutions been created within a relatively homogeneous cultural space.

Fourth, virtually all states include within their boundaries a multiplicity of cultures. Indeed the term 'nation state' is a misnomer. Modern states include a large number of national groups, ethnicities, 'tribes', languages and religions, i.e. ways of life. The modern state is irreversibly a multi-cultural institution. Pluralism is a fact of life of the contemporary world, a fact which has yet to be properly digested by analysts and policy makers alike. Some states (Israel, Pakistan, Iran) behave as if they contained a homogeneous population of uniform religious belief; few states (Switzerland is an obvious exception) have constructed institutions which explicitly take into account the linguistic, religious and ethnic diversity of citizens.

Many states have made attempts, of varying degrees of effort and success, to reduce discrimination against minority groups, to integrate those of different 'race' into the mainstream and to assimilate the foreign-born, the indigenous population and other minorities into the dominant society. Diversity, pluralism and multi-culturalism within states, however, raise issues which go beyond assimilation, integration, affirmative action, anti-discrimination and the like. They raise questions of access to resources and institutions, participation in the wider life of the polity and society, as well as issues of fairness and equity. Cultural diversity raises the questions of how best to protect the interests and rights of minorities, how to avoid the tyranny of the majority, and how best to secure adequate representation of minorities in decision-making institutions.

How one approaches these questions depends in part on how one views the role of multi-culturalism within states. At one end of the spectrum of opinion are those who view pluralism as a disadvantage. Diversity is a source of conflict; it often leads to violence and bloodshed; it results in political instability; and it makes it hard for people to get along together in their daily life. Multi-culturalism is something that must be contained or managed, preferably by making 'them' as much like 'us' as possible. Far from contributing to economic growth and human development, cultural diversity is an obstacle that in one way or another must be overcome or got around.

At the other end of the spectrum are those who regard cultural diversity not as a liability but as an asset. Different ways of life, different ways of looking at the world, different ways of thinking are indeed challenging and a source of dissonance and tension that can lead to conflict and violence. But those challenges and tensions are also a source of creativity (in all its forms) and it is creativity (not capital in any of its forms) which is the fountainhead of economic growth and human development. That is, it is new knowledge, new technology and new institutional arrangements which are the ultimate sources of growth and development[24] and it is a plausible hypothesis that cultural diversity acts as a stimulus to innovative activities of all sorts. That is, one can view cultures as 'experiments' which are sources of knowledge. The more experiments humanity conducts, i.e. the greater is cultural diversity, the more knowledgeable and innovative we are likely to be.

It has long been recognized that minorities often are highly innovative in business and account for a disproportionate number of entrepreneurs. Think of the Chinese in South-east Asia, the Lebanese in West Africa, the Indians in East Africa and the Quakers in the United Kingdom. The claim being made here, however, is more general, namely, that pluralism contributes to creativity in all fields of endeavour. If this is true, then over the very long run multi-cultural states have more potential than states with a relatively homogeneous population. A potential for human and material progress does not of course imply that the potential inevitably will be realized. The translation of potential into actual achievement depends on whether in a particular time and place the advantages of pluralism can be brought into play and the disadvantages minimized. At any given moment some culturally homogeneous societies (e.g. Japan, South Korea) may appear on balance to be less divisive and more dynamic than some pluralist societies, but given a longer time horizon, pluralism is likely to be more advantageous than homogeneity.

## Globalization and cultural interchange

Cultural diversity is of course much greater at the global than at the country level. It might have been possible once upon a time to imagine cultures as being separated from one another – with room to breathe and to develop independently – but technological change in transport and communications has for centuries been dissolving time and space, breaking down the barriers which surround even the most isolated cultures. This process has accelerated dramatically in the last 50 years and is part of a wider tendency towards globalization. One consequence of globalization is that cultures are coming into increasingly close contact with one another. The Chinese culture rubs against the Indian culture. The Indian culture rubs against the European culture. The European culture rubs against African cultures, and so on.[25]

The 'rubbing' of cultures is not a question of physical proximity and, indeed, strictly speaking cultures do not have fixed boundaries. They interpenetrate and for this reason cultures are not homogeneous; they are, rather, hybrids.[26] It is thus particular cultural attributes that rub against one another and not one particular reified culture (much less a singular national or state culture) that rubs against another.

Be that as it may, this 'rubbing' has been going on for a long time and before considering the implications for the contemporary world, it is worth glancing back at history. It would be fatuous to claim that technological change and the cultural interchange that follows it have been universally beneficial. Development has been uneven and, more important, the impact of cultural interchange has often been asymmetrical, some groups and cultures losing absolutely, not just relatively. Central Asia, for instance, long occupied a strategic position on the caravan trade routes connecting China with the eastern Mediterranean and Europe. Its cities of Samarkand, Bukhara and Khiva (now in Uzbekistan) were centres of economic, political and cultural activity where the arts and architecture, the natural sciences and mathematics and theology flourished. Beginning in the fifteenth century, the development of transoceanic transport, however, made overland transport through Central Asia unprofitable and the region fell into a steep decline. The maritime regions of Asia were brought into closer contact with Europe while parts of the interior of Asia became increasingly isolated.

Closer contact, however, has been a mixed blessing. Whether one considers the explosive conquests of Islam beginning in the seventh century, which from the epicentre in Arabia covered the whole of the Middle East, all of North Africa and the Iberian peninsula in Europe, or the westward migration of the Mongol 'hordes' of the thirteenth century, which ended at the Danube River and the outskirts of Budapest, or the unrelenting expansion of Western Europe from the fifteenth century onwards to virtually every corner of the globe, cultural interchange often seems more like a one-way street than a dual carriageway highway. Cultural contact often has been a by-product of military encounters and has been associated with violence, pillage, war, enslavement,[27] conquest, colonialism and imperialism.[28] It has led to the introduction of alien diseases to those who had no natural resistance to them and in some cases to the decimation of indigenous populations. It has helped to spread racism;[29] occasionally it has resulted in genocide; more often it has led to the destruction of pre-existing social structures and the system of beliefs that sustained them.[30] Historically, globalization often had a fatal impact.[31]

Yet there is another side to the story: cultural contact was indeed a mixed blessing. The initial effects of cultures rubbing against one another may well be accurately described by the phrase 'a fatal impact',[32] but the longer-term effects were more positive. Contacts between cultures led to a myriad of exchanges and adaptations that were of benefit to all parties. Consider foodstuffs and primary commodities. Latin America gave us maize, potatoes, the tomato and natural rubber; Ethiopia and Yemen gave us coffee; India gave us sugar; China gave us tea and noodles (which the Italians transformed into pasta), and so on. The world's pharmacopoeia similarly draws on botanical products from many different regions. The same is true of our domesticated animals.

Early Chinese science led the world and in the field of technology China gave us paper, porcelain (or fine 'china'), the compass, gunpowder and much else.[33] The Arabs gave us our system of numerals. The Central Asians gave us algebra and taught us how to measure the motions of the heavens. Indeed 'from about 750 to 1100, Islamic science and technology surpassed those of Europe'.[34] During this period, 'Islam was Europe's teacher',[35] and Cordoba was the greatest centre of learning in Europe. The pupil, however, eventually began to outshine the teacher. In the Islamic world, as in Europe, there arose a conflict between science and theology, but in the Islamic world, theology won. One sign of this, perhaps Islam's 'greatest mistake ... was the refusal of the printing press'[36] and the consequent retardation in the spread of knowledge.

In religion, India gave us Buddhism, the Arabian peninsula Islam and Palestine Christianity. Mutual influences in art and architecture, music and dance, crafts and household technology are too numerous to recount. All our cultures have been immeasurably enriched by contact with others.

Similar processes can be observed today. Indeed, whatever may have been the case in the past, today no culture, no society is completely closed.[37] The questions revolve around the degree of openness and the terms on which a culture interacts with other cultures. That is, whether the relationship is one of subordination, domination and exploitation or one of equality, mutual respect and beneficial exchange. The difference today is that globalization has made cultural interchange more frequent than in the past, deeper and more rapid. Some have speculated that we are witnessing the emergence of a 'global culture' and submerging local cultures under an irresistible tide of Western influence. Culture worldwide is becoming more homogeneous: Coca-Cola, blue jeans and North American popular music rule the roost. Local dialects and entire languages are disappearing by the hundreds, local cuisines are being replaced by Western-style fast foods, traditional ways of life are being abandoned in favour of pale images of the American way of life.

While there is some truth to this, cultural interchange in the modern world is a two-way exchange. Capital, technology and even labour circulate globally. Science is universal and accessible to all to a greater degree than ever before. Ideas, information and knowledge are transmitted much more rapidly and more widely than in the past. The result is an increase in diversity: greater heterogeneity, not greater homogeneity. This evidently is true at any given location, as more and more ways of life learn to coexist, and it also is true globally, as cultural interpenetration multiplies the number of permutations and in the process creates new ways of life, new cultures. This increased diversity, in turn, has led to an acceleration in creativity and innovation.

There has been an explosive growth of knowledge and technology in the last 50 years and this has greatly contributed to the rapid advances in human development that have occurred and to the rapid economic growth we have enjoyed, a pace of growth worldwide that is unprecedented in human history. Cultural interchange has indeed been a mixed blessing, but the positive contribution of interchange has been extraordinarily large.

## The intrinsic and instrumental values of culture

Culture (or the communal aspect of life) is analogous to human development (which focuses on the individual) in that culture is valued in itself and also as a means to obtain other things which are desired or valued. That is, culture possesses both intrinsic and instrumental value. The intrinsic value of culture has long been recognized and is reflected in many ways: in concerns to preserve cultural heritage, to respect our traditions and the preceding generations who passed them on to us, to record spoken languages before they disappear, to conserve, restore and maintain historical monuments, art objects and ancient artefacts. Culture as our way of life is something most of us treasure and wish to preserve in a recognizable form; it contributes to our sense of self or who we are and to our sense of satisfaction or well being.

In addition, however, culture as a means is becoming widely recognized. Increasingly the instrumental value of culture is being used by leaders in various areas of life to achieve economic, social and political purposes. This includes the appeal to tradition to forge new alliances based on ethnicity or nationality, sometimes with the objective of creating new, culturally homogeneous states, as with the Serbs in Bosnia. It also includes the revival of religious and other traditions in an attempt to re-establish an old order, to re-create a 'golden age' and to impose ancient, fundamental values on a society regarded as immoral and godless. The Christian, Jewish, Islamic and Hindu 'fundamentalist' movements can be interpreted in this way.

Thus culture has been used in places for sectarian and reactionary purposes and as a weapon to preserve or create a particular way of life. These uses of culture reflect 'a politics of nostalgia'.[38] These uses of culture, however, are only part of the global picture. As argued above, globalization has led to an intensification of cultural interchange and this, in turn, is transforming local cultures without necessarily producing cultural uniformity. For example, culture is being used to create new forms of expression: English is becoming the *lingua franca*, yet spoken English is evolving in different directions in different regions of the world while at the same time, the number of people who are bilingual or multi-lingual is increasing rapidly. Similarly, cultural interchange has led to new ways of communicating (e.g. via the fax and internet), new types of music, new ways of doing business (the transnational corporation), new forms of political organization (e.g. the European Union), new channels of international crime and even new ways of finding a spouse (e.g. by advertising in the international media). This burst of cultural creativity or cultural vitality, although uneven across space, is very widespread and indeed is reshaping the world, simultaneously creating elements of a 'global culture' while strengthening many features of 'local culture' and 'popular culture'.

One can think of culture as the glue that binds people together and enables them to interact. But cultures may not be equally successful in enabling people to live well, in peace and harmony, and to exercise their creativity. A culture of peace and harmony, for instance, is something that must be created, not just taken for granted. Genocide, ethnic cleansing, civil conflict, repression of minorities, domestic violence – today as in the past, nationally and internationally – are a reproach to our political cultures. Far too many people on this planet experience violence as an undesired aspect of their 'way of life'. Indeed, for many, violence or the threat of violence have become routine, a commonplace.

Yet at another level the glue provided by culture makes human development and economic growth possible. At this more profound level, culture is the most valuable instrument of all. Culture gives people a sense of identity and helps to define one's place in the world. It provides a degree of psychological security by enclosing each person within symbolically visible cultural boundaries. It fosters trust and cooperation within the group and thereby facilitates collective agreements, working together and market exchange. It makes people's behaviour and reactions more predictable than otherwise and this, too, facilitates cooperation, exchange and economic transactions in general. It inhibits (or at least contains) interpersonal, interkinship and intercommunity conflict while at times accentuating conflict with those of other cultures, particularly when 'the other' is sharply defined or differentiated.

Globalization is bringing cultures into increasingly close and frequent contact with one another. This 'rubbing' produces friction and the possibility of conflict,[39] which in turn require further cultural adaptation and institutional innovation. But cultural contact also leads to cultural exchange, to mutually profitable borrowing and lending, and to cultural adaptation. These, in turn, result in cultural vitality for all concerned, in aesthetic, scientific and technological creativity and in economic expansion. Indeed it is quite possible that cultural exchange is one of the roots, perhaps the principal root, of global dynamism and the ultimate source of human creativity, human development and economic growth.

If one adopts a culture-centred rather than a state-centred view of the world, things look rather different. Culture seen from a global perspective can be regarded as human 'software'.[40] This is a global asset which in principle is accessible to all, although in practice some groups have much greater ease of access than others. Access to this 'software' takes place when cultures interpenetrate, a historical process that goes back as far as one can see. Today, however, cultural interpenetration is more frequent, more rapid and more pervasive than ever before. This aspect of globalization ultimately may be more significant than other features of the process that receive so much attention, namely, the rapid growth of international trade, the investments by transnational corporations, the huge flows of financial capital, the migration of labour and the political and institutional transformations occurring at supranational levels. The reason cultural interpenetration is so important is that it implies cultural exchange and this, in turn, implies diversity, heterogeneity and a breaking down of mental and conceptual boundaries. That is, cultural exchange can be understood as 'a translocal learning process'[41] which stimulates creativity and is the fountainhead of material progress and human development.

# 3
# Globalization and the Shape of Things to Come*

We are participants in a long march to a global economy. Since the end of the Second World War economic forces have been unleashed which are creating for the first time a worldwide economic system which is regulated largely by market forces. Government-imposed restraints on the free flow of trade, investment and technology have diminished sharply and a liberal international economic order has been created which has profound implications for the shape of things to come. Indeed I shall argue that economic globalization is bound to affect not only the way we earn our living but also our political institutions, the natural environment and the pace of cultural interchange.

Globalization is a consequence partly of policy changes, partly of technological changes which have reduced the costs of integration and partly of the disintegration of the European, Japanese and Russian empires which fragmented the world into separate spheres of influence. These processes have transformed the world economy in a remarkably short period of time. World income and output since 1950 have grown about 3 per cent a year, faster than at any time in recorded history. World trade has grown more than twice as fast as this and individual countries have become much more 'open' to external influences. Between 1950 and 1996, for example, exports increased from 7 per cent of total global output to 21 per cent.

Foreign direct investment grew half again as fast as foreign trade and three times as fast as world output. Global financial investment in stocks, bonds and foreign currencies grew ten times as fast as world output. No one born after 1914 can have witnessed such a high speed of economic integration or such a high degree of integration.

## Is globalization a new phenomenon?

Sceptics might retort that only those ignorant of history could claim that globalization is a new phenomenon. The present period of rapid integration, according to the sceptics, should be seen as a return to the past, and particularly to the economic conditions that prevailed in the second half of the nineteenth century and the first 13 years of the twentieth century. Prior to the First World War, international commerce was relatively free, overseas investment was a commonplace and, moreover, there was widespread international migration of labour, unlike today. All of this was interrupted by the two world wars and the great depression of the 1930s. Now, at last, we are returning to the earlier trend of closer global economic integration.

While there is some truth to this sceptical view, there are several factors that suggest that the process of globalization today is qualitatively different from the processes operating in the nineteenth century. We must not forget that a high proportion of the world's population participated only marginally in the global economy of the nineteenth century. Because of the high cost of transport and communication, countries experienced high levels of 'natural' protection and the degree of economic integration necessarily was rather low. Furthermore, a majority of the world's population lived under colonial regimes where trade and investment were regulated in the interest of the imperial power.

This situation began to change radically with decolonization, starting in 1947 with the independence of India and Pakistan. When China began to open its economy in late 1978, another billion people – roughly one-fifth of the world's population – became more closely integrated into the global economy. The process continued with the disintegration of the USSR in 1991, when another 400 million people were added. Thus the spatial dimension of globalization is much larger than in the past.

On the conceptual plane, too, globalization is much broader than ever before. Indeed it is virtually all embracing.[1] The penetration of market forces to every corner of the globe is affecting everything: our social relations and politics, our culture, even our global climate. True, human activity in the past has altered microclimates, reduced biological diversity and resulted in the extinction of certain species, but the effects usually were localized whereas now they often are generalized. Equally important, we lack institutions of global governance which even in principle could enable us to take collective action to correct or mitigate the undesirable effects of globalization.

How did this state of affairs arise? Let us begin with policy-induced liberalization. Since 1947 there have been eight rounds of global negotiations to reduce tariffs and other restrictions on international trade. The most recent negotiations – in the so-called Uruguay round – were completed in 1993. Initially trade liberalization concentrated on manufactured goods and on trade among the rich countries. The results have been highly successful and tariffs on manufactured goods imported into rich countries are today only about 4 per cent on average. Moreover, trade liberalization has gradually been extended to cover agricultural products as well as services and to include the developing countries, so that trade liberalization now is universal even if not complete.

Restrictions on the international movement of capital were removed more slowly. The United States generally eschewed capital controls from the beginning, but elsewhere capital controls were not abolished until 1979 in Britain, 1980 in Japan and 1990 in France and Italy. Capital account liberalization was even more gradual in the developing countries, but after 1982 the process accelerated dramatically, indeed in my view too rapidly, particularly in Latin America and sub-Saharan Africa where liberalization was made a condition for international assistance to stabilization and restructuring programmes.

There has not been a comparable liberalization of the global labour market. On the contrary, policies have become less liberal in recent years, as we shall see below.

Technological changes have reinforced policy changes in fostering globalization. The costs of freight and passenger transport, communications and computing have fallen dramatically and as a result the pattern of global production is changing beyond recognition. A product may be designed in one country, its components produced in a second, the parts assembled in a third and the final product exported to a fourth. Lower transport costs have reduced 'natural' protection and this has permitted a much more dispersed location of production worldwide. Indeed labels of national origin on manufactured products are becoming meaningless.

Primary products, which are transport intensive, are of declining relative importance in world trade whereas trade in services and in manufactured goods has been growing very rapidly. Some services, e.g. computer software, can be 'shipped' over a telephone line, and containerization has greatly reduced the cost of shipping manufactured goods. New technologies have reduced both space and time.

These new technologies also have helped to make globalization irreversible. Electronic transfers of funds make it more difficult for governments to reimpose capital controls. The fax and e-mail make it more difficult to restrict flows of information services. The large volume of intra-firm trade within multinational corporations and the ability of multinational corporations to shift resources readily throughout the world make it more difficult to reimpose trade barriers. Globalization and liberalization will be with us for as far ahead as one can see.

## Asymmetrical liberalization

Whether we like it or not, we live in a liberal world where markets are allowed to work their magic, except for one curious asymmetry. There are free flows internationally of primary commodities, manufactured goods and many services. There are free flows of technology and intellectual property rights. There are free flows of capital. The flow of labour, however, is severely restricted and the rich countries are becoming not more liberal but less liberal.

In this respect globalization is moving backwards. There was a time when international migration was massive and forced. In the seventeenth and eighteenth centuries the Atlantic slave trade led directly to the deaths of over 50 million Africans and to the importation of some 15 million slaves into North America, the Caribbean islands and Brazil. In the nineteenth century between 10 and 40 million indentured workers, mostly from China and India, were transported around the world, mostly to colonial territories where labour was scarce. In the second half of the nineteenth century and the first decades of the twentieth there was massive but free migration from Europe, when 60 million people left for the United States, Canada, Australia, New Zealand, South Africa and parts of Latin America.

Since the early 1970s, however, the global labour market has become less free. Controls over immigration have been tightened, the annual flows of immigrants into the rich countries have declined and a bias against the migration of low-skilled labour has been introduced. There is a fragmented global market for high-skilled workers, technicians and professionals but there is no real, legal global market for low-skilled workers. The result in the United States, for example, is that the foreign born account for a much smaller proportion of the US population today (9.3 per cent) than they did a century ago (about 15 per cent).

The restrictions on the movement of workers make no economic sense. Greater international labour mobility, particularly of low-skilled labour, would benefit everyone, host countries and sending countries alike. Greater mobility of labour would raise total output and incomes in the rich, host countries. It would increase efficiency in the use of the world's resources all round, in rich and poor countries alike. It would increase the supply of entrepreneurship and reinvigorate the economies of Western Europe and Japan and help to sustain growth in North America. It would stimulate the creation of small businesses on which the health of economies depends. It would increase savings, investment and human capital formation in the rich countries, while increasing the flow of remittances to poor countries. It would accelerate the pace of innovation. And all these things combined would accelerate the growth of average incomes in both rich countries and poor.

Think of the growth of Western Europe in the 1960s, the growth of the Middle East in the 1970s and the growth in the United States in the late nineteenth and early twentieth centuries: all of these periods of rapid growth were fuelled by large-scale immigration. Indeed the United States could not have developed at the speed it did without the enormous contribution of foreign labour.[2]

Finally, for those of you who might be worried about social security entitlements in your old age, immigration would alleviate the economic problems associated with the ageing population in rich countries. By reducing the dependency ratio, i.e. by raising the ratio of active workers to retired people, immigration permits a lower tax burden on the employed population or a higher level of state-financed pensions, or both. Hence the elderly should be strong defenders of free labour markets.

What, then, is the problem about immigration? Why all the fuss? The advocates of restricting the mobility of labour usually fall back on three arguments.

First, it is claimed that migration increases unemployment. This is not true. Most migrants enter low-wage occupations that are not attractive to the indigenous population. That is, they often do not compete directly with local labour. Furthermore, a high proportion of migrants create their own jobs by becoming self-employed. Most important, by stimulating growth, migration actually reduces unemployment rather than increases it. It is a great fallacy to think that the number of jobs is fixed and that migrant workers deprive local workers of a livelihood. This is a fear on which demagogues feast, but the truth is that migrants create jobs for themselves and others that otherwise would not exist.

Second, it is claimed that migration increases inequality. It is indeed plausible to argue that in the host country immigration lowers the wages of some categories of low-skilled labour and accentuates inequality in the distribution of income, but the quantitative effect is slight. In particular, the huge rise in recent years in inequality in the United States, Western Europe and the ex-socialist countries associated with the former Soviet Union has almost nothing to do with the migration of labour. Attempts sometimes are made to use migrants as scapegoats, but it is quite wrong to blame them for the injustices of our societies. Moreover, if one is seriously concerned about increasing equality, measures that create a more liberal labour market internationally should be welcomed. The reason for this is that from a world perspective, migration reduces global inequality rather than increases it. The egalitarians among us should be staunch advocates of open borders.

Third, it is claimed that migration increases the tax burden. While this is true at some times and in some places, in general this proposition is false. Most migrants are of prime working age. They are neither very young nor old. They therefore place few demands on public education, public health services or state old age pensions. In fact, on balance migrants tend to pay more in taxes than they receive in benefits. The fiscally prudent among us should be warm advocates of free labour markets.

One of the consequences of globalization, however, is that whether one supports or opposes greater freedom of movement, there is not much that can be done about it. Migration is a response to very powerful market forces. Falling costs of travel and rising incomes in the developing countries have made migration much easier, and widening income differentials between rich countries and poor have made migration more attractive. The incentives to migrate are strong. The measures to nullify the incentives are costly and ineffective. Many borders are porous. Erecting fences, lengthy checks at crossing points, floodlighting illegal routes of entry, sending troops to patrol borders have all been of little avail. The pragmatists among us might well ask, 'why waste resources trying to prevent what is good for us when we know that in any case we are bound to fail?'

I conclude, then, that fewer restrictions on immigration would benefit everyone, that the alleged harmful effects of migration are greatly exaggerated and that policies intended to prevent immigration, at least in the United States, merely squander taxpayers' money. It is hard to imagine anything more foolish. Good sense however may eventually prevail and, if so, the shape of things to come, in this area at least, will differ substantially from what we see today.

## Globalization and economic space

Let us turn now to consider the economic consequences of globalization. Has globalization produced prosperity? Has it reduced global inequality? Has it affected all regions of the globe similarly?

Viewed from outer space, economic prosperity has increased substantially during recent decades. The world's per capita income rose about 1.2 per cent a year from 1965 to 1996.[3] Seen in historical perspective, this represents rapid growth of the world economy. Angus Maddison, for example, estimates that between 1400 and 1820 world GDP per capita increased only 0.07 per cent a year.[4]

It is widely believed that globalization has been accompanied by greater inequality in the distribution of the world's income. The facts are unclear and the causal relationships are not well understood, but one way of looking at the issue is to divide the world into three groups classified by average income per head. This is the convention that has been followed by the World Bank for a number of years, and is somewhat analogous to dividing society into three classes of low-, middle- and upper-income groups. If we do this, it transpires that during the period 1965–96, average incomes in the low-income countries increased 3.1 per cent a year as compared to 2.2 per cent a year in the high-income countries; in the middle-income countries average income increased only 0.9 per cent a year. That is, growth rates were bimodally distributed across countries classified by level of per capita income. The poorest countries grew faster than the richest and, in this sense, global inequality diminished.[5]

This is slightly misleading, however, because inequality within the group of low-income countries increased dramatically. The countries of sub-Saharan Africa experienced a decline in average incomes (−0.2 per cent a year) whereas the two largest and poor Asian countries, China and India, enjoyed much faster growth (6.7 and 2.3 per cent a year, respectively). This illustrates the more general point that growth has been distributed very unevenly among the major regions of the developing world. Growth rates were negative not only in sub-Saharan Africa but also in the Middle East and North Africa (−1.8 per cent a year) and in the ex-socialist developing countries of Europe and Central Asia (−1.3 per cent a year). In Latin America and the Caribbean the rate of growth was positive but rather low (1.1 per cent a year), whereas in South Asia (2.2 per cent a year) growth was twice as fast as in Latin America and in East Asia and the Pacific (5.5 per cent a year) it was five times as fast.

These large variations in long-term growth rates cannot be attributed entirely to the process of global integration and liberalization. The decline in incomes in the ex-socialist countries arises in the first instance from the political collapse of the former Soviet Union. The transition from central planning to a more market-oriented economic system and the way the Soviet bloc countries were reintegrated into the world economy often were handled poorly, but this has little to do with globalization as such. China, after all, handled the processes of transition and reintegration smoothly and experienced no fall in income. On the contrary, growth accelerated.[6] The same is true of Vietnam. Similarly, the steep decline in average incomes in the Middle East and North Africa reflects the political turmoil in the region (civil conflict in Algeria, wars in Iraq, Iran and Kuwait) at least as much as falling oil prices. Yet it is only the latter that is connected directly to economic globalization.

Falling incomes in sub-Saharan Africa and the slow growth of incomes in Latin America can more plausibly be linked to globalization. The debt crisis of the 1980s hit these two regions particularly hard and the recovery from the crisis-induced depressions was slow and difficult. And in many parts of Africa, civil conflicts of various sorts greatly aggravated the region's economic difficulties.

At the other end of the spectrum, the best growth performance, until 1997, clearly was in East Asia. Indeed many commentators cite East Asia as evidence that globalization is a powerful force for economic progress. But just as globalization cannot be blamed entirely for a region's failure, so too it cannot be credited for another region's success. There is much more to East Asia's outstanding economic performance than trade liberalization, low exchange rates and exploitation of its comparative advantage in labour intensive exports of manufactured goods.[7] Several countries in the region (China, South Korea, Taiwan) had major land reforms and several others (including Hong Kong and Singapore) began the development process with a reasonably equitable distribution of income. East Asia also emphasized human capital formation – notably basic education and health services – and this contributed both to rapid growth and low inequality. Rates of physical capital formation were high and this investment was financed largely by domestic savings; foreign capital was relatively unimportant. In other words, 'domestic' economic factors were at least as important as 'global' factors in explaining East Asia's success.

So far we have concentrated on the spatial distribution of the outcomes of globalization, namely, variations in economic growth.

But what are the global forces that affect these outcomes? The two most important are flows of international capital, particularly foreign direct investment, and international trade in goods and services. Consider first foreign direct investment.

Despite the liberalization of global capital markets, foreign investment is rather small. In the rich countries, foreign direct investment accounts for only about 6 per cent of total investment. Most investment continues to be financed by domestic savings. Despite the great scarcity of capital in developing countries and its apparent abundance in the rich countries, the largest recipient of foreign direct investment is the United States. In fact, most foreign investment consists of one rich country investing in another rich country. Roughly 60 per cent of all foreign direct investment circulates among the small number of rich countries and only 40 per cent is directed to the large number of poor countries that account for 85 per cent of the world's population.

Within this large group of developing countries, most foreign investment is directed to the middle-income countries. In 1995, for example, the low-income countries received only 43.5 per cent of the foreign direct investment that was channelled to developing countries. Moreover, one country, China, received 86.4 per cent of all the foreign capital invested in low-income countries. In other words, most poor countries received virtually no foreign capital.[8]

Despite the liberalization of the world's capital markets, foreign investment has not become an engine of growth in the poor countries. If anything, flows of foreign capital, because they are concentrated in the rich countries, have helped to widen global inequalities. Foreign investment does not flow to countries where capital is 'scarce' in a physical sense; rather it flows to countries where expected profits are high. In the developing countries this implies that foreign direct investment is most likely to be attracted to countries that have rich mineral deposits (especially oil) or to countries that have succeeded in achieving rapid growth of exports (particularly manufacturing exports)[9] or more generally to countries which already are enjoying a rapid rate of growth of total output and income.[10] Foreign direct investment, in summary, is not a cause of growth; it is a consequence of growth.

The same is true, broadly speaking, of foreign trade. Most of the world's trade consists of exports from one rich country to another. The high-income countries currently account for more than three-quarters of total world merchandise exports. The share of the developing countries is less than 22 per cent and the share of sub-Saharan Africa and South Asia combined is a paltry 2.4 per cent. In other words, most of the very poor countries are out of the trade loop; they are effectively delinked from the global economy.

During the first half of the 1990s the volume of world trade grew 6.0 per cent a year. Merchandise exports originating in the high-income countries grew somewhat less rapidly than this, namely 5.4 per cent a year, indicating that the rest of the world was becoming more closely integrated into the global economy. This was especially true of East and South Asia, where exports increased 17.8 and 8.6 per cent a year, respectively. In sub-Saharan Africa and in the Middle East and North Africa, however, trade increased only about 1 per cent a year. These two regions are becoming increasingly marginalized.

Thus the forces propelling globalization – trade and investment – have had a very uneven spatial impact. The rich countries have participated fully in the process and the middle-income countries are becoming increasingly integrated into the global system, but among the low-income countries, only China has become a large recipient of foreign capital and a major trading nation. Most of the poor countries have benefited neither from a rapid growth of exports nor from a large inflow of foreign investment. The most important economic consequence of globalization in these countries has been the exodus of much of their human capital through the emigration of professional, technical and managerial personnel.

The processes of globalization, positive and negative, have enormous implications for politics and for our dominant political institution, the territorial state. Let us examine some of these implications.

## The squeeze on the state

The state as an economic entity is being squeezed from above by the forces of globalization and from below by the forces of sub-nationalist and ethnic politics.[11] The creation of a unified global economic system is eroding the ability of the state to manage the domestic economy, i.e. to impose its will on enterprises with subsidiaries in a number of countries, on investors with access to international capital markets and on employed persons with internationally marketable skills. Increased mobility of goods and services, assets and individuals has made it increasingly difficult for the state to impose its authority on persons and entities that in principle fall under its jurisdiction.

Just as the state of Minnesota, within the context of the US economy, has limited freedom of action in economic affairs, so too one can imagine a time when, say, Canada, within the context of a global economy, will have lost much of its power to regulate its own economy. The state as the locus of economic control may be slowly withering away. The French learned during the Mitterrand government that Keynesian macroeconomic policy no longer is possible in one country. The Thais have recently learned that exchange rate policy in a globally integrated economy is severely constrained. Most central bankers know that integration of world bond markets sets limits on their ability to lower interest rates. Microeconomic policy is similarly constrained. For example, the ability of large firms to locate their fixed investment almost anywhere in the world has reduced the power of the state to regulate industry be it through taxation, the imposition of minimum wage legislation, environmental controls, health and safety provisions or anything else.

One must not exaggerate the argument, however. In some cases, globalization affects not so much what governments do as how they do it. Consider taxation as an example. The relatively greater mobility of capital as compared to labour has led to a shift in the burden of taxation in the rich countries from capital to labour. Within the capital category, governments have an incentive to tax fixed capital and immobile natural capital (land, real estate, mineral deposits) more highly than internationally mobile financial capital. Indeed governments often offer subsidies to attract finance capital. And within the labour category, we have witnessed in recent years a tendency for governments to reduce the marginal rates of income taxation on high-income earners (who are internationally more mobile) while actually increasing effective tax rates on less mobile ordinary wage earners. Thus globalization has had a discriminatory and disequalizing effect by weakening the ability of the state to impose or increase certain types of taxation.

Even the ability of the state to police its own frontiers is being undermined. Smuggling of goods into and out of countries is a commonplace and occurs on a massive scale. In some countries in Africa it is thought that over half of international trade consists of smuggled goods. The most notorious example of the inability of the state to control the production and trade of commodities is of course narcotic drugs. In many parts of Latin America and South-east Asia the illegal production of drugs accounts for a significant proportion of total output, most of which is exported. Indeed it is estimated that the retail value of trade in illegal drugs is second only to the weapons trade and exceeds international trade in oil.

The flow of 'bads' is equally difficult to control. Pollution no longer respects international boundaries. In some cases pollution threatens the globe as a whole (as in the rise in average global temperature caused by burning fossil fuels); in other cases pollution affects a large number of countries in a specific region (as in the explosion of a nuclear power plant at Chernobyl, Ukraine); and in still other cases pollution may affect a single neighbouring country (as with air pollution from power stations coming down as acid rain hundreds of miles away). Globalization, in other words, implies not only the universal dissemination of goods but also the dissemination of 'bads'.

Lastly, as suggested earlier, the state also is losing control over the flow of labour across its borders. It is now cheaper and faster than ever before for people to move from one country to another, and they are doing so in the millions. Most migration, contrary to popular perception, consists of poor people moving from one low-income country to another, often as refugees or as irregular, unrecorded, illegal migrants. Despite strenuous efforts, there is little the state can do about these flows of people and in the end there may be no alternative but to accept the situation, declare an amnesty and regularize the position of the irregular migrants.

In summary, slowly but surely, globalization is weakening the economic sovereignty of states. Freedom of manoeuvre has diminished and policy mistakes can be severely punished by global market forces. Increased mobility of enterprises, assets and individuals has made it easier for economic agents to escape controls or at least to mitigate them. And when attempts are made to prohibit an activity, as with trade in narcotic drugs and the immigration of labour, the outcome is unlikely to be a cessation of the activity but rather its transfer to the underground economy.

In addition to the forces of globalization coming from above, the state is being squeezed from below by other forces which can loosely be described as sub-nationalism. These forces challenge the political legitimacy of existing states and threaten their territorial integrity. Examples include the separation of Bangladesh from Pakistan; the separation of Eritrea from Ethiopia; the disintegration of the former Soviet Union into 15 independent states; the continuing disintegration of the former Yugoslavia; and separatist movements in a large number of states, including Indonesia, the Philippines, India, Sri Lanka and the Sudan. The Palestinian struggle for nationhood can be included here. Cases can also be found of nationalist movements that cut across existing state boundaries and that aspire to create a new state of their own from portions of existing states. The movements for Irish reunification, greater Serbia and a greater Kurdistan (potentially absorbing territory from Iran, Iraq, Syria and Turkey) are obvious examples.

These movements can be viewed in a variety of ways, e.g. as inspired by nationalist, ethnic or cultural demands, but at their heart is a search for community or identity different from the community or identity offered by shared citizenship of an existing state. In some cases sub-nationalist movements centre on differences in language and culture, as in the Basque movement in Spain, the conflict between the Flemings and Walloons in Belgium and the separatist movement in Quebec, Canada. In other cases the search for community has revolved around a resurgence of religious identity. Examples include the separatist movement by the Sikhs in north-western India and the revival of Islam in many parts of the world. In still other cases broader 'ethnic' demands have become a source of conflict, as in many parts of sub-Saharan Africa, in Central America and in the Andean region of South America.

How should one interpret the rise of ethnicity as a political force? First, it is evident that ethnicity can undermine state power and pose a threat from below to the legitimacy of existing states. Second, sub-nationalist movements can be intolerant of outsiders, narrow and exclusive, socially divisive and sources of communal strife. But, third, at their best they can be inclusive and sharing; they can encourage strong loyalties and commitment; and they can permit a high degree of participation in the life of the community. Sub-nationalist movements can be seen as creating an opportunity for more self-determination, as enabling people to choose the polity under which they wish to live, and as enlarging personal and group freedoms. These are things which should be welcomed. I shall argue below, however, that if taken to an extreme, sub-nationalist politics are doomed to failure: the construction of a community around a homogeneous culture is neither possible nor desirable.

Sub-nationalist political movements, if they attain their objectives, are likely to lead to smaller political units, i.e. loose federations in large states or an increase in the number of small states. It is indeed the reduction in scale of the polity that permits greater participatory democracy. This raises the possibility of a trade-off between the political desirability of small states and a loss of economic efficiency. That is, it forces us to consider whether small states are likely to suffer from diseconomies of scale.

There are two areas where one can plausibly argue that small states are at an economic disadvantage, namely in providing the basic machinery of government and in supplying defence services. Every country will need a head of state, an array of ministries, a tax-collecting bureaucracy, a central bank, etc. The costs of providing these essential services may well rise less than proportionately as the size of state increases. Particularly in very small states, including many islands in the South Pacific and the Caribbean, the costs may be disproportionately high. In other words, there may be a range over which there are economies of scale in public administration. If so, very small states will be at an economic disadvantage.

The same is true when it comes to military expenditure and warfare. Small states are at a disadvantage compared to large. This does not mean that all small states are incapable of defending themselves (Switzerland suggests otherwise), or that no small state can defeat a major power (Vietnam has shown that it can be done), or that all small states need armed forces (Costa Rica has survived and prospered without an army), but if military power is an objective, large states enjoy an economic advantage in the form of lower unit costs.

There are also economies of scale in production and this, too, puts small countries at an economic disadvantage to the extent that they rely on their domestic market. It is here, however, that globalization comes to the aid of sub-nationalist forces. Liberalization of economic transactions and the creation of an integrated global market are making it easier for small states to exploit economies of scale in production. Globalization means that small states need not pay a penalty in the form of reduced efficiency and lower incomes. Similarly, national alliances, collective security and international mechanisms for keeping the peace – if they are credible – provide alternative ways for small states to achieve a degree of military security.

In other words, globalization is reducing the economic disadvantages of small states. Globalization also has made smaller states politically more attractive to many sub-nationalist groups. Thus the costs of smallness are falling and the perceived benefits are rising. This implies that the squeeze on existing states is likely to continue. Processes of globalization are becoming increasingly compatible with the search for identity based on smaller communities.

## Global governance

If one accepts the argument that globalization has reduced the ability of the state to manage economic affairs, then it is important to reconsider our institutions for global governance. It does not follow automatically that if the state is weaker, global institutions should be strengthened. It is possible to imagine an alternative response in which groups of countries come together to create strong regional institutions. Indeed this is happening in the European Union and it is conceivable that something similar could occur in South-east Asia and parts of Latin America. One can also imagine a multi-layered system of governance beginning with global institutions but embracing regional and state institutions as well as institutions of provincial and local government. Great Britain, for example, has decided simultaneously to become more closely integrated into the European Union and to devolve some authority now held by the central government to newly created institutions in Scotland and Wales. In such a multi-layered system it should be possible to locate responsibility at that layer of governance where economies of scale are exhausted. In Europe this is called the principle of subsidiarity.

Thus we are not talking about world government but rather about a set of institutions at the global level that are needed to manage the forces of globalization. Our existing system of global governance emerged higgledy-piggledy in response to a series of crises and global events, foremost among which were the First World War, the Second World War, the collapse of imperialism and the associated dramatic increase in the number of newly independent countries. The linchpin of the present system is the United Nations Organization with its headquarters in New York.

Although the United States was the moving spirit behind the creation of the UN, and to this day has the dominant position within the Organization, the United States in the last two decades has been ambivalent in its attitude towards international multilateral cooperation. On the one hand, the United States in principle remains committed to multilateral solutions to global problems and is quick to use the UN when it is in its interest to do so, as in the recent confrontation with Iraq over weapons inspection. On the other hand, the United States has so far refused to pay the $1.5 billion it owes to the UN and is demanding that its share of the regular budget be reduced by a fifth (from 25 to 20 per cent). The United States has not hesitated to act unilaterally when it was convenient to do so, e.g. in disregarding the dispute resolution procedures of the World Trade Organization (WTO), and on two occasions it has withdrawn from two major specialized agencies, namely, the International Labour Organization (ILO) and the United Nations Educational, Scientific and Cultural Organization (UNESCO).

This behaviour has put the United States at odds with the vast majority of other member countries, undermined the cohesion of the Organization and seriously eroded the financial viability of the entire United Nations system. Precisely at a time when globalization has increased the need for an effective system of global governance, the ability of our existing institutions to undertake collective action on a global scale has been reduced. Only anarchists and nihilists can be content with this state of affairs. The combination of an enfeebled system of global governance and an increasing number of states which find it increasingly difficult to manage their economies is almost certain to result in periodic crises and poor performance over the long run. Reforms are essential. The question is what sorts of reforms are most urgently needed.

First, our institutions of global governance should be more democratic. The present system of voting is a bizarre and indefensible mixture in which in the Security Council the five countries which happened to be on the winning side at the end of the Second World War have a veto, in the General Assembly each state has the same vote and influence whether its population is less than 1 million people or more than 1 billion, and in the International Monetary Fund and World Bank votes are weighted by a country's financial contribution. Something more closely approximating the principle of one person, one vote is needed to confer political legitimacy on our global institutions.

Second, the finances of our global institutions must be given secure foundations. The assessment of budgetary contributions should be based on agreed principles, payment should be punctual and obligatory and a mechanism for enforcement should be created, including penalties for non-compliance. A clause in the United Nations charter deprives a country of its vote in the General Assembly if it does not adhere to the financial rules and is two years or more in arrears. This clause has never been applied. At the very least, it should be strictly enforced. Third, global governance should be based increasingly on the rule of law. States should be bound by their international commitments and should be prevented from oscillating between multilateralism and unilateralism whenever it suits them. Disputes should be settled by the International Court of Justice or by specialized tribunals created for the purpose, and judgments should be binding on all parties. It is highly regrettable that the United States along with a small number of other countries recently refused to support the creation of a permanent international court of criminal justice.

Fourth, serious consideration should be given to the proposal of the previous Secretary-General to create a small but permanent United Nations peace-keeping and peace-making force. Interventions in conflict situations have so far been on an *ad hoc* basis and have largely depended on the political interests of one or more of the major powers rather than on the intrinsic merits of the case. We need a proper global police force but one which is accountable to the global community as a whole. This is especially true today because the distinction between internal and external conflicts is rapidly ceasing to be useful: refugees from civil conflicts spill across international borders, armed bands seek temporary sanctuary in adjacent territories, neighbouring countries get drawn into the conflict, one or more of the great powers intervenes and the United Nations is then called in to clean up the mess. Surely we can do better than this.

These issues of global governance are connected to the question discussed earlier of the size of the state. The design of mechanisms that reduce the likelihood of armed conflict and increase security, the creation of more effective global organizations and the continuation of economic liberalization all permit a small size of state when that is what people desire.

Turning to issues of economic governance, there are just a few points I wish to make.[12] First, it is evident that the International Monetary Fund is much too small to act as a world central bank and lender of last resort. The elimination of controls over international trade and capital account transactions is bound to result in periods of instability and there is a danger that instability in one country will be transferred to another. This in fact is what we are witnessing today. Hence the demand on the resources of the IMF to finance short-term stabilization programmes is certain to increase. Recent evidence from Mexico to South Korea, Indonesia and Russia, however, has shown that the funds available to the IMF are woefully inadequate. Increasingly the resources the IMF can lend to a country have had to be supplemented by funds from the United States and other countries. In the 1997 stabilization programme in South Korea, for example, the IMF provided less than 40 per cent of the total funds required, namely, $21 billion out of a total of $55 billion. The rest was provided by the World Bank ($10 billion), the Asian Development Bank ($4 billion) and seven individual countries led by Japan ($10 billion) and the United States ($5 billion). This need to rely on multiple sources of financing weakens the authority and autonomy of the IMF and injects an external political element into decisions about what countries to assist, how much funding to provide and what policy conditions should be imposed. None of this is desirable and I believe a strong case can be made for a very substantial increase in the resources of the IMF. At the same time, the IMF needs to be reformed and to become less secretive about its policies and more accountable for its actions.

Second, the World Bank and the various regional development banks may have outlived their usefulness. Foreign aid in all its forms is shrinking and has become dwarfed by international flows of private capital. The world market for long-term capital is functioning reasonably well and profitable projects have little difficulty in attracting private capital. True, private foreign capital, as we have seen, does not flow in large amounts to the poorest of the developing countries, but their needs can best be met by direct transfers of grants rather than through loans on favourable terms. The time has come to privatize the World Bank and the other intergovernmental financial aid agencies.

If we do this, it will be necessary to create a new mechanism for providing foreign assistance to the lowest-income countries to replace the dying conventional aid programmes. One possibility would be a pure international tax and transfer mechanism. Resources could be raised through a low and mildly progressive international income tax on the gross national product of high-income countries. These resources would then be disbursed automatically through a negative income tax. That is, foreign assistance would be distributed to low-income countries in inverse proportion to the recipients' income per head. Such a scheme would ensure that the burden of foreign assistance is equitably distributed among the rich countries, that the available funds are distributed among eligible poor countries in accordance with their need and that foreign assistance is insulated from the political, commercial and other interests of rich countries.

A separate mechanism is needed to facilitate mutually beneficial intergovernmental transactions where the global market mechanism works poorly. Examples include environmental programmes in developing countries which are at least in part of benefit to developed countries, the management of the global commons in Antarctica, the oceans and outer space and public health measures in developing countries designed to prevent the spread of the AIDS epidemic and other communicable diseases such as tuberculosis. There are numerous cases where economic and technological globalization generate 'externalities' and 'free rider' problems, particularly but not exclusively for the environment. Where there are cases of 'market failure', alternative institutions will have to be created to facilitate the negotiation of advantageous agreements and monitor the results.[13] When an agreement includes side payments for services rendered by one party to another, provision will also have to be made for the transfer of funds.

Lastly, we need to strengthen rule-based systems governing international economic intercourse. If liberalism is to be taken seriously, countries must be discouraged from acting arbitrarily and unilaterally and harming the interests of their trading partners. An example of unilateral action is the proliferation of anti-dumping measures in some countries as a disguised form of protection, now that tariffs have been reduced to very low levels. In 1996 there were 311 anti-dumping measures in force in the United States and 153 in the European Union; at the other extreme, there were only three anti-dumping measures in force in Japan, two in Singapore and none in Chile. A mechanism is needed to enforce good behaviour and to provide compensation for damages when one country breaks the rules of the game and inflicts economic injury on another.

The suggestion, in other words, is that the principles which govern economic intercourse within a country should be extended worldwide. Discrimination against workers on grounds of race, for example, is illegal in many countries. The injured party may take the offender to court and claim substantial damages. There is a remedy in law. In the international arena, however, there is no effective remedy when one country arbitrarily violates the rules of good conduct. The new World Trade Organization does contain some provision for compensation, but the coverage is narrow and the process of adjudication slow and cumbersome. Much more needs to be done.

## Globalization, culture and development: the long view

Globalization, as we have seen, has major implications for economics, politics and institutional transformation. It also has implications for culture, and the ways cultures interact and adapt to changing circumstances.[14] Some analysts claim to observe the emergence of a global culture and the spread of Western values, political forms of organization and ways of life. I believe this view is too simple. Indeed if one looks deeply it will be evident that globalization is creating greater cultural diversity, not less.

Moreover, almost all countries are culturally diverse, whether they like it or not. Some, it must be admitted, do not. At one end of the spectrum are those who believe pluralism is a disadvantage. Diversity leads to conflict, violence and bloodshed and to political instability.

Multi-culturalism is something that must be contained or managed, preferably by making 'them' as much like 'us' as possible. Far from contributing to economic growth and human development, cultural diversity is an obstacle that in one way or another must be overcome.

At the other end of the spectrum are those who regard cultural diversity as an asset. Different ways of life, different ways of looking at the world, different ways of thinking pose challenges and tensions which are a source of creativity and it is creativity which is the fountainhead of economic growth and human development. Cultures can be seen as 'experiments' which lead to new knowledge, new technology and new institutional arrangements, and it is these experiments with different ways of being and doing that are the ultimate sources of human betterment.

I do not wish to deny that historically cultural contact has sometimes had highly negative consequences, including conquest, the spread of racism and the destruction of indigenous societies. But in the long run, cultural interchange has been very beneficial and in fact has made us what we are, affecting what we eat, how we preserve or regain our health, what we believe, how we discover the truths of nature, what languages we speak, the ways we calculate and the scripts we use to communicate with one another.

What was true in the past is even more true today. Globalization has made cultural interchange more frequent than in the past, deeper and more rapid. Furthermore, cultural interchange in the modern world is characterized by greater reciprocity, by more of a two-way exchange. As we have seen, capital, technology and even labour circulate globally. Science is accessible to all to a greater degree than ever before. Ideas, information and knowledge flow more quickly and widely than ever before. And the result is greater diversity than ever before, locally and globally. This increased diversity, in turn, has resulted in a faster pace of technical innovation and social creativity. There has been an explosive growth of knowledge and technology in the last 50 years and this has greatly contributed to the rapid advances in human development that have occurred and to the rapid economic growth we have enjoyed, a pace of growth worldwide that is unprecedented.

# 4
# Human Development: Origins, Evolution and Impact*

Modern development economics, that is, that branch of economics concerned with improving conditions in low-income countries, can be traced back to the 1940s.[1] From its inception development economics has largely been about material enrichment, that is, expanding the volume of production of goods and services. It was usually assumed, explicitly or implicitly, that an increase in aggregate output, say, the growth of gross domestic product per capita, would reduce poverty and raise the general well being of the population. This assumption was rooted in utilitarianism and the view that production generated incomes and higher incomes, in turn, resulted in greater utility or economic welfare. Indeed the connection between increased output and decreased poverty was thought to be so strong that many economists believed that a concentration on growth alone would suffice to achieve the goal of development. Growth, in other words, became not just the means for achieving development but the end of development itself. True, there were always dissenters, but the dissenters tended to qualify the emphasis on growth by underlining the importance of the distribution of the benefits of growth, rather than challenging the importance of growth as such. Debates about alternative development strategies often were debates about how best to accelerate the growth of production of goods and services.[2]

## Origins

The human development approach as it emerged in the late 1980s represented a radical departure in two ways. First, it challenged the utilitarian assumption on which much of development economics rests. Above all, following the path-breaking work of Amartya Sen, the process of development is seen as a process of expanding the 'capabilities' of people rather than increasing utility or economic welfare or satisfaction.[3] That is, the objective of development is not to increase output but to enable people to increase their range of choice, to do more things, to live a long life, to escape avoidable illness, to have access to the world's stock of knowledge, and so forth. Notice that capabilities and choices are closely linked and these, in turn, are closely linked to freedom, both negative freedom (e.g. freedom from hunger) and positive freedom (e.g. freedom to achieve more fully the life of one's choice).[4]

An increase in the supply of commodities in this formulation may help to increase human capabilities, but it does so indirectly and is not an end in itself. The human development approach, in other words, dethrones national product as the primary indicator of the level of development. Moreover, although rising output and incomes do increase human development, they do so at a diminishing rate. That is, there are diminishing returns to the ability of material enrichment to increase human capabilities. This is not the same as assuming diminishing marginal utility of income, although several critics have confused the two points.

Second, the human development approach also has challenged the common assumption that the means to development is the accumulation of physical capital, that is, investment in plant and equipment. Following the equally path-breaking work of T.W. Schultz, human development places great emphasis on the accumulation of human capital.[5] A large number of empirical studies have shown that expenditure on education often produces economic returns which are as high as or higher than the returns from investing in physical capital.[6] The concept of human capital formation includes more than expenditure on education, however. It has been extended to cover research and development expenditures which generate new knowledge and technologies, the provision of basic health services, expenditures on nutrition programmes and the provision of family planning services.[7] That is, investment in human beings in all these forms is regarded as productive, whether the objective is to increase national product or expand human capabilities.

Taken together, the shift in the objective of development combined with an emphasis on human capital as the means to development have far-reaching implications for the overall strategy of development. People are placed firmly in the centre of the stage: they are simultaneously the object of policy and a major instrument of their own development. A commodity-centred view of development is replaced by a people-centred view of development.

## Evolution

Dissatisfaction with gross national product as an indicator of development and with commodity-centred approaches in general is long standing. The World Bank in the early 1970s advocated a marginal redistribution of income, using part of the additional output created by a growth process to benefit the poor by investing in assets of particular importance to them. This strategy of 'redistribution from growth' was important because of its tacit recognition that the expansion of production was not enough to reduce poverty and achieve development.[8] The International Labour Organization, in an effort with which I was associated, attempted in the mid-1970s to take the analysis a step further, arguing that development priorities should be altered in favour of employment creation and the satisfaction of basic human needs such as the need for food, shelter, clothing, primary and secondary education and primary health care.[9] Both 'redistribution from growth' and 'basic needs', however, remained within a commodity-centred perspective of development: they merely wanted to ensure that more of the benefits from increased production reached low-income groups.

By the 1980s it became evident that growth could no longer be taken for granted. Much of Africa and Latin America in particular were in deep crisis and development policy was concerned in large part with 'stabilization' and 'structural adjustment'. The standard policies of stabilization and adjustment, however, not only resulted in stagnation or, worse, economic decline, but the brunt of adjustment invariably fell on the less well off, thereby accentuating inequality and poverty. UNICEF reacted to orthodoxy by insisting it was both possible and desirable to design an adjustment programme that protected the poor from a severe decline in income and preserved basic health, nutrition, child care and education services from reductions in public expenditure. This approach, called 'adjustment with a human face', became a major challenge to mainstream views and did more than any prior publication to 'put people first'.[10]

By then the intellectual building blocks of human development were in place and the time was ripe for its acceptance outside academic circles. The impetus came from the United Nations Committee for Development Planning in 1987. The Committee decided that in its 1988 report it would address the human costs of structural adjustment. A working group was created, chaired by the late Mahbub ul Haq, and I was asked to be the rapporteur. I was given a small budget to commission a few research papers and organize, with John Knight of Oxford

University, a research seminar in Geneva. The papers were subsequently published as a special issue of the *Journal of Development Planning* and reprinted in book form.[11] A synthesis of this material became the draft of my report for the Committee for Development Planning, which was published with minor modifications under the innocuous title of *Human Resources Development: a Neglected Dimension of Development Strategy.*[12] The acorn was planted, but it was not obvious it would grow into an oak.

Human development took root a year later when Mahbub ul Haq moved to UNDP as the Special Advisor to the Administrator and persuaded UNDP to endorse the human development approach.[13] Beginning in 1990 the UNDP issued an annual *Human Development Report* which expanded the concept of human development and attempted to show how the strategy could be translated into operational terms for policy makers. *The Human Development Report*, quite deliberately, was printed in the same format as the World Bank's flagship publication, the *World Development Report*. The *Human Development Report*, however, was written in an entertaining style and was much more forthright in its analysis and provocative in its recommendations. It has attracted an enormous amount of interest worldwide and has become highly influential.

Mahbub ul Haq was keen from the beginning that the human development approach should provide clear policy guidance to developing countries. He asked me and Terry McKinley to write a report on problems of implementation and this ultimately was published as a short book entitled *Implementing a Human Development Strategy.*[14] UNDP then invited me to lead teams of economists and other social scientists to Mongolia, Uzbekistan and Vietnam to formulate concrete policies within a human development framework.[15] The countries chosen turned out to be among the poorest in the world and to face daunting economic and social problems. The experiences were invaluable, at least to me, in demonstrating that the insights of the human development approach could indeed be applied even under very difficult circumstances. There is an alternative to the mainstream prescriptions and UNDP can provide a valuable service in offering a 'second opinion' on development issues to low-income countries.

## Measurement

Per capita income had long been the primary indicator of the level of development and changes in per capita income were traditionally the most important indicator of progress in achieving development. Economic welfare since the days of Pigou had been subjected to the 'measuring rod of money', although other social scientists often argued that money income was too narrow a conception of well being.[16] The most serious challenge to GNP per capita as the index of development was the Physical Quality of Life Index, invented by M.D. Morris in the 1970s.[17]

The PQLI, as it is known, tried to measure well being or the 'quality of life' directly rather than indirectly by aggregating the output of goods and services and dividing the total by the size of the population. The index itself is very simple, being the unweighted average of (i) infant mortality per thousand births, on a scale of 0–100, where the poorest performance is given a score of zero and the expected best performance (viz. 7/1000) a score of 100; (ii) life expectancy at age one, on a scale of 0–100, where the poorest performance in each year is given a score of zero and the best a score of 100; and (iii) the adult literacy rate in percentage terms. The PQLI, however, never succeeded in capturing the imagination of development practitioners and failed to dislodge GNP from its lofty perch.

Indeed the dethronement of GNP per capita had to wait until Meghnad Desai (now Lord Desai) and Amartya Sen invented the Human Development Index (HDI) and UNDP incorporated it into the annual *Human Development Report*. Almost instantly the HDI became a widely accepted alternative indicator of development. It is important to recognize, however, that the HDI and GNP per capita are not trying to measure the same thing. GNP per capita is an indicator of utility, well being or economic welfare, while the Human Development Index represents an attempt to measure the level of human capabilities. Well being and capabilities are not the same thing.

A person may have the capability to acquire adequate nutrition (and the well being obtained from nourishment) and yet choose to go on a hunger strike. A person may have the capacity to travel and enjoy mobility and yet choose to stay at home, even if staying at home implies high risks, as during a civil war. Similarly, a person may have the capability to live a long life and yet choose to commit suicide. The Human Development Index is trying to measure capabilities, the set of choices people have available to them, and ultimately the freedoms people have, whereas GNP per capita tries to measure the subjective enjoyment people obtain from consumption. Thus the HDI and GNP per capita should be seen as complementary indicators providing different information and not as substitutes for one another.

The HDI has four components, namely, life expectancy at birth, the adult literacy rate, the combined enrolment ratio in primary, secondary and tertiary education and real income measured in purchasing power parity terms. Note that several of the components of the HDI also are part of the PQLI, but the interpretation of the two indicators is quite different, the former purporting to measure capabilities and the latter well being. The HDI also includes GNP per capita as one of its components, although it is expressed in purchasing power parity terms. Once again, however, the interpretation is rather different: in the HDI income is not used as an indicator of well being but as something which enhances human capabilities.

This is a key point in understanding the human development approach. Higher incomes increase capabilities, but as mentioned earlier, they do so at a diminishing rate. That is, there are diminishing returns to income in terms of the ability of rising incomes to enhance human capabilities. In the HDI there have been experiments with several different ways to introduce the idea of diminishing returns. Currently it is assumed that diminishing returns begin only when real income reaches the global average.[18] This assumption evidently is rather arbitrary, but the principle of diminishing returns to income is important.

One would expect that country rankings on the Human Development Index would be broadly similar to country rankings in terms of GNP per capita, both because in theory rising incomes increase capabilities and because in practice per capita income (in purchasing power parity terms) is incorporated into the HDI and given a weight of one-third. What is interesting is not that the correlation between the two indicators is high and positive but that it is far from perfect. Indeed in a surprising number of cases there is a very substantial difference between country rankings on the two scales.

In 1995, for example, out of a total of 174 countries for which we have data, there were 18 countries in which the difference between the two rankings was 25 places or more. Some countries clearly do much better in terms of human development than their level of income would lead one to predict. Costa Rica, for instance, ranks 34 on the HDI whereas in terms of per capita income it ranks only 62, a difference of 28. Similarly, Vietnam ranks 122 on the HDI whereas its per capita income rank is 148, a difference of 26. Four other countries, three of them ex-socialist countries, have performed relatively better in terms of human development than in terms of their ability to produce the goods and services measured in GDP and GNP. A relatively low income, in other words, need not prevent countries from adopting policies which result in relatively high levels of human development.

The opposite also is true. Some countries, despite a high level of income per head, have underperformed in terms of human development. Kuwait, for example, ranks fifth out of 174 countries in the world on a real GDP per capita scale, yet it ranks only 54 on the HDI scale, a difference of 49 places. The pattern is similar in Morocco, Mauritius, Senegal and eight other countries which have performed very poorly on the HDI scale compared to the ranking on a real income scale. A high average income, in other words, is no guarantee of a high level of human development. Hence if one agrees that an expansion of human capabilities should be the objective of development policy, the strategy of development will have to be broadened to include much more than the growth of GNP.

One of these additional dimensions is the distribution of income. Greater inequality reduces average capabilities, partly because it deprives low-income people of the material means for enhancing their capabilities and partly because diminishing returns to income implies that high-income recipients gain relatively little in terms of increased capabilities from their higher incomes. This phenomenon can be reflected by producing a 'distribution adjusted' HDI, either by weighting the income component of the HDI by one minus the Gini coefficient (the original procedure) or by weighting it by the ratio of the shares of income received by the poorest and richest quintiles of the population (the current procedure). In either case, a country is penalized for inequality and this is reflected in the value of its HDI.

Similarly, the Human Development Index can be adjusted to take gender issues into account. The UNDP has produced a 'gender sensitive' HDI to reflect differences between women and men in life expectancy, literacy and earnings.

The HDI has thus proved to be a flexible tool, capable of measuring differences in levels of human development across countries and changes in human development over time; it has also been possible to measure the impact on human development of inequality in the distribution of income and discrimination against women. Beyond this, some scholars have disaggregated the national HDI and calculated regional or provincial HDIs in an attempt to measure spatial differences in human development. The UNDP, consistent with its advocacy of *sustainable* human development, has experimented with incorporating environmental variables into the HDI, but so far it has not proved possible to produce a 'green' Human Development Index.

The human development approach has led to a reconceptualization of the notion of poverty. Mainstream development economics, with its commodity-centred view of the world, has defined poverty as insufficient income, and often as a level of income which is insufficient to permit an individual or household to acquire the number of calories needed for a nutritious diet. That is, poverty has been reduced to income poverty, and income poverty has been reduced to undernutrition. The human development approach, while not denying the importance of adequate nutrition, takes a broader view of poverty, regarding it as a form of deprivation along several dimensions.

In 1996 the UNDP published its first attempt to measure poverty within a human development framework.[19] The Capability Poverty Measure (CPM), as it was called, is a simple composite index that attempts to measure shortfalls in three basic dimensions of human development, namely, (i) being literate and having access to knowledge, (ii) having adequate nourishment and (iii) being able to give birth in a safe and healthy way. Shortfalls in these dimensions are measured by the percentage of women who are illiterate, the proportion of children under five years of age who are underweight and the percentage of births unattended by trained health personnel. The CPM is calculated by adding these three percentages and dividing by three, i.e. each indicator of deprivation is given equal weight.

Although the procedure is remarkably simple, the indicators rather crude and the weights arbitrary, the results are illuminating. The ranking of countries varies depending on whether the CPM is used or a head count measure of income poverty. Vietnam, for example, has a poverty incidence of 20.1 per cent according to the CPM and 50.9 per cent according to the World Bank's head count estimate of income poverty.[20]

A second experiment in measuring poverty was published by UNDP in 1997. The number of variables was expanded to five in compiling the Human Poverty Index and a greater attempt was made to select indicators of deprivation which are mirror images of the HDI. The five variables are (i) the percentage of the population not expected to reach age 40, (ii) the adult illiteracy rate, (iii) the percentage of the population without access to safe water, (iv) the percentage of the population without access to health services, and (v) the percentage of children under five years of age who are underweight. As before, the five variables in the composite index are given equal weight.

The Human Poverty Index does not differ all that much from the Capability Poverty Measure and it is not clear which better captures the notion of human deprivation. Further experimentation with alternative specifications of human poverty indicators is likely to be worthwhile. Enough progress has been made however to suggest that the broader concept of poverty embedded within the human development approach has both analytical and policy-making advantages. This does not imply that estimates of income poverty are no longer useful, for they surely are, but in future they are likely to be regarded as complementary to other poverty indicators which between them give us a more rounded view of the human condition.

## Institutionalization

The success of the human development approach is due partly to the power of the underlying ideas and partly to the fact that human development rapidly became institutionalized within the United Nations system. UNDP, and specifically Mahbub ul Haq, deserve much credit for this. The annual *Human Development Report*, starting in 1990, expanded and elaborated upon the concept of human development and did so in a lively way which attracted large numbers of readers. The team of consultants that worked with Mahbub ul Haq included many experienced and innovative development economists who helped ensure that academic standards were not sacrificed in order to reach a large audience.

Each *Human Development Report* adopts a global perspective. Trends in human development are regularly monitored; much effort is devoted to measurement and quantification, with the results being presented in an attractive manner; and an elaborate statistical annex is included at the back of each *Report*. In addition, each volume contains a discussion of a specific issue, often a subject on which there is considerable controversy or is of international importance. The first issue of the *Human Development Report* (1990) concentrated on defining and measuring human development and presenting the Human Development Index. The basic point was made that there is no automatic link between economic growth and the enhancement of people's capabilities. The next year (1991) the gender sensitive HDI was introduced[21] and, much more controversially, the concept of human development was enlarged to include a wide range of human freedoms. Indeed a Human Freedom Index was published and it was shown that there is a high correlation between human freedom and human development. A number of developing countries objected strongly to printing a Human Freedom Index and for a time there was a danger that UNDP would be forced to discontinue the series of *Human Development Reports* after only two issues.

The developing countries were mollified by the third issue (1992), which concentrated on North–South relations. The themes in this issue were unequal partnership between rich and poor countries, very large global inequalities and the widening gap in global opportunities. The inadequacies of our system of global economic governance were underlined and a number of constructive proposals were made. This was followed in 1993 by a *Report* which implicitly was critical of excessive reliance on market mechanisms and the neglect of institutional and equity issues. The importance of people's participation in economic, civic and political life was a red thread which ran throughout the report. Markets are of course necessary, but they should be reformed in many cases to make them more people-friendly. The emphasis on military security, which dominated the Cold War, should be replaced by an emphasis on human security. This in turn would require giving higher priority to employment creation, investment in people, an equitable distribution of assets and construction of stronger social safety nets.

The 1994 *Human Development Report* was devoted to the issues on the agenda for the Social Summit that met in Copenhagen, namely, poverty reduction, employment creation and social integration. The theme of human security was continued from the previous report and the social programmes needed to ensure security, it was argued, could be financed by the 'peace dividend' made possible by the end of the Cold War. New forms of international cooperation for development were proposed, including one mechanism that would provide compensation for damages (e.g. when developed countries broke the rules of the liberal international trade regime) and another mechanism for facilitating international negotiations and payments for services rendered (e.g. in the case of externalities arising, say, from one country bearing the costs of an environmental programme that benefited several other countries). It was also suggested that international transfer programmes, i.e. foreign aid, should henceforth be financed by a scheme of global taxation rather than on an *ad hoc* basis by national governments operating independently.

The 1995 *Report*, in anticipation of the global conference on women and development in Beijing, concentrated on gender issues. The multiple dimensions of gender inequalities were examined, including innovative research on the distribution across tasks of work effort (or time) as between men and women as compared to the distribution of the rewards from work (or income) as between men and women. The *Report* demonstrated that women provide considerably more than half the world's work while receiving considerably less than half the world's income. The *Report* also contained two new indicators: the gender-related development index (GDI), which purports to measure capabilities after adjusting for gender inequalities, and the gender empowerment measure (GEM), which attempts to measure the degree of participation of women in economic and political life.

The topics covered in the most recent *Human Development Reports* are the relationship between economic growth and human development (1996); human poverty, conceptualized as the denial of choices and opportunities (1997); and the linkages between human development and patterns of consumption (1998).

This sequence of themes in UNDP's flagship publication did much to institutionalize the human development approach at the global level. Analysis was extended to the country level when UNDP began to help developing countries produce annual national human development reports. This has now been done in 108 countries. In Bangladesh as many as six national human development reports have been produced and four have been produced in many other countries, all following a broadly similar format to that used in the global report. The volume of information and analysis is thus quite considerable. Indeed a stage has now been reached when it is possible to launch a specialized journal devoted exclusively to human development. UNDP, continuing its pattern of entrepreneurial initiative, has decided to publish a new *Journal of Human Development*, the first issue of which should appear this year. This will complete the circle: academic ideas initiated by Professors Sen and Schultz were first institutionalized in the international development community and now are being institutionalized through a new journal in the academic community.

## Impact

Finally, let us consider what impact the human development approach has had on the lives of people in developing countries. This is equivalent to asking how useful is the idea ten years on? Perhaps its greatest contribution has been to offer a 'second opinion' to the Bretton Woods orthodoxy. Human development has injected an element of competition in the market for ideas and the monopoly of the IMF and World Bank in providing advice on development strategies has been broken. Indeed in some respects the Bretton Woods institutions have been forced on to the defensive and one can observe today a struggle of orthodoxy to absorb new ideas rather than be transformed by them. For example, in 'stabilization' and 'structural adjustment' programmes the IMF and World Bank have added 'safety nets' to the standard package. These 'safety nets' often appear to be afterthoughts – a concession to outside critics – rather than recognition that human security should be an integral part of a government's overall objective.

Similarly, greater prominence is now given to the 'social sectors' than was once the case, but the acknowledgement of their importance has been rather grudging. World Bank policy as regards education, health and pensions for the elderly is that public expenditure on these items should be reduced to the minimum, that state-financed programmes should be carefully targeted on the most deserving and that the private sector should be encouraged to become the main provider. It still is not recognized that the distinction between 'economic' and 'social' sectors is artificial, that 'social' expenditures are a major vehicle for enhancing capabilities, that the enhancement of capabilities is the ultimate objective of development and that 'social' expenditure is really a form of human capital expenditure which enjoys high rates of return.

The World Bank has gone further than the IMF in absorbing the new ideas. Indeed the danger is that the Bank will co-opt the vocabulary of human development while ignoring the substance. The IMF has not even gone that far. The IMF-designed stabilization programmes in South-east Asia have made virtually no provision to safeguard human security, to protect expenditure on the social sectors or to construct even minimal social safety nets. The consequences for development have been horrific and surely the time has come for the member countries of the IMF to insist that the organization become much less secretive, more open about publishing the advice it gives and more accountable for its actions. There is in fact an alternative to the IMF's orthodoxy and the Fund should be compelled to defend its approach in open debate.

The World Bank deserves some credit for acknowledging that development is about people and not about GDP. In the 1998 issue of *World Development Indicators*, for instance, the Bank first presents a 'World View' (which contains both economic and human development indicators); this is followed by groups of tables on 'People' and 'Environment'; data on the 'Economy' are not presented until one reaches the fourth group of tables. It would be easy to dismiss this as window-dressing, but presentation matters and the sequencing of material in the Bank's main statistical publication indicates the priorities of the users even if not of the Bank.

The human development approach will continue to challenge the status quo with new ideas. For example, the transition in the former Soviet Union from central planning to a more market-oriented economic system has been dominated by the Bretton Woods orthodoxy – price liberalization, reduction in public expenditure and privatization of state-owned enterprises – and the results have been a disaster. China and Vietnam, in contrast, ignored the Western orthodoxy and designed their own reform programme, which was much more consistent with the human development approach and which has enjoyed remarkable success.[22] There are lessons to be learned even now, both by the Bretton Woods institutions and by the countries of the former Soviet Union.

Another example is the role in development of a redistribution of income and wealth. The mainstream view is sceptical of redistributive policies on grounds that they harm incentives, create inefficiency in the allocation of resources and reduce savings. The human development approach, however, is sympathetic to redistributive policies, and particularly favours an equitable distribution of productive assets. The benefits of an egalitarian distribution of human capital in enhancing capabilities are evident, but there are reasons to believe that a more equal distribution of natural capital (e.g. land) and physical capital (e.g. by encouraging small and medium-sized enterprises) also would promote human development.[23] If this turns out to be true, mainstream views may not be able to recover from the challenge of the human development approach. Human development would then become the new orthodoxy.

# 5
# The Distribution of Wealth and the Pace of Development*

*with Amy Ickowitz*


Economists have long been interested in the relationship between the distribution of income and the rate of economic growth. Two propositions have tended to dominate the literature. The first, associated with the name of Simon Kuznets, asserts that the degree of inequality varies systematically with the level of income per head, initially increasing as incomes rise and then, beyond some point, decreasing with further increases in income per head.[1] The second proposition, often associated with Arthur Okun, asserts that there is a 'great trade-off' between equality and efficiency and hence policy interventions intended to reduce inequality have a high cost in terms of a lower average income.[2] Taken together, the two propositions have been used to argue against public policies intended to create a less unequal society, since the Kuznets proposition indicates that in the long run policy interventions are unnecessary and the Okun proposition indicates that in the short run they are harmful.

In this chapter we attempt to do three things. First, we reconsider the evidence behind the Kuznets and Okun propositions. Second, we explore the implications for development of shifting the focus of analysis from the distribution of income to the distribution of productive assets or wealth. Third, we consider where appropriate the implications for the analysis of substituting human development for an expansion of gross national product (GNP) as the objective of development policy. Our conclusion is that a more equal distribution of wealth is more likely to accelerate the pace of human development than retard it and hence the earlier view that emphasized a conflict between equality and development is seriously misleading.

The belief in a trade-off between equity and growth, in both developed and developing economies, is widely held. Recent evidence, however, indicates not only that the two are compatible but that they are mutually reinforcing. Traditional analyses of the relationship between inequality and growth have focused on the relationship between income inequality and the growth of GNP. In this essay, in contrast, we will examine inequality not only in terms of income but also in terms of the distribution of productive assets, i.e. natural, physical and human capital. Furthermore, while all of the empirical testing thus far defines growth as an increase in GNP, the results will have to be carefully reinterpreted if one assumes that growth of GNP is not the ultimate goal of development but simply a means to the end of increasing human development. Economic growth may help to advance human development, and per capita income enters into the human development index, but the two are not synonymous.

First, we examine the empirical evidence that has been gathered to date on the relationship between growth and inequality. We begin with a review of the evidence on income inequality and then discuss the evidence on inequality in the distribution of assets. Second, we explore some of the current theories which try to explain why growth and inequality might be inversely related. Third, we consider some of the evidence from individual countries. Finally, we raise some of the policy implications that arise from this re-examination of the data, the theories and actual experience. Our ultimate objective is to show that a redistribution of productive assets could serve as a catalyst for growth, both in terms of an expansion of GNP and in terms of higher levels of human development.

## Empirical evidence

Discussion of the empirical evidence begins with the famous Kuznets hypothesis. We then consider more recent work on the distribution of income and its link to economic growth. Next, we consider the importance of natural capital, concentrating on the distribution of landownership. Lastly, we consider human capital, taking as an example the distribution of education.

### The Kuznets hypothesis

For nearly four decades the Kuznets hypothesis was accepted as a stylized fact by most economists. The well known inverted U-shaped relationship between income inequality and the level of income affected the way economists approached theory as well as policy. In the early 1990s, however, economists increasingly began to question the idea that there was a close relationship between the level of income per head and the degree of inequality. The need for a re-evaluation had been apparent for quite some time. The insights from human capital theory, the refinement of endogenous growth theory and apparent real world anomalies combined to encourage scholars to take a second look at the Kuznets hypothesis. Several papers were published in the early 1990s which claimed that not only was there no inverse relationship between growth and income equality during the first stages of development but that on the contrary, initial inequality in the distribution of income was inimical to growth.

Simon Kuznets, writing in the 1950s and 1960s, developed his hypothesis that income inequality tends first to rise and then fall with increases in real income per capita after examining the historical experience of the developed countries and a very small sample of developing countries for which data were available. He believed that the historical record showed that such a relationship existed, but he was very careful to point out that this did not mean that there was an inherent trade-off between growth and equality, as he is sometimes interpreted to have argued:

> All we can say is that the unequal distribution of income in the earlier decades in the presently developed countries did not prevent rapid economic growth. But our data do not reveal the specific social and economic circumstances, and we cannot say that a somewhat less (or more) unequal size distribution might not have contributed to even faster growth.[3]

During the years after Kuznets first published his observations regarding the historical relationships between growth and income equality, several empirical studies were done using cross-sectional data to test whether this inverse relationship held, using the larger amount of data that had become available from the developing countries. In 1973, Felix Paukert, using cross-sectional data on 56 countries originally gathered by Adelman and Taft Morris,[4] concluded that 'the data ... support the hypothesis expressed but not fully tested by Kuznets that with economic development income inequality tends to increase, then becomes stable and then decrease'.[5] Perhaps the most well known of the empirical studies is that done by Ahluwalia[6] using cross-sectional data from 60 countries. He was convinced enough by the data of the existence of a U-shaped relationship between equality and growth to call it a 'stylized fact'. Sherman Robinson went even further and claimed that the U hypothesis 'has gathered the force of economic law'.[7]

Not all economists agreed that the empirical tests were convincing enough to elevate the status of the U hypothesis to 'stylized fact', let alone 'economic law'. In 1983, Ashwanti Saith criticized Paukert and Ahluwalia's use of cross-sectional data to test what is really a secular relationship. By using cross-sectional data they implicitly assumed that every country travelled along 'one well-trodden U-path'. They thus ignored the fundamental inter-country differences pointed out by Kuznets in 'size, historical heritage, and timing of their industrialization process'[8] among other things. Saith proceeded to question the robustness of Ahluwalia's results. He reran Ahluwalia's regression on his sample of developing countries, dropping those observations which he considered to be outliers and Spain since he believed that it could not really be called a developing country. He found that Ahluwalia's coefficients were no longer significant and concluded that 'Ahluwalia's quadratic fit, and hence the U-curve, are the products of a few outliers, and if these are excluded from the sample, the U-curve fades into insignificance'.[9]

Ahluwalia and the authors of later studies performed in the 1970s and 1980s relied on a data set assembled by Shail Jain.[10] Much of these data is of poor quality and therefore calls the conclusions of these investigations into question. Deininger and Squire[11] have specified three basic criteria that data must meet in order for them to qualify as 'quality' data:

1. the data must come from nationally representative household surveys;
2. all sources of income (or uses of expenditure) must be included (and not, for example, only wage income);
3. the survey must be representative of the country's entire population and results must not be based on extrapolations from information gathered only from specific subgroups (e.g. it should not be a survey of only the urban population or only whites).

These appear to be reasonable criteria, but much of the data used in past empirical investigations of the relationship between inequality and growth have not met these basic standards. Only 61 of Jain's original 405 observations, for example, meet the minimum requirements set by Deininger and Squire.

### The world turned upside down

More recent empirical research not only questions the validity of the Kuznets hypothesis but seems to reverse the conclusions. Persson and

Tabellini were perhaps the first to find econometric evidence that there might be a negative relationship between initial income inequality and the rate of growth. They used two sets of data, one based on historical data from nine developed countries and the other cross-sectional data from 56 countries since the end of the Second World War. On their historical sample, they performed what has become a standard growth regression of GDP growth on various variables including the income share of the top 20 per cent of the population as a measure of inequality. In their sample for the post-war period, they focus on the median voter and therefore, rather unpersuasively, use the income share of the third quintile as their measure of inequality. They reported that 'a strong negative relation between income inequality at the start of the period and growth in the subsequent period is present in both samples'.[12] That is, high initial inequality is associated with slow growth of output and incomes.

Alesina and Rodrik perform similar regressions for two periods, namely 1960–85 and 1970–85. In addition to using a Gini coefficient on income as a measure of inequality, however, they also include a Gini coefficient on land as one of their regressors. Their high-quality data set uses Jain's data from the OECD countries and data from Fields[13] for 29 developing countries. 'The results indicate that income inequality is negatively correlated with subsequent growth.'[14] When they use the Gini coefficients for land and for income separately, they find both to be significant at the 5 per cent level or higher, depending on the sample. When they use them both together, however, the Gini coefficient for land stays significant at the 1 per cent level, but the significance of the Gini coefficient for income declines to 10 per cent for the sample from the longer period and to 5 per cent for the shorter period. George Clarke runs similar regressions using various income inequality measures and then performs sensitivity analysis to test the robustness of the negative relationship between income inequality and growth. His results 'confirm a robust and negative relationship between inequality and growth'.[15]

It seems that the most recent work using more and better data comes to a different conclusion regarding the relationship between inequality and income growth from those studies done in the past. However even the data used in the most recent studies are still far from perfect. Deininger and Squire question the quality of Persson and Tabellini's data on quintile shares of income. Only 18 out of Persson and Tabellini's 56 data points meet their criteria for quality data. 'The negative relationship between income inequality and growth evaporates if, for example, we rerun the regressions by Persson and Tabellini using only the eighteen ... high-quality observations contained in their sample.'[16]

Deininger and Squire are also critical of the data in Alesina and Rodrik as well as in unpublished work by Perotti.[17] Both studies include observations for developed countries from Jain's data set. Some of the income figures for these countries are based on wage income, which can create the impression of high disparities in countries which may have low inequality of net household income. Also, a large number of observations from developed countries (36 out of the 69 in Alesina and Rodrik and 50 out of Perotti's 67) 'gives rise to the suspicion that the statistical analysis captures structural differences between developed and developing countries more than regularities that are equally valid for both groups'.[18] Deaton also argues that 'Jain's figures are not a sound basis on which to make international comparisons, and results that rely on them should be viewed with great skepticism, although the lesson is widely ignored in the recent political economy literature, for example Persson and Tabellini (1990) and Alesina and Perotti, (1992).'[19]

Deininger and Squire use a new data set on income distribution to re-examine the relationship between growth and inequality. They collected as many observations of income distribution as they could from both primary and reliable secondary sources and obtained a total of 2600. After applying their criteria for quality data outlined above, they were left with 682 high-quality observations, which is substantially more than are contained in the data sets used in previous studies. Not only do they have more cross-sectional observations, they also have a significantly greater number of time series observations for each country. This is crucial because the empirical testing of the Kuznets hypothesis in the past used cross-sectional data to try to draw conclusions about what is, in reality, a longitudinal relationship. According to Deininger and Squire, 'Indeed, our data provide little support for an inverted-U relationship between levels of income and inequality when tested on a country-by-country basis, with no support for the existence of a Kuznets curve in about 90 per cent of the countries investigated.'[20]

When they run the standard growth regression used in the past but with their high-quality data, Deininger and Squire's results appear at first to corroborate those of Persson and Tabellini, Alesina and Rodrik, and Perotti, in showing that initial inequality has a negative effect on future growth. This effect, however, is no longer significant when regional dummies are introduced into the regression. This suggests to them that 'a wide range of region-specific characteristics which may, but need not, include inequality, could be at the root of the relationship that has been observed in much of the literature'.[21] While their results do not confirm that there is an inverse relationship between initial income inequality and growth, they do confirm that initial income inequality is not positively correlated with growth. Thus the idea that income redistribution is incompatible with growth receives no support from the cross-section evidence and the view that inequality is a precondition for growth is increasingly untenable.

Even though Deininger and Squire do not find a significant correlation between aggregate growth and overall income inequality, they do find a significant and positive correlation between growth and increases in income of all but the top quintile. The relationship is strongest for the bottom quintile, implying that growth is associated with a reduction of poverty. They found that during decadal growth episodes, the incomes of the bottom quintile increased in more than 85 per cent of the cases they examined.[22]

What does this imply for human development? It is reasonable to suppose that an increase in income increases human capabilities but that it does so at a diminishing rate. That is, there are diminishing returns to income in terms of its ability to increase human development. This assumption, in fact, is incorporated into the construction of the human development index. It follows from this that, for any given increase in the average level of income, the more evenly distributed is the increase in income, the greater will be its contribution to raising human development. In other words, an egalitarian pattern of economic growth contributes more to human development than an inegalitarian pattern (see Chapter 2 above).

### The distribution of land

As we have seen, empirical testing of the relationship between inequality and growth has traditionally been done using data on the distribution of income. Like Alesina and Rodrik, however, Deininger and Squire have also used data on the distribution of land. They hoped to use these data as a proxy for the distribution of assets in general. Quite apart from the problem of using land as a proxy for productive assets as a whole, data on the distribution of land almost always understate the degree of inequality. There are several reasons for this.

First, measures of land concentration ignore those who own no land at all, e.g. landless agricultural wage labourers. That is, the data refer to the distribution of land among landowners and not among the entire rural population. Second, most of the data refer to the distribution of land holdings and not to units of ownership. Thus, for instance, an estate that is divided into ten tenant farms would be counted as ten holdings and not as one unit of ownership. This results in an underestimate of the degree of inequality since land holdings tend to be distributed more equally than landownership. Many owners of large farms prefer to rent out their land to tenants rather than cultivate the entire area themselves. Third, measures of land concentration ignore those who own more than one farm by counting each farm as a separate unit of ownership. This, too, results in an underestimate of the degree of inequality. Finally, land is treated as a homogeneous asset of uniform quality. That is, measures of land concentration are in practice measures of inequality in surface area and not measures of inequality in the value of land as a productive asset. If, as is often the case, most of the best land is owned by large landowners, the degree of inequality will be understated by most conventional measurements.

Despite these problems, Deininger and Squire are right to underline the importance of land inequality, particularly since the 'possession of land could be a major determinant of an individual's productive capacity and their ability to invest, especially in agrarian societies where land is a major asset'.[23] Using regression analysis, Deininger and Squire find that the relationship between the initial degree of inequality in the distribution of land and subsequent growth is negative, significant and robust. Greater land inequality leads to slower growth. When regional dummies are added to the regression, the significance of the coefficient on land distribution is reduced, but it remains statistically significant. Given the fact that the degree of inequality as measured by the Gini coefficient for land distribution is almost certainly understated, the true relationship would be even stronger than the estimated relationship.

## The distribution of human capital

While land is an important asset in most developing countries, human capital is perhaps an even more important determinant of a country's growth potential. Recent evidence suggests that the contribution of human capital to growth is higher than that of either natural or physical capital, and perhaps more than the two combined (Chapter 2 above).[24] This is especially true if one reinterprets growth to mean an increase in human development, since improvements in health and education contribute directly to human development as well as indirectly through their effects on increasing the growth of output and incomes.

Using data on 98 countries from the period 1960–85, Robert Barro finds that the growth rate of real GDP per capita is positively related to the initial stock of human capital as proxied by primary and secondary school enrolment rates.[25] Thus the more equitably distributed are educational opportunities, i.e. the higher is the percentage of the population enrolled in primary and secondary schools, the higher is the growth rate. The effects on raising human development would be stronger still, because of the direct contribution of education to human development.

The microeconomic evidence supports these findings. Rati Ram estimates that the returns to schooling are 13 per cent on average for all countries, with a higher return in developing countries compared to developed countries.[26] Evidence also indicates that the returns to primary and secondary education are higher than the returns to tertiary education. George Psacharopoulos explains that 'for primary education, unit costs are small relative to the extra lifetime income or productivity associated with literacy. For university education, the opposite is true.'[27] Given that tertiary education usually favours the elite in developing countries – and even in developed countries the middle and upper classes are disproportionately represented – a more equal distribution of expenditures on education would increase efficiency and growth as well as equity. Indeed in another paper Psacharopoulos finds that in developing countries the rates of return on investments in primary education are more than 25 per cent, whereas they fall sharply at higher levels, namely to 15–18 per cent in secondary education and to 13–16 per cent in tertiary education.[28]

A recent study by the Asian Development Bank enables one to estimate the contribution of various factors to the difference in the rate of growth of per capita income in East and South-east Asia during the period 1965–90, on the one hand, and three other regions during the same period, on the other hand. Consider, for example, sub-Saharan Africa. During the 25 years under examination, the rate of growth of output per head in sub-Saharan Africa was four percentage points a year slower than in East and South-east Asia. This difference of four percentage points can be decomposed as follows: 2.3 percentage points are due to differences in human capital (namely 'schooling' and 'demography'), one percentage point is due to differences in natural capital (namely, 'resources and geography') and 0.1 percentage points are due to differences in physical capital (specifically, 'government savings rate'). The remaining 0.6 points are attributed to other factors.[29] A broadly similar result was found in South Asia but not, curiously, in Latin

America, where 'initial conditions' and 'openness' appear to have been much more important.

While such decomposition exercises must be treated with some scepticism, the Asian Development Bank study confirms the importance of human capital in accelerating economic growth and, in the cases of East and South-east Asia and South Asia, suggests that human capital was more than twice as important as natural and physical capital combined in explaining differences in economic performance. These results are therefore consistent with other recent empirical findings.

## Theoretical explanations

Why might one expect that inequality in the distribution of income and wealth could harm development and that reduced inequality could accelerate it? Both political and economic explanations have been put forward. Let us begin with the insights of political theory and then turn our attention to possible economic reasons.

### Political insights

There are three separate strands of argument to the analysis which connects inequality in the distribution of income and wealth to political instability. First, it has been argued that inequality can result in redistributive taxation which is harmful to growth of output. Second, it has been argued that inequality can result in a change in the composition of public expenditure which increases unproductive outlays and in the process reduces both the rate of growth of output and human development. Third, it has been argued that inequality can result in class conflict and uncooperative behaviour which reduces technical and institutional change and the growth of output.

Several papers published in the early 1990s examined the possible link between inequality and growth through the channel of voting behaviour. Each of these papers involves the construction of a theoretical model designed to capture both the economic and the political choices of the members of an economy and a polity. All of the papers make use of the median voter theorem which purports to demonstrate that when people vote on different possible tax rates, the tax rate preferred by the median voter will be the one chosen.

Persson and Tabellini were the first to set up such a model and used an overlapping generations framework in which different individuals are assumed to have different incomes. An individual acts as an economic agent as well as a voting citizen. It is assumed that the role of the government is to redistribute income from those who invest more than the average to those who invest less than the average. Agents work and invest in human capital. Individuals with more skills accumulate more capital. The government levies taxes at a rate proportional to income, while the revenues are redistributed in a lump sum manner to all agents so that poor agents benefit as much as rich ones but pay a relatively smaller amount in taxes.

The authors assume that the more of the returns on her investment an individual can retain, the higher will be the growth rate. This is because investment (and hence growth) is sensitive to the after-tax rate of return. On this basis the authors conclude that inequality is harmful to growth and offer the following explanation:

> ... if the median voter coincides with the average investor, he prefers a nonredistributive policy, whereas he prefers a tax (a subsidy) on investment if he is poorer (richer) than the average. More generally a median voter with higher individual skills ... and therefore a higher $k^m$ (median voter's capital accumulation) prefers more private appropriability. A higher average skill level ... gives higher average accumulation and hence increases the cost of redistribution, so that the voter prefers a less interventionist policy.[30]

The chain of causality is thus lower income inequality leads to less voter preference for redistributive tax intervention; less government intervention leads to more investment and hence to faster growth.

The idea behind Alesina and Rodrik's model is similar to that in Persson and Tabellini, but the technical details are slightly different. They use an endogenous growth model and instead of differentiating between individuals based on income, they focus on differences in the relative shares of labour and capital endowments. The government, in their model, uses proportional taxation of capital income to finance public investment. A large increase in taxation lowers the after-tax return on private capital investment and thus reduces the incentive for agents to invest and therefore reduces the growth rate of the economy. They too make use of the median voter theorem and argue that 'the higher the proportion of capital income to total income of the median voter, the lower the tax rate chosen by the voting process and the higher the rate of investment and growth. In terms of income distribution, the poorer the median voter in relation to the voter with average income, the higher the equilibrium tax rate and the lower the growth rate.'[31]

Like Alesina and Rodrik, Bertola[32] uses an endogenous growth model and focuses on relative capital and labour shares. The government's role in his model, however, is not public expenditure, but redistribution from capital to labour through a proportional tax on capital. The intuition of the results is similar to that in Alesina and Rodrik. The higher the level of taxation, the lower the after-tax return on capital which results in a lower investment rate and a lower growth rate. The higher the ratio of profit income to wages for an individual, the less likely she is to vote for a high tax rate. Again using the median voter theorem, the tax rate that will emerge will be inversely related to the profits–wages ratio of the median voter. An implication of both papers is that the more even is the initial distribution of profits, and hence of productive wealth, the more rapid is likely to be the rate of growth. This follows from an assumption that government interventions are harmful to growth, e.g. that taxes reduce the return on private investment, that the return on public investment is lower than the return on private investment or that public investment is a very small share of total public expenditure on the margin.

A surprising implication of the idea that political behaviour is the crucial link between equality and growth is that this relationship is likely to be stronger in democracies than in authoritarian regimes since it is only in democracies that the median voter can vote on tax policies. Persson and Tabellini divided their sample into two groups – democratic and non-democratic – and found that indeed the positive relationship between equality and growth held only for their democratic sample. Alesina and Rodrik, however, in performing a similar test with their data found that the coefficient on the dummy variable for democracy in their regression 'is not statistically significant, rejecting the hypothesis that the relationship between inequality and growth is different in democracies and nondemocracies'.[33] While Deininger and Squire take this as incontrovertible evidence that the political instability argument fails to explain the reason for the inverse relationship between inequality and growth, Alesina and Rodrik offer an alternative interpretation of their result. They argue that it is possible that 'the pressure for redistribution coming from the majority is felt not only in democracies but also in other regimes... some dictators are subject to political influences similar to those experienced by elected representatives'.[34]

Alesina and Rodrik are correct to point out that even a highly authoritarian regime is unlikely to be totalitarian and hence often will have to respond to political pressures in one way or another. In some cases the response may be accommodating, e.g. through adjustments of tax rates or the level of transfer payments. In other cases, however, the response may be increased repression, e.g. through higher spending on police, prisons, the judiciary, secret police and perhaps the armed forces. That is, the adjustment may occur not on the revenue side but via changes in government expenditure which reduce resources available for redistribution and accelerating growth. In this second case, 'inequality can be costly to maintain'.[35] Bowles and Gintis argue in a similar vein that one explanation for 'the sharply contrasting economic performances of the very unequal Latin American and less unequal East Asian economies over the 1980s and early 1990s is related to the high enforcement cost of economic inequality'.[36]

Moreover, countries with a highly unequal distribution of wealth are likely to be characterized by sharp class conflict and periodic civil violence. Quite apart from the costs of repression, such conflicted and polarized societies will find cooperation between workers and asset owners to be difficult, be the asset owners large landowners or urban capitalists. 'Each will be suspicious of the other; each will resist changes proposed by the other. The result will be greater risk, lower levels of investment, slower rates of technological and institutional change and a slower long term rate of growth.'[37]

Thus there are several political channels which can link inequality and growth. Statistical regularities that can be captured in a regression equation probably do not exist and if they do exist, they are likely to be hard to detect.

### Insights from economic theory

Economic theory offers a number of insights that help one to understand why reduced inequality of income and wealth could increase the pace of development, whether measured in terms of growth of GNP or expansion of human capabilities. We shall concentrate on investment in human capital, asset distribution and the rate of savings, and employment and the distribution of physical assets.

Stiglitz and Weiss[38] have argued that because of imperfect information about the characteristics and future behaviour of borrowers, the loanable funds market does not produce a market-clearing price in equilibrium but instead is characterized by credit rationing. One consequence of this is that agents (individuals and firms) are able to borrow only if they own an asset that can be used as collateral. This restricts the number of investors in general and in particular makes it difficult to finance human capital formation.

Investments in human capital are lumpy and usually require either accumulated savings or credit. If credit rationing limits access to funds, then those who have more initial wealth are better able to invest in human capital, partly because they have more of their own funds to use and partly because their wealth provides collateral which, in turn, gives them greater access to credit. The distribution of wealth will thus affect investments in human capital which, in turn, will affect output and growth.[39] 'A more unequal initial distribution of assets would then imply that, for any given level of per capita income, a greater number of people are credit constrained. In an economy where individuals make indivisible investments – in schooling and education for example – that have to be financed through credit, this would imply lower aggregate growth.'[40] This is even more true if by 'growth' one means human development since education contributes directly to enhanced capabilities. Hence if the poor were to own more assets that could be used as collateral, e.g. land, they could borrow money to invest in the human capital of their families and thereby become more educated, healthier and more prosperous citizens.

Deininger and Squire believe that credit market imperfections provide a stronger link between inequality and growth than do the political channels discussed above. They cite two pieces of evidence in support of this view. First, in the advanced economies where one would not expect land to be an important source of collateral, the initial distribution of land does not in fact appear to be a significant determinant of growth. Second, in the developing countries the initial degree of land inequality is significantly and negatively associated with the average educational attainment of the population. This lends credence to the proposition that assets such as land may make it easier for people in developing countries to obtain access to credit which can be used to finance education.

While a greater supply of educated workers may be necessary for a faster pace of development, it is not sufficient. The human development approach sometimes ignores the importance of demand for an educated labour force. From the human development perspective, the enhancement of human capital is of course a goal in itself, independent of its impact on accelerating the growth of output. However the impact of improvements in human capital on human development would be magnified if human capital formation were also to accelerate growth of GNP since economic growth contributes to an enhancement of human development. If investment in people is to have the desired impact on growth, there must be a demand for the skills created.

Increasing the number of taxi drivers with advanced degrees is unlikely to have a strong effect on the growth rate. Hence it is important to take into account the social rate of return on different types of human capital when allocating resources. It is equally important that macroeconomic and trade policies, i.e. the development strategy in general, be supportive of an employment intensive pattern of growth.

In some developing countries enrolment ratios for women are still far below those of men. Enhancing the human capital of women through education bestows the same direct benefits on society as educating men in terms of having a more skilled and productive workforce. Birdsall, Ross and Sabot have shown that 'substituting gender-specific primary-school enrollment rates into the original Barro model [produces] no significant difference between the coefficient values for males and females'.[41] There are, however, indirect effects or positive externalities of education associated with its effect on reducing fertility rates. It is widely known that rapid population growth rates have been an obstacle to development in many poor countries, even in those which have managed to achieve reasonable rates of growth of GNP. In all countries the education of women confers triple benefits: it raises human development directly, it contributes to a faster growth of output and, by reducing the fertility rate, it increases the rate of growth of per capita income.

Another possible link between asset inequality and growth arises from incentive compatibility problems which are common in highly unequal economies. Bowles and Gintis offer an example of how inefficient incentive structures can affect productivity and growth.

> Consider an agrarian economy of a hundred households in which most of the land is owned by a single landowner who hires labor and/or leases land under share-cropping tenancy. Both of these forms of employment have adverse incentive effects. Wage workers have little intrinsic work motivation, since they do not own the results of their work. As a result, the cost of supervising agricultural labor may be considerable. Share-croppers, too, have diluted incentives as they are only partial owners of their work. They will thus allocate less effort and care to their rented land than they would if they owned it themselves.[42]

A redistribution of land would clearly result in greater efficiency in the presence of these incentive and monitoring problems. One reason why this does not come about through the market mechanism is because of the credit market imperfections discussed above.

Let us turn now to the question of savings.

One theoretical justification for the Kuznets hypothesis was proposed by Nicholas Kaldor.[43] He made two crucial assumptions: (i) that a high savings rate is essential for growth and (ii) that rich people have a higher marginal propensity to save than poor people. It follows from these assumptions that in order to ensure a high savings rate and hence rapid growth, income should be concentrated in the hands of the rich. We have already qualified the first of Kaldor's assumptions by arguing that the returns on human capital can be as high as the returns on saving and investing in physical capital. The second assumption also can be questioned, since it is not obvious that rich people always save proportionally more than poor.

Particularly in developing countries, the amount an individual or household saves is likely to be strongly influenced by available investment opportunities.[44] The reason for this, as with investment in education, has much to do with the incomplete coverage and malfunctioning of capital markets. Because of the extreme credit market imperfections in most developing countries – in the rural sector and in the informal urban sector – most poor people have virtually no access to the formal credit market. They can neither save (deposit funds) through the banking system nor can they obtain loans (borrow funds) from formal sector commercial banks. In the developed countries, in contrast, the credit market intermediates between an investor and a saver, in principle (although not in practice) allowing all those with commercially viable projects to obtain finance capital.

In developing countries, for those who do not have access to the credit market, notably the poor, the investor and the saver must be the same individual, and the decision to save becomes identical to the decision to invest. In such cases an individual is likely to save only if she has a profitable investment opportunity within reach. A landless agricultural labourer, for example, has few investment opportunities and hence can be expected to save little whereas a small peasant landowner with a similar level of income can invest in the land and hence can be expected to save relatively more. The implication is that a more even distribution of assets could increase the overall savings rate by giving land or other productive assets to the currently assetless-poor and thereby provide them with profitable outlets for their savings.

Some of the earlier literature suggests that this may be true. A study of rural savings rates in India, for example, showed that farmers with access to land ('cultivating families') saved on average 13 per cent of their income (not including direct investment of labour in their land, which would have raised the estimate to 20 per cent); landless house-holds (or 'non-cultivating families'), in contrast, saved less than 4 per cent of their income, presumably for precautionary motives.[45] In other words, those who had an outlet for their savings actually saved three to five times more than those who did not. A study in then undivided Pakistan showed that rural inequality and average incomes were lower in East Pakistan than in West Pakistan, but personal savings rates were higher in rural East Pakistan (12 per cent) than in rural West Pakistan (9 per cent).[46] That is, according to the conventional view, rural sav-ings should have been higher in West Pakistan than in East Pakistan since the former was both less poor and had a greater concentration of income, but the opposite was the case.

Finally, there is some evidence that among those who do have land, there is no systematic tendency for large farmers to save more than small. A study of 72 holdings in Ludhiana District in the Punjab, in 1969–70, showed that net savings were highest on medium-sized farms (26.5 per cent of total income), followed by large farms (25.1 per cent) and then small (16.7 per cent). In the Hissar District of Haryana, a study of 108 holdings again showed that net savings were proportion-ately highest on medium-sized farms (35.5 per cent of total income), but small farms were a close second (34.2 per cent) followed by large farms (31.3 per cent).[47] These data suggest that a redistribution of land among already existing landowners would not reduce the savings rate. These conjectures are supported by the redistributive land reforms in Taiwan and mainland China, where if anything, savings rates increased after assets were redistributed.

It is reasonable to ask, however, whether arguments that apply to the distribution of land apply with equal force to the distribution of physi-cal capital such as machinery and buildings. The empirical studies by Deininger and Squire use land as a proxy for all assets and find that there is a positive relationship between a more equal distribution of assets and growth. Furthermore, as argued above, the true relationship is likely to be even stronger than the estimated relationship since the measurements used for empirical testing understate the true degree of land inequality. One must be cautious, however, before making a leap from the distribution of land to the distribution of productive assets in general. It is conceivable that there are peculiar features of land that make its equitable distribution more favourable to growth than might be true of other productive assets. It is well established, for example, that 'output per hectare tends to be higher on small farms than on large, because small farmers use their land more intensively and utilise more labour-intensive techniques of production'.[48] It does not follow from this that small businesses tend to adopt more labour intensive techniques than large or obtain a higher output per unit of capital. That is something that needs to be established.

As far as we know, there has not been a systematic attempt to test empirically the relationship between the distribution of physical assets and growth. There are reasons to believe, however, that this relationship is positive as well. First, there is abundant case study evidence that indicates that small and medium enterprises create more employment per unit of capital than large enterprises. A smaller average size of enterprise is therefore likely to be associated with greater labour intensity, a higher productivity of capital and, of course, a more equal distribution of income. Second, in most developing countries – particularly those which followed an import substituting pattern of industrialization – the industrial sector is dominated by large, monopolistic enterprises which are highly inefficient. A more equitable distribution of physical capital could lead to a more competitive market, greater efficiency and higher average incomes. Since most developing countries have a comparative advantage in relatively labour intensive processes and products, greater emphasis on small and medium-sized enterprises would enable them to exploit their resources more efficiently and, in addition, accentuate human development by increasing the demand for skilled labour, i.e. human capital.

Third, as argued above, if savings in developing countries are in part a function of investment opportunities, then policies which give the majority of people greater access to physical assets will simultaneously give them an important reason to save and invest. Even adequate shelter can provide an investment opportunity, since many poor families can use a room in their house to establish a business, e.g. a restaurant, bar or teahouse, a repair shop or a microenterprise (see Chapter 8 below). Home-based enterprises can be a stepping-stone to larger activities and they certainly are an advance over ambulatory vendors and sales by squatters on the pavement.

There are thus several advantages of basing industrial development on small and medium enterprises. The practical problems that have impeded the development of small-scale, labour intensive enterprises in the past have been credit market imperfections discussed above, onerous government regulations, controls and licences, and policies that have favoured large enterprises, including protection from imports, subsidized bank credit and tax benefits. Taiwan is a counter-example. It avoided a heavy bias in favour of large, capital intensive enterprise and instead emphasized the expansion of small-scale industry. The results, in terms of equity and growth, were remarkable.[49]

## Evidence from country studies

While the theoretical insights and the econometric studies discussed above have been instrumental in encouraging a re-evaluation of the relationship between growth and inequality, perhaps the greatest blow to the Kuznets hypothesis and the Okun proposition came from the blatant anomalies represented by the experiences of several East Asian economies such as Japan, China, South Korea and Taiwan. A South-east Asian country, namely Vietnam, probably should also be added to this list. These countries experienced outstanding achievements as measured by almost all indicators of development while they managed for long periods to maintain and even at times to improve their performance with respect to equality. Speaking specifically of South Korea and Taiwan, Tibor Scitovsky claims, rightly we believe, that 'by the double criterion of growth and equity, they have been the most successful of all the developing nations'.[50] During the 1980s in particular, their performance was in stark contrast to those countries in Latin America and sub-Saharan Africa that experienced both slow (and in some cases negative) growth rates and worsening inequality. Do any of the theories discussed in the previous section shed any light as to why the East Asian and, say, Latin American countries performed so differently with respect to growth and equality?

Those theories which focus on class conflict and political instability do not appear at first glance to be relevant in the East Asian context. While there were indeed redistributive measures in several countries of the region, they did not take the form of income redistribution as described in the models, nor were the redistributive measures the outcome of a voting process. If, however, one thinks of the models as metaphors that express the advantages of redistribution in a political economy context, then perhaps some insights can be gained. The East Asian governments did not redistribute income or use tax-financed transfer policies, they redistributed assets instead. Taiwan, South Korea, China and Japan all implemented major land reforms following the Second World War. These redistributions of wealth, however, were not a result of the voting process but of historical circumstances. Indeed the threat of communism, and the example of the land reform in China, provided strong political incentives to introduce land reforms first in Japan, then in Taiwan and last in South Korea.

In Latin America, in contrast, the elites were not as threatened by a communist revolution and could afford to disregard the alienation of the poor. Even so, the modest land redistribution in Mexico during the interwar period and the much more radical land reform in Bolivia in 1952 were warnings that social injustice could not be ignored completely. Pressure for land reform increased after the Cuban revolution, but only in Chile (during the Frei and Allende administrations) was there a significant redistribution of land, and even there land reform was reversed during the Pinochet dictatorship. Indeed, the usual response to inequality in Latin America was repression, unlike East Asia where several governments attempted to 'ensure that all groups in the population benefitted visibly from growth'.[51]

More generally, East Asian governments were more vigorous in promoting agricultural and rural development, partly by encouraging technological change (the green revolution) and partly by creating a more appropriate policy environment. While the Latin American countries tended, for example, to overvalue their exchange rates to the detriment of the agricultural and export sectors, in East Asia the exchange rate was either kept close to its free market value or even in some cases undervalued. This benefited a large proportion of the working population, and particularly the poor, a majority of whom were employed in agriculture and the export sector.

Birdsall, Ross and Sabot emphasize human capital as providing the crucial link between development and equality when comparing the relative performances of East Asia and Latin America. After regressing primary and secondary school enrolment rates on income per capita for over 90 countries during the period 1965–87, they found that 'countries in East Asia, with the exception of Thailand, had significantly higher primary and secondary enrolment rates than predicted by cross-country comparisons. The performance of Latin American countries is not nearly as strong as that of East Asia and is mixed relative to the international norms'.[52] Moreover, while enrolment rates in both regions increased over time, the quality of education in East Asia has continuously improved, while the quality of education in Latin America has declined, as evidenced by lower completion rates.

The difference in performance between the two regions does not seem to reflect differences in government commitment to education, at least as represented by differences in public expenditure on education as a percentage of GNP. In fact, the differences are not great. For example, in 1960 public expenditure on education as a percentage of GNP was 2.0 per cent in South Korea and 1.9 per cent in Brazil, while in 1992 the figures were 4.2 per cent in South Korea and even higher in Brazil, namely 4.6 per cent.[53] The East Asian countries, however, enjoyed the benefits of both rapid growth and rapid declines in fertility rates. These two factors combined to ensure that absolute expenditure per child on education was much higher in East Asia than in Latin America.

Compared to East Asia, slow economic growth in Latin America and a much less rapid decline in fertility rates meant that resources for spending on education increased slowly while the size of the school-age population expanded rapidly. Since fertility rates are inversely related to the level of education (particularly female education), there is a virtuous circle wherein increased education leads to lower fertility which in turn results in greater education expenditures per child, which lowers fertility further.[54] East Asia was caught in this virtuous circle whereas Latin America was not.

Latin America's relative disadvantage was exacerbated by differences in the composition of educational expenditure. Consider South Korea and Brazil again. In 1992, about 7 per cent of expenditure on education in South Korea was allocated to higher education whereas in Brazil it was 26 per cent. Yet we know that expenditures on primary and secondary education have a stronger impact on economic growth, human development and equality than expenditure on tertiary education. Brazil, in other words, chose her priorities within education unwisely. This does not necessarily mean that the priorities were irrational. Large investments in tertiary education usually subsidize the education of the elites, who are able to capture the resources of the state and use them to their advantage. It should not be surprising that in Latin America, where inequality is very great, the proportion of education expenditures allocated to tertiary education tends to be much higher than in East Asia.

Low enrolment rates are both a result of and a cause of inequality. Once again, there is cumulative causality. Williamson finds that much of the difference in secondary school enrolment rates between South Korea and Brazil can be explained by differences in inequality.[55] By educating only part of a population, the human capital of that group is enhanced and as a consequence that section of the population has an asset which gives them an advantage over those who remain uneducated, thus exacerbating inequality.

Birdsall, Ross and Sabot describe two virtuous circles in East Asia wherein 'education contributed to economic growth, which, in turn, stimulated investment in education' and then 'education contributed to low levels of income inequality which, in turn, stimulated investment in education'.[56] Latin America, alas, was caught in two vicious circles where poor educational performance and inappropriate development strategies combined to impede growth. Slow economic growth then contributed to relatively low investment in education. At the same time, poor educational performance contributed to high income inequality which in turn limited investments in education.

Not only did the East Asian countries do better than other developing countries in terms of improvements in the supply of education – both quantity and quality – they also stand out as examples of countries which created a strong demand for labour. By promoting their agricultural and export sectors through investment in infrastructure, by adopting favourable exchange rate policies and by reducing distortions in factor markets, the East Asian countries encouraged labour intensive methods of production. These policies not only helped to increase living standards in the agricultural sector, they also raised wages in the non-agricultural sector by raising the reservation wage. This was especially true in countries which had a redistributive land reform. That is, redistributive measures in agriculture also reduced inequality in the urban, industrial sectors of the economy.

The export sectors in most countries of East Asia initially relied on intensive use of low-skilled labour, but over time exporting became more and more skill intensive. The combination of expanding employment opportunities and increasing real wage rates ensured that the returns to education at the level of the individual remained high. In Latin America, on the other hand, the demand for labour remained weak. Many of the Latin American countries adopted an import-substituting industrialization strategy in the 1960s and 1970s which discriminated against agriculture. Industrial production was highly capital intensive and thus did not require large numbers of educated and skilled workers. As a result, the private returns to education were reduced and hence the incentives for individuals and families to invest in education were lower than they might have been had the development strategy been different. Birdsall, Ross and Sabot underscore the importance not only of enhancing human capital by increasing educational opportunities, but also of ensuring that there is a demand for the skills created. They argue that 'weak demand for educated labor may help to explain why countries such as Peru and Argentina, which like East Asia, had greater than predicted human capital endowments, nevertheless have tended to underperform, with respect to growth'.[57]

Finally, the extensive land reforms that took place in South Korea and Taiwan provided the majority of households with a valuable asset

in which to invest. In addition, in Taiwan, the process of industrialization was not concentrated in urban areas as is usually the case, but
encompassed the rural areas as well. Indeed Taiwan (like China and the
Punjab of India) industrialized the countryside. This pattern of development gave farmers and their families an additional source of
employment and income. In 1975, for instance, 53.7 per cent of farm
incomes in Taiwan came from jobs off the farm.[58] The industrialization
process in Taiwan also was unusual in that much of the growth in
industry originated as a result of increases in the number of small
firms. That is, industrialization in Taiwan was led by small and
medium enterprises, not by large private oligopolies or state enterprises
as in most developing countries. John Mellor notes that 'an extraordinarily high proportion of total nonagricultural output takes place in
small firms. Indeed, 60 percent of all exports come from firms of less
than 100 employees. Those firms are broadly distributed through the
previously rural areas.'[59] Thus the combination of land reform and
small enterprise development in the countryside meant that natural
and physical capital and hence investment opportunities in Taiwan
were widely distributed among households. In addition, the labour
intensive pattern of growth ensured that human capital was a valuable
asset and this, in turn, ensured that investment in education would
enjoy a high rate of return.

## Policy implications

The focus of attention in this essay has been on the microeconomics
of asset redistribution. A supportive general development strategy is,
however, essential. Macroeconomic policy must ensure that the rate of
inflation is not so high that the functioning of the price mechanism is
impaired; and it must ensure that the pressure of demand is not so low
that investment incentives and the overall level of employment are
depressed. International trade policy must not be strongly biased either
against exporting or import substitution. Most important, a high level
of investment is desirable to give flexibility to the economy and to
enable the structure of incentives to operate effectively in allocating
resources. In such an environment the opportunities created by asset
redistribution are most likely to be grasped.

Economic theory, econometric evidence and historical experience
combine to produce an eloquent message: relative equality in the distribution of wealth contributes to faster economic growth and enhanced
human development. It goes without saying that a redistribution of

assets in favour of the poor would reduce poverty, both once-for-all and over time, because of its effect on the rate of economic growth. This would be true whether poverty is conceptualized as insufficient income or as a deficit in capabilities. The question of how best to achieve this more equitable distribution of productive assets still remains. The answer is bound to be affected by the characteristics of the three types of productive assets, viz. natural capital, human capital and physical capital. In the abstract it appears that there are two possible paths which governments can take to redistribute wealth. One is the more direct route of an immediate, once-for-all redistribution of the stock of existing assets. The other involves a more circuitous path of redistributing the flow of investments so that on the margin, new additions to the stock of assets are equitably distributed.

Of the three types of productive assets, only existing stocks of natural capital can be redistributed quickly and relatively easily. The class of natural capital, however, is large – including farm land, forests and plantations, pastures, water rights, fishing rights – and the importance of natural capital in the total stock of capital tends to vary inversely with the level of income per head. That is, the poorer the country, the more significant is natural capital likely to be in determining the overall distribution of wealth. At the other extreme, existing stocks of human capital evidently cannot be immediately redistributed since most human capital is embodied in human beings. An improvement in the distribution of human capital will consequently depend on reallocating and increasing expenditure on such things as education, training, health, nutrition programmes and family planning services. This redirection of the flow of investment in human capital, however, need not take long to have an impact on the composition of the stock of human capital. It takes less than a decade, for example, to provide primary and some secondary education to a child, and the provision of basic health services takes even less time. One should not imagine therefore that a redistribution of human capital is necessarily a long–term objective; much can be achieved rather quickly.

A redistribution of the stock of physical capital is more complicated than a redistribution of natural capital. Direct investment by the state in the manufacturing sector once was common in developing countries. In addition, partial or complete nationalization of assets has been attempted in many countries and the consequences for distributive equity have depended on whether the value added of the nationalized enterprises rose or fell and on how the value added was distributed among the population. Many formerly socialist countries have pursued the opposite strategy, denationalizing or privatizing state-owned enter-prises, but the experience so far is not particularly encouraging. Indeed in many formerly socialist countries privatization has resulted in an extremely unequal distribution of productive wealth with no compensat-ing pay-off in terms of a sharp acceleration in the pace of development.[60]

The most promising approach is to ensure that access to finance cap-ital is widespread, that obstacles to the creation and growth of small and medium enterprises are removed, and that relative factor prices provide incentives to adopt employment intensive patterns of growth. Beyond this, it may be possible to help the poor accumulate assets, e.g. where appropriate, by turning the assets constructed on public works programmes over to a cooperative composed of those who laboured to build them.[61] Similarly, housing policy can be designed to promote widespread ownership of dwellings and a house plot, which can provide not only shelter but a place of business.

The argument that savings are a function of investment opportuni-ties, and that a redistribution of productive assets would accelerate growth and human development and reduce poverty, rests on an assumption that there are slack resources in poor households which can be mobilized. There is surplus labour that can be used for invest-ment. There is a margin of consumption above physical subsistence that can be squeezed if attractive investments are available. There is a potential for savings to rise if access to financial markets can be improved. In other words, the poor are quantity constrained rather than price constrained, and opportunities for employment, investment and borrowing are more influential in determining the pace of capital accumulation and savings by the poor than the wage rate, the profit rate and the real rate of interest. Asset redistribution in effect, eases the quantity constraint and permits savings and the employment of labour to increase, thereby raising the level of investment.

It is sometimes argued that although a land reform would increase the rate of growth, a rise in aggregate investment would have an even greater effect, and if a land reform were to lead to social unrest and a decline in overall investment, a redistribution of assets might not be worthwhile.[62] However a classic study of Latin America by William Cline comes to the opposite conclusion.[63] He argues that even if one makes pessimistic assumptions about the effect of redistribution on aggregate savings and investment, a redistribution of income in Argentina, Brazil and Mexico to roughly the then British level of equality would bene-fit the poor. Assuming there is a fall in the annual growth rate by 0.66 per cent in Argentina and by approximately 1 per cent in Brazil and

Mexico, the incomes of the bottom 70 per cent of the population nevertheless would rise considerably. In fact, for the poorest 70 per cent to reach the post-redistribution level of income with the undiminished pre-redistribution rate of growth would require 34 years in Argentina, 56 years in Brazil and 49 years in Mexico. By then, most of the poor would have died.

Moreover, theory and empirical evidence since the time Cline wrote suggests that a redistribution of productive assets could in some circumstances increase investment and accelerate the rate of growth. If correct, this strengthens the case for redistribution. Similarly, while redistribution of land and other assets, or the threat of redistribution, could lead to social unrest and lower investment, as Deininger and Squire suggest, the perpetuation of inequality also can be costly in terms of resource use and this can lower the level of investment and the rate of growth. At the very least, the case against a redistribution of wealth is much weaker than once thought and the case in favour of redistribution is much stronger. Finally, asset redistribution is occurring willy-nilly in the ex-socialist countries and in many others (particularly in Africa and Central America) racked by civil conflict. The redistribution of wealth in these cases is disorderly and arbitrary rather than purposive and an opportunity is being missed to redistribute on a more systematic basis to encourage equity and long-term material and human development. In economies entering a period of post-war reconstruction or a transition from central planning to a more market-oriented economic system, the fluidity of politics may provide a brief opening for imaginative policies which link the distribution of wealth to the pace of development.

# Part II

# Systemic Transformation and Macroeconomic Reform

# 6
# Economic Policy during the Transition to a Market-Oriented Economy*

The transition economies which are the subject of this chapter include 26 countries with a total population of 413 million people. These countries are divided into three groups: the 11 countries of Central and Eastern Europe (118 million), the three Baltic States (8 million) and the 12 successor states to the former Soviet Union (287 million). The largest state by far is the Russian Federation with 148 million people, while the smallest is Estonia with only 1 million inhabitants. Twelve other countries, however, have 5 million people or less. Three countries – the Russian Federation, Ukraine and Poland – account for nearly 58 per cent of the total population.

Table 6.1 contains data on population size and two estimates of gross national product per capita. The first estimate is derived by converting GNP in local currency to the equivalent in US dollars by using the official exchange rate (following the World Bank's so-called Atlas method). The second attempts to measure 'real' differences in living standards by valuing output with a set of constant international prices intended to reflect purchasing power parity. Both estimates should be treated with caution, but they do provide a rough indication of how average incomes vary across countries. The use of the purchasing power parity method results in a narrower range of average incomes than does the method which uses exchange rates, but the latter is more transparent and more widely understood. In what follows we shall almost always use the estimates of GNP per capita obtained by applying the official exchange rate to local currency values.

It can be seen at a glance that average incomes in Eastern and Central Europe are higher than in either of the other two regions. The range, however, also is the greatest, since Eastern and Central Europe contains both the richest of the transition economies (Slovenia, $8200)

*Table 6.1*   Population and per capita gross national product in 26 transition economies, 1995

|  | Population (*millions*) | GNP per capita | |
|---|---|---|---|
|  |  | *$ 1995* | *PPP$ 1995* |
| Central and Eastern Europe |  |  |  |
| Albania | 3 | 670 | n.a. |
| Bulgaria | 8 | 1330 | 4480 |
| Croatia | 5 | 3250 | n.a. |
| Czech Republic | 10 | 3870 | 9770 |
| Slovakia | 5 | 2950 | 3610 |
| Hungary | 10 | 4120 | 6410 |
| Macedonia | 2 | 860 | n.a. |
| Poland | 39 | 2790 | 5400 |
| Romania | 23 | 1480 | 4360 |
| Slovenia | 2 | 8200 | n.a. |
| FR of Yugoslavia | 11 | n.a. | n.a. |
| Baltic States |  |  |  |
| Estonia | 1 | 2860 | 4220 |
| Latvia | 3 | 2270 | 3370 |
| Lithuania | 4 | 1900 | 4120 |
| Former Soviet Union/ Commonwealth of Independent States |  |  |  |
| Armenia | 4 | 730 | 2260 |
| Azerbaijan | 8 | 480 | 1460 |
| Belarus | 10 | 2070 | 4220 |
| Georgia | 5 | 440 | 1470 |
| Kazakhstan | 17 | 1330 | 3010 |
| Kyrgyzstan | 5 | 700 | 1800 |
| Moldova | 4 | 920 | n.a. |
| Russian Federation | 148 | 2240 | 4480 |
| Tajikistan | 6 | 340 | 920 |
| Turkmenistan | 5 | 920 | n.a. |
| Ukraine | 52 | 1630 | 2400 |
| Uzbekistan | 23 | 970 | 2370 |

*Source:* World Bank, *World Development Indicators 1997*, Washington, DC: World Bank, 1997, Table 1.1, pp. 6–9 and Table 2.1, pp. 34–6.

and one of the poorest (Albania, $670). Next in order of average income come the three Baltic States, with the smallest and richest (Estonia, $2860) having an income about 50 per cent higher than the largest and poorest (Lithuania, $1900). Finally, there is the former Soviet Union, with a low average income and considerable variation around the average. Indeed development in the Soviet Union was so uneven that the successor states fall naturally into three distinct groups: the Slavic countries (the Russian Federation, Belarus and Ukraine), the Central Asian republics (Kazakhstan, Uzbekistan, Turkmenistan, Kyrgyzstan and Tajikistan) and the Caucasus (Armenia, Azerbaijan and Georgia). Note that Moldova does not fit neatly into any of these groups.

Average incomes in the three Slavic countries are more than twice as high as average incomes in the five Central Asian republics, and average incomes in Central Asia are twice as high as in the three countries of the Caucasus. The poorest of the Slavic countries (Ukraine, $1630) is richer than the richest of the Central Asian countries (Kazakhstan, $1330). And only Tajikistan ($340) in Central Asia is noticeably poorer than the countries of the Caucasus.

The 26 countries that interest us are thus very heterogeneous in terms of population size and income per head. The things they have in common are, first, that they were part of a closely integrated economic and political system centred on the Soviet Union and, second, that they began a transition from central planning to a market-oriented regime at approximately the same time. Simultaneous systemic change in so many and in such diverse countries is unique in world history: nothing like it has been witnessed before. This does not imply, however, that policy makers in the 26 countries were navigating without a compass and sailing into uncharted seas. There was in fact considerable relevant experience that could have been drawn upon if those in authority had wished to do so. China began a similar systemic change in late 1978 and the decade of experience there could have been of great value. In addition, a number of developing countries, particularly in Latin America and sub-Saharan Africa, embarked upon radical structural adjustment programmes in the early 1980s and the difficulties they encountered were warning signs that unfortunately were ignored. Lastly, there was the experience in Western Europe after the end of the Second World War when a market economy was re-created and wartime controls and planning institutions were dismantled. All of this experience was overlooked when the transition began, with consequences we shall describe in the next section.

## Economic performance during the transition

In this section we present the basic facts and describe what occurred during the transition from a centrally planned economic system to a more market-oriented economy. Analysis of the facts will be undertaken in the next section. Here we cover inflation, economic growth, poverty and inequality, demographic indicators of distress and social indicators of societal collapse.

## The explosion of prices

The price mechanism under central planning performed no allocative function. Prices did not reflect, and were not intended to reflect, social costs and benefits and planners did not use price signals to determine what would be produced, what methods of production would be used or how national income would be distributed. Prices reflected administrative decisions and many prices remained fixed year after year. Inflation was not a problem.

In the 1980s, however, many countries experimented with partial price liberalization and inflation began to appear, although the rate of increase in the level of prices was low. The situation changed dramatically in the 1990s after the collapse of the Soviet Union and the disintegration of the former Yugoslavia. Price controls were removed, often suddenly and across the board, and the result was an explosion of prices that is unprecedented for its duration and the number of countries affected. Table 6.2 contains information on the annual rate of increase of consumer prices for 25 countries for the period 1990–95. In only three countries (the Czech Republic, Hungary and Slovakia) was the peak rate of inflation kept below 62 per cent; in 22 countries the rate of inflation was 100 per cent or more for at least one year; and in 15 countries the peak rate of inflation was at least 1000 per cent a year. In Georgia in 1994 the rate of inflation was 18 000 per cent. By 1995 only four countries (Albania, Croatia, the Czech Republic and Slovakia) had succeeded in bringing the rate of inflation down to less than 10 per cent a year.

In most transition economies the government lost control over the level of prices and the price mechanism consequently functioned poorly. The systemic change from central planning to a market-oriented regime, intended to improve economic efficiency in resource use and accelerate growth, had the opposite effect. Relative prices fluctuated erratically, long-term investment decision making became impossible, and the distribution of income became arbitrary. As a result, investment collapsed, output and incomes fell sharply and growth rates became negative. The acute macroeconomic instability created by rapid inflation undermined the entire reform effort.

There were a number of factors that contributed to the debacle. First, the decision to liberalize prices instantaneously and indiscriminately

*Table 6.2*  Percentage annual rates of inflation, 1990–95

|  | 1990 | 1991 | 1992 | 1993 | 1994 | 1995 |
|---|---|---|---|---|---|---|
| Central and Eastern Europe |  |  |  |  |  |  |
| Albania | 0.0 | 35.5 | 225.9 | 85.0 | 28.0 | 8.0 |
| Bulgaria | 22.0 | 333.5 | 82.0 | 72.8 | 89.0 | 62.0 |
| Croatia | 135.6 | 249.5 | 938.2 | 1 516.0 | 98.0 | 4.1 |
| Czech Republic | 10.8 | 56.7 | 11.1 | 20.8 | 10.2 | 9.1 |
| Slovakia | 10.8 | 61.2 | 10.1 | 23.0 | 14.0 | 9.9 |
| Hungary | 29.0 | 34.2 | 22.9 | 22.5 | 19.0 | 28.2 |
| Macedonia | 120.5 | 229.7 | 1 925.2 | 248.0 | 65.0 | 50.0 |
| Poland | 586.0 | 70.3 | 43.0 | 35.3 | 32.2 | 27.8 |
| Romania | 5.1 | 174.5 | 210.9 | 256.0 | 131.0 | 32.3 |
| Slovenia | 549.7 | 117.7 | 201.0 | 32.0 | 19.8 | 12.6 |
| Baltic States |  |  |  |  |  |  |
| Estonia | 23.1 | 210.6 | 1 069.0 | 89.0 | 48.0 | 29.0 |
| Latvia | 10.5 | 124.4 | 951.2 | 109.0 | 36.0 | 25.0 |
| Lithuania | 8.4 | 224.7 | 1 020.3 | 390.0 | 72.0 | 35.0 |
| Former Soviet Union/ Commonwealth of Independent States |  |  |  |  |  |  |
| Armenia | 10.3 | 100.0 | 825.0 | 3 732.0 | 5 458.0 | 175.0 |
| Azerbaijan | 7.8 | 105.6 | 616.0 | 833.0 | 1 500.0 | 412.0 |
| Belarus | 4.5 | 83.5 | 969.0 | 1 188.0 | 2 200.0 | 800.0 |
| Georgia | 3.3 | 78.5 | 913.0 | 3 126.0 | 18 000.0 | 160.0 |
| Kazakhstan | 4.2 | 91.0 | 1 610.0 | 1 760.0 | 1 980.0 | 180.0 |
| Kyrgyzstan | 3.0 | 85.0 | 824.6 | 1 208.7 | 280.0 | 45.0 |
| Moldova | 4.2 | 98.0 | 1 276.0 | 789.0 | 327.0 | 30.0 |
| Russian Federation | 5.6 | 92.7 | 1 353.0 | 896.0 | 303.0 | 190.0 |
| Tajikistan | 4.0 | 111.6 | 1 157.0 | 2 195.0 | 452.0 | 635.0 |
| Turkmenistan | 4.6 | 102.5 | 492.9 | 3 102.0 | 2 400.0 | 1 800.0 |
| Ukraine | 4.0 | 91.2 | 1 210.0 | 4 735.0 | 842.0 | 375.0 |
| Uzbekistan | 3.1 | 82.2 | 645.0 | 534.0 | 746.0 | 315.0 |

*Source*: World Bank, *World Development Report 1996*, New York: Oxford University Press, 1996, Table A.3, p. 174.

turned out to be a serious mistake. The alternative was to liberalize selectively and gradually. This was the approach adopted in China and Vietnam with considerable success. In China, for instance, the rate of inflation was less than 3.0 per cent a year during the first six years of reform; in 1988, ten years after the transition began, inflation reached 20.7 per cent a year, but it was quickly brought down to 2.2 per cent in 1990. In other words, the authorities never lost control of the situation. Similarly, in Vietnam the reforms began in earnest in 1989 and during the period 1990–95 inflation averaged 30.5 per cent a year, with a peak of 67.6 per cent in 1991.

Second, many of the transition economies became embroiled in violent conflict: the economy was disrupted, many goods became scarce and prices were subjected to upward pressure. The civil war that accompanied the break-up of Yugoslavia undoubtedly contributed to the rapid inflation in Croatia, Macedonia and Slovenia. The peaceful division of Czechoslovakia into the Czech Republic and Slovakia, and the relative price stability in those two countries, stands in sharp contrast to the bloodshed in the former Yugoslavia. There was also civil war in Georgia and Tajikistan and a war between Armenia and Ajerbaijan; in the Russian Federation there was a violent conflict with the Chechens. All of these conflicts contributed to rapid inflation.

Third, there was the legacy of the past. Price controls and rationing often led to a form of 'forced savings' and the accumulation by households of liquid funds in bank accounts. These cash balances or 'monetary overhang' represented pent-up demand that was released by rapid price liberalization. The result was a price explosion in Poland, the first country to adopt wholesale liberalization, of 586 per cent in 1990. This was followed by similar explosions in 1992, after the disintegration of the Soviet Union. Prices in that year rose 1353 per cent in the Russian Federation and 1210 per cent in Ukraine, for example.

Fourth, price liberalization occurred in an uncompetitive environment. Industrial and trading enterprises, whether state owned or newly privatized, often were the sole supplier of the goods and services they produced. That is, they were monopolies which enjoyed considerable market power and they were not subjected to market disciplines and the incentives created by competition to reduce costs and restrain price increases. On the contrary, once released from administrative controls, the monopolistic enterprises used their new freedom to increase prices and exploit their dominant position in the market. This exacerbated the inflationary tendencies that already existed. Equally important, in the absence of competition there can be no assurance that reliance on the price mechanism will result in an improved allocation of resources.

Finally, inflation was fuelled by large and persistent public sector deficits that were monetized by the central banks. The deficits, in turn, were caused partly by a steep decline in government revenues that accompanied liberalization and partly by the decision of most governments to cover the losses of those state-owned enterprises that ran into financial difficulty when prices were liberalized and relative prices changed radically. Thus there were pressures on both the revenue and expenditure sides of the public accounts that contributed to rapid inflation. The implication is that tax reform and reform of the state-owned enterprises are integral to the success of price reform. The failure to address this linkage helps to explain why the transition economies experienced simultaneously rapid inflation and a contraction of aggregate demand.

## Output, income and economic growth

It was widely believed that the transition from central planning to a more market-oriented economic system would result in faster economic growth and a rapid improvement in the standard of living of the great majority of the population. Few analysts at the time anticipated either the depth or the duration of the decline in incomes or the extent to which inequality in the distribution of income increased. Several hundred million people became impoverished, economic output collapsed and the social services proved to be incapable of coping with the calamity. Not even the Great Depression of the 1930s witnessed such a severe fall in incomes.[1]

Output began to fall as early as 1988 in Albania, Hungary, Romania and Yugoslavia. In 1989 output also began to fall in Bulgaria. By 1990 production was falling everywhere, most rapidly in Poland (by 11.6 per cent a year) and least rapidly in the then Czechoslovakia (by 1.5 per cent a year). As can be seen in Table 6.3, in most countries output did not begin to recover until 1993 or 1994. The recovery was earlier in Poland (1992) and much later in the Commonwealth of Independent States. Indeed in the Russian Federation the bottom of the decline was not reached until 1997 and in Ukraine, the second largest country, the end still is not in sight.

The hardships experienced by the 26 countries with which we are concerned were also experienced by Mongolia, a country whose economy was closely integrated into that of the former Soviet Union.[2] Output fell sharply during the early years of the transition and did not begin to rise until 1994. Between 1989 and 1993 the cumulative decline in gross domestic product was roughly 20 per cent. In China, in contrast, the transition began much earlier (in late 1978) and was much more successful.[3] The average rate of growth accelerated and in no year did output fail to rise. In the ten years starting in 1979 the average rate of growth of GDP was 9.0 per cent per annum. The same is true in Vietnam.[4] The economic reforms began *de facto* in 1989 and between 1990 and 1995 gross domestic product increased 7.6 per cent a year. Moreover, there was not a single year in which output and incomes failed to rise.

*Table 6.3*    Year when growth rate first became positive

| | |
|---|---|
| Central and Eastern Europe | 1994 |
|   Albania | 1993 |
|   Bulgaria | 1994 |
|   Croatia | 1994 |
|   Czech Republic | 1993 |
|   Slovakia | 1994 |
|   Hungary | 1994 |
|   Macedonia | 1996 |
|   Poland | 1992 |
|   Romania | 1993 |
|   Slovenia | 1993 |
|   FR of Yugoslavia | 1994 |
| Baltic States | 1994 |
|   Estonia | 1995 |
|   Latvia | 1994 |
|   Lithuania | 1994 |
| Former Soviet Union/ Commonwealth of   Independent States | 1998? |
|   Armenia | 1994 |
|   Azerbaijan | 1996 |
|   Belarus | 1996 |
|   Georgia | 1994 |
|   Kazakhstan | 1996 |
|   Kyrgyzstan | 1996 |
|   Moldova | 1998? |
|   Russian Federation | 1997 |
|   Tajikistan | 1998? |
|   Turkmenistan | 1992 |
|   Ukraine | ? |
|   Uzbekistan | 1996 |

*Source:* United Nations, Department of Economic and Social Affairs, *The World Economy at the Beginning of 1998*, document E/1998/INF/1, Table A.5, p. 31.

Elsewhere the story is very different. (See Table 6.4.) Total output in Central and Eastern Europe has yet to regain the level achieved in 1990. In Slovenia output is 4 per cent higher than in 1990 and in Poland it is 25 per cent higher, but in every other country of the region it is lower. On average GDP in Central and Eastern Europe in 1997 was nearly 12 per cent lower than in 1990. The situation in the Baltic States, especially Latvia and Lithuania, is much worse. In 1997 GDP was only 59 per cent of the 1990 level. Worse still is the Commonwealth of Independent

*Table 6.4*  Cumulative change in real GDP, 1990–97 (index: 1990 = 100)

| | 1990 | 1991 | 1992 | 1993 | 1994 | 1995 | 1996 | 1997 |
|---|---|---|---|---|---|---|---|---|
| Central and Eastern Europe | 100 | 88.7 | 80.3 | 75.7 | 78.7 | 82.6 | 85.8 | 88.4 |
| Albania | 100 | 72 | 66.7 | 73.2 | 80.1 | 86.5 | 94.4 | 84.9 |
| Bulgaria | 100 | 88.2 | 81.8 | 80.6 | 82.1 | 83.8 | 74.7 | 70.6 |
| Croatia | 100 | 81.1 | 79.5 | 77.4 | 82.1 | 84.2 | 88.5 | 93.5 |
| Former Czechoslovakia | 100 | 85.7 | 80 | | | | | |
| Czech Republic | | | | 80.4 | 82.6 | 86.6 | 90.1 | 91.4 |
| Slovakia | | | | 76.8 | 80.7 | 86.1 | 92.1 | 97.4 |
| Hungary | 100 | 88.3 | 85.6 | 85 | 87.5 | 88.8 | 90 | 93.2 |
| Macedonia | 100 | 93 | 85.7 | 77.9 | 76.4 | 75.5 | 78 | 81.2 |
| Poland | 100 | 93 | 95.5 | 99.1 | 104.4 | 111.6 | 118.3 | 125.2 |
| Romania | 100 | 87.1 | 79.6 | 80.7 | 83.9 | 89.8 | 93.5 | 91.4 |
| Slovenia | 100 | 91.1 | 86.1 | 88.6 | 93.3 | 97.2 | 100.1 | 104.1 |
| FR of Yugoslavia | 100 | 88.4 | 64.4 | 44.6 | 45.8 | 47.5 | 49.6 | 50.1 |
| Baltic States | n.a. | 100 | 68.6 | 53.3 | 53.4 | 54.5 | 56.4 | 59 |
| Estonia | n.a. | 100 | 85.9 | 78.6 | 72.5 | 75.5 | 78.6 | 83.3 |
| Latvia | n.a. | 100 | 65.1 | 55.4 | 55.8 | 55.3 | 56.9 | 59 |
| Lithuania | n.a. | 100 | 66 | 46 | 46.4 | 47.7 | 49.4 | 51.7 |
| Former Soviet Union/ Commonwealth of Independent States | 100 | 93.8 | 81.2 | 72.7 | 61.6 | 57.5 | 54.6 | 54.6 |
| Armenia | | | 54.7 | 49.9 | 52.6 | 56.2 | 59.5 | 63 |
| Azerbaijan | | | 72.6 | 55.8 | 44.8 | 39.5 | 40 | 42.2 |
| Belarus | | | 84.7 | 78.3 | 68.4 | 61.4 | 62.9 | 66 |
| Georgia | | | 51.7 | 36.5 | 39.8 | 41 | 45.7 | 50.2 |
| Kazakhstan | | | 88.8 | 80.7 | 65.6 | 60.3 | 60.6 | 61.8 |
| Kyrgyzstan | | | 80.8 | 68.2 | 54.5 | 51.6 | 54.5 | 56.2 |
| Moldova | | | 66.6 | 65.8 | 45.3 | 44.5 | 40.9 | 40.1 |
| Russian Federation | | | 80.2 | 73.3 | 63.9 | 61.3 | 57.9 | 58.2 |
| Tajikistan | | | 64.7 | 53.5 | 46.7 | 40.9 | 34 | 32.7 |
| Turkmenistan | | | 127.3 | 129.1 | 107 | 96.3 | 96.4 | 92.5 |
| Ukraine | | | 84.5 | 72.5 | 56 | 49.2 | 44.3 | 42 |
| Uzbekistan | | | 83.5 | 81.2 | 77.1 | 76.2 | 77.4 | 79.9 |

*Source:* United Nations, Department of Economic and Social Affairs, *The World Economy at the Beginning of 1998*, document E/1998/INF/1, Table A.5, p. 31.

States, where GDP in 1997 was only 55 per cent of the 1990 level. Two of the Central Asian countries, Turkmenistan and Uzbekistan, experienced a less severe decline than the other CIS countries, while a third Central Asian country, Tajikistan, racked by civil war, saw its GDP fall by two-thirds.

The Russian Federation and Ukraine account for nearly 70 per cent of the population of the CIS countries and the performance of their economies inevitably influences the performance of their neighbours. Unfortunately both countries have experienced unusually serious difficulties. As we have seen, output in the Russian Federation continued to fall until 1997 and in Ukraine output is still falling. Furthermore, the extent of the fall was very great: 58 per cent in Ukraine so far and 42 per cent in the Russian Federation. A full economic recovery in these two countries would make an enormous difference not only to the well being of their citizens but to the entire region.

The fall in output and incomes was due in large part to a collapse in aggregate demand, and in particular to a sharp fall in investment. In Table 6.5 we compare the investment ratio in 1990 and 1995 for the 21 countries for which data are available. Only in two countries did the investment ratio rise, namely in Croatia and Slovenia. In the other 19 countries the investment ratio fell, in a number of cases by a third or more. This fall in the investment ratio occurred in a context of falling GDP and as a result, there was a precipitous fall in the absolute level of investment.

Consider the Russian Federation. Between 1990 and 1995 the investment ratio fell by one-sixth: from 30.1 per cent of GDP to 25 per cent of GDP. Total output, however, fell by 38.7 per cent during that period and hence investment was a smaller share of a much smaller GDP. The level of investment in 1995 was in fact only half what it was in 1990. In some countries, e.g. Kazakhstan, the decline in gross investment was so great that it was impossible to maintain the initial stock of capital intact. That is, net investment was negative.[5] This almost certainly was true, too, in Armenia, Georgia, Lithuania and Moldova.

It is often argued, with considerable justification, that the centrally planned economies were characterized by a high investment ratio but by a low (and falling) productivity of investment. The growth rate, consequently, was not as rapid as it could have been if investment had been allocated efficiently and the level of consumption consequently was unnecessarily low. A fall in the investment ratio, by this reasoning, was not necessarily undesirable. The problem, however, is that not only did the ratio of investment to GDP fall, but the level of gross investment fell dramatically, indeed to such a low level that output and incomes could not be sustained and, in some cases, the stock of fixed productive assets could not be maintained.

*Table 6.5*   Gross domestic investment, 1990 and 1995 (per cent of GDP)

|  | 1990 | 1995 |
|---|---|---|
| **Central and Eastern Europe** | | |
| Albania | 28.9 | 16 |
| Bulgaria | 25.6 | 21 |
| Croatia | 13.4 | 14 |
| Czech Republic | 28.6 | 25 |
| Slovakia | 33.5 | 28 |
| Hungary | 25.4 | 23 |
| Macedonia | 32.0 | 15 |
| Poland | 25.6 | 17 |
| Romania | 30.2 | 26 |
| Slovenia | 16.9 | 22 |
| F.R. of Yugoslavia | n.a. | n.a. |
| **Baltic States** | | |
| Estonia | 30.2 | 27 |
| Latvia | 40.1 | 21 |
| Lithuania | 34.3 | 19 |
| **Former Soviet Union/ Commonwealth of Independent States** | | |
| Armenia | 47.1 | 9 |
| Azerbaijan | 27.8 | 16 |
| Belarus | 27.4 | 25 |
| Georgia | n.a. | 3 |
| Kazakhstan | 42.6 | 22 |
| Kyrgyzstan | 23.8 | 16 |
| Moldova | n.a. | 7 |
| Russian Federation | 30.1 | 25 |
| Tajikistan | 23.4 | 17 |
| Turkmenistan | 40.0 | n.a. |
| Ukraine | 27.5 | n.a. |
| Uzbekistan | 32.2 | 23 |

*Sources*: World Bank, *World Development Report 1996*, New York: Oxford University Press, 1996, Table A.2, p. 173; World Bank, *World Development Indicators 1997*, Washington, DC: World Bank, Table 4.12, pp. 174–6.

## Income inequality and income poverty

In addition to the fall in the level of income, there was also a remarkable increase in inequality in the distribution of income. (See Table 6.6.) Before the process of economic reform began, the centrally planned economies enjoyed a relatively egalitarian distribution of

*Table 6.6*    Income inequality and poverty

| | Gini coefficient | | Per cent change | Population in poverty | |
|---|---|---|---|---|---|
| | *1987–88* | *1993* | | *Year* | *Percentage* |
| Central and Eastern Europe | | | | | |
| Albania | | | | 1996 | 19.6 |
| Bulgaria | 0.23 | 0.38[a] | 65 | 1995 | 19.1 |
| Czech Republic | 0.19 | 0.27 | 42 | | |
| Slovakia | | 0.20[b] | | | |
| Hungary | 0.21 | 0.27 | 29 | 1989–94 | 25 |
| Poland | 0.25 | 0.30 | 20 | 1993 | 23.8 |
| Romania | | 0.26[b] | | 1994 | 21.5 |
| Slovenia | 0.24 | 0.28 | 17 | | |
| FR of Yugoslavia | | 0.26[a] | | 1995 | 28.9 |
| Baltic States | | | | | |
| Estonia | 0.23 | 0.40 | 43 | 1994 | 8.9 |
| Latvia | | 0.27 | | | |
| Lithuania | | 0.34 | | | |
| Former Soviet Union/ Commonwealth of Independent States | | | | | |
| Azerbaijan | | | | 1995 | 61.5 |
| Belarus | | 0.22 | | 1989–94 | 37 |
| Georgia | | | | 1989–94 | 30 |
| Kazakhstan | 0.30[c] | 0.33 | 10 | 1993–94 | 50 |
| Kyrgyzstan | 0.17–0.41 | about 0.50 | 22–194 | 1993 | 45.4 |
| Moldova | | 0.34[b] | | | |
| Russian Federation | 0.24–0.34 | 0.50 | 47–108 | 1994 | 30.9 |
| Turkmenistan | 0.26 | 0.36 | 38 | 1993–94 | 48 |
| Ukraine | | 0.26[b] | | 1995 | 31.7 |
| Uzbekistan | 0.29 | 0.34[a] | 17 | 1993–94 | 29 |

[a] 1995.
[b] 1992.
[c] 1990.

*Sources*: World Bank, *World Development Report 1996*, New York: Oxford University Press, 1996, Table 4.1, p. 69; World Bank, *World Development Indicators 1997*, Washington, DC: World Bank, 1997, Table 2.5, pp. 50–2 and Table 2.6, pp. 54–6; United Nations Development Programme, *Uzbekistan Human Development Report 1996*, Tashkent: UNDP, 1996; United Nations, *Economic Survey of Europe in 1996–1997*, Geneva and New York: United Nations, June 1997, Ch. 4; United Nations Development Programme, *Human Development Report 1997*, New York: Oxford University Press, 1997, Annex Table A2.1, pp. 53–5; United Nations Development Programme, *Azerbaijan Human Development Report 1996*, Baku: UNDP, 1996; UNDP, *Bulgaria Human Development Report 1997*, Sofia: UNDP, 1997; United Nations Development Programme, *Turkmenistan Human Development Report 1996*, Ashgabat: UNDP, 1996; United Nations Development Programme, *Yugoslavia Human Development Report 1997*, Belgrade: UNDP, 1997.

income, compared both to the developing economies and to the advanced market economy countries. During the transition period, however, income differentials widened considerably and in a number of countries the degree of inequality, as measured by the Gini coefficient, approached that of the most inegalitarian of the developing countries. This is conspicuously the case in the largest country, the Russian Federation, where inequality is now comparable to that in some Latin American countries.

In 11 cases it is possible to make a rough estimate of the change in inequality by calculating the percentage increase in the Gini coefficient between 1987–88 (before the reforms began) and 1993 (by when the reforms were well under way). In five countries (Bulgaria, the Czech Republic, Estonia, Kyrgyzstan and the Russian Federation) the Gini coefficient increased by 40 per cent or more in just half a decade, and in three others (Hungary, Poland and Turkmenistan) inequality increased by 20–38 per cent. Inequality appears to have increased least in Kazakhstan, but in this case the period covered (1990–93) is only three years and hence is not comparable to the other nine countries.

Although quantitative evidence is lacking, it is clear that the transition also has been accompanied by an increase in inequality in the distribution of productive assets. Prior to the reforms, most productive assets were owned either by the state or by collective or cooperative institutions; the distribution of wealth among households was consequently highly equal. Since 1991, however, state-owned enterprises have been sold to the private sector. Privatization has proceeded more rapidly in some countries than in others, and the method of asset disposal has been more equitable in some countries than in others, but the net result has been to create a small and wealthy capitalist class and a highly polarized society. The market economies being created will begin life with a very unequal distribution of wealth.

Income inequality also increased in China, Mongolia and Vietnam and thus the experience of the 26 countries with which we are primarily concerned is not unique. In China, for example, the Gini coefficient increased from about 0.33 in 1979–80 to 0.38 in 1988, a rise of 15 per cent and much less than the increase in the early stages of transition in the countries that concern us.[6] After that, however, inequality increased sharply and by 1995 the Gini coefficient had risen to 0.45, implying an increase in income inequality since 1979–80 of roughly 36 per cent.[7] This is broadly comparable to the increase experienced in the other transition economies although in China the increase occurred over a much longer period.

The combination of a fall in average incomes and a rise in inequality resulted in a very substantial increase in the incidence of income poverty. Using a poverty line of $4 a day (in 1990 purchasing power parity dollars), the UNDP estimates that poverty in Eastern Europe and the CIS countries increased from 4 per cent of the population in 1988 to 32 per cent in 1994, or from 13.6 million people to 119.2 million.[8] In other words, prior to the transition to a market economy, mass poverty was unknown: all able-bodied people had a job and hence a source of livelihood and an elaborate system of social services ensured that the elderly, the ill and the handicapped were protected from hardship. During the transition, however, the system of social protection became much weaker, unemployment increased and real wages fell. The inevitable consequence was the emergence of widespread poverty and destitution.

The estimates of poverty in the final column of Table 6.6 are based on national standards and hence are not necessarily comparable across countries. Nevertheless the data are of considerable interest. The six observations from Central and Eastern Europe suggest that poverty in that region afflicts about 20 per cent of the population or more. This is true even in Poland which by 1993 had virtually regained the 1990 level of output. Poverty in Estonia is limited apparently to only 8.9 per cent of the population but the incidence of poverty almost certainly is higher in the other two Baltic States since the fall in average income was much greater in Latvia and Lithuania than in Estonia. In the nine CIS countries for which we have data, poverty is uniformly high, rising from 29 per cent of the population in Uzbekistan to nearly 62 per cent in Azerbaijan. It is noteworthy that in the two largest countries, Ukraine and the Russian Federation, the incidence of poverty is about 31 per cent.

Thus the data suggest that with the possible exception of Estonia, the incidence of income poverty increased sharply and in most countries affects between a fifth and a third of the population. This deterioration in the standard of living of the lowest-income groups is due in part to a decline in average incomes and in part to greater inequality in the distribution of income. There can be little doubt that for 100 million people or more in poverty, living conditions today are much worse than they were before the transition began.

## Demographic consequences of the economic collapse

It is sometimes claimed that estimates of output in the transition economies are unreliable and that the decline in incomes is exaggerated.

Three reasons are advanced to support these views. First, it is argued that the value of output in the pre-reform period was overstated and hence that average incomes were much lower than the official data indicate. Second, after the reforms were introduced there was a breakdown in the statistical system and the output of many private sector activities was not fully recorded, particularly in the case of small and medium enterprises. Third, a number of illegal activities flourished, including smuggling across international borders, and this activity was not reflected in the national income accounts. Hence output and incomes during the early years of the transition were higher than the official data indicate. Moreover, since many of the unrecorded incomes are thought to have accrued primarily to lower-income groups, e.g. incomes generated in informal sector activities, it is argued that the reported increase in inequality also is exaggerated.

While there is an element of truth in all three propositions, other types of evidence support the view that in most countries the economy did indeed perform very poorly during the transition and that this had serious negative consequences for human development. The demographic data in particular indicate that the transition economies as a group experienced a crisis of major magnitude.

Let us begin with the data on life expectancy at birth. (See Table 6.7.) Consider the period between 1980 (long before the beginning of the transition) and 1995 (the most recent year for which data are available). In Central and Eastern Europe life expectancy for males declined in two countries (Bulgaria and Romania) and remained unchanged in two others (Hungary and Poland); life expectancy for females rose in all ten countries for which we have data. In the Baltic States male life expectancy declined in Latvia and Lithuania and female life expectancy in Lithuania. In the Commonwealth of Independent States life expectancy for males declined in four countries (Armenia, Belarus, the Russian Federation and Ukraine) while life expectancy for females declined in four countries (Armenia, Belarus, the Russian Federation and Tajikistan) and remained unchanged in another (Ukraine).

The most alarming statistic is the sharp fall in life expectancy among Russian men. Between 1980 and 1995 life expectancy fell by four years, more than in any other country, and today life expectancy for males in the Russian Federation is only 58 years. This is ten years less than the life expectancy of men in China!

The decline in average incomes, the rise in income inequality, the increase in insecurity, uncertainty and unemployment, and the deterioration of the social services, including the health services, led to a

*Table 6.7*   Life expectancy at birth, 1980 and 1995 (years)

| | Males | | | Females | | |
|---|---|---|---|---|---|---|
| | *1980* | *1995* | *Change* | *1980* | *1995* | *Change* |
| Central and Eastern Europe | | | | | | |
| Albania | 68 | 70 | 2 | 72 | 76 | 4 |
| Bulgaria | 69 | 68 | −1 | 74 | 75 | 1 |
| Croatia | 66 | 70 | 4 | 74 | 78 | 4 |
| Czech Republic | 67 | 70 | 3 | 74 | 77 | 3 |
| Slovakia | 67 | 68 | 1 | 74 | 76 | 2 |
| Hungary | 66 | 66 | 0 | 73 | 74 | 1 |
| Macedonia | n.a. | 71 | n.a. | n.a. | 75 | n.a. |
| Poland | 67 | 67 | 0 | 75 | 76 | 1 |
| Romania | 67 | 66 | −1 | 72 | 74 | 2 |
| Slovenia | 66 | 70 | 4 | 75 | 78 | 3 |
| FR of Yugoslavia | 68 | 70 | 2 | 73 | 75 | 2 |
| Baltic States | | | | | | |
| Estonia | 64 | 65 | 1 | 74 | 76 | 2 |
| Latvia | 64 | 63 | −1 | 74 | 75 | 1 |
| Lithuania | 66 | 63 | −3 | 76 | 75 | −1 |
| Former Soviet Union/ Commonwealth of Independent States | | | | | | |
| Armenia | 70 | 68 | −2 | 76 | 74 | −2 |
| Azerbaijan | 64 | 66 | 2 | 72 | 75 | 3 |
| Belarus | 66 | 64 | −2 | 76 | 75 | −1 |
| Georgia | 67 | 69 | 2 | 75 | 78 | 3 |
| Kazakhstan | 62 | 64 | 2 | 72 | 74 | 2 |
| Kyrgyzstan | 61 | 63 | 2 | 70 | 72 | 2 |
| Moldova | 62 | 65 | 3 | 69 | 73 | 4 |
| Russian Federation | 62 | 58 | −4 | 73 | 72 | −1 |
| Tajikistan | 64 | 66 | 2 | 69 | 66 | −3 |
| Turkmenistan | 61 | 62 | 1 | 68 | 69 | 1 |
| Ukraine | 65 | 64 | −1 | 74 | 74 | 0 |
| Uzbekistan | 64 | 66 | 2 | 71 | 72 | 1 |
| Other | | | | | | |
| China | 66 | 68 | 2 | 68 | 71 | 3 |
| Mongolia | 57 | 64 | 7 | 59 | 66 | 7 |
| Vietnam | 61 | 65 | 4 | 65 | 70 | 5 |

*Source*: World Bank, *World Development Indicators 1997*, Washington, DC: World Bank, 1997, Table 2.14, pp. 86–8.

sharp decline in birth rates in almost all of the transition economies and to a rise in mortality rates in many countries. (See Table 6.8.) Between 1980 and 1995 the birth rate fell by 21–38 per cent in Central and Eastern Europe, by a third in the Baltic States and by 8–44 per cent in the Commonwealth of Independent States. There is a clear association between the extent of the decline in average incomes and the sharpness of the fall in birth rates. Marriage rates fell, divorce rates increased, married couples postponed having children and more and more women had to resort to abortion. In other parts of the world a decline in the birth rate is a sign of improved economic conditions, but in the transition economies the collapse of the birth rate is a sign of acute economic distress.

This interpretation is supported by the evidence on mortality rates. Between 1980 and 1995 the death rate declined in only one country of Central and Eastern Europe; it remained unchanged in seven and rose in two (Bulgaria and Romania). The death rate rose in all three of the Baltic States. In the Commonwealth of Independent States the death rate declined in four countries, remained unchanged in two and rose in the remaining six countries. That is, the mortality rate increased in half the CIS countries and the rise was especially great in Ukraine and the Russian Federation, by far the two largest countries in the group. In 1995 the death rate was lower in China, Mongolia and Vietnam than in 9 of the 11 Central and Eastern European countries, all 3 of the Baltic States and 7 of the 12 CIS countries. In fact only in Albania and Uzbekistan was the mortality rate lower than in China, Mongolia and Vietnam.

The combination of a fall in the birth rate and a rise in the death rate was such that in ten of the transition economies the natural rate of growth of the population became negative by 1995. Economic collapse led to demographic contraction. In Central and Eastern Europe the population growth rate was negative in Bulgaria, the Czech Republic, Hungary and Romania; it was also negative in all three Baltic States; in the Commonwealth of Independent States it was negative in Belarus, the Russian Federation and Ukraine. In other words, in countries which account for 65 per cent of the total population of the transition economies, the death rate exceeds the birth rate. It is hard to imagine that something similar could have happened ever before over such a large region during peacetime conditions.

The brunt of the demographic impact often fell on men. This is reflected in an abnormally low ratio of men to women in the total population. (See Table 6.9.) Using as a standard of comparison the

*Table 6.8*  Death and birth rates, 1980 and 1995 (per 1000 people)

| | Crude death rate | | | Crude birth rate | | |
|---|---|---|---|---|---|---|
| | *1980* | *1995* | *Change* | *1980* | *1995* | *Change* |
| Central and Eastern Europe | | | | | | |
| Albania | 6 | 6 | 0 | 29 | 21 | −8 |
| Bulgaria | 11 | 13 | +2 | 15 | 10 | −5 |
| Croatia | n.a. | 11 | n.a. | n.a. | 11 | n.a. |
| Czech Republic | 13 | 11 | −2 | 15 | 10 | −5 |
| Slovakia | 10 | 10 | 0 | 19 | 12 | −7 |
| Hungary | 14 | 14 | 0 | 14 | 11 | −3 |
| Macedonia | 7 | 7 | 0 | 21 | 16 | −5 |
| Poland | 10 | 10 | 0 | 19 | 13 | −6 |
| Romania | 10 | 12 | +2 | 18 | 11 | −7 |
| Slovenia | 10 | 10 | 0 | 15 | 10 | −5 |
| FR of Yugoslavia | 10 | 10 | 0 | 18 | 14 | −4 |
| Baltic States | | | | | | |
| Estonia | 12 | 14 | +2 | 15 | 10 | −5 |
| Latvia | 13 | 16 | +3 | 15 | 9 | −6 |
| Lithuania | 10 | 12 | +2 | 16 | 11 | −5 |
| Former Soviet Union/ Commonwealth of Independent States | | | | | | |
| Armenia | 6 | 7 | +1 | 23 | 14 | −9 |
| Azerbaijan | 7 | 7 | 0 | 25 | 21 | −4 |
| Belarus | 10 | 12 | +2 | 16 | 11 | −5 |
| Georgia | 9 | 9 | 0 | 18 | 11 | −7 |
| Kazakhstan | 8 | 9 | +1 | 24 | 18 | −6 |
| Kyrgyzstan | 9 | 8 | −1 | 30 | 25 | −5 |
| Moldova | 10 | 11 | +1 | 20 | 14 | −6 |
| Russian Federation | 11 | 15 | +4 | 16 | 9 | −7 |
| Tajikistan | 8 | 7 | −1 | 37 | 28 | −9 |
| Turkmenistan | 8 | 7 | −1 | 34 | 31 | −3 |
| Ukraine | 11 | 14 | +3 | 15 | 10 | −5 |
| Uzbekistan | 8 | 6 | −2 | 34 | 29 | −5 |
| Other | | | | | | |
| China | 6 | 7 | +1 | 18 | 17 | −1 |
| Mongolia | 11 | 7 | −4 | 38 | 27 | −11 |
| Vietnam | 8 | 7 | −1 | 36 | 26 | −10 |

*Source*: World Bank, *World Development Indicators 1997*, Washington, DC: World Bank, 1997, Table 2.2, pp. 38–40.

*Table 6.9*   Missing men

| | Year | Number of men per 100 women | Number of missing men |
|---|---|---|---|
| **Central and Eastern Europe** | | | |
| Bulgaria | 1993 | 96 | 0 |
| Czech Republic | 1994 | 94 | 0 |
| Hungary | 1994 | 92 | 220 749 |
| Macedonia | 1992 | 102 | 0 |
| Poland | 1994 | 95 | 0 |
| Romania | 1994 | 96 | 0 |
| Slovenia | 1994 | 94 | 0 |
| **Baltic States** | | | |
| Estonia | 1993 | 88 | 67 520 |
| Latvia | 1994 | 86 | 241 812 |
| Lithuania | 1993 | 90 | 121 918 |
| **Commonwealth of Independent States** | | | |
| Armenia | 1992 | 94 | 0 |
| Belarus | 1993 | 89 | 404 155 |
| Kyrgyzstan | 1995 | 97 | 0 |
| Moldova | 1992 | 91 | 107 226 |
| Russian Federation | 1994 | 89 | 5 869 096 |
| Ukraine | 1993 | 87 | 2 635 973 |

*Source*: United Nations, *Demographic Yearbook 1997*, New York: United Nations, 1997.

number of men per 100 women in the United Kingdom and Japan, namely 96, it transpires that in 12 of the 16 transition economies for which we have data, the sex ratio was unfavourable to men. In two countries (Bulgaria and Romania) the sex ratio was the same as our standard and in two others (Macedonia and Kyrgyzstan) the sex ratio was higher than our standard.

One way to gauge the effects on men of the transition from a centrally planned to a more market-oriented economic system is to calculate the number of 'missing men' in each country. We define missing men as the difference between the number of men one would expect to find if the sex ratio were normal (i.e. 96 men per 100 women) and the actual number of men in the population. That is,

$$MM = 0.96W - M,$$

where        $W$ = number of women in the population,
        $M$ = number of men in the population, and
        $MM$ = number of missing men in the population.

In making the calculations presented in Table 6.9, we selected only those countries where the male:female sex ratio is less than 94. In other words, we assume there are no 'missing men' in the Czech Republic, Slovenia and Armenia where the sex ratio of 94 is only slightly lower (and possibly not significantly lower) than our standard of 96. This leaves us with eight countries where there are missing men.

One of the eight countries is in Central and Eastern Europe, namely Hungary, where there are 220 749 missing men. There are missing men in each of the three Baltic States and the total for the region is 370 480. The heart of the problem is in the Commonwealth of Independent States, where there are four countries with missing men, namely Belarus, Moldova, the Russian Federation and Ukraine. There are nearly 5.9 million missing men in the Russian Federation alone and another 2.6 million in Ukraine. The total for the CIS countries is 9.0 million and the grand total for the transition economies as a whole is nearly 9.7 million. This is one measure of the toll on men of the policies followed during the transition.

## Social pathology during the transition

The transition imposed a heavy cost on the people of the region not only in terms of increased illness, higher mortality and lower life expectancy but also in terms of social breakdown as reflected in increased alcohol consumption, a dramatic rise in drug addition, an explosion of criminal activity of all sorts and an increase in the suicide rate. Homicides, for example, increased by more than 50 per cent between 1989 and 1994 in Poland and Belarus; in the Russian Federation they increased by more than 100 per cent during the same period; and in Estonia, Lithuania and Latvia homicides increased by more than 150 per cent.[9]

Despair sometimes led to suicide, especially by men, and in some countries the suicide rate was three times higher than in the European Union. In Table 6.10 we present data on suicide rates for 15 countries, including five Central and Eastern European countries, the three Baltic States and seven CIS countries. The suicide rates in the table can perhaps best be compared with those in the European Union which are 20 per 100 000 people for males and 7 per 100 000 people for females.

One can see at a glance that in all the countries in Table 6.10 the suicide rate for women is much lower than that for men, as is true everywhere. In some countries, however, the suicide rate for men is four or five times as high as that for women. This is the case in Poland, all three Baltic States, Belarus, Kazakhstan, the Russian Federation and

*Table 6.10*  Number of suicides, 1989–93 (per 100 000 people)

|  | *Male* | *Female* |
|---|---|---|
| Central and Eastern Europe | | |
| Albania | 2 | 1 |
| Bulgaria | 25 | 10 |
| Czech Republic | 28 | 10 |
| Hungary | 55 | 18 |
| Poland | 25 | 5 |
| Baltic States | | |
| Estonia | 64 | 15 |
| Latvia | 72 | 17 |
| Lithuania | 74 | 14 |
| Commonwealth of Independent States | | |
| Armenia | 4 | 1 |
| Belarus | 49 | 10 |
| Kazakhstan | 38 | 9 |
| Russian Federation | 66 | 13 |
| Tajikistan | 5 | 2 |
| Ukraine | 38 | 9 |
| Uzbekistan | 9 | 3 |

*Source*: United Nations Development Programme, *Human Development Report 1997*, New York: Oxford University Press, 1997, Table 36, p. 213.

Ukraine. The abnormally high male : female ratios are further evidence suggesting that the burden of adjustment was especially heavy for men.

In every country except Albania, Armenia, Tajikistan and Uzbekistan the suicide rate for men is higher than in the European Union. In Hungary it is nearly three times as high; in Estonia, the Russian Federation, Latvia and Lithuania it is more than three times as high. In the case of women, suicide rates are twice as high, or more, as those in the European Union in Hungary and the Baltic States; in the Russian Federation the suicide rate for women is not quite twice as high as in the European Union. The transition to a market economy has literally been lethal for a great many people.

The transition to a market economy has thus been accompanied by a demographic collapse, a dramatic increase in anti-social behaviour and a rise in self-destructive behaviour, especially among men. The causes are multiple and complex and almost certainly include (i) a loss of earnings, as represented by a decline in real wages; (ii) a rise in economic uncertainty, particularly in the early period of hyper-inflation; (iii) a loss of economic security, as represented by a rise in unemployment for working people and a fall in the purchasing power of pensions for retired people; and (iv) a decline in the coverage of social services, including of course the health services. This combination of events varied from one country to another, but in general was widespread and had serious consequences for human development.

## Alternative reform strategies

Systemic transformation implies fundamental reforms in a great many areas. The transition from central planning to a market-guided economy consequently has profound implications for the role of the state. It is not simply a matter of reducing the size of the state but of reconsidering the very purpose of the state. The state in a market economy not only does fewer things than in a centrally planned economy, it also does different things. Moreover, during the transition from plan to market the responsibilities of the state actually increase, for the state then becomes the engine of reform. The state cannot abdicate its responsibilities or relinquish previously held tasks in the expectation that market forces will spontaneously fill the vacuum: the creation of a market economy requires an active state and a clearly defined set of priorities.

The essential reforms evidently will vary from one country to another depending upon the initial conditions at the beginning of the transition. Several countries in Central and Eastern Europe, for example, had a long history of experimentation with price reforms (Hungary, Poland) and in two cases (Poland and Yugoslavia) the agricultural sector included private as well as collective forms of ownership. In the former Soviet Union, in contrast, there had been no experiments with market institutions or private ownership prior to 1989. Furthermore, the planning system was more deeply embedded into the Soviet economy and had a long history (the First Five Year Plan having been launched in 1928) whereas in Central and Eastern Europe the planned economy was not adopted until the late 1940s. Hence at the start of the transition in Central and Eastern Europe there were many people still alive who remembered how a market economy worked; that was not true in the Soviet Union and consequently the learning process was bound to be longer.

## The essential reforms

There are seven sets of reforms that are widely regarded as essential to the success of the transition process. We list them in approximate order of priority. First in order of importance is the creation of domestic markets. This sounds obvious and simple, but it is not. Macroeconomic stability must be established so that markets produce clear and accurate signals. A legal framework must be created so that contracts can be enforced and 'mafia capitalism' avoided. Property rights must be reasonably secure, whether for state, collective or private property, so that assets can be used as collateral when raising funds for investment and claims to the residual income of an enterprise can be clearly established. Market institutions must be created, particularly for factor markets, and above all a properly regulated, financially viable and efficient commercial banking system must be created. Capitalism without capital markets will not work well. In other words, there is much more to creating a market economy than simply removing controls and allowing prices rather than administrative measures to determine the allocation of resources.

Unfortunately, many transition economies neglected these issues in a rush to liberalize prices. As we have seen, very high rates of inflation undermined the transition in many countries. Equally common, the banking system was poorly regulated and fragile and was unable to allocate investment funds efficiently. Fraud, widespread criminal behaviour and bankruptcy extended from Latvia to Albania to the Russian Federation to Kazakhstan. Commercial law was poorly developed and the judicial system often was unable to enforce contracts. The basic institutions of a market economy were lacking and hence it is no surprise that the results of price liberalization were so disappointing.

Second, once domestic markets have been created and are functioning properly, liberalization of international trade becomes an essential reform. Recall that most of the transition economies that interest us are rather small. Indeed only two countries (Ukraine and the Russian Federation) have more than 40 million people and hence a domestic market that could support an array of industries at an efficient scale. All of the others have little alternative to relying on international markets to exploit their comparative advantages. Trade permits specialization and division of labour, the exploitation of economies of scale in industry and the transfer of technology embodied in capital equipment. The integration of the transition economies into the global economy is therefore a high priority.

In practice, alas, integration often has proved to be difficult. Under the Soviet planning system many enterprises producing intermediate and capital goods had a single buyer or customer for their output and a single source of supply. Moreover, many towns were heavily dependent on a single enterprise for employment: they were in effect company towns. Trade among the Soviet bloc countries occurred within the Council for Mutual Economic Assistance (CMEA) and this system worked reasonably well, although the pattern of trade within CMEA did not reflect comparative advantage in the conventional sense nor were the prices under which trade was conducted similar to world prices.

The planning system and CMEA were dismantled when the Soviet Union disintegrated in 1991 and this severely disrupted trading relationships, particularly among the countries of the former Soviet Union. Enterprises suddenly lost their traditional markets for both inputs and outputs and were unable instantaneously to find new trading partners, in part because marketing channels did not exist and in part because the quality of the goods produced did not meet world standards. International trade declined precipitously and this contributed greatly to the sharp fall in output. Had the CMEA continued in operation during the early years of the transition and trade liberalization been introduced more gradually, it is likely that the creation of a market economy would have occurred more smoothly.

Third, opportunities should be created for a private sector to emerge. New enterprises require access to land and premises, raw materials, foreign exchange and bank credit on commercial terms; they also must be allowed to hire labour. In principle there are many activities that could attract private entrepreneurial initiative – personal services, domestic and foreign trading, small workshops and repair facilities, tourism, small-scale farming, etc. – but administrative obstacles and controls must be removed so that private enterprise is not inhibited. New private sector activities have several features which make them especially attractive during the early stages of a transition: they usually are small in scale, widely dispersed and labour intensive, and thus the benefits of private sector activity contribute to employment creation and a relatively equal distribution of income. In addition, small-scale activities usually have a relatively short gestation period and hence contribute quickly to increased output and incomes. New enterprises also are largely self-financed and thereby contribute to maintaining the savings and investment rates. For all these reasons the reform strategy should give a high priority to encouraging the establishment of new private sector enterprises.

Reforming the existing state enterprises is the fourth essential reform. Managers will have to learn to respond to market signals rather than simply implement instructions received from the planning authorities. Firms will have to learn to formulate investment plans, assess risk and undertake their own investment projects. Marketing outlets will have to be developed. New accounting systems will have to be designed which enable profit and loss calculations to be made. Irrespective of the system of ownership, the firm under a market economy operates very differently from the firm under a planned economy and it is unrealistic to suppose that state enterprises can flourish under a market economy without substantial adaptation. Indeed the alternative to adaptation often is bankruptcy or large losses which have to be financed by the state.

Fifth, reform of the state enterprises also implies reform of the system of taxation, including introduction of a profits tax that applies equally to state and private enterprise, introduction of sales or value added taxes and possibly also the introduction of an income tax. This is especially important in those countries where state-owned enterprises provide social services elsewhere provided by local and central government. It is very common for state enterprises to finance child care and kindergarten facilities, supply housing for their workers, primary schooling, medical care and clinics, and even vacation facilities. The cost structure of state enterprises therefore reflects not only the costs of production but also the costs of providing basic social services. This cost structure cannot be sustained in a competitive market economy and hence alternative arrangements will have to be made to finance and provide social services. If this is not done, state enterprises will go out of business, or essential social services will disappear or state enterprises will run huge deficits which, if covered by the state, will contribute to rapid inflation. In many countries we have witnessed a combination of the three responses.

Privatization of state-owned enterprises is the sixth reform. Small enterprises and the stock of housing often can be transferred to private ownership straight away without disrupting the economy or causing hardship. Indeed privatization may well result in greater efficiency, improved customer service and higher private savings and investment. Privatization of medium and large enterprises is much more complicated, however, and should proceed on a case-by-case basis. Preconditions for success include the creation of well functioning markets, reform of the management and *modus operandi* of state enterprises, reform of the system of corporate taxation and reform of the social services. Careful attention should be paid to the method of transfer of state-owned assets (e.g. by voucher, by sale to the existing managers, by sale to the workers of the enterprise, by sale to the general public, by sale to foreigners) and to the effects on the distribution of income and wealth. Even in the best of cases one should not expect too much from privatization: the benefits, if any, will arise primarily from a once-for-all improvement in the use of existing resources whereas the long-term objective of the transition is continuing improvements arising from an acceleration in the rate of growth of output and incomes.

Finally, there is the question of liberalization of the external capital account. It is natural that transition economies would wish to attract foreign capital to help restructure the economy and accelerate the pace of expansion. Foreign direct investment can be particularly useful and a case can be made for reducing obstacles to an inflow of direct invest-ment and liberal provision for profit repatriation. It is less clear, how-ever, that short-term foreign borrowing or portfolio investments should be liberalized until the transition is completed, and particularly not until macroeconomic stability is achieved, the commercial banking system is reformed, markets are functioning well (including the market for foreign exchange) and the state-owned enterprises have been reformed. Experience in Latin America, then in South-east Asia and most recently in the Russian Federation has shown that premature lib-eralization of the capital account exposes a country to potentially highly destabilizing movements of short-term capital that can under-mine the economic reform process.

### Simultaneous reform: the big bang

The most widely advocated reform strategy at the time of the collapse of the Soviet Union is known as 'shock therapy' or the 'big bang'. The central idea behind shock therapy is that countries should effect the traverse from central planning to a market economy as quickly as pos-sible by introducing market reforms simultaneously, in a big bang. It was recognized that a certain amount of 'pain' would be suffered, but it was believed that the duration of pain would be brief and the subse-quent gains would be considerable. These gains depended upon creat-ing a full set of markets which produced equilibrium market clearing prices that reflected the forces of supply and demand. Markets, in turn, would be efficient only if there were well defined property rights, which was interpreted to mean private property rights.

The big bang strategy thus was reduced to three components. First, state-owned enterprises should be privatized and, in effect, a capitalist

class should be created without the prior necessity of the private accumulation of capital. Second, all prices should be completely liberalized,
domestic and foreign, so that price signals could be used to allocate
resources and increase economic efficiency. Third, foreign capital
should be used to ease the pain caused by falling output and incomes.
It was hoped that liberalization and the sale of state-owned enterprises
would attract substantial amounts of foreign private investment, but
failing that, large amounts of foreign aid would have to be provided by
bilateral donors and the international financial institutions.

In practice, of course, no country followed the big bang strategy
in all its details. Privatization occurred in fits and starts, price liberalization was never instantaneous or uniform across all sectors, and
foreign capital failed to materialize in sufficient volume to prevent a
sharp fall in output and incomes and a dramatic increase in poverty.
Nevertheless the majority of countries in the former Soviet Union and
in Central and Eastern Europe adopted what can best be described as
shock therapy or the big bang approach and they were noticeably slow
to implement the other reforms indicated above to be essential for the
success of the reform process (e.g. creating space for new private sector
firms to emerge, reforming the state enterprises, restructuring the
social services and creating a viable commercial banking system).

In retrospect it is clear that the big bang strategy was seriously
flawed. Foreign capital was not integral to the strategy but was a *deus
ex machina* introduced to temper the hardships caused by the failure of
shock therapy (price liberalization and privatization) to be in fact ther-
apeutic. Privatization was even more problematic. Its role was largely
political, namely 'to cut the government-controlled sector down to a
size that would make a return to the totalitarian state and its central
planning impossible'.[10] In other words, privatization was not necessary
from an economic perspective to ensure the success of the transition.
The energies devoted to privatization were misplaced and the claim
that privatization deserved top priority was based on faulty reasoning.
The big bang, as an economic strategy, thus becomes reduced to rapid
price liberalization.

The evidence now is clear: price liberalization by itself is unlikely
to work well. There is more to a market economy than the absence
of administrative controls. As indicated above, a legal framework must
be in place, market institutions must be created, a dense network of
suppliers and customers must be established, competitive conditions
must be ensured and where this is not feasible, monopolistic enterprises
must be regulated in the public interest. None of this can be achieved

instantaneously – reform takes time – and an attempt to do everything at once is likely to produce an outcome in which nothing is done properly.

## Sequential reform and the management of a disequilibrium system

The alternative to simultaneous reform is not to postpone the inevitable or do nothing or avoid taking difficult decisions in the hope that something positive will turn up. Procrastination has been tried in several countries – Turkmenistan, Uzbekistan, Belarus – and the results leave much to be desired. The realistic alternative is to introduce reforms in sequence, to do first things first. This has two implications. First, priorities have to be identified and an optimal sequence of reforms implemented. Second, the government must learn to manage a disequilibrium system and abandon the illusion that a general equilibrium – a full set of market clearing prices – can be created quickly. Let us consider each of these points in more detail.

Macroeconomic stabilization is the first priority. An environment of low to moderate inflation is a precondition for creating an efficient market economy, as previously explained. This implies that monetary and fiscal policies should be relatively tight and that price controls should be retained until the monetary overhang is eliminated and markets begin to function properly. The danger of tight monetary and fiscal policies, however, is that they will depress output and plunge the economy into a deep recession. This danger should be counteracted by measures intended to stimulate output in selected sectors. Reform efforts should be concentrated on increasing production in areas where the elasticity of supply is high.

China and Vietnam began in the agricultural sector, where a combination of institutional reforms and improved terms of trade led to a rapid increase in output and a dramatic increase in average incomes in the rural areas. Agriculture is not unique, however, in being responsive to newly created opportunities. Small and medium enterprises also are characterized by high supply elasticities and the activities where these types of enterprises predominate (services, workshops, small batch manufacturing) should be candidates for early price liberalization. Small and medium enterprises also have the advantage that capital expenditure is modest and can be largely self-financed. Hence the creation of opportunities for new private enterprises to emerge and grow should have high priority. Again, in China, small private enterprises grew like mushrooms in the urban areas while in the rural areas township and village enterprises experienced explosive growth. Indeed in

China today, the state enterprises account for less than half of industrial output, although state enterprises have continued to grow rapidly throughout the transition period.

Tourism is another sector where supply elasticities can be high, and both China and Vietnam have been successful in developing a large tourist industry quickly. Housing is yet another activity where potential demand is great and supply elasticities are high. In addition, housing activity tends to be widely dispersed geographically and hence the benefits of growth are distributed to all parts of the country. Housing can stimulate the building materials industries and local construction companies, both of which usually are organized around small and medium size enterprises. Finally, housing, too, can be largely self-financed and hence expansion in this sector helps to sustain saving and investment. In fact the world's largest housing boom occurred in the rural areas of China during the early years of the transition to a market economy.

A concentration on activities with high supply elasticities will help to sustain employment and output and prevent a fall in incomes. The next priority should be to maintain and if possible accelerate the rate of growth. The key here is to maintain a high level of investment. In some cases, as indicated above, creating opportunities for small and medium enterprises will help to raise private savings and investment. Reform of the capital market, however, particularly the creation of an efficient commercial banking sector also will be essential. In addition, the state-owned enterprises should be reformed so that their costs are reduced, their profitability increased and a reasonable portion of their profits is retained to help finance their investment. Finally, state investment in infrastructure such as transport, power and communications should be maintained throughout the transition period and this implies that taxation and expenditure policies should be designed so that government expenditure gives priority to capital formation.

Growth during the transition is vitally important because it is through growth that economies are able to restructure production and increase efficiency. High levels of investment allow resources to be shifted quickly in response to price signals and enable profit opportunities to be translated into a rapid increase in output. Declining output, in contrast, reduces the incentive to invest and makes restructuring much more difficult. In other words, the effectiveness of price liberalization, and the resulting change in relative prices, largely depends upon the rate of investment.

If the reform strategy is limited to price stabilization and price liberalization, output, employment and incomes are likely to fall. That, in turn, will lower investment and growth, reduce the flexibility of the economy and retard necessary changes in the composition of output. It is for these reasons that expanding sectors with high supply elasticities and maintaining a high level of investment merit such high priority in the sequence of reforms.

Reform of the social services and the creation of an effective safety net then become feasible. If employment and average incomes are rising during the transition, the proportion of the population that falls into poverty is likely to be small, even if the distribution of income becomes more unequal, as is probable. The combination of a low incidence of poverty and generally improving standards of living means that a relatively modest income transfer will be sufficient to contain poverty to tolerable levels and that a modest increase in taxation on the better off will be all that is required to finance the transfer payments. If, on the other hand, poverty is widespread and average incomes are falling, the volume of transfers needed to assist the poor will be large and the resistance of the non-poor will be great. An effective safety net will not be financially or politically possible.

It is for this reason that in the sequence of reforms an expansion of incomes, employment and output and an increase in investment and the rate of growth should have a higher priority than increased transfer payments to the poor and a restructuring of the social services. Both production reforms and reforms of the social services are terribly important, but if the latter are given priority over the former, there is a danger that the entire reform effort will fail.

Let us turn now to the problem of managing a disequilibrium system. Sequential reform usually entails only partial price liberalization during the early stages of the transition. For example, price controls (and quota deliveries) might be retained for basic foodstuffs but above quota output might be allowed to be sold on the free market at whatever price market forces determine. This 'dual price system' has several advantages. It provides a strong incentive on the margin to increase production and in effect 'stretches' the elasticity of supply. At the same time it ensures that consumers can obtain essential supplies of food at controlled prices. This prevents real wages from falling precipitously and poverty from increasing. Similarly, in the case of raw materials and intermediate products, industrial enterprises are able to acquire necessary inputs at controlled prices. This prevents their costs from rising sharply in response to changes in relative prices which could suddenly make them uncompetitive. The dual prices also ensure that deliveries of inputs continue normally and hence production is not disrupted by a breakdown in the input supply system. All of this helps to sustain aggregate output and employment. Lastly, the dual price system helps the government to maintain control over the general level of prices and prevent the emergence of rapid inflation during the liberalization process.

The disadvantages of operating a dual price system are, first, that corruption is encouraged and, second, that price signals are distorted. Corruption is encouraged because whenever there is more than one price for a product, participants in the market have a strong incentive to engage in arbitrage, i.e. purchase the product at the low controlled price for resale in the free market at a high price. The dual price system also distorts price signals because neither the controlled price nor the free market price corresponds to the long run equilibrium price. The former is too low and the latter too high. This disequilibrium system can move the economy in the right direction but it will not produce an optimal outcome.

In practice the disequilibrium system is likely to be even more complex than we have intimated. At any given moment in time during the transition, in the economy as a whole, prices in some markets will be completely controlled, in other markets there will be dual prices and in still other markets prices may be completely free. This set of relative prices will not be as irrational as under a centrally planned economy where all prices are administratively controlled, but nor will there be a fully consistent set of market clearing prices which produces an optimum allocation of resources. Individual markets will not produce equilibrium prices and the economy will not be in a 'general equilibrium'.

## The false distinction between gradual and rapid reform

Sequential reform often is described by its critics as gradual reform and simultaneous reform is described by its advocates as rapid reform. This is a false and very misleading distinction. Those countries which have adopted a strategy of sequential reform, notably China and Vietnam, have progressed much more rapidly than those countries, such as the Russian Federation and even Poland, which adopted a strategy of simultaneous reform and shock therapy. Indeed, as we have seen, many countries moved backwards after the big bang and have yet to recover fully: income per head declined, demographic indicators moved into reverse and the social structure came under severe stress.

The fundamental difference between simultaneous and sequential reform strategies turns on whether one is primarily concerned with the ultimate destination at the end of the transition or whether one is primarily concerned with the path taken by the economy during the transition process. The simultaneous reform strategy focuses on the desired end result; it is based on a comparative static perspective, i.e. a comparison between the initial position (central planning) and the final destination (a market economy in general equilibrium). The objective is to get from the initial position to the desired final destination as quickly as possible by liberalizing all markets simultaneously and establishing private property rights in all sectors of the economy, and specifically through the privatization of state-owned enterprises. The underlying assumption is that the details of the trajectory are of secondary importance: any disruption experienced by the economy is likely to be short-lived and can be neglected (or assuaged by an inflow of foreign aid).

The sequential reform strategy, in contrast, focuses on the transition process itself. The objective of policy is to create a smooth transition from central planning to a functioning market economy. This strategy is based on a dynamic perspective in which at any moment in time the economy will be in disequilibrium and it is the task of government to manage this disequilibrium so that the economy continues to move in the desired direction. The underlying assumption is that the details of the trajectory are of critical importance because they in fact determine the speed at which the economy travels and the ultimate destination towards which it is moving. Indeed the notion of a specific general equilibrium as the ultimate destination of the transition is regarded as an abstraction which has no operational significance.

What matters is the journey, not the destination.[11] There is now abundant evidence from about 30 countries that details are important, that the sequence in which reforms are introduced has major implications for the outcome and that it is wishful thinking to assume that if all controls are removed at once, markets will emerge spontaneously and the economy will quickly attain equilibrium. In practice this has not happened; big bang strategies have caused the economy to implode: gross inefficiencies have persisted, output and incomes have fallen, domestically financed investment has collapsed and growth rates have been negative for years on end. This massive policy experiment has caused widespread misery, insecurity and poverty. The irony is that the first transition strategy, which began in China from 1978 onwards, was based on sequential reforms and was highly successful. The transition strategies in the former Soviet Union and in Central and Eastern Europe began more than a decade later and were based largely on simultaneous reforms. Those transition strategies have been a failure. It is a tragedy that so little was learned from the Chinese experience: the failures could have been avoided; the hardships need not have occurred.

## The role of the state

Both the size of the state and the role of the state have changed during the transition from central planning to a more market-oriented economic system. Several tendencies stand out. First, the absolute size of the central government has shrunk quite considerably.[12] This is not surprising given the decline in gross domestic product that has occurred in nearly all transition economies. Second, central government expenditure has tended to decline more rapidly than GDP and hence there has also been a relative contraction of public expenditure. In Romania, for example, central government expenditure declined from 44.7 per cent of GDP in 1980 to 31.9 per cent in 1994, a fall of nearly 29 per cent. Third, government revenues have fallen even more rapidly than government expenditure and as a result severe fiscal imbalances have arisen in a number of countries.

In Table 6.11 we present data for 17 countries as regards revenue and 16 countries as regards expenditure. Only in Croatia and Estonia does revenue exceed expenditure; in the other 14 countries the government is operating with a deficit. In seven countries expenditure exceeds revenue by more than 20 per cent, namely in Armenia, Azerbaijan, Belarus, Kyrgyzstan, the Russian Federation, Ukraine and Uzbekistan. All of these countries were part of the Soviet Union and the large deficits they are running is evidence of the difficulty they have encountered in creating an efficient tax system after independence.

The size of the state as measured by government expenditure as a percentage of GDP varies from one group to another. The three Baltic States cluster around 30 per cent. The state in this group tends to be significantly smaller than in Scandinavia, the European region closest to the Baltic States. In Central and Eastern Europe the state tends to be considerably larger, accounting for slightly more than 40 per cent of GDP. That is, the state in Central and Eastern Europe is about the same size as in Scandinavia. The successor states to the former Soviet Union show much greater variation. The range is from 14 per cent in Azerbaijan to 49 per cent in Ukraine, with most clustering between 27 and 39 per cent.

The defenders of 'shock therapy' tend to play down the role of the state during the transition and emphasize instead the 'initial conditions'

*Table 6.11*    Central government revenue and expenditure, 1994 (per cent of GDP)

|  | Revenue | Expenditure |
|---|---|---|
| Central and Eastern Europe | | |
| Bulgaria | 37.4 | 43.1 |
| Croatia | 42.8 | 41.1 |
| Czech Republic | 41.0 | 42.5 |
| Poland | 41.7 | 44.1 |
| Romania | 29.9 | 31.9 |
| FR of Yugoslavia[a] | 39.3 | 43.9 |
| Baltic States | | |
| Estonia | 35.0 | 31.9 |
| Latvia | 25.5 | 27.6 |
| Lithuania | 25.3 | 27.2 |
| Former Soviet Union/ Commonwealth of Independent States | | |
| Armenia[b] | 14.0 | 39.0 |
| Azerbaijan[a] | 10.0 | 14.0 |
| Belarus | 31.4 | 37.8 |
| Kyrgyzstan[a] | 15.0 | 29.0 |
| Russian Federation | 20.2 | 27.0 |
| Turkmenistan | 14.7 | n.a. |
| Ukraine[b] | 40.5 | 49.0 |
| Uzbekistan[c] | 28.1 | 35.6 |

[a] 1995.
[b] 1993.
[c] 1996.

*Sources*: World Bank, *World Development Indicators 1997*, Washington, DC: World Bank, 1997; *Azerbaijan Human Development Report 1996*, Baku: UNDP, 1996; *Armenia Human Development Report 1995*, Yerevan: UNDP, 1995; *Kyrgyzstan Human Development Report 1997*, Bishkek: UNDP, 1997; *Turkmenistan Human Development Report 1996*, Ashgabat: UNDP, 1996; *Ukraine Human Development Report 1996*, Kiev: UNDP, 1996; *Uzbekistan Human Development Report 1997*, Tashkent: UNDP, 1997; *Yugoslavia Human Development Report 1997*, Belgrade: UNDP, 1997.

that prevailed at the beginning of the reform process. In drawing lessons from the economic transitions in Asia and Eastern Europe, Parker, Tritt and Woo, for example, claim that 'the first lesson is that initial country conditions determine the output response of a centrally planned economy upon its marketization, be it of the all-out or phased-in variety'.[13] Comparing explicitly Hungary, Poland and Russia (where output collapsed) with China and Vietnam (where output grew), the authors conclude that 'the difference in output performance likely comes from the difference in initial structural conditions'.[14]

What are these initial 'structural conditions' that led to growing prosperity in China and Vietnam and impoverishment in Central and Eastern Europe and the former Soviet Union? Two points are emphasized. First, both China and Vietnam had 'a predominantly agricultural economy with a huge surplus labor force'[15] and in addition, Vietnam 'had the good fortune to discover oil'.[16] These are curious explanations based on *ad hoc* arguments. True, Vietnam did discover a relatively small amount of oil, but the oil sector is much larger in Azerbaijan, Kazakhstan, the Russian Federation and Turkmenistan, in all of which economic performance was poor. It is true, too, that China and Vietnam had large agricultural sectors and much surplus labour, but an abundance of low-productivity, low-skilled and underemployed labour usually is regarded as a handicap to be overcome, not a cause of success, and a relatively large industrial sector, such as the other transition economies possessed, usually is regarded as an asset, not an excuse for failure. Surely differences in structure mattered less than differences in government policy.

What, then, is the role of the state in the transition process? First, as repeatedly emphasized, the state must ensure macroeconomic stability and create an environment in which price signals can work effectively. The prevention of rapid inflation is an essential precondition for success. This will require firm monetary policies, the avoidance of large public sector deficits and probably tax reforms. The volume of government expenditure is a secondary matter, provided tax revenues are adequate to finance it.

Second, market institutions must be created, in sequence, following a set of priorities, so that markets function properly. More is at stake here than simply removing controls and expecting market forces to emerge spontaneously. A system of commercial law will be needed so that contracts can be enforced and lawlessness contained. The public administration will have to be reorganized and primary emphasis shifted from implementing production plans to creating incentives to guide the private sector. Policies to create competitive conditions are central to a well functioning market economy, and where competition is absent, a system of government regulation will have to be designed and put in place.

Factor markets will have to be organized to replace centralized allocations of capital, urban and agricultural land, and labour. The banking system and other financial institutions will have to be developed to spread investment risks through financial intermediation, to provide access to credit to those seeking to finance profitable investment projects and to enable interest rates and screening procedures to ensure that scarce loanable funds are allocated to the most profitable projects. Landownership need not be privatized, but a functioning market in land use rights should be created. That is, land should be 'commercialized' so that industrialists can obtain factory sites, providers of services can obtain urban premises, house builders can obtain construction land, etc.

Some goods and services will have to continue to be supplied by local, provincial or central government because the market mechanism on its own would fail to provide the socially optimal output. Markets can be excellent in supplying private goods, but whenever a good is not depleted or 'used up' in the process of use, and whenever it is impossible or very costly to exclude those who do not wish to pay from using the good, markets will not function well. These 'public goods' include the legal system and the courts, information systems (e.g. market information, weather forecasts, research institutions) and much physical infrastructure (including urban water supply and sewage disposal services). Price liberalization and competition are not relevant in such cases; the state will have to retain responsibility for providing public goods.

Markets also fail when there are 'externalities', i.e. when some benefits or costs are not reflected in market prices. Certain types of expenditure on education and health, for example, confer benefits not only on the purchaser but on the community at large and thereby contribute more to the level and rate of growth of output than a free market price would indicate. In such instances a strong case can be made for government intervention in the market to increase the volume of educational and health services. Unfortunately, governments in many transition economies have begun to privatize these services and there is a danger not only that the well being of the population will decline but that long-term growth will be adversely affected.

Similarly, some activities inflict costs on the society at large that are not reflected in market prices. In this case, government might well be justified in intervening in the market to reduce output, e.g. by imposing a tax, establishing minimum standards of, say, water and air pollution or in some cases, assigning property rights to a resource so that the owner has an incentive to take into account all the consequences of using a resource in a particular way. There are many examples of large negative externalities in the transition economies left over from the period of central planning, including severe industrial pollution in Baku, Azerbaijan and many industrial cities in Poland, nuclear contamination in parts of Kazakhstan, chemical pollution of ground water in

Uzbekistan, and damage to coastal fisheries in Vietnam. The danger now is that market failures will add to the failures of central planning to degrade further the environment. The state thus has an important role to play in cleaning up the inherited mess and preventing new problems from arising.

### Property relations

The third task for the state during the transition period is to establish a new set of property relations. Many analysts have reduced this task to the privatization of state-owned enterprises, and indeed it is a common view that there are 'two indispensable functions in the dismantling of state socialism, namely the stabilization and privatization of the economy'.[17] Consistent with the shock therapy approach, many countries (the Czech Republic, Hungary, Poland, Romania, Slovakia) announced their intention at the beginning of the transition to privatize between a third and half of the state enterprises within three years.[18] But much more is involved in creating a new set of property relations than transferring ownership of state enterprises to the private sector.

By now it is generally agreed that in every transition economy the growth of new private enterprises has been much more significant than the transfer of ownership of old enterprises. Even so, in many countries the growth of the private sector has been hampered because property rights are unclear and consequently access to finance capital, foreign exchange and land have been obstructed. In Uzbekistan and Kazakhstan, for example, the private sector has not been able to contribute its full potential because property relations still are unclear.

Land rights have been a particular problem in many countries. In China and Vietnam the ownership of land has not been privatized. Instead households have been given use-rights, i.e. long leases which provide security of tenure. In effect, a small peasant farming system has been created, but because use-rights generally are not transferable, a land market has failed to emerge. In Kazakhstan, where there is political resistance to the privatization of land, it was suggested that ownership should remain with the state but that leases should be sold, possibly at auctions, so that land becomes 'commercialized' and the state is able to generate revenues by appropriating the rent through lease charges.[19] In Mongolia, where a nomadic livestock sector continues to be important, it was suggested that pasture land be allocated through group leases.[20] There are, in other words, several ways to commercialize land and create an efficient land market without changing ownership titles.

The stock of housing, particularly in urban areas, belonged either to the state or to state enterprises prior to the beginning of the transition. Privatization of housing by transferring ownership to sitting occupants can be done rather easily and usually makes economic sense, partly because it increases the mobility of labour. If done properly, it can also contribute to a relatively equitable distribution of wealth.

The governments of most transition economies also have privatized large numbers of small state enterprises, most of which are in the service sector. This, too, is sensible: it usually results in better customer service, improved quality, more efficient use of resources and more rapid growth. The controversy arises over what to do with the medium and large state-owned enterprises.[21]

In Vietnam there has been no privatization of large state enterprises although there have been joint ventures with large foreign enterprises. In China some state enterprises were transformed into collective enterprises and in 1997 the government announced that in future there would be some privatization of state enterprises on a case-by-case basis. Some state enterprises have become partially privatized by issuing stock to their employees and over 300 state enterprises list their shares on domestic and even foreign stock exchanges. Expansion of the private sector, however, has come largely from the growth of new enterprises and, indeed, the non-state sector now accounts for well over 60 per cent of industrial output.

Much of the growth has come from township and village enterprises (TVEs). The World Bank has correctly described the property rights of TVEs as 'fuzzy',[22] but this has not prevented their vigorous expansion. Some TVEs are private in ownership and operation but register themselves as collectively owned in order to escape legal discrimination. These TVEs are said to be 'wearing the red cap'. Others follow the 'Zhejiang Model': the TVEs are registered with the local authorities and make an annual contribution to the village funds, but otherwise the firms enjoy complete autonomy. Still others follow the 'Jiangsu Model' under which the local authorities exercise tight control over the TVEs.[23] This demonstrates yet again that there are several alternatives to privatization and these alternatives can be highly successful.

The majority of countries in Central and Eastern Europe and in the former Soviet Union are committed to privatizing all state enterprises, even the large ones. In practice, privatization 'has progressed much more slowly than originally intended and has proved much more problematic'.[24] Where state enterprises have been sold (as opposed to given away) there has been a problem of valuation of assets, since future profitability of the firms is difficult to assess until relative prices are stabilized. On the liabilities side of the accounts, the complex web of inter-enterprise loans that emerged in the early stage of the transition has made it difficult for potential investors to assess the debt position of state enterprises. And the lack of well developed capital markets has added to the problem of valuing state assets.

In any case the financial wealth of citizens in the transition economies is very low compared to the potential value of the state enterprises. This lack of purchasing power means that if sales are limited to citizens, the market price of state assets is bound to be very low and the contribution of privatization to government revenues (and the resolution of the fiscal crisis) will be meagre. The alternative is to sell the state enterprises to foreigners, if buyers can be found, but this implies that the transition economies will end with a market economy in which the major assets are owned by foreigners while the native born supply the labour. Capitalism without domestic capitalists is unlikely to be attractive.

More generally, the property relations that have been created through privatization often have resulted in great inequalities in the distribution of wealth. Moreover, there is a potential conflict between equity (which requires that the ownership of state assets be distributed evenly among the population whose sacrifices created the assets in the first place) and efficiency (which requires that ownership be concentrated so that the owners can exercise effective control over the enterprise). So far, alas, privatization in practice has not allowed the state to achieve any of its objectives. 'Privatization in the transition economies has resulted neither in tangible increases in government revenue nor in better corporate governance, nor even in equity.'[25]

Data on the privatization of medium and large state enterprises in seven countries are presented in Table 6.12. The table contains information on the proportion of medium and large enterprises still under state ownership in 1995, the dominant method used to dispose of state assets and the proportion of state assets distributed to private owners under the dominant method of disposal. In Lithuania, for example, 35 per cent of the large and medium enterprises still are in the hands of the state, 60 per cent were distributed to the private sector through vouchers, and 5 per cent through other means.

In the Russian Federation just over a third of the medium and large enterprises still remain under state ownership. Most of the privatized firms were turned over to insiders through management–employee buyouts. This ownership structure essentially preserved the status quo

*Table 6.12*   Privatization of medium and large state enterprises, 1995 (percentage of total value)

|  | Still in state hands | Dominant method of privatization | Percentage |
|---|---|---|---|
| Czech Republic | 40 | Vouchers | 50 |
| Hungary | 42 | Sale to outsiders | 40 |
| Poland[a] | 54 | Other[b] | 23 |
| Estonia | 15 | Sale to outsiders | 60 |
| Lithuania | 35 | Vouchers | 60 |
| Russia[a] | 34 | Management–employee buyout | 55 |
| Mongolia | 45 | Vouchers | 55 |

[a] Percentages refer to the number of enterprises, not their value.
[b] Includes transfers to municipalities or social insurance organizations, debt–equity swaps, and sales through insolvency proceedings.
*Source*: World Bank, *World Development Report 1996*, New York: Oxford University Press, 1996, Table 3.2, p. 53.

as regards management and as a result in Russia the 'privatized compa-nies do not perform or behave differently from state-owned enter-prises'.[26] The change in property relations, however, has been highly inequitable. It has accentuated income differentials among workers because 'insider privatization has made the already privileged workers in efficient, modern enterprises richer by giving them a bigger share of the capital income, and has impoverished the workers of inefficient, technologically backward enterprises by replacing the budget subsidies they have been receiving with ownership claims on what is effectively a rusting scrap heap'.[27] Even worse, insider privatization has resulted in 'nomenclatura privatization' on a vast scale, control of the firms by the former state enterprise managers, and massive fraud and theft. One enthusiast for privatization is so outraged by what has happened that he recommends that where large state enterprises were stolen by the managers, they 'ought to be re-nationalized in order to be re-privatized using the proper official privatization procedures'.[28] Those who were less enthusiastic about privatization in the first place can only note the irony.

In Poland, a majority of large and medium enterprises still are owned by the state. Those firms which have been privatized, as in Russia, are dominated by insiders.[29] In Hungary, attempts were first made to sell large state enterprises to outsiders, specifically to foreigners, on a case-by-case basis, but there was a poor response from foreign investors and the attempt was abandoned. The revived privatization programme, although still ostensibly based on sales to outsiders, effectively was based on insider privatization. In the Czech Republic (as in Lithuania and Mongolia) a voucher scheme was implemented which at first appeared to be highly successful. About 70 per cent of the voucher-privatized shares, however, soon came under the control of a small number of investment funds. The largest investment funds were founded by majority state-owned banks and other financial institutions in which the state had a dominant interest, and as a result, privatization in the Czech Republic 'meant a transfer of ownership from the state to partly state-owned financial institutions'.[30]

This brief survey indicates that privatization is more difficult than the 'big bang' strategists anticipated and the results less beneficial. The creation of a new set of property relations is indeed an important element in a transition strategy, but those countries which have concentrated on creating favourable conditions for the growth of new enterprises have been more successful than those which concentrated on the transfer of ownership of existing state enterprises. Similarly, where ownership and control have been retained by the state, the more successful countries have taken steps to 'commercialize' land and state enterprises and to ensure that investors have access to bank credit and foreign exchange. The important point is that conditions should be created so that markets function well, not that all assets be privatized.

## Poverty, inequality and human development

Finally, the state has a vital role to play during the transition to a market economy in promoting human development, preventing large inequalities from emerging and containing the increase in poverty within tolerable limits. Unfortunately, the record under these three headings has so far been poor. Price liberalization, privatization of state enterprises and a general bias towards *laissez-faire* have combined to undermine previous achievements in human development, to create in many countries a high degree of inequality in the distribution of wealth and income, and to impoverish large sections of the population. Market forces alone cannot be relied upon to produce an equitable society; the most one can ask of market forces is that they produce an efficient allocation of resources. How those resources are distributed among the members of society depends in large part on the role played by the state.

It is important that the transition strategy rest on firm foundations. It is the responsibility of the state to prevent an explosive inflation, to maintain an adequate rate of investment, to channel effort into activities where supply can increase rapidly and substantially, and to ensure that 'key prices' in strategic markets reflect social opportunity costs, including bank interest rates, the price of foreign exchange, the wage rate for low-skilled labour, the price of energy and, depending on the country, the price of irrigation water. If these things are done, the growth rate will be positive, the pattern of growth will permit an expansion of employment opportunities, average incomes will rise and any increase in inequality probably will be modest.

Even so, some groups may fall into poverty, but the incidence of poverty is likely to be low. It will then be feasible for the government to design and implement short-term policies to cope with impoverishment. Depending on the circumstances in each case, governments may wish to organize emergency, labour intensive public works schemes or credit programmes aimed at encouraging microenterprises or credit channelled to specific groups such as women, all of which would contribute to accelerated growth as well as to a reduction in poverty. Some transfer payments may be necessary, e.g. to the elderly or the handicapped, but whenever possible the anti-poverty programmes should be designed to reinforce or complement other policies intended to create an equitable and efficient market economy. An egalitarian land reform, for instance, would combine equity, greater efficiency and rural poverty reduction.

All of the countries that interest us began the transition to a market economy with a level of human development that was higher than one would have predicted on the basis of their per capita incomes alone. That was still true in 1994 at the nadir of the economic collapse in most countries. In Table 6.13 we indicate the rank (out of 175 countries) of 28 transition economies on the human development index (HDI) and then compare the HDI rank with the countries' rank in terms of real GDP per capita. Albania, for instance, ranks 102 on the HDI; its per capita GDP rank, however, is 106 and thus its GDP per capita rank minus its HDI rank is 4. In other words, Albania is 4 rungs higher up the ladder of human development than it is on the ladder of per capita income. As can be seen at a glance, all of the countries in the table except Mongolia perform relatively better on a human development scale than on an income scale, and some countries (Tajikistan, Georgia, Moldova) perform spectacularly better.

The problem in many transition economies is that human development has begun to decline. Between 1993 and 1994, for example, the HDI value fell in at least one of the Baltic States (Latvia), in four of the Central Asian republics (Kazakhstan, Kyrgyzstan, Tajikistan and Uzbekistan), in two countries of the Caucasus (Armenia and Azerbaijan)

*Table 6.13*   Relative ranking of human development and real GDP per capita in 28 transition economies, 1994

|  | HDI rank[a] | GDP per capita rank minus HDI rank[b] |
|---|---|---|
| Central and Eastern Europe |  |  |
| Albania | 102 | 4 |
| Bulgaria | 69 | 9 |
| Croatia | 77 | 10 |
| Czech Republic | 39 | 3 |
| Slovakia | 42 | 12 |
| Hungary | 48 | 5 |
| Macedonia | 80 | 5 |
| Poland | 58 | 14 |
| Romania | 79 | 3 |
| Slovenia | 35 | 3 |
| Baltic States |  |  |
| Estonia | 71 | 8 |
| Latvia | 92 | 6 |
| Lithuania | 76 | 8 |
| Former Soviet Union/ Commonwealth of Independent States |  |  |
| Armenia | 103 | 24 |
| Azerbaijan | 106 | 25 |
| Belarus | 62 | 13 |
| Georgia | 105 | 31 |
| Kazakhstan | 93 | 6 |
| Kyrgyzstan | 107 | 18 |
| Moldova | 110 | 28 |
| Russian Federation | 67 | 7 |
| Tajikistan | 115 | 35 |
| Turkmenistan | 85 | 12 |
| Ukraine | 95 | 14 |
| Uzbekistan | 100 | 14 |
| Other |  |  |
| China | 108 | 3 |
| Mongolia | 101 | − 10 |
| Vietnam | 121 | 26 |

[a] The ranking on the human development index (HDI) is out of a total of 175 countries.
[b] GDP per capita is measured in terms of purchasing power parity dollars (PPP$).
*Source*: UNDP, *Human Development Report 1997*, New York: Oxford University Press, 1997, Annex Table 1, pp. 146–8.

and in three other former republics of the Soviet Union (Moldova, Ukraine and the Russian Federation).[31] In effect, these ten countries, and perhaps others for which we have no data, have begun to consume part of their human capital. If this continues, not only will the capabilities of the population decline further, but the prospects for long-term growth will be damaged.

Governments may be tempted to reduce expenditure on human development – particularly spending on health and education – as part of a stabilization programme. In some cases the justification may be the belief that since the stock of human capital initially was relatively large, a temporary cut in spending would do little harm. In other cases policy makers may believe that the private sector, i.e. the market, can replace public provision of health and educational services. And in still other cases, there may be a hope that foreign aid will come to the rescue. All of these views are short-sighted.

Certainly there is a need to reconsider the role of the state in promoting human development. The structure of the health and education systems may well have to be adapted to the requirements of a market economy where, for example, the rigid requirements of a system of manpower planning must give way to the requirements of a much more flexible labour market. Similarly, there may be a case to reconsider the composition of expenditure on human development, reallocating resources away from a hospital-based system of health care towards, say, preventive medicine. There is also a need to rethink the methods of providing services, reducing the responsibilities of state-owned enterprises to supply a wide range of welfare services and increasing the responsibility of local, provincial and central government and, in some cases, the private sector. Finally, responsibilities for financing human development expenditures will have to be reconsidered, notably the division of responsibility between the state, employers and the individuals concerned.

Thus there is much to be done, and countries cannot simply 'leave it to the market' to sort things out. Equally, the state cannot postpone decisions about human development until the transition is well under way because human development expenditures will affect the trajectory of the transition itself, both its speed and the ultimate destination. Poverty, inequality and human development are inextricably connected and in formulating economic policy during the transition to a market-oriented economy, the long-term implications of short-term measures should not be overlooked. Indeed, contrary to the believers in shock therapy, there may be no end to the transition: it is a permanent journey.

# 7
# Macroeconomic Reform and Employment: an Investment-Led Strategy of Structural Adjustment in Sub-Saharan Africa*

There are 50 countries in sub-Saharan Africa.[1] These countries, containing over 600 million people, are among the poorest in the world. Indeed the World Bank classifies 74 per cent of the countries of sub-Saharan Africa as 'low-income economies' and the United Nations Development Programme classifies 79 per cent as being 'low human development' countries. In most cases low income and low human development coincide, but in Angola, Cameroon and Senegal medium incomes are none the less associated with low human development whereas in Zimbabwe and Congo medium human development has been achieved despite their low incomes. (See Table 7.1.)

The conclusion is inescapable: the great majority of countries in sub-Saharan Africa are poor regardless of the standard of evaluation used. In fact only eight countries are classified as having achieved a 'medium' level of development by both UNDP and the World Bank. Three of these (Cape Verde, Seychelles and Swaziland) have less than 1 million people and four (Mauritius, Gabon, Botswana and Namibia) have less than 2 million. Only South Africa (40.5 million) has a large population and because of the legacy of apartheid, there is great inequality and poverty.

At least in a qualitative sense one can be certain that the level of development in sub-Saharan Africa is low. It is more difficult to be certain about trends in production and incomes. In Table 7.2 we present estimates of the rates of growth of gross domestic product (GDP), population and GDP per capita for the period 1980–94. Let us consider these three macroeconomic phenomena in order.

In the case of 17 out of the 50 countries there is no estimate of the rate of growth of GDP for the period that interests us. That leaves us with 33 countries. In many, perhaps most, of these countries the

*Table 7.1*   Classification of countries in sub-Saharan Africa

| Country | Low-income (World bank) | Low human development (UNDP) |
|---|---|---|
| Angola | | × |
| Benin | × | × |
| Botswana | | |
| Burkina Faso | × | × |
| Burundi | × | × |
| Cameroon | | × |
| Cape Verde | | |
| Central African Republic | × | × |
| Chad | × | × |
| Comoros | × | × |
| Congo | × | |
| Côte d'Ivoire | × | × |
| Djibouti | × | × |
| Equatorial Guinea | × | × |
| Eritrea | × | n.a. |
| Ethiopia | × | × |
| Gabon | | |
| Gambia | × | × |
| Ghana | × | × |
| Guinea | × | × |
| Guinea-Bissau | × | × |
| Kenya | × | × |
| Lesotho | × | × |
| Liberia | × | × |
| Madagascar | × | × |
| Malawi | × | × |
| Mali | × | × |
| Mauritania | × | × |
| Mauritius | | |
| Mayotte | | n.a. |
| Mozambique | × | × |
| Namibia | | |
| Niger | × | × |
| Nigeria | × | × |
| Reunion | | n.a. |
| Rwanda | × | × |
| São Tomé and Principe | × | × |
| Senegal | | × |
| Seychelles | | |
| Sierra Leone | × | × |
| Somalia | × | × |
| South Africa | | |
| Sudan | × | × |
| Swaziland | | |

*Table 7.1* (*Continued*)

| Country | Low-income (World bank) | Low human development (UNDP) |
|---|---|---|
| Tanzania | × | × |
| Togo | × | × |
| Uganda | × | × |
| Zaire | × | × |
| Zambia | × | × |
| Zimbabwe | × | |

*Table 7.2*   Growth rates in sub-Saharan Africa: 1980–94 (per cent per annum)

| Country | GDP | Population | GDP per capita |
|---|---|---|---|
| Angola | n.a. | n.a. | n.a. |
| Benin | 3.0 | 3.0 | 0.0 |
| Botswana | 8.6 | 3.4 | 5.2 |
| Burkina Faso | 3.4 | 2.7 | 0.7 |
| Burundi | 2.7 | 2.9 | −0.2 |
| Cameroon | 0.2 | 2.9 | −2.7 |
| Cape Verde | n.a. | n.a. | n.a. |
| Central African Republic | 1.2 | 2.4 | −1.2 |
| Chad | 4.9 | 2.4 | 2.5 |
| Comoros | n.a. | n.a. | n.a. |
| Congo | 2.5 | 3.1 | −0.6 |
| Côte d'Ivoire | −0.1 | 3.7 | −3.8 |
| Djibouti | n.a. | n.a. | n.a. |
| Equatorial Guinea | n.a. | n.a. | n.a. |
| Eritrea | n.a. | n.a. | n.a. |
| Ethiopia | n.a. | 2.7 | n.a. |
| Gabon | −0.3 | 3.4 | −3.7 |
| Gambia | 2.8 | 3.7 | −0.9 |
| Ghana | 3.4 | 3.2 | 0.2 |
| Guinea | n.a. | 2.6 | n.a. |
| Guinea-Bissau | 4.2 | 1.9 | 2.3 |
| Kenya | 3.2 | 3.2 | 0.0 |
| Lesotho | 4.8 | 2.7 | 2.1 |
| Liberia | n.a. | n.a. | n.a. |
| Madagascar | 0.7 | 2.9 | −2.2 |
| Malawi | 1.7 | 3.2 | −1.5 |
| Mali | 2.1 | 2.6 | −0.5 |
| Mauritania | 2.3 | 2.6 | −0.3 |
| Mauritius | 6.2 | 1.0 | 5.2 |
| Mayotte | n.a. | n.a. | n.a. |
| Mozambique | 2.0 | 1.8 | 0.2 |

*Table 7.2  (Continued)*

| Country | GDP | Population | GDP per capita |
|---------|-----|------------|----------------|
| Namibia | 2.0 | 2.7 | −0.7 |
| Niger | −0.9 | 3.3 | −4.2 |
| Nigeria | 1.8 | 3.0 | −1.2 |
| Reunion | n.a. | n.a. | n.a. |
| Rwanda | −2.9 | 2.9 | 0.0 |
| São Tomé and Principe | n.a. | n.a. | n.a. |
| Senegal | 2.3 | 2.8 | −0.5 |
| Seychelles | n.a. | n.a. | n.a. |
| Sierra Leone | 0.8 | 2.2 | −1.4 |
| Somalia | n.a. | n.a. | n.a. |
| South Africa | 0.9 | 2.3 | −1.4 |
| Sudan | n.a. | n.a. | n.a. |
| Swaziland | n.a. | n.a. | n.a. |
| Tanzania | 3.6 | 3.1 | 0.5 |
| Togo | 0.3 | 3.1 | −2.8 |
| Uganda | 3.8 | 2.6 | 1.8 |
| Zaire | n.a. | n.a. | n.a. |
| Zambia | 0.5 | 3.4 | −2.9 |
| Zimbabwe | 2.8 | 3.1 | −0.3 |

*Source*: Calculated from data in World Bank, *World Development Report 1996*, New York: Oxford University Press, 1996.

estimates of domestic production are not terribly reliable, in part because much production is for subsistence consumption and does not pass through a market and in part because market prices often are highly distorted. Thus quantitative estimates must be treated with caution. The simple average[2] rate of growth of GDP for the 33 countries for which data are available was about 2.3 per cent a year during the 14-year period 1980–94. This is low compared to most other developing regions of the world. Moreover the 2.3 per cent average rate of growth for our 33 countries may overstate the average for sub-Saharan Africa as a whole. The reason for this is that there was serious political violence in several of the countries for which data are lacking – Eritrea, Ethiopia, Liberia, Somalia, Sudan, Angola – and it is likely that civil war and ethnic conflict in those countries reduced the rate of growth below the average in the rest of sub-Saharan Africa. Thus our estimated growth rate of 2.3 per cent a year should be regarded as an upper limit.

There was considerable variation in growth performance among the 33 countries for which we have data. A few grew quite rapidly and two countries, both small, enjoyed outstanding performances, namely

Mauritius (6.2 per cent a year) and Botswana (8.6 per cent a year). At the other extreme, four countries experienced a negative rate of growth of production and two of these, Niger and Rwanda, suffered a precipitous decline in output of −0.9 and −2.9 per cent a year, respectively.

Turning to estimates of demographic expansion, it will be seen in Table 7.2 that in the case of 15 countries there is no estimate of the rate of growth of the population. Even in the remaining 35 countries demographic data should be interpreted with caution. Censuses often are infrequent and somewhat unreliable. Inter-census estimates are even less reliable. In many countries accurate estimates of the size of the population and its rate of growth are unavailable. Keeping this warning in mind, the average rate of growth of the population in the 35 countries of sub-Saharan Africa for which we have some information was 2.8 per cent a year between 1980 and 1994.

This is very rapid demographic growth compared to the growth rates in the rest of the developing world. In only three countries – Guinea-Bissau, Mauritius and Mozambique – was the rate of growth of the population less than 2 per cent a year and in 15 it was 3 per cent a year or more. Birth rates and population growth rates have, however, begun to fall in sub-Saharan Africa and with sensible economic policies which focus on improving the health, education and income-earning opportunities open to women, these rates should fall further.

The combination of a slow rate of growth of output and a rapid rate of growth of the population has produced a negative rate of growth of GDP per head. During the period 1980–94 the simple average rate of growth of output per head in sub-Saharan Africa was −0.4 per cent a year. This average is based on information from 33 countries; in 17 countries no information is available. Of the 33 countries, 11 had positive growth rates, two had a zero growth rate and 20 experienced a negative growth of per capita output. Once again, the average rate of −0.4 per cent probably understates the rate of decline in sub-Saharan Africa as a whole since many of the countries where data are absent probably performed even worse than average because of civil conflicts of various sorts.[3] Our estimate should therefore be regarded as a minimum: the true average rate of decline probably was faster than our estimate suggests.

Assuming that the average country in sub-Saharan Africa experienced a fall in output per head of about 0.4 per cent a year for 14 years, this implies that per capita output fell about 5 or 6 per cent during the period. Average incomes fell even more sharply than output because in the majority of countries, as we shall see below, there was a significant deterioration in the external terms of trade. Given that average incomes already were very low at the beginning of the period, the incidence and depth of poverty must have increased quite considerably. In so far as the decline in average incomes was accompanied by increased inequality in the distribution of income, as fragmentary evidence suggests in some countries,[4] the rise in poverty must have been exacerbated.

The World Bank reports that 47 per cent of the total population of sub-Saharan Africa were poor in 1985[5] and the International Fund for Agricultural Development reports that 60 per cent of the rural population of sub-Saharan Africa were poor in 1988.[6] The economic situation has continued to deteriorate since these estimates were made and it is therefore highly likely that poverty is even greater today.

Macroeconomic performance in sub-Saharan Africa since 1980 thus has been remarkably bad. The rate of growth has been slow, output per head has declined, average incomes have fallen, inequality probably has increased and the proportion of the population living in poverty has risen. The outcome has not been uniformly bad, some countries have performed better than others and in a few countries performance has been good, but seen as a whole, the economies of sub-Saharan Africa compare unfavourably with the rest of the world, with the possible exception since 1989 of the economies of the former Soviet Union.

Those concerned about the acute and increasing hardship in Africa, particularly external advisors and international financial agencies, have recommended policies of 'stabilization' and 'structural adjustment'.[7] The meaning of these phrases is not unambiguous and it is useful to examine them with some care. This we do in the next two sections.

## Stabilization

The purpose of stabilization policies is to restore macroeconomic balance. In the African context severe imbalances are reflected in high and possibly accelerating rates of inflation, a large and possibly increasing balance of payments deficit and perhaps, too, in a large public sector deficit, including deficits of public sector enterprises. The general policy recommendation in such a situation is to reduce the level of aggregate demand so that it corresponds more closely to the economy's production potential and to lower inflationary expectations by establishing the 'credibility' of strong anti-inflation measures by the government.

Specific policies recommended usually include a reduction in the supply of money and an increase in nominal interest rates; a reduction in government expenditure and, less frequently, an increase in tax revenues; privatization of state-owned enterprises or, again less frequently, reform of state enterprises to reduce losses or increase profits; and unification of exchange rates and devaluation of the currency. The primary purpose of the policies is to stabilize the price level and, secondarily, to restore balance to the external trading account and to the public sector's income and expenditure accounts. In fact, most countries in sub-Saharan Africa (35 according to the latest count) have introduced stabilization and structural adjustment programmes and it is now possible in general terms to evaluate the outcomes.

Before doing so, however, it is necessary to be specific about the standard of evaluation. High rates of inflation undoubtedly are harmful to an economy. First, they lead to inefficiencies in the allocation of resources and consequently to a lower level of output and income than would otherwise be possible. Second, high rates of inflation also make it more difficult to make long-term investment decisions and this leads to a lower rate of capital formation and to a pattern of investment biased in favour of projects with a quick pay-off. The result is a lower rate of growth of output, incomes and employment. Third, rapid inflation usually is accompanied by large and arbitrary changes in the distribution of income and this damages economic incentives and leads to a widespread sense of injustice.

It does not follow from this, however, that 'stabilization' should be taken literally, i.e. that the objective of policy should be to stabilize the price level and achieve a zero rate of inflation. Such an objective, if attained, probably would increase inefficiency and reduce the rate of growth. The reason for this is that a well functioning price system depends for its success on the flexibility of relative prices and relative prices are likely to be more flexible if the rate of inflation is positive but moderate.

An illustration may clarify the point. If the demand for bicycles diminishes while that for radios increases, the price of bicycles should fall and the price of radios should rise, i.e. relative prices should move against bicycles. Similarly, if the demand for carpenters declines while the demand for electricians increases, relative wages should shift against carpenters. The problem is that many prices (e.g. in the manufacturing sector) and many wages (notably in the urban formal sector) are 'sticky' downwards; a nominal cut in some prices and wages is difficult to achieve. Yet if the aggregate level of prices is stable, i.e. there is zero inflation, a change in relative prices implies that for every price rise there must be a compensating price fall elsewhere. Sticky prices and wages may make this impossible unless stabilization measures are pushed to such an extreme that the level of effective aggregate demand falls below the potential level of production of the economy.

Rather than allow that to happen, it would be better to tolerate mild inflation so that relative prices can adjust with some prices rising faster than others but without the necessity of some prices falling absolutely while others rise. Exactly how much inflation should be tolerated on grounds of economic efficiency and growth is impossible to say, but the answer presumably depends on the degree of downward stickiness of prices and on the extent of relative price adjustments that are necessary. That is, the more sticky are prices and the greater the required changes in relative prices, the higher the rate of inflation that should be tolerated. Given the highly 'distorted' structures of prices in many sub-Saharan countries, an upper limit of the rate of inflation of 20 per cent a year might be a reasonable objective of a 'stabilization' programme.[8]

This would allow the government some margin to run a modest fiscal deficit. This margin of flexibility should be used to finance public investment, not to cover the deficits of state enterprises or to finance current operating expenditure. Higher public investment, as emphasized below, should raise incomes and accelerate growth directly and, in addition, stimulate investment and growth in the private sector. Government borrowing, in moderation and if used for the right purposes, thus could play a constructive role.

Table 7.3 contains data on the rate of inflation (as measured by the GDP deflator) in the 33 countries of sub-Saharan Africa for which information is available. The data cover three periods, namely, the decade of the 1980s, the first four years of the 1990s and the entire period 1980–94. One possible test of the success of stabilization efforts would be whether the rate of inflation has diminished over time, regardless of the initial or terminal rate of inflation. That is, non-accelerating inflation might well be an objective of macroeconomic policy.

Unfortunately, sub-Saharan Africa has not done particularly well by this test. The rate of inflation actually accelerated between the first and second periods in 18 of the 33 countries. In the remaining 15 countries the rate of inflation did indeed diminish. In most of the countries where inflation accelerated, there is little cause for concern because even after the acceleration the rate of inflation was well below our cut-off point of 20 per cent a year. In only three countries (Malawi, Nigeria and Zimbabwe) did the acceleration in inflation move the country from below the threshold level to above it, and in only one country (Mozambique) was inflation initially above the threshold level and

*Table 7.3*   Indicators of stabilization

| Country | GDP deflator (average annual percentage rate of growth) | | | Nominal lending rate of banks, 1994 (% per annum) |
|---|---|---|---|---|
| | *1980–90* | *1990–94* | *1980–94* | |
| Angola | n.a. | n.a. | n.a. | n.a. |
| Benin | 1.6 | 7.9 | 3.8 | 16.8 |
| Botswana | 13.1 | 8.4 | 11.7 | 13.9 |
| Burkina Faso | 3.1 | 4.0 | 3.4 | 16.8 |
| Burundi | 4.4 | 7.1 | 5.2 | n.a. |
| Cameroon | 5.7 | 2.7 | 4.8 | 17.5 |
| Cape Verde | n.a. | n.a. | n.a. | n.a. |
| Central African Republic | 5.6 | 6.2 | 5.8 | 17.5 |
| Chad | 1.1 | 6.6 | 2.7 | 17.5 |
| Comoros | n.a. | n.a. | n.a. | n.a. |
| Congo | 0.3 | 2.1 | 0.8 | 17.5 |
| Côte d'Ivoire | 3.1 | 6.8 | 4.2 | 16.8 |
| Djibouti | n.a. | n.a. | n.a. | n.a. |
| Equatorial Guinea | n.a. | n.a. | n.a. | n.a. |
| Eritrea | n.a. | n.a. | n.a. | n.a. |
| Ethiopia | n.a. | n.a. | n.a. | 14.3 |
| Gabon | 1.9 | 10.5 | 4.4 | 17.5 |
| Gambia | 8.7 | 5.6 | 14.9 | 25.0 |
| Ghana | 42.4 | 20.7 | 36.1 | n.a. |
| Guinea | n.a. | 11.7 | n.a. | 22.0 |
| Guinea-Bissau | 56.1 | 53.4 | 55.3 | 36.3 |
| Kenya | 9.0 | 17.7 | 11.5 | n.a. |
| Lesotho | 13.6 | 11.9 | 13.1 | 14.3 |
| Liberia | n.a. | n.a. | n.a. | n.a. |
| Madagascar | 17.1 | 16.8 | 17.0 | n.a. |
| Malawi | 14.6 | 22.8 | 17.0 | 31.0 |
| Mali | 5.6 | 8.0 | 6.3 | 16.8 |
| Mauritania | 8.6 | 7.6 | 8.3 | 10.0 |
| Mauritius | 8.7 | 7.2 | 8.3 | 18.9 |
| Mayotte | n.a. | n.a. | n.a. | n.a. |
| Mozambique | 38.4 | 49.3 | 41.6 | n.a. |
| Namibia | 13.6 | 9.5 | 12.4 | 17.1 |
| Niger | 2.9 | 4.7 | 3.4 | 16.8 |
| Nigeria | 16.6 | 37.4 | 22.6 | 20.5 |
| Reunion | n.a. | n.a. | n.a. | n.a. |
| Rwanda | 3.3 | 9.7 | 5.2 | 15.0 |
| São Tomé and Principe | n.a. | n.a. | n.a. | n.a. |
| Senegal | 6.4 | 7.1 | 6.6 | 16.8 |
| Seychelles | n.a. | n.a. | n.a. | n.a. |
| Sierra Leone | 56.0 | 55.9 | 56.0 | 27.3 |
| Somalia | n.a. | n.a. | n.a. | n.a. |
| South Africa | 14.8 | 11.9 | 14.0 | 15.6 |

*(Continued)*

*Table 7.3    (Continued)*

| Country | GDP deflator (average annual percentage rate of growth) | | | Nominal lending rate of banks, 1994 (% per annum) |
|---|---|---|---|---|
| | 1980–90 | 1990–94 | 1980–94 | |
| Sudan | n.a. | n.a. | n.a. | n.a. |
| Swaziland | n.a. | n.a. | n.a. | n.a. |
| Tanzania | 35.7 | 20.4 | 31.3 | 39.0 |
| Togo | 4.7 | 5.7 | 5.0 | 17.5 |
| Uganda | 125.6 | 28.8 | 97.5 | n.a. |
| Zaire | n.a. | n.a. | n.a. | n.a. |
| Zambia | 42.4 | 124.2 | 66.1 | 113.3 |
| Zimbabwe | 11.5 | 27.0 | 16.0 | 34.9 |

*Source*: Calculated from data in World Bank, *World Development Report 1996*, New York: Oxford University Press, 1996, Tables 2 and 11.

then accelerated further. Thus one can safely say that, in general, accelerating inflation is not a major problem in Africa, at least in those countries where data are available.

A second test of the success of stabilization efforts would be whether the rate of inflation during the second period (the 1990s) is below the threshold level of 20 per cent a year. The results of this test are quite encouraging: 23 out of the 33 countries for which data are available are below the threshold and only ten are above it. Half of the ten countries above the threshold (Ghana, Malawi, Tanzania, Uganda and Zimbabwe) have rates of inflation below 30 per cent a year and hence the extent of price instability may not be alarming; the remaining five countries, however (Guinea-Bissau, Mozambique, Nigeria, Sierra Leone and Zambia) clearly do have serious inflationary problems and require further stabilization efforts in order to improve their macroeconomic performance.

So far we have used the word 'stabilization' to refer to changes in the general level of prices, i.e. to the rate of inflation. We have argued that 'stabilization' ought to imply a rate of inflation no higher than 20 per cent per annum and have used this standard to evaluate performance in Africa. There is, however, a second sense in which the word 'stabilization' could be used, namely stability of certain strategic or key prices. The word is seldom used in this second sense, but a case can be made that stability in this second sense is even more important than stability in the first sense of moderate inflation.

Two obvious candidates for strategic prices that ought to be kept stable are the real rate of interest and the real exchange rate. Let us consider each in turn.

The real rate of interest is the nominal (or market) rate of interest adjusted for expected or anticipated inflation. Since anticipated inflation is hard to measure, in practice the real rate of interest usually is calculated as the nominal rate of interest minus the current rate of inflation. Thus if the nominal rate of interest is 8 per cent a year and the rate of inflation is 10 per cent, the real rate of interest is a negative 2 per cent. In most discussions of macroeconomic policy emphasis is placed on the role of interest rates (that is, the deposit rate of interest) in providing an incentive to save (particularly through formal sector financial institutions) and in reducing aggregate consumption demand (and hence contributing to price stabilization). Negative or low but positive real deposit rates of interest are criticized for discouraging savings. Given the low (and even negative[9]) savings rates in many sub-Saharan countries, this criticism is not without merit. The problem with this argument, however, is that most of the empirical evidence suggests that savings are not very sensitive to changes in interest rates.

More significant in our view is the effect of interest rates on the efficiency of investment. That is, the strategic price is the real lending rate of interest. If the rate of interest charged by banks to their customers is negative in real terms, the risk to the borrower disappears and the demand for credit will greatly exceed the available funds. Price (i.e. interest rates) will play no role in allocating credit and the banks will have to rely on credit-rationing devices to distribute funds among enthusiastic would-be borrowers. The temptation for bankers to lend to their friends or to those with political influence or to engage in corrupt practices will be very great. Since the banks will not run a risk of default on their loans, bankers will have no incentive to select the best projects (those with the highest rates of return) and to weed out the worst projects (those with a high likelihood of failure). The result is that the composition of investment will be adversely affected and the return on investment will be reduced. This, in turn, will lower the average rate of growth.

It is thus important that the real lending rate of interest should be positive, moderately high and stable. While it is true that gross domestic investment in sub-Saharan Africa has been lower than in other developing regions, and in addition the rate of investment has fallen substantially (from 23 per cent of GDP in 1980 to 17 per cent in 1994), the most serious problem is the low return on investment as reflected in the large number of 'white elephants', economically non-viable projects and a poor project mix.

The real lending rate of interest influences not only what projects will be undertaken but also the degree of labour intensity of production.

A low real rate of interest introduces a bias against the employment of labour, a factor in relative abundance in Africa, and instead creates incentives for producers to adopt relatively capital intensive methods of production. Given that the great majority of countries in sub-Saharan Africa obtain their capital goods from abroad, low real rates of interest in effect represent a subsidy by Africa to employment in the capital goods industries of the rest of the world. This is hardly a desirable macroeconomic policy.

As a rough rule of thumb, a sensible policy in sub-Saharan Africa might be a real lending rate of interest of a minimum of 10 per cent per annum. This would not reduce demand for investment below the available funding but it would increase the incentive to allocate funds for investment more efficiently. How well have our countries done according to this test? In the last column of Table 7.3 there is information on the nominal lending rate of banks in 1994. This nominal rate of interest can be compared with the actual rate of inflation in 1990–94 as reported in the second column of the table. This comparison will give us a crude approximation to the real lending rate of interest and is the best that can be done in the absence of detailed country studies.

A comparison of nominal lending rates with the actual rate of inflation is possible in 28 countries. In 24 of the 28 countries the real rate of interest is positive; only in Guinea-Bissau, Nigeria, Sierra Leone and Zambia is it negative. This is encouraging. On the other hand, in only 12 countries is the real rate of interest at least 10 per cent a year. In other words, 16 out of 28 countries fail to pass the test. This implies that throughout much of sub-Saharan Africa 'stabilization' is being hampered by less than optimal interest rate policies.

A second strategic price that ought to be kept stable is the real rate of exchange. The real rate of exchange is the nominal rate of exchange adjusted for rates of inflation in the domestic economy and in the country's trading partners. In effect the nominal exchange rate is adjusted to take into account the difference between the domestic and foreign rates of inflation. A stable real exchange rate means that the structure of incentives as regards importing and exporting is held constant.

Once a unified 'equilibrium' exchange rate is established which brings the balance of payments deficit to a level which can be sustained by long-term inflows of foreign capital, both public and private, the rate of exchange should be stabilized, i.e. the real rate of exchange should remain roughly constant until fundamental economic conditions change. This is especially important in small countries where dependence on foreign trade is high. Unfortunately, there is no evidence on the evolution over time in the real exchange rate in the sub-Saharan countries, but as we shall see below, the behaviour of exports suggests that real exchange rates in many countries have been allowed to appreciate, to the detriment of the countries' balance of payments position.[10]

The argument in favour of stabilizing strategic prices such as the real rate of exchange and the real borrowing rate of interest can be extended to the policy regime as a whole. Investment is inherently a risky undertaking: it requires a commitment of funds 'today' in the expectation of rewards 'tomorrow', sometimes in a rather distant tomorrow. If risks are high and uncertainty is great, the volume of investment will diminish and the time horizon of investors will shrink: investors will be unwilling to commit large sums of money over long periods of time. Volatile government policies – and arbitrary changes in policies – increase risk and harm investment whereas stable policies and a 'credible' policy regime, by reducing uncertainty, create a more favourable economic environment and can help to stimulate private investment and growth.

## Structural adjustment

Structural adjustment policies have three major purposes. First, they are designed to effect a substantial change in the composition of output, primarily through a radical alteration in the structure of relative prices. The intention is to reform the market mechanism so that prices reflect marginal costs and benefits, in the expectation that this in turn would induce a change in the pattern of production in favour of products in which the country has or can rapidly acquire a comparative advantage. An improvement in the internal terms of trade of the rural sector, for example, would be expected to reverse the decline in per capita agricultural production. Second, structural adjustment is intended to integrate the countries of sub-Saharan Africa more closely into the global economy. Exports were expected to grow rapidly and to increase their share of GDP. Foreign trade was expected to become a leading sector, reversing the import-substituting industrialization strategy adopted in the early post-independence period. Third, structural adjustment is intended to raise the rate of investment and improve the allocation of investment, thereby increasing the rate of growth of output, incomes and employment. Poverty would decline as average incomes rose. The ultimate consequence of the economic reforms thus would be a fundamental restructuring of the economy and a marked improvement in its performance.

We shall analyse below each of the three components of structural adjustment policies in sub-Saharan Africa. Before doing so, however, it is important to distinguish between those outcomes which are the result of exogenous 'shocks' and those which can be attributed to the policy reforms and the way they were introduced. Many analysts have argued that the distressing macroeconomic performance in Africa is due in large part to external shocks, notably a dramatic deterioration in the external trading environment. The decline in the terms of trade often is singled out as a major contributing factor.

In the second column of Table 7.4 data are presented on the change in the external terms of trade for 33 countries between 1985 and 1994. In two cases (Burkina Faso and Senegal) there was no change in the terms of trade; in eight cases the terms of trade improved, usually only moderately but in Botswana and Mauritius dramatically. In the remaining 23 countries the terms of trade declined, often very sharply indeed, as in Burundi, Uganda, Nigeria, Rwanda and Gabon. Clearly there was an external trade shock in many countries and the shock was serious. Inspection of the data in Table 7.4 shows, however, that there is no close association between the change in the terms of trade and the rate of growth either of exports or of investment.

In Cameroon, for example, the terms of trade declined 30.1 per cent but the value of exports none the less increased 6.3 per cent a year during the period 1980–94. In Niger the terms of trade improved by 11 per cent but the rate of growth of exports was negative, namely −5.2 per cent a year. Turning to investment, in Malawi the terms of trade deteriorated by 12.1 per cent but investment grew by 7.0 per cent a year. In South Africa, in contrast, the terms of trade improved fractionally (by 0.9 per cent) but investment declined by 2.7 per cent a year.

A second exogenous shock frequently emphasized is internal, namely the widespread ethnic conflict and civil discord in sub-Saharan Africa. The direction of causality almost always is said to run from ethnic conflict to economic disruption. The conflict and violence in countries such as Angola, Mozambique, Ethiopia, Somalia, the Sudan, Liberia and Rwanda undoubtedly did severely damage the economy (or large parts of it) contributing mightily to the economic crisis in those countries. But the relationship between ethnic conflict and economic performance is more subtle than this implies: it can be argued that the economic crises in sub-Saharan Africa increased the likelihood of domestic conflicts and, once started, increased the intensity of conflict. According to this view, ethnic conflict is at least in part endogenous.

*Table 7.4*   Indicators of restructuring in sub-Saharan Africa

| Country | Growth of exports 1980–94 (% per annum) | Change in the Terms of trade, 1985–94 (%) | Growth of investment 1980–94 (% per annum) |
|---|---|---|---|
| Angola | n.a. | n.a. | −0.9 |
| Benin | −1.0 | −0.9 | n.a. |
| Botswana | n.a. | +56.7 | 1.7 |
| Burkina Faso | −1.1 | 0.0 | 2.0 |
| Burundi | 2.5 | −60.9 | n.a. |
| Cameroon | 6.3 | −30.1 | −3.7 |
| Cape Verde | n.a. | n.a. | n.a. |
| Central African Republic | −1.4 | −16.5 | 0.9 |
| Chad | 0.9 | +4.0 | 12.6 |
| Comoros | n.a. | n.a. | n.a. |
| Congo | 5.1 | −38.0 | −10.4 |
| Côte d'Ivoire | −1.1 | −25.7 | −7.3 |
| Djibouti | n.a. | n.a. | n.a. |
| Equatorial Guinea | n.a. | n.a. | n.a. |
| Eritrea | n.a. | n.a. | n.a. |
| Ethiopia | n.a. | −37.8 | n.a. |
| Gabon | 3.3 | −41.6 | −4.1 |
| Gambia | −1.2 | −19.0 | 1.4 |
| Ghana | 4.0 | −31.2 | 2.1 |
| Guinea | n.a. | −24.2 | n.a. |
| Guinea-Bissau | −2.9 | +1.1 | 4.3 |
| Kenya | 3.2 | −35.5 | −0.1 |
| Lesotho | 6.0 | n.a. | 7.9 |
| Liberia | n.a. | n.a. | n.a. |
| Madagascar | −0.1 | −33.9 | 1.3 |
| Malawi | 1.9 | −12.1 | 7.0 |
| Mali | 4.6 | +3.0 | 5.3 |
| Mauritania | 1.3 | −3.6 | −2.0 |
| Mauritius | 8.7 | +57.1 | 10.0 |
| Mayotte | n.a. | n.a. | n.a. |
| Mozambique | −1.5 | +9.7 | 0.7 |
| Namibia | 1.9 | n.a. | 7.6 |
| Niger | −5.2 | +11.0 | −6.2 |
| Nigeria | 0.3 | −48.5 | −9.1 |
| Reunion | n.a. | n.a. | n.a. |
| Rwanda | 3.5 | −44.9 | −0.9 |
| São Tomé and Principe | n.a. | n.a. | n.a. |
| Senegal | 2.4 | 0.0 | 2.5 |

*Table 7.4    (Continued)*

| Country | Growth of exports 1980–94 (% per annum) | Change in the Terms of trade, 1985–94 (%) | Growth of investment 1980–94 (% per annum) |
|---------|------------------|------------------|------------------|
| Seychelles | n.a. | n.a. | n.a. |
| Sierra Leone | − 3.8 | − 18.3 | − 2.5 |
| Somalia | n.a. | n.a. | n.a. |
| South Africa | 2.0 | + 0.9 | − 2.7 |
| Sudan | n.a. | n.a. | n.a. |
| Swaziland | n.a. | n.a. | n.a. |
| Tanzania | n.a. | − 34.1 | n.a. |
| Togo | − 3.5 | − 35.3 | − 8.5 |
| Uganda | 3.2 | − 61.1 | 7.4 |
| Zaire | n.a. | n.a. | n.a. |
| Zambia | 1.6 | − 4.5 | − 6.8 |
| Zimbabwe | 5.1 | − 16.0 | 1.0 |

*Source*: Calculated from data in World Bank, *World Development Report 1996*, New York: Oxford University Press, 1996, Tables 3 and 11.

During the 1960s, in the immediate post-independence era, growth in sub-Saharan Africa was encouraging, human development indicators improved substantially, incomes and general well being increased and poverty began to decline. The import-substituting industrialization strategy that was adopted, however, soon reached its limits, particularly in the smaller countries, and in the 1970s per capita incomes stagnated and began to decline. By the 1980s, as we have seen, most of sub-Saharan Africa found itself in the midst of a severe economic crisis. Per capita output declined steadily, average incomes sometimes fell sharply, foreign indebtedness rose precipitously, food production per head declined and hunger became chronic. In some countries (Ethiopia, Somalia, southern Sudan and the Sahelian countries) famines occurred. Competition for food, jobs (particularly in the formal sector), income-earning opportunities in general and productive resources intensified. Livestock operators, for example, attempting to preserve traditional grazing and water rights, often found themselves in conflict with peasant farmers attempting to expand the cultivated area into lands previously regarded as marginal.

The intensification of competition over livelihoods, resources and opportunities in not a few instances resulted in social conflicts of a bewildering variety: between Asian traders and indigenous peoples;

between one 'tribe' and another; between groups from different regions, or of different religious orientations; between pastoralists and farmers; between people of different 'race', and so on. Military dictatorship, civil war, banditry, ethnic confrontation and even genocide and ethnic cleansing became a commonplace. Economic failure often had horrible political consequences. Restructuring became essential.

There are, however, three very distinct ways of bringing about structural adjustment – of radically changing the composition of output – and these three ways or paths have markedly different consequences for the people concerned. The first path is the one that is usually implicit in conventional policy advice given to sub-Saharan African countries. It is assumed that changes in the composition of output occur as a result of a reallocation of the existing stocks of productive assets. That is, physical, human and natural capital can be reassigned and combined in different proportions to produce a new mix of products from the set of feasible alternatives. Movement occurs along a given 'production possibilities frontier' in response to changes in relative product prices. This movement is assumed to be frictionless and rapid and consequently full utilization of resources is ensured and structural adjustment is achieved without significant lags.

This first path is illustrated in Figure 7.1 as a movement from point A to point B. The initial composition of output at A reflects a development strategy which gives priority to manufacturing and promotes growth along an expansion path represented by the ray OA. Structural adjustment entails a new development strategy – one that gives higher priority, say, to the minerals sector – and an attempt to move along a different expansion path represented by the ray OD. This expansion path is intersected by a segment of the production possibilities frontier at B and the purpose of the economic reforms is to effect a shift from A to B by reallocating existing resources.

This story is not implausible. Assume, for instance, that the price of millet falls relative to the price of maize. Farmers are likely to reallocate their land, labour power and mechanical equipment from the production of millet to that of maize. The output of millet will decline and the output of maize will increase and, moreover, this change in the cropping pattern will occur quickly (namely within one crop season) and without a decline in the degree of utilization of land, physical capital or labour. A change in relative crop prices is sufficient in this case to bring about a change in the composition of output.

Consider another example: a fall in the price of cocoa relative to alternative crops. In this case there may be no supply response, i.e. a

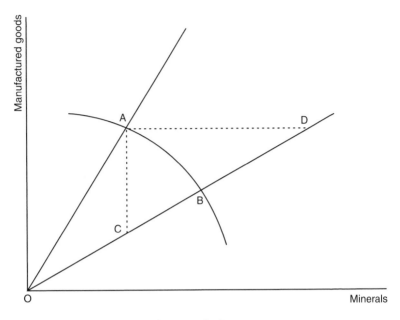

*Figure 7.1*   Alternative paths of structural adjustment

fall in cocoa production and a corresponding rise in the output of alternative crops. That is, there may be no reallocation of resources, no structural adjustment. The reason for this is that once the heavy investment in cocoa trees has occurred, the marginal cost of harvesting the output may be very low and hence even if prices fall sharply it may pay the farmer to maintain production. The failure to respond to the price disincentive may persist indefinitely, or until it is necessary to replace the old cocoa trees by replanting young ones.

Consider, finally, the opposite case of a rise in the price of a tree crop (say, coffee) relative to the price of an annual crop (say, beans). It is not possible merely to reallocate the land and labour used to grow beans in order to increase coffee production. Considerable investment is needed: the farmer must purchase and plant coffee saplings and then wait several years for the trees to mature to a fruit-bearing age. This investment will not occur unless (a) the farmer expects the relatively favourable price of coffee to be semi-permanent and (b) the farmer is able to finance the investment, including the consumption needs of himself and his family while waiting for the coffee trees to yield their first harvest. That is, structural adjustment in this case is heavily dependent upon the rate of investment.

We have deliberately selected examples from agriculture to illustrate the first path of structural adjustment – namely adjustment through reallocation – because conditions in agriculture more closely approximate the assumptions that lie behind the conventional view. Even so, it is evident that once specific capital is introduced, as was the case with cocoa and coffee trees, the conventional story becomes much more complicated.

Let us turn now to the second path of structural adjustment. This is the path that comes closest to describing the path actually followed in much of sub-Saharan Africa and this path can be called structural adjustment through contraction. Imagine, as in Figure 7.1, that structural adjustment is interpreted to mean a shift in the composition of output away from manufactured goods and in favour of minerals (petroleum, natural gas, copper, diamonds, platinum, gold, etc.). How might this shift occur within a context of decreased aggregate demand and price stabilization and of a radical change in relative prices?

Clearly both the demand effects and the relative price effects would reduce the profitability of the manufacturing sector. Labour would be discharged, idle manufacturing capacity would increase, unwanted capital equipment would be released for use elsewhere or sold as scrap, output of manufactured goods would decline. So far so good: production in the low priority sector would contract and the resources used in that sector would in principle become available to facilitate the expansion of the minerals sector, the high priority sector. But could the resources formerly used in manufacturing profitably be reabsorbed in the minerals sector? There is reason for doubt, and the doubt centres on the specificity of much physical and human capital.

The physical capital used in a brewery, or a textile mill or a food processing plant cannot rapidly be converted for use down a mine shaft, to cut a seam of coal, to sift diamonds, to transport ores on a conveyor belt or to separate the economically valuable minerals from the surrounding rock. Each economic activity requires specific types of capital equipment, specific tools, even sometimes specific buildings and this physical capital cannot readily be reallocated for other purposes.

The same is true of much human capital. Indeed the existence of firm-specific human capital is one reason why industrial enterprises often pay their experienced and skilled employees more than a 'market clearing' wage. It is worthwhile for firms to pay a premium in order to retain their human capital. The worker on an electronics assembly line (who could well be female) cannot be transformed into an underground miner (where physical strength is important). The worker in a furniture factory does not possess the skills needed on an oil rig. The worker in a pharmaceutical company, the salesperson in a kitchen utensils factory, or the quality control inspector in a meat processing plant can only with difficulty be absorbed in a totally different occupation. Resources, in other words, cannot normally be reallocated quickly and without friction. Expansion of newly profitable activities (minerals in our example) usually requires investment both in plant and equipment (physical capital) and in the education and training of the labour force (human capital). Moreover, the greater the desired transformation of the economy, the more essential it is to achieve a high rate of investment in physical and human capital.

Structural adjustment can still occur, but it occurs through contraction of unprofitable activities combined with stagnation of output in the profitable activities. This is depicted in Figure 7.1 as a movement from A to C. Note that C is on the same expansion path as B (namely the ray OD) and hence the proportion of manufactured goods and minerals is the same as at point B, but the level of production of both manufactured goods and minerals is much lower. Structural adjustment is purchased at the price of economic contraction, high unemployment and massive poverty. This essentially is what has happened in large parts of sub-Saharan Africa.

The response of well meaning advisors and aid donors has been to advocate the construction of a 'safety net' to alleviate the worst forms of hardship. This advocacy, however, is based on a misconception about the nature of the problem. A safety net would be appropriate if the increased unemployment and poverty were temporary and constituted a small deviation from the path of structural adjustment through resource allocation, i.e. a movement from A to B. In fact, however, sub-Saharan Africa is on a quite different path – a path of structural adjustment through contraction – and the human distress associated with this path is neither of short duration nor small in magnitude. The resources required to construct an effective safety net would consequently be enormous and such an undertaking is not feasible given the sharp decline in available resources. What is needed is not so much a safety net as policies that put the economy on a different path of adjustment.

Here, too, well meaning advisors and aid donors have an inkling of what is required, namely a sharp acceleration in the rate of growth of investment. There has been a proliferation of so-called structural adjustment loans and, indeed, the amount of foreign aid received in sub-Saharan Africa, when expressed as a proportion of GDP, is relatively high in many countries.[11] The problem is that foreign capital inflows have not been used to increase the level of investment but instead they have been used to finance current public and private expenditure. This reflects not the foolishness of donors but inappropriate government policies during the transition.

This brings us to the third path of structural adjustment – namely adjustment through investment. In Figure 7.1 this is illustrated by the movement from A to D. Point D is on the ray OD and hence the expansion path and the composition of output are the same as at points B and C. The difference is that the movement to D, i.e. the path to structural adjustment, occurs without any reallocation of pre-existing resources and without any decline in the level of output in the manufacturing sector. Structural adjustment along this path is part of a growth strategy, a strategy designed to increase investment in physical, human and natural capital and to channel that investment into economic activities which have become highly profitable as a result of changes in the structure of incentives.

The third path – structural adjustment through investment – does not result in a rise in unemployment, a fall in average real incomes or an increase in poverty. On the contrary, the rate of growth of GDP accelerates and average incomes rise rapidly. Moreover, as the experiences of China and Vietnam illustrate during their transition from central planning to a more market-oriented economic system, an investment-dominated path of structural adjustment is compatible with a simultaneous expansion of all sectors of the economy, but of course expansion at different rates. In terms of our diagram, this implies a movement in a north-easterly direction from A rather than the movement due east from A to D. Far too much attention has been devoted to adjustment through reallocation in sub-Saharan Africa; much more attention should in future be devoted to adjustment through investment.

## Structural adjustment in the external sector

As mentioned earlier, one of the objectives of structural adjustment policies in Africa is to improve performance in the foreign trade sector and in particular to increase the rate of growth of exports. In the first column of Table 7.4 we report figures for the rate of growth of the value of exports for the 31 countries for which data are available. The simple average rate of growth of exports ($G_x$) for these 31 countries

*Table 7.5* Export performance in 31 countries of sub-Saharan Africa, 1980–94 (number of countries)

|  | *Yes* | *No* | *Total* |
|---|---|---|---|
| $G_x < 0$ | 11 | 20 | 31 |
| $G_x \leqslant G_{pop}$ | 22 | 9 | 31 |
| $G_x \leqslant G_{gdp}$ | 18 | 13 | 31 |

during the period 1980–94 was 1.5 per cent a year. There was of course considerable variation around this average, but taken at face value the rate of growth does appear to be remarkably slow.

A clearer understanding of the significance of the export growth figures can be obtained by comparing them with other relevant parameters. This is done in Table 7.5. We ask in the first row of the table whether the rate of growth of export earnings was negative ($G_x < 0$). The answer is that in 11 countries the value of exports declined absolutely. These 11 countries in 1994 had less foreign exchange from exporting to finance the imports needed for development than they did 14 years earlier. These unfortunate countries included Côte d'Ivoire, Burkina Faso and Niger, among others. In the other 20 countries the rate of growth was at least positive. Nevertheless, the evidence suggests that about a third of the countries of sub-Saharan Africa face a potentially crippling foreign exchange constraint on development.

In the second row of Table 7.5 we ask whether the rate of growth of exports was slower than the rate of growth of the population ($G_{pop}$). In 22 countries – more than two-thirds of the total – the answer was yes. That is, the per capita availability of foreign exchange earned from exporting was less in 1994 than in 1980 in a large majority of sub-Saharan African countries. The people of Africa have become less integrated into the world economy and instead have become more dependent (in the absence of foreign aid) on domestic production to satisfy their needs for capital, intermediate and consumption goods.[12] In only nine countries did export earnings per head of the population increase.

Finally, in the third row we consider whether exports grew more slowly than GDP ($G_{gdp}$). If structural adjustment in the foreign trade sector is to be a success, one would expect the ratio of exports to GDP to rise. Alas, in 18 countries it fell. At least in these countries, it is perhaps unlikely that exports could be the engine of growth, as some advocates of structural adjustment have hoped. Given the small size of most of the countries in the region, it is unrealistic to imagine that national self-sufficiency is consistent with high levels of development. The trend in the 18 countries where exports have grown less rapidly than total output is therefore cause for concern. On the other hand, there are 13 countries in sub-Saharan Africa where exports have grown more rapidly than GDP. While it would be premature to herald this as evidence of export-led growth, relative growth rates in some of these countries at least are moving in the right direction.

## Investment: the neglected path to adjustment

This brings us closer to the heart of the matter, the urgent need to increase investment and improve its allocation among sectors and projects. This should be the primary task of macroeconomic policy in sub-Saharan Africa. Indeed, unless this can be achieved, structural adjustment will fail. The task is formidable.

The third column of Table 7.4 contains data on the annual rate of growth of investment in 31 countries during the period 1980–94. The simple average for these 31 countries is a miserable 0.3 per cent a year. Even this low figure probably overstates the true rate of growth of investment in sub-Saharan Africa as a whole since many of the countries for which data are lacking have been wracked by civil wars and have suffered considerable destruction of and damage to the stock of physical capital.

As usual in so large and diverse a group of countries, there are several which have performed much better than average and several which are much worse than average. Uganda, Namibia and Lesotho have experienced rates of growth of investment in excess of 7.0 per cent a year; in Mauritius investment has grown 10 per cent a year and in Chad it has increased 12.6 per cent a year. If these rates can be sustained in the decades ahead, these five countries have a good chance of achieving structural adjustment through investment. At the other extreme are five countries – Zambia, Côte d'Ivoire, Togo, Nigeria and Congo – where investment has declined between 6.8 and 10.4 per cent a year. These are classic cases of structural adjustment through contraction.

In Table 7.6 we ask and answer questions about investment performance similar to the questions posed about export performance in Table 7.5. In the first row of Table 7.6 we ask whether the rate of growth of investment ($G_i$) was negative. The answer, surprisingly, is that in 14 out of the 31 countries for which we have data the rate of growth was indeed negative. That is, in those countries the stock of physical capital assets was smaller in 1994 than it was in 1980.

*Table 7.6* Investment performance in 31 countries of sub-Saharan Africa, 1980–94 (number of countries)

|  | *Yes* | *No* | *Total* |
|---|---|---|---|
| $G_i < 0$ | 14 | 17 | 31 |
| $G_i \leqslant G_{pop}$ | 22 | 9 | 31 |
| $G_i \leqslant G_{gdp}$ | 20 | 11 | 31 |

There was an absolute decline in the value of such things as the number of dwellings and commercial buildings, the stock of machinery and transport equipment, the quality and length of the road and railroad networks, the size of inventories, and so on. The productive potential of the economy, in other words, was slowly shrinking. In the other 17 countries, fortunately, the stock of capital assets was increasing, even if the rate of growth in most cases was rather low.

In the second row of Table 7.6 we ask whether investment was growing less rapidly than the population ($G_{pop}$). In more than two-thirds of the cases (22 countries) the per capita rate of growth of investment was negative. In the remaining nine countries it was positive. The implication is that the amount of physical capital per person was declining in most of sub-Saharan Africa. Assuming that in the long run average incomes are closely correlated with the amount of capital available per person, the data suggest that even the currently low levels of income in sub-Saharan Africa are not sustainable unless trends in population growth and investment are reversed.

Finally, in the third row of Table 7.6 we address an issue that is central to structural adjustment through investment. Is the rate of growth of investment less rapid than the rate of growth of GDP ($G_{gdp}$)? In 20 out of 31 countries it turns out that investment is growing less rapidly than total output, implying that the investment ratio is declining in about two-thirds of the countries of sub-Saharan Africa. In 11 countries the investment ratio is rising.

A falling investment ratio would not matter if the ratio were high at the beginning of the period of structural adjustment and per capita incomes were growing rapidly. But in most of sub-Saharan Africa the investment ratio is low and per capita incomes are falling. In these circumstances it is essential to increase the rate of growth of investment and raise the proportion of output that is devoted to capital formation. Only thus can employment be generated and the long slide in living standards be halted and reversed.

## Labour and adjustment through contraction

The three paths to structural adjustment obviously have very different implications for employment and the remuneration of labour. The path followed in most of sub-Saharan Africa, unlike the other two possible paths, is highly disadvantageous. Those who were working in 1980 suffered the consequences of a decline in output per head; those who entered the workforce between 1980 and 1994 found it more difficult than their predecessors to obtain full-time employment and, when employed, they found that on average they were less well rewarded for their efforts than the previous generation.

The labour force in sub-Saharan Africa is growing exceptionally fast. Indeed only in the Middle East and North Africa is the labour force increasing more rapidly. Between 1980 and 1994 the simple average annual rate of growth of the labour force in 35 countries of sub-Saharan Africa for which we have data was 2.7 per cent. The lowest rate of growth was in Guinea-Bissau and Mozambique (1.6 per cent a year) and the highest was in Kenya (3.6 per cent). (See Table 7.7.) In 12 countries the workforce increased 3.0 per cent a year or more.

Rapid growth in the numbers of those seeking employment combined with slow growth of investment has resulted in a fall in the capital–labour ratio in most countries. This has undermined the ability of the economy to sustain production at previously attained levels. As can be seen in Table 7.8, the capital–labour ratio was constant in one country and rose in eight; in the other 22 countries for which we have data, it fell. That is, in two-thirds of the countries of sub-Saharan Africa the amount of capital available to equip each member of the labour force actually declined over a 14-year period.

This negative trend in capital–labour ratios is reflected in trends in the productivity of labour and hence in the income received by working people. If the labour force rises more rapidly than output, the average productivity of labour will fall and, in fact, this is what occurred in much of sub-Saharan Africa. In 12 of the 33 countries for which we have data, the average productivity of labour increased, but in the remaining 21 countries it fell. This downward trend in productivity, extending over 14 years in 21 countries, means that it was impossible to maintain the real incomes of workers and, primarily because of this, poverty increased.

Structural adjustment through contraction, in other words, resulted in a contraction of employment opportunities and real incomes. This contraction of the labour market took various forms which differed in

*Table 7.7*   The labour force

| Country | Growth of the labour force, 1980–94 (% per annum) | Percentage of the labour force in agriculture, 1990 |
|---|---|---|
| Angola | n.a. | n.a. |
| Benin | 2.6 | 64 |
| Botswana | 3.3 | 46 |
| Burkina Faso | 2.0 | 92 |
| Burundi | 2.8 | 92 |
| Cameroon | 2.6 | 70 |
| Cape Verde | n.a. | 31 |
| Central African Republic | 1.8 | 80 |
| Chad | 2.1 | 83 |
| Comoros | n.a. | 77 |
| Congo | 2.8 | 49 |
| Côte d'Ivoire | 3.0 | 60 |
| Djibouti | n.a. | n.a. |
| Equatorial Guinea | n.a. | 77 |
| Eritrea | n.a. | n.a. |
| Ethiopia | 2.6 | 86 |
| Gabon | 2.4 | 52 |
| Gambia | 3.4 | 82 |
| Ghana | 3.1 | 59 |
| Guinea | 2.3 | 87 |
| Guinea-Bissau | 1.6 | 85 |
| Kenya | 3.6 | 80 |
| Lesotho | 2.6 | 40 |
| Liberia | n.a. | 72 |
| Madagascar | 3.0 | 78 |
| Malawi | 3.5 | 87 |
| Mali | 2.7 | 86 |
| Mauritania | 2.2 | 55 |
| Mauritius | 2.1 | 17 |
| Mayotte | n.a. | n.a. |
| Mozambique | 1.6 | 83 |
| Namibia | 2.4 | 49 |
| Niger | 3.0 | 90 |
| Nigeria | 2.6 | 43 |
| Reunion | n.a. | n.a. |
| Rwanda | 3.1 | 92 |
| São Tomé and Principe | n.a. | n.a. |
| Senegal | 2.5 | 77 |
| Seychelles | n.a. | n.a. |
| Sierra Leone | 1.9 | 67 |
| Somalia | n.a. | 75 |
| South Africa | 2.6 | 14 |

Table 7.7   (*Continued*)

| Country | Growth of the labour force, 1980–94 (% per annum) | Percentage of the labour force in agriculture, 1990 |
|---|---|---|
| Sudan | n.a. | 69 |
| Swaziland | n.a. | 39 |
| Tanzania | 3.2 | 84 |
| Togo | 2.7 | 66 |
| Uganda | 2.9 | 85 |
| Zaire | n.a. | 68 |
| Zambia | 3.4 | 75 |
| Zimbabwe | 3.3 | 68 |

*Source*: World Bank, *World Development Report 1996*, New York: Oxford University Press, 1996 and UNDP, *Human Development Report 1996*, New York: Oxford University Press, 1996.

*Table 7.8*   Changes in the capital–labour ratio and the productivity of labour, 1980–94 (number of countries)

| | Rising | Constant | Falling | Total |
|---|---|---|---|---|
| Capital–labour ratio | 8 | 1 | 22 | 33 |
| Productivity of labour | 12 | 0 | 21 | 33 |

urban and rural areas. In the urban areas the formal sector declined absolutely in terms of output and employment.[13] This is especially true of public sector activities. Those who remained in formal sector employment usually experienced a fall in real wages,[14] demonstrating that wage rates may be sticky but that they are not rigidly fixed.[15]

Some of those who lost formal sector jobs became openly unemployed and some of the new entrants into the labour market who were unable to obtain formal sector jobs continued to search and meanwhile joined the ranks of the openly unemployed. Rates of open unemployment, however, have not risen dramatically in sub-Saharan Africa. Instead there has been a large increase in part-time employment and a rapid 'informalization' of the urban economy in response to the contraction of formal sector activities. Indeed the 'informalization' of the economy is the most notable, or at least the most visible, consequence of the prolonged economic crisis. Finally, unable to find productive employment, some workers became discouraged and withdrew from the labour force; they simply dropped out.

The implication is that although there is not a lot of idle labour in Africa's cities, there is an enormous amount of slack in the labour market. That is, there is a great deal of labour that potentially could be employed in more productive activities, including of course investment activities. We shall argue below that this potential should be exploited by organizing investment projects in the public sector.

Although the rate of urbanization in Africa is the most rapid in the world, the proportion of the labour force engaged in agriculture also is the highest in the world. The second column of Table 7.7 contains information for 43 countries. On average, 68 per cent of the labour force in these countries obtains a livelihood from agriculture. The range is very wide. At the top end of the distribution, three countries (Burkina Faso, Burundi and Rwanda) employ 92 per cent of the labour force in agriculture whereas at the lower end of the distribution only 14 per cent of the working population is engaged in agriculture in South Africa. In 34 out of the 43 countries, however, more than 50 per cent of the labour force is in the agricultural sector. The economies of sub-Saharan Africa, in other words, still are predominantly rural.

Worsening labour market conditions in the rural areas were in large part a manifestation of a fall in labour productivity in agriculture – and of a decline in food output per capita. Small farmers, tenants and wage workers experienced a fall in real incomes because of a fall in output per worker per year. Structural adjustment policies, contrary to the expectations of many, seem to have been associated with a decline in the rate of growth of agricultural output. In the decade of the 1980s, agriculture in sub-Saharan Africa grew 1.8 per cent a year on average, but in the period 1990–94 the rate of growth declined by more than half, to 0.7 per cent a year.

Structural adjustment brought about a change in relative prices which favoured agriculture (as opposed to manufacturing) and, within agriculture, export crops (as opposed to food crops). Careful studies of Sierra Leone, Tanzania and Zambia, however, indicate that the change in relative prices was not sufficient to induce (i) an acceleration of agricultural output as a whole, or (ii) a switch from food production to export crops or (iii) a reverse flow of labour from urban to rural areas.[16] The failure of changes in relative prices to reallocate resources in the predicated direction could of course be attributed to the presence of long lags in the system, but a more natural interpretation of the evidence, consistent with the view presented above, would be that reallocation of resources is extremely difficult in the absence of high rates of investment.[17] Getting prices right is not enough.

# The structure of incentives

Structural adjustment through reallocation places primary emphasis on improving the structure of incentives by reforming and liberalizing prices. Specific policies advocated include the removal of price controls and government subsidies, removal of quotas and other non-tariff barriers to international trade combined with a reduction of tariffs to a uniform modest level, and unification and liberalization of the foreign exchange rate. The broad purpose is to eliminate 'distortions' so that prices accurately reflect social costs and benefits. We have no quarrel with this broad objective, but we would make three qualifications.

First, if one supports a programme of structural adjustment through investment, then the most important aspect of the structure of incentives is its effect on the efficiency of investment. The challenge of economic reform is to produce a set of price signals that channel new investments into the socially most profitable sectors and projects. Had the allocation of investment in sub-Saharan Africa been better, the rates of growth of output and incomes would have been much higher, even if the level of investment had remained relatively low. The primary objective of a new structure of incentives should be to correct this glaring deficiency.

Second, it would be a serious mistake to equate price liberalization with *laissez-faire*. Prices convey information. When markets work well they convey accurate information about social costs and social benefits, but markets often do not work well – they convey misleading information – and when this occurs there is a possible argument for government intervention. For example, strong cases can be made to tax the consumption of tobacco products (to protect public health), or to tax the consumption of alcoholic beverages (to prevent injury or death to others in automobile accidents) or to tax the use of hydrocarbon fuels (to reduce damage to the environment). These are examples of negative 'externalities' which result in market failure.

Most important from our perspective are market failures that lead to a severe misallocation of investment. Consider education. It is widely recognized that expenditure on education is a form of investment in human capital that confers substantial benefits both on the person being educated and on society at large. That is, there are large positive 'externalities' associated with education which are not taken into account by a free market. Hence there is a good reason, on grounds of efficiency in investment allocation, for governments to subsidize the cost of education. The same is true of some types of vocational training. Governments which reduce expenditure on primary and secondary education, either on grounds that they are reducing subsidies and thereby improving the structure of incentives or on grounds that they are reducing the fiscal deficit and thereby promoting stabilization, are implicitly turning their backs on structural adjustment through investment and following a path of structural adjustment through contraction.[18]

A similar argument can be made for government expenditure on public health and nutrition programmes. The benefits of measures to prevent the spread of communicable diseases (cholera, yellow fever, typhoid), malaria and, above all, AIDS are reaped by the community as a whole and not just by the individual receiving treatment. There is thus a case for collective provision of disease prevention and eradication services; if left to the market these services will be underprovided. More generally, well nourished children and a healthy working population will absorb knowledge more quickly and be more innovative and productive. This will raise the average productivity of labour and benefit directly the workers concerned and indirectly their dependants, co-workers and fellow citizens.

Thus public subsidy of certain types of expenditure on education, training, nutrition and health should be seen as improving the allocation of investment. These are investments in human capital with potentially high rates of return. The experience of East Asia demonstrates that this form of market intervention contributes to faster, more sustainable and equitable growth. The same almost certainly would be true in sub-Saharan Africa. Where there are major market failures (as in education and health) selective government intervention can improve the structure of incentives.

The third qualification to more conventional ways of thinking about incentives is to note that there is much more to the structure of incentives than relative prices.[19] The price structure is only a part, albeit an important part, of the structure of incentives. Equally important are barriers which exclude people from participating in some markets, as happens with licensing regulations which restrict a number of informal sector activities in many cities in sub-Saharan Africa; or features of an economy which restrict the ease of access of some people to markets, such as the restricted access of small farmers and small businesspeople to formal sector credit markets; or overt discrimination, which reduces occupational mobility and income-enhancing opportunities of some people because of their gender, ethnic or other characteristics. There are also many cases of missing markets in sub-Saharan Africa, where economic activity occurs without market mediation and consequently the output that is produced is not explicitly valued. Important examples include food produced for household consumption, in urban as well as rural areas, by unpaid female labour and, more generally, labour performed by female labour within a household economy in a wide range of activities that include food preparation, child raising, assistance to the elderly and provision of medical services.[20]

The structure of incentives includes all activities, whether mediated by the market or not, and in the case of market-mediated activities, it includes discrimination, barriers to entry, market access and, of course, relative prices. The essential point, however, is that even if one is a believer in structural adjustment through reallocation, and hence focuses on changing incentives, 'getting prices right' will not suffice. Particularly in sub-Saharan Africa the phenomenon of missing markets is widespread. Unpaid women producing unpriced goods and services account for a high proportion of productive labour. The price system – the structure of incentives narrowly defined – often is biased against the crops grown by women (and other goods and services they produce) as well as against innovations which reduce the time and effort spent by women in crop cultivation (and other activities), since the labour of women is not valued by the market. It is hardly surprising that an incentive system, broadly defined, that is strongly biased against half the population has produced such unsatisfactory outcomes.

Consistent with our theme of giving high priority to a better allocation of investment, there are two areas where substantial improvements are possible.[21] First, public sector investment often is poorly allocated. It is excessively capital intensive and hence creates less employment than it could; there is enormous scope for labour intensive public investment programmes, as we shall see below. In addition, public investment is excessively concentrated in the capital and hence rural–urban and regional inequalities are accentuated. Further, public investment often is directed to projects that have low rates of return and hence produces less income than it should. Fresh thinking is needed on the role of the state in domestic resource mobilization and the financing of investment, on project selection and evaluation, and on the objectives and management of state enterprises. The 'commercialization' of state-owned enterprises may be more important than the 'privatization' of state enterprises.

Second, private sector investment also is poorly allocated in sub-Saharan Africa. The reason for this is the underdevelopment of capital markets and the concentration of the banking system. The problem is partly a matter of inappropriate pricing, namely low real borrowing rates of interest, as discussed above. In addition there is a problem about the sectoral allocation of credit. Most people in Africa do not in fact have access to formal sector credit at any price and large sectors of the economy are starved of finance. Small and medium-sized urban businesses have much difficulty obtaining credit; agriculture and live-stock are under-supplied, apart from large plantations and ranches, and small farmers obtain virtually no credit from banks. Fishermen and rural artisans cannot obtain loans from commercial banks; the informal sector as a whole has little access to credit; new enterprises in any sector are rarely able to obtain start-up capital. The great majority of people in Africa either are self-financed or use the informal credit market supplied by traders, moneylenders, friends and relatives. Most formal sector credit, in effect, is reserved for large, well established urban enterprises. The consequence of this massive defect in the structure of incentives is that many highly profitable private sector enterprises fail to get established and many small but established enterprises are unable to grow rapidly for lack of credit.

The pace and efficacy of structural adjustment would be much increased by improvements in the functioning of capital markets in Africa – by institutional innovation, by improved regulation of the banking sector, by supporting credit programmes targeted at specific groups such as women, informal sector entrepreneurs and small farm-ers and by increasing the supply of 'venture capital'. The emphasis should be on encouraging new private sector enterprises to emerge (particularly those which are small in scale and labour intensive) and on enabling small private sector enterprises to expand, innovate and penetrate new markets, including of course export markets. Changing the structure of incentives, in other words, is about accelerating growth by creating new productive assets; a more efficient allocation of the existing stock of resources, while not unimportant, is of secondary significance.

## Investment and the role of the state

The obvious question to ask of an investment-led strategy of structural adjustment in sub-Saharan Africa is how an acceleration of investment can be financed. There are three possible sources we shall examine: (a) foreign financing, (b) private sector saving and investment and (c) the public sector. Let us consider each of these in turn.

It is always tempting to look abroad for a solution to financial problems. In the case of sub-Saharan Africa, however, it is unlikely that a solution will be found there. Foreign direct investment in the region is negligible and is likely to remain so. A few countries with rich mineral deposits to exploit may be able to attract private foreign capital and South Africa's relatively large urban market may attract some foreign investors, but most countries with small markets, falling incomes and poorly educated workers will be avoided by foreign capital. The evidence from China and the market economies of East and South-east Asia is that foreign capital flows to a country in large volume only after the country has succeeded in attaining rapid rates of growth. That is, inflows of private foreign capital are a consequence of successful development, not a cause of it.

There is of course foreign aid, but total aid allocations have been falling rapidly and it is perhaps improbable that the trend will be reversed in the near future. In principle Africa's share of a declining total could increase, so that aid inflows actually rose or at least remained constant, but it would seem unwise to plan on this when designing a strategy for structural adjustment. If foreign aid is available, and it is thought to be useful,[22] it would be a welcome addition to domestic resources, but when it comes to financing national development, governments in sub-Saharan Africa should make conservative assumptions and choose self-reliance.

Foreign debt is a major problem in many countries of the region. In sub-Saharan Africa as a whole total external indebtedness increased by 153 per cent between 1980 and 1994 and external debt as a percentage of GNP rose during the same period from 30.6 to 78.7 per cent. Debt servicing in some countries (Côte d'Ivoire, Congo, Burundi, Uganda, Kenya) absorbs well over 30 per cent of export earnings and a combination of debt forgiveness, a moratorium on repayment and unilateral default could release large sums of foreign exchange to help finance an investment-led structural adjustment programme.[23] Countries contemplating unilateral action, however, should consider carefully the possible consequences, namely termination of aid programmes and a reduction in the already meagre inflows of private foreign capital.

Despite the low and even negative savings rates that characterize sub-Saharan Africa, the private domestic sector could under the right conditions finance a much higher level of investment. A change in the structure of incentives along the lines suggested, including greatly widening access of potential investors to formal sector credit institutions, could increase the incentive to save and improve the allocation of savings. Because some saving by a would-be borrower almost always is required before obtaining a loan, widening access to lending institutions should increase the number of savers and the rate of savings.

It is customary to think of the savings decision as being separate from the investment decision. The two are guided by different incentives and are brought into balance by price adjustments in financial markets and variations in the level of national income. This is only a partial view of the savings process however. In many sectors of a sub-Saharan economy the amount saved by an enterprise, household or individual depends upon the specific investment opportunities open to that enterprise or household. If those engaged in a small family-owned and family-operated firm, for example, see a promising opportunity for expansion, they may seize the opportunity by reinvesting some of the firm's profits rather than using them to increase current consumption. That is, it is the presence of a profit opportunity that determines simultaneously the amount of investment and saving that occurs. The saving and investment decisions merge into one. People restrict their consumption not in order to 'save' but in order to finance a desired investment. In such a situation, the role of government policy should not be to try to induce people to consume less (save more) but rather to create a development environment in which there are large numbers of profitable investment opportunities.

This way of examining the problem of how to finance investment in sub-Saharan Africa can be extended further. In many instances investment requires little more than the direct application of labour: digging an irrigation or drainage ditch; planting a tea garden, coffee bushes or fruit trees; clearing, levelling or terracing a field; constructing a wall, animal shelter or home out of earth bricks. Whether a household will expend labour on such tasks depends on whether it is worthwhile or profitable. If there is plenty of slack in the labour market, e.g. in the form of seasonal rural unemployment, potentially profitable investments can be 'financed' not by consuming less (i.e. saving) but by working longer. That is, surplus labour at the level of the household can be used to finance household level investment projects. The problem is not how to save more but how to create investment opportunities. If there is an abundance of investment opportunities, the savings problem will take care of itself.

The issue then is not savings in a narrow sense but domestic resource mobilization. This way of posing the problem sheds new light on the question of the right balance between public and private sector investment. Governments which have attempted to follow a path of structural adjustment through reallocation have regarded public sector investment, and indeed public spending in general, as competitive with private sector investment. Public spending is said to 'crowd out' private investment. This view, however, urgently needs to be reassessed.

In the conditions which prevail in sub-Saharan Africa, many types of public expenditure are likely to be complementary to private sector investment.[24] This is likely to be true of public investment in rural and urban infrastructure (transport, power, water and sewerage facilities) and of public expenditure on several kinds of human capital investment (primary and secondary education, certain types of vocational training, basic health and nutrition, applied agricultural research). Expenditure in these areas can increase investment opportunities in the private sector and raise, not lower, private sector 'savings'. That is, public investment can increase the profitability of private investment and this, in turn, will increase private savings and domestic resource mobilization more generally.

The state thus has a leading role to play. This presupposes of course that there is a functioning state that is able to evaluate policies, choose from among them and implement programmes that bear some resemblance to what was planned. Where the state has disintegrated (Liberia, Somalia) or is in rapid decay (Zaire, Sudan), development is impossible and the first order of business must be to reconstruct the state (as is happening in Uganda and Mozambique). Any strategy of adjustment, i.e. any set of policies deliberately selected to achieve a specified objective, even *laissez-faire*, requires a functioning state. The alternative is anarchy, not the spontaneous order of well functioning markets.

A strategy of structural adjustment through investment implies that the composition of government expenditure, at all levels, should be shifted as far as possible in the direction of investment in human, physical and natural capital. There has been much debate about whether the state in sub-Saharan Africa is 'too large' and should be reduced in size. A more fruitful debate would be over the role of the state, directly and indirectly, in promoting a rapid rate of growth of investment and ensuring an efficient allocation of investment funds. It is not sufficient that government spending be heavily biased towards capital formation, it is equally important that within each spending category, funds be allocated to achieve the highest possible rate of return.

Let us consider spending on human capital as an example. It is well established that investing in education yields a high return, often comparable to or higher than the returns from investing in physical capital. Within education, the rate of return is highest on expenditures on primary education, followed by secondary education. The returns on university and other forms of tertiary education tend to be lower than the returns on primary and secondary education. Yet when one examines the composition of public expenditure on education, it often turns out to be the case that funds are allocated in inverse proportion to the rate of return: university education receives the largest amount of funds, followed by secondary and then primary education. It follows from this that if budgetary priorities were reversed, some of the funds now allocated to universities being transferred to primary education, the rate of return on investment in education as a whole would rise and the overall efficiency of investment would increase. Similarly, if governments are forced to cut spending on education, e.g. because of the need to stabilize the economy, the damage-minimizing strategy would be to cut university budgets first and leave spending on primary and secondary education intact.

The same arguments apply to public spending on health. Investing in the health of the people can be an excellent use of a country's resources, but not all forms of health expenditure are equally profitable. Some types of medical treatment are costly and produce modest results whereas other types are inexpensive and produce large benefits. Particularly in sub-Saharan Africa where resources are very scarce, it is important to allocate government expenditure on health services so as to maximize the returns. In general this implies favouring preventive health programmes, primary health care centres, mother and child nutrition programmes and pre- and post-natal maternity services and family planning programmes. In practice, however, government health expenditure pyramids often are inverted: most of the funds are allocated to the less beneficial activities while those with high returns are starved of resources. Large urban hospitals in particular absorb a disproportionate amount of the budget, to the neglect of primary health centres in the rural areas and preventive programmes in general. The overall impact of investments in health could be increased substantially if funds were better allocated.

Consider next government-financed investment in physical capital. There is an enormous need in sub-Saharan Africa for investment in

infrastructure, in both rural and urban areas. Much public investment at present, however, uses relatively capital intensive methods of
production (which require imported equipment), relies on large, well
established contractors (and thus excludes small and medium-sized
African-owned businesses) and even uses imported construction materials (which denies investment opportunities to local suppliers). The
result is that public investment is costly and the returns are rather low.
Numerous opportunities are overlooked to generate a large amount of
employment for low-skilled labour at very low wages, to encourage
the emergence and growth of small local contractors by providing a bit
of training and credit, and to foster a large, rapidly expanding local
construction materials industry.

The state can play a leading role in mobilizing domestic resources
for investment. The key is the organization of labour intensive public
investment projects. Such projects can generate a lot of employment
both during the construction phase and in maintenance activities.
They can help to economize on the use of foreign exchange by reducing the demand for imported capital equipment and construction
materials and hence they can help to ease the severe balance of payments constraint on development. And, if procurement and bid ten-
dering policies are revised, that can encourage saving and investment
in the private sector, directly in the construction and building materials industries and indirectly in industries which support construction
activities (e.g. transport) and supply wage goods to construction workers (clothing, footwear, processed food, etc.).

Moreover, labour intensive public investment in infrastructure can
be used to improve the distribution of income by choosing projects
whose benefits accrue more than proportionately to the poor. Examples
include the provision of water, drainage and sewerage facilities in the
poorest neighbourhoods of large cities, construction of schools, health
clinics and civic buildings in small towns and the rural areas, and giving priority to investment in farm-to-market roads and rural electrifica-
tion rather than to major highways and to providing more power
stations in the large cities. The combination of high labour intensity of
construction and selection of investment projects to benefit the poor
can do much to reduce poverty and inequality in sub-Saharan Africa.

Where it is practicable to do so, user fees and charges should be
levied to enable the state to recover its costs of investment and maintenance. When given the choice between services plus modest user fees,
on the one hand, and no services and no charges, on the other, the evidence suggests that the poor are willing to pay fees for services that

genuinely improve their lives. Thus a large public investment programme in sub-Saharan Africa could be inexpensive (in so far as it concentrates on mobilizing abundant low-skilled labour and pays a low
wage) and it could also be partly self-financing (by imposing user fees
to recover costs).

Finally, let us consider the role that could be played by state-owned
enterprises in financing structural adjustment through investment. In
many parts of sub-Saharan Africa the formal sector consists largely of
the public administration and public sector enterprises. Private formal
sector activity in comparison is very small. State enterprises, however,
typically operate at a loss, in part because they are seen as providing an
essential service (e.g. telephone services), in part because they are used
to increase distributive equity (e.g. subsidized public transport) and in
part because the revenues of state enterprises have been diverted from
their proper purposes. Whatever the causes may be, the deficits of state
enterprises have contributed to the economic crisis in Africa and have
propelled the economy along a path of structural adjustment through
contraction.

The deficits of state enterprises are a form of negative savings. They
constitute a drain on the resources available for productive investment
and for this reason the state enterprises as presently organized are a
major obstacle to structural adjustment through investment. This
obstacle must be removed.

There are two ways to do this. First, the state can dispose of the state
enterprises through gift or sale. This is known as 'privatization' and is
widely recommended. There are, however, several difficulties with this
approach. If after transfer to the private sector the ex-state enterprises
continue to operate at a loss, there will be demands for state subsidies
and various forms of protection to cover the losses. Negative savings
will persist and the drain on the economy will continue; the change in
the form of ownership will make no difference to the macroeconomic
performance of the economy. Moreover, if the transfer of ownership
occurs through gift or through sale at less than full market value, some
individuals, namely the new owners of the enterprise, will become
enriched at the expense of the general public. This almost certainly
will result in a more unequal distribution of income and wealth.
Furthermore, if the state uses the receipts from the sale of state enterprises to reduce its current operating deficit rather than to reinvest in
other more productive activities, the rate of investment in the economy actually could fall. Capital assets, in effect, would be transformed
into current consumption.

These undesirable consequences of privatization can be avoided if (a) state enterprises are sold at their full market value, (b) the sales proceeds are used by the government to finance other kinds of investment and (c) the newly privatized companies are allowed to go bankrupt if they are unable to operate at a profit. These are stringent conditions for the success of a privatization programme and few if any countries in sub-Saharan Africa have met them. None the less, countries continue to be advised to adopt privatization programmes, on the grounds that this sends an attractive 'signal' to domestic and foreign investors that the economic climate has improved. A better signal than inefficient privatization, however, would be evidence of a reformed policy regime and abundant investment opportunities.

The alternative to privatization is the 'commercialization' of state enterprises. Rather than sell loss-making enterprises, or give them away, this approach concentrates on reforming the state enterprises: separating the firms from ministerial control so that they become independent entities, transforming the managers of state enterprises from civil servants to commercially minded businessmen, or if necessary replacing them; introducing profit making as the principal objective of the firms; subjecting them to greater competition by eliminating barriers to entry; and if all else fails, allowing them to become bankrupt.

The assumption of course is that reform is possible, that commercialization of the state enterprises would produce high returns for the government in the form of a steady flow of profits which could be used to finance investment in the state enterprises themselves, in labour intensive infrastructure and in human capital. If this happened, the state enterprises, far from being an obstacle to structural adjustment, would become a major source of finance for development. If, however, state enterprises turn out to be incorrigible – a herd of white elephants causing havoc, trampling crops and threatening life and limb – then indeed privatization might be the better solution. In extreme instances some state enterprises might not be viable under a sensible structure of incentives. That is, neither commercialization nor privatization would result in a profitable outcome. In such instances the only alternative is to sell the firm for its scrap value. But it is premature to come to such pessimistic conclusions.

The optimistic view is that public investment can be the leading sector in structural adjustment in sub-Saharan Africa and, because of complementarities with the private sector, can stimulate a rise in aggregate saving and investment and in the overall rate of growth. This approach presupposes reform of the state enterprises which transforms them into a source of profit, the organization of a large labour intensive investment programme in physical infrastructure and an inversion of the expenditure pyramid for education and health in order to increase the returns on investment in human capital. This three-pronged initiative should be feasible in the conditions that beset sub-Saharan Africa and, if successfully implemented, could transform for the better the lives of millions of desperately poor people.

# 8
# Domestic Resource Mobilization and Enterprise Development in Sub-Saharan Africa

*with Mark D. Brenner*

Since the early 1980s much of sub-Saharan Africa has been in the throes of economic crisis. Growth rates in real terms have remained stubbornly low or negative, real income per capita has fallen precipitously and despite repeated reassurances that prosperity was just around the corner, stabilization and structural adjustment policies have not delivered Africa from its misery. Humbled by this recent history, many are now seeking answers for why orthodox economic policy has failed to live up to its claims, and an active research effort is under way to find alternative solutions to the persistent problems of poverty and low levels of human development that afflict so much of Africa. This chapter should be seen as a contribution to the search for more effective policies. Specifically, we propose to analyse the questions of domestic resource mobilization and enterprise development in sub-Saharan Africa, within the context of an investment-led strategy for structural adjustment.[1]

Our work proceeds as follows. In the first section we briefly summarize the logic of stabilization and structural adjustment and develop the concept of investment-led structural adjustment which will serve as the organizing framework for the remainder of the chapter. In the second we identify and discuss the external sources for financing such an investment-led strategy. We find much evidence to support the belief that Africa is unlikely to achieve desired rates of growth of output and of human development based on external sources of finance. Hence we next begin to consider domestic sources of finance for such a strategy. We start by considering the role of the private sector. Specific attention is paid to the role of private savings and its relationship to the investment decision. In addition we underline the considerable possibilities for mobilizing household labour. Then we consider the public sector. Here we analyse the controversial issue of the size of the public sector and we discuss the possibilities for 'crowding-in' due to complementarities between the public and private sectors. In the fifth section we discuss the informal sector and its role in enterprise development. Then we turn to some possible programmatic elements of an investment-led strategy. Access to technical training and credit are given much consideration, as is the financing of housing as a productive asset. In addition policies such as targeted credit schemes, guaranteed employment programmes and the 'commercialization' of state-owned enterprises are considered. Finally, we present our concluding remarks.

## Stabilization, structural adjustment and an investment-led strategy

Many concerned with the acute and increasing hardship in Africa, particularly external advisors and international financial agencies, have recommended policies of stabilization and structural adjustment. It is in the context of these policies that Africa now operates, for better or worse, and from which our analysis emerges. However, these policies are not unambiguous and thus a brief statement of what we mean by stabilization and structural adjustment is provided below.

### Stabilization

The primary purpose of stabilization policies is to restore macroeconomic balance. This includes the price level, the public sector's revenue and expenditure accounts and the external trading account. Imbalances may be due to high and possibly accelerating inflation, to large and possibly increasing balance of payments deficits or to large public sector deficits, including the deficits of state-owned enterprises. Policy recommendations centre around lowering levels of aggregate demand, so that spending corresponds more closely to the economy's production potential, as well as lowering inflationary expectations with 'credible' anti-inflationary measures by the government. Specific policy recommendations may include such things as a reduction in the money supply and an increase in nominal interest rates; reductions in government expenditure; privatization of state-owned enterprises; and unification of exchange rates and currency devaluation. Much can be said about these objectives, their translation into specific policies and their relevance to the African context. For the purposes of this chapter, however, such issues are left unaddressed and we move on to a consideration of structural adjustment.[2]

## Structural adjustment

Structural adjustment policies serve three principal purposes. First and foremost, they are designed to induce a substantial change in the composition of domestic output, primarily through shifts in the structure of relative prices. Second, they are intended to integrate countries more fully into the global economy. Third, structural adjustment policies are intended to raise the rate of investment and simultaneously improve its allocation, resulting in increasing rates of growth of output, incomes and employment.

While on the surface it may seem obvious, the purpose of changing the composition of domestic output deserves more elaboration. Indeed, we see three pathways along which structural adjustment can alter the composition of output, each with dramatically different implications for the economy. The first path underlies, explicitly or implicitly, most neoclassical policy prescriptions in developing countries. It is assumed that the existing stocks of productive assets can be reallocated relatively easily among the various sectors, in order to reflect more accurately domestic factor endowments and relative world prices. In the neoclassical parable, this path corresponds to shifts along a given 'production possibilities frontier' in response to changes in the relative prices of final products. This shift is assumed to be frictionless and rapid and consequently resources remain fully utilized and adjustment is achieved without significant lags. In the second path, certain conditions inhibit the frictionless shifts associated with the first path. This is the path most representative of the African experience, and can be called structural adjustment through contraction. Here, the specificity of much human and physical capital, combined with factor price rigidities, serve to inhibit the utilization of newly freed resources in the now more attractive sector, and consequently there is a reduction of aggregate demand that pulls the country inside its 'production frontier'. The manufacturing sector in Kano, Nigeria serves as an illuminating example of such an adjustment process. Adebayo Olukoshi reports that in July 1992 capacity utilization in manufacturing was as low as 35 per cent and no higher than 60 per cent in the firms surveyed, with 78 per cent of the manufacturers operating below 50 per cent of capacity.[3] Table 8.1 depicts the sectoral composition of these capacity utilization figures.

Finally, there is the third pathway for changing the composition of domestic output, namely, investment-led structural adjustment.

*Table 8.1*   Manufacturing capacity utilization in Kano, Nigeria, July 1992 (subsectoral average[4])

| Subsector | Capacity utilization (%) |
| --- | --- |
| Leather tanning and processing | 51 |
| Plastic, plastic products, including footwear | 45 |
| Soap, perfumes, toiletries and cosmetics | 48 |
| Mineral water, packaged juices, beer and spirits | 41 |
| Food, beverages and vegetable oil | 60 |
| Paper, paper products and stationery | 43 |
| Foam and rubber products, including rubber footwear | 40 |
| Glass products | 35 |
| Electrical and communication equipment | 38 |
| Cardboard packaging materials, suitcases | 41 |
| Miscellaneous manufactured products | 44 |
| Metal processing and fabrication | 41 |
| Motor vehicle and assembly, spare parts | 45 |
| Textiles, weaving, knitting, spinning | 42 |
| Steel and steel products | 36 |
| Candles, paints, pharmaceuticals, batteries, chemicals | 45 |
| Sweets and confectionery | 49 |
| Burnt bricks, floor and wall tiles, ceramic ware | 60 |
| Cement, asbestos, concrete products | 54 |
| Wood processing and wooden products | 48 |
| Enamelware and aluminium products | 46 |

*Source*: Adebayo Olukoshi, *Economic Crisis, Structural Adjustment and The Coping Strategies of Manufacturers in Kano, Nigeria*, UNRISD Discussion Paper 77, September 1996.

Along this path, structural adjustment is seen as part of a general growth strategy for the entire economy, one which seeks to increase investment in physical, human and natural capital. An important element of a general growth strategy should be to ensure that investment is channelled into activities which have become more profitable as a result of changes in the structure of incentives. Rather than the high unemployment and falling real incomes so typical of adjustment through contraction, investment-led adjustment can result in rising real incomes and accelerated growth of gross domestic product. Furthermore, as the Chinese and Vietnamese transition experiences demonstrate, this can be accomplished with the simultaneous expansion of all sectors of the economy, albeit at different rates.[5] In terms of the neoclassical parable, this is equivalent to an expansion of the 'production possibilities frontier'. It is this path of adjustment which we take as most desirable, and which informs the following discussion.

## Financing investment-led adjustment: external sources

Foreign advisors and aid donors are not ignorant of the need to increase dramatically the rate of investment in sub-Saharan Africa. Indeed, they have sometimes seen themselves, and other external actors such as multinational corporations, as central to the process. There are problems with such a logic, which we explore in the following two subsections. We find, first, that foreign aid, even in relatively large amounts (whether expressed in per capita terms or as a percentage of GNP), has failed to spur overall investment, and, second, that foreign direct investment has not been forthcoming. Much of this can be attributed to problems internal to the countries of sub-Saharan Africa, but we also believe that to an important degree the problem resides in the inverted nature of the neoclassical logic.

African governments typically are offered specific assistance and unspecific hopes, namely, structural and sectoral adjustment loans by the international financial institutions to assist during the transition associated with resource reallocation, and the hope that foreign direct investment will follow, presumably attracted by profit opportunities associated with domestic restructuring and specific stabilization and structural adjustment policies. Indeed, the relationship between the two is critical to the logic of the neoclassical approach. It is implicitly assumed that 'getting prices right', along with other specific policies that accompany structural adjustment loans, will be sufficient to produce a structure of incentives that will attract foreign investment (often in export-oriented activities), which will then contribute to faster growth of the economy. Such an approach also assumes implicitly that adjustment follows the relatively frictionless path of resource reallocation, and thus structural and sectoral adjustment loans become part of the construction of a 'safety net' to alleviate the worst forms of hardship during the transition. These two assumptions, both incorrect in our view, reflect a misdiagnosis of the problem. In what follows we attempt to explain why that is the case, and to assess the ability of foreign aid and private foreign direct investment to finance the investment-led adjustment which we advocate. We begin with a consideration of foreign aid.

### Official development assistance

Foreign aid, or official development assistance (ODA), has been widely viewed as a critical element in the adjustment process. Indeed, structural adjustment loans have proliferated, and ODA has been abundant in many respects. Consider, for example, Table 8.2, which contains estimates of ODA per capita for three periods since 1980.[6] For the 38 countries where data are available, overall ODA per capita has risen from an average of $45.82 in the period 1980–85 to $71.71 in 1991–94, or by more than 56 per cent. In a region where many countries' per capita incomes fall well below $500 these numbers are not insignificant. Moreover, while not uniformly the case, this upward trend in

*Table 8.2*  Overseas development assistance per person (annual average in US dollars)

| Country | 1980–85 | 1986–90 | 1991–94 |
|---|---|---|---|
| Angola | n.a. | n.a. | n.a. |
| Benin | 22.81 | 42.88 | 53.82 |
| Botswana | 103.70 | 122.31 | 86.03 |
| Burkina Faso | 31.50 | 34.61 | 45.80 |
| Burundi | 29.87 | 40.47 | 46.53 |
| Cameroon | 20.36 | 29.25 | 50.55 |
| Cape Verde | 194.28 | 261.62 | 316.47 |
| Central African Republic | 41.98 | 66.46 | 54.95 |
| Chad | 19.46 | 43.90 | 39.73 |
| Comoros | 116.00 | 110.22 | 106.82 |
| Congo | 51.16 | 61.47 | 75.52 |
| Côte d'Ivoire | 7.94 | 42.90 | 71.14 |
| Djibouti | n.a. | n.a. | n.a. |
| Equatorial Guinea | n.a. | n.a. | n.a. |
| Eritrea | n.a. | n.a. | n.a. |
| Ethiopia | 8.52 | 16.81 | 21.30 |
| Gabon | 76.28 | 64.34 | 28.75 |
| Gambia | 73.87 | 115.70 | 92.02 |
| Ghana | 14.26 | 33.42 | 41.12 |
| Guinea | 16.51 | 47.85 | 64.69 |
| Guinea-Bissau | 72.24 | 108.61 | 122.45 |
| Kenya | 23.32 | 35.49 | 33.59 |
| Lesotho | 68.44 | 68.42 | 69.34 |
| Liberia | 53.99 | 34.19 | 41.43 |
| Madagascar | 20.25 | 30.55 | 29.34 |
| Malawi | 20.16 | 43.92 | 51.29 |
| Mali | 37.47 | 52.69 | 46.69 |
| Mauritania | 112.62 | 113.16 | 119.75 |
| Mauritius | 41.12 | 62.41 | 35.08 |
| Mayotte | n.a. | n.a. | n.a. |
| Mozambique | n.a. | n.a. | n.a. |
| Namibia | n.a. | n.a. | n.a. |
| Niger | 35.61 | 47.65 | 43.97 |

*Table 8.2*   (*Continued*)

| Country | 1980–85 | 1986–90 | 1991–94 |
|---|---|---|---|
| Nigeria | 0.41 | 1.53 | 2.39 |
| Reunion | n.a. | n.a. | n.a. |
| Rwanda | 28.66 | 37.34 | 59.60 |
| São Tomé and Principe | 89.63 | 241.62 | 428.95 |
| Senegal | 52.63 | 92.82 | 78.68 |
| Seychelles | n.a. | n.a. | n.a. |
| Sierra Leone | 20.03 | 21.40 | 41.03 |
| Somalia | n.a. | n.a. | n.a. |
| South Africa | n.a. | n.a. | n.a. |
| Sudan | 38.65 | 36.63 | 21.73 |
| Swaziland | 48.83 | 55.13 | 62.34 |
| Tanzania | 29.71 | 38.10 | 39.74 |
| Togo | 33.71 | 55.71 | 42.08 |
| Uganda | n.a. | n.a. | n.a. |
| Zaire | 12.45 | 19.08 | 7.20 |
| Zambia | 44.26 | 59.35 | 99.74 |
| Zimbabwe | 29.11 | 30.12 | 53.21 |

*Source*: Authors' calculations based on OECD, *Geographical Distribution of Financial Flows to Developing Countries*, Paris, various years.

ODA per person can be found in 25 of the 38 individual countries for which we have data.

An even more dramatic picture emerges from Table 8.3, which depicts ODA as a percentage of GNP for the three periods in question. For the 31 countries with available data, we record an average ODA as a percentage of GNP that rises from 13.75 per cent in the period 1980–85 to 15.80 per cent in the period 1986–90 and finally to 16.59 per cent in the period 1991–94.[7] That is, over the entire period the aid ratio increased by more than a fifth, from levels that already were high. Moreover, if all of the ODA had been productively invested, aid inflows alone would have been sufficient to finance a rapid rate of growth, even if domestic savings had been zero.

Unfortunately, however, these exceptionally high levels of ODA have not produced concomitant levels of growth or human development. In fact, for the 33 countries for which data are available, the simple average rate of growth of GDP was roughly 2.3 per cent per annum during the period 1980–94. Furthermore, the United Nations Development Programme classifies 79 per cent of sub-Saharan African countries as experiencing 'low human development'.[8] More importantly, the large aid inflows have yet to result in the levels of investment that are

*Table 8.3*   ODA as a percentage of GNP (annual average)

| Country | 1980–85 | 1986–90 | 1991–94 |
|---|---|---|---|
| Angola | n.a. | n.a. | n.a. |
| Benin | 8.08 | 11.68 | 14.42 |
| Botswana | 12.74 | 8.04 | 3.18 |
| Burkina Faso | 17.36 | 12.32 | 15.65 |
| Burundi | 13.17 | 18.70 | 26.62 |
| Cameroon | 2.66 | 2.91 | 6.63 |
| Cape Verde | 61.54 | 38.75 | 37.73 |
| Central African Republic | 15.12 | 17.67 | 15.00 |
| Chad | n.a. | n.a. | n.a. |
| Comoros | 34.66 | 24.43 | 20.87 |
| Congo | 4.82 | 6.67 | 8.59 |
| Côte d'Ivoire | 2.07 | 4.30 | 12.30 |
| Djibouti | n.a. | n.a. | n.a. |
| Equatorial Guinea | n.a. | n.a. | n.a. |
| Eritrea | n.a. | n.a. | n.a. |
| Ethiopia | 7.69 | 14.14 | 16.56 |
| Gabon | 1.83 | 3.23 | 2.87 |
| Gambia | 26.39 | 49.17 | 26.14 |
| Ghana | 3.68 | 8.80 | 11.10 |
| Guinea | 5.43 | 11.60 | 13.52 |
| Guinea-Bissau | 43.19 | 65.77 | 56.84 |
| Kenya | 7.08 | 10.09 | 12.28 |
| Lesotho | 14.29 | 15.44 | 10.92 |
| Liberia | n.a. | n.a. | n.a. |
| Madagascar | 7.13 | 12.90 | 13.92 |
| Malawi | 12.16 | 25.53 | 29.26 |
| Mali | 24.49 | 21.47 | 17.46 |
| Mauritania | 26.14 | 24.24 | 25.45 |
| Mauritius | 3.89 | 3.43 | 1.24 |
| Mayotte | n.a. | n.a. | n.a. |
| Mozambique | n.a. | n.a. | n.a. |
| Namibia | n.a. | n.a. | n.a. |
| Niger | 14.79 | 16.44 | 17.62 |
| Nigeria | 0.05 | 0.62 | 0.87 |
| Reunion | n.a. | n.a. | n.a. |
| Rwanda | 10.94 | 11.55 | 31.96 |
| São Tomé and Principe | n.a. | n.a. | n.a. |
| Senegal | 13.06 | 14.48 | 12.02 |
| Seychelles | n.a. | n.a. | n.a. |
| Sierra Leone | 6.86 | 8.81 | 25.26 |
| Somalia | n.a. | n.a. | n.a. |
| South Africa | n.a. | n.a. | n.a. |
| Sudan | n.a. | n.a. | n.a. |
| Swaziland | 6.21 | 6.54 | 5.51 |

*Table 8.3*   (*Continued*)

| Country | 1980–85 | 1986–90 | 1991–94 |
|---------|---------|---------|---------|
| Tanzania | n.a. | n.a. | n.a. |
| Togo | 14.54 | 14.95 | 11.93 |
| Uganda | n.a. | n.a. | n.a. |
| Zaire | n.a. | n.a. | n.a. |
| Zambia | n.a. | n.a. | n.a. |
| Zimbabwe | 4.03 | 5.04 | 10.46 |

*Source*: Authors' calculations based on OECD, *Geographical Distribution of Financial Flows to Developing Countries*, Paris, various years.

necessary to move the process of adjustment along any path other than that of contraction. This is in part due to inappropriate government policies which have directed foreign capital inflows to the financing of current public and private expenditures. It is remarkable, for instance, that between 1980 and 1994 government and private consumption increased as a proportion of GDP in sub-Saharan Africa while the weighted savings rate fell in the same period from 27 to 16 per cent.[9] Low levels of investment are also in part due to the curious logic of adjustment embodied in the neoclassical orthodoxy.

By assuming a relatively frictionless reallocation of resources in the process of adjustment, economic hardship appears, at worst, to be a temporary by-product of the process. This necessitates, at most, the construction of a 'safety net' to alleviate the worst aspects of the transition. Such an outlook appears to have engendered a certain amount of complacency about current expenditure patterns, resting on the neoclassical faith that restoring macroeconomic balance and 'getting prices right' will provide sufficient incentives for an increase in domestic savings and foreign direct investment. An implicit assumption of frictionless adjustment excludes the possibility of adjustment through contraction, as well as the severe, long-term human distress that accompanies it, and hence the approach ignores the fact that the resources required to construct an effective safety net in the face of such distress are immense, precisely at a time of dwindling available resources. Indeed, more than a safety net, we find Africa in need of a different path of adjustment.

### Foreign direct investment

A second important element in the neoclassical adjustment strategy is foreign direct investment (FDI). FDI, along with ODA, is often thought to help close the gap between domestic savings, both public and private, and the desired level of domestic investment. This logic, as alluded to above, holds that domestic adjustment, through 'getting prices right' and other specific policies, will create incentives sufficient to attract FDI. Moreover, foreign capital is frequently seen as a critical link to international technology and world markets, as well as a complement to, rather than competitor with, domestic capital formation. Consequently, it is regularly described, uncritically in our view, as beneficial to the receiving country. In this subsection we set aside questions of the desirability of or benefit from FDI and instead concern ourselves with the more narrow question of whether FDI will be adequate to meet the needs of an investment-led adjustment process in sub-Saharan Africa.

The first measure of this adequacy which we will consider is an estimate of FDI per capita for three periods since 1980. In considering Table 8.4, which contains these estimates, it must first be noted that

*Table 8.4*   Foreign direct investment per person (annual average in US dollars)

| Country | 1980–85 | 1986–90 | 1991–94 |
|---|---|---|---|
| Angola | n.a. | n.a. | n.a. |
| Benin | 0.11 | 0.11 | 0.70 |
| Botswana | −8.96 | −1.76 | 7.77 |
| Burkina Faso | −0.07 | 0.09 | 0.45 |
| Burundi | 0.42 | 0.09 | −0.11 |
| Cameroon | 3.91 | 1.31 | −0.85 |
| Cape Verde | n.a. | n.a. | n.a. |
| Central African Republic | n.a. | n.a. | n.a. |
| Chad | n.a. | n.a. | n.a. |
| Comoros | n.a. | n.a. | n.a. |
| Congo | −3.28 | 2.33 | 16.76 |
| Côte d'Ivoire | 1.73 | 1.07 | 1.68 |
| Djibouti | n.a. | n.a. | n.a. |
| Equatorial Guinea | n.a. | n.a. | n.a. |
| Eritrea | n.a. | n.a. | n.a. |
| Ethiopia | n.a. | n.a. | n.a. |
| Gabon | 59.58 | 65.35 | 41.40 |
| Gambia | n.a. | n.a. | n.a. |
| Ghana | 0.33 | 1.12 | 2.32 |
| Guinea | n.a. | n.a. | n.a. |
| Guinea-Bissau | n.a. | n.a. | n.a. |
| Kenya | 0.35 | 2.01 | 1.72 |
| Lesotho | n.a. | n.a. | n.a. |
| Liberia | n.a. | n.a. | n.a. |
| Madagascar | 0.19 | 0.49 | 0.03 |

*Table 8.4*   (*Continued*)

| Country | 1980–85 | 1986–90 | 1991–94 |
|---|---|---|---|
| Malawi | 0.40 | 1.60 | 0.70 |
| Mali | 0.07 | −0.14 | 0.38 |
| Mauritania | −0.92 | −0.04 | −0.07 |
| Mauritius | 3.72 | 10.67 | −2.59 |
| Mayotte | n.a. | n.a. | n.a. |
| Mozambique | n.a. | n.a. | n.a. |
| Namibia | n.a. | n.a. | n.a. |
| Niger | −0.34 | 1.56 | 0.13 |
| Nigeria | 1.23 | 2.46 | 3.72 |
| Reunion | n.a. | n.a. | n.a. |
| Rwanda | 0.19 | 0.25 | 0.33 |
| São Tomé and Principe | n.a. | n.a. | n.a. |
| Senegal | 0.35 | 0.25 | 2.08 |
| Seychelles | n.a. | n.a. | n.a. |
| Sierra Leone | n.a. | n.a. | n.a. |
| Somalia | n.a. | n.a. | n.a. |
| South Africa | n.a. | n.a. | n.a. |
| Sudan | n.a. | n.a. | n.a. |
| Swaziland | n.a. | n.a. | n.a. |
| Tanzania | n.a. | n.a. | n.a. |
| Togo | −0.05 | −0.22 | 0.33 |
| Uganda | n.a. | n.a. | n.a. |
| Zaire | n.a. | n.a. | n.a. |
| Zambia | n.a. | n.a. | n.a. |
| Zimbabwe | n.a. | n.a. | n.a. |

*Source*: Authors' calculations based on OECD, *Geographical Distribution of Financial Flows to Developing Countries*, Paris, various years.

relatively few of the countries in sub-Saharan Africa have data available on FDI. This, along with the fact that measurement of FDI is often a more complicated and contentious issue than ODA for example, implies that these data should be interpreted with caution. For the 20 countries for which data are available, overall FDI per capita has risen steadily, from an average of $2.95 in the period 1980–85 to $4.43 in the period 1986–90 to $7.38 in the period 1991–94. Despite these minuscule absolute values of FDI per capita, the averages present a misleading picture of the importance of direct investment in a typical country in sub-Saharan Africa because of the concentration of direct investment in Gabon. Indeed, 14 of the 20 countries for which we have data never achieved a level of FDI per capita as large as the average for 1980–85, the period when average inflows were smallest at $2.95. In addition, half the countries where data are available have at least one period where flows of direct investment were negative, representing a net outflow of productive resources. Finally, a word must be said about the upward trend of these three period averages. This too is misleading because in only 7 of the 20 countries under consideration did FDI per capita increase steadily over the three periods.

An exercise perhaps even more revealing is to put the levels of FDI in the context of the national economies of the region, using FDI as a percentage of GNP as one measure. Table 8.5 contains these figures for the

*Table 8.5*  Foreign direct investment as a percentage of GNP (annual average)

| Country | 1980–85 | 1986–90 | 1991–94 |
|---|---|---|---|
| Angola | n.a. | n.a. | n.a. |
| Benin | 0.04 | 0.03 | 0.19 |
| Botswana | −1.11 | −0.12 | 0.29 |
| Burkina Faso | −0.04 | 0.03 | 0.15 |
| Burundi | 0.18 | 0.04 | −0.06 |
| Cameroon | 0.51 | 0.13 | −0.11 |
| Cape Verde | n.a. | n.a. | n.a. |
| Central African Republic | n.a. | n.a. | n.a. |
| Chad | n.a. | n.a. | n.a. |
| Comoros | n.a. | n.a. | n.a. |
| Congo | −0.31 | 0.25 | 1.91 |
| Côte d'Ivoire | 0.45 | 0.11 | 0.29 |
| Djibouti | n.a. | n.a. | n.a. |
| Equatorial Guinea | n.a. | n.a. | n.a. |
| Eritrea | n.a. | n.a. | n.a. |
| Ethiopia | n.a. | n.a. | n.a. |
| Gabon | 1.43 | 3.29 | 4.14 |
| Gambia | n.a. | n.a. | n.a. |
| Ghana | 0.08 | 0.29 | 0.63 |
| Guinea | n.a. | n.a. | n.a. |
| Guinea-Bissau | n.a. | n.a. | n.a. |
| Kenya | 0.11 | 0.57 | 0.63 |
| Lesotho | n.a. | n.a. | n.a. |
| Liberia | n.a. | n.a. | n.a. |
| Madagascar | 0.07 | 0.21 | 0.01 |
| Malawi | 0.24 | 0.93 | 0.40 |
| Mali | 0.05 | −0.06 | 0.14 |
| Mauritania | −0.21 | −0.01 | −0.01 |
| Mauritius | 0.35 | 0.59 | −0.09 |
| Mayotte | n.a. | n.a. | n.a. |
| Mozambique | n.a. | n.a. | n.a. |
| Namibia | n.a. | n.a. | n.a. |
| Niger | −0.14 | 0.54 | 0.05 |

*Table 8.5 (Continued)*

| Country | 1980–85 | 1986–90 | 1991–94 |
|---|---|---|---|
| Nigeria | 0.15 | 0.99 | 1.35 |
| Reunion | n.a. | n.a. | n.a. |
| Rwanda | 0.07 | 0.08 | 0.18 |
| São Tomé and Principe | n.a. | n.a. | n.a. |
| Senegal | 0.09 | 0.04 | 0.32 |
| Seychelles | n.a. | n.a. | n.a. |
| Sierra Leone | n.a. | n.a. | n.a. |
| Somalia | n.a. | n.a. | n.a. |
| South Africa | n.a. | n.a. | n.a. |
| Sudan | n.a. | n.a. | n.a. |
| Swaziland | n.a. | n.a. | n.a. |
| Tanzania | n.a. | n.a. | n.a. |
| Togo | − 0.02 | − 0.06 | 0.09 |
| Uganda | n.a. | n.a. | n.a. |
| Zaire | n.a. | n.a. | n.a. |
| Zambia | n.a. | n.a. | n.a. |
| Zimbabwe | n.a. | n.a. | n.a. |

*Source*: Authors' calculations based on OECD, *Geographical Distribution of Financial Flows to Developing Countries*, Paris, various years.

20 countries for which data are available. Here we see that on average FDI was 0.1 per cent of GNP during the period 1980–85; it rose to 0.39 per cent of GNP during the period 1986–90 and reached a level of 0.49 per cent of GNP in the period 1991–94. As before, these numbers indicate the relatively minor role that direct investment has played in the adjustment process. Indeed, in over half the countries for which data are available FDI never rose above 0.5 per cent of GNP. As with FDI per person, the apparent upward trend is representative only of a minority of the countries in question, with 8 out of 20 countries demonstrating an upward trend. Moreover, in three of these eight countries the initial period was negative, depicting a net capital outflow which improved over the two subsequent periods.

Thus, as these figures along with those from Table 8.4 indicate, foreign direct investment has not contributed in any significant way to the adjustment process in sub-Saharan Africa, nor can we expect it to do so in future. On the contrary, we find much to support the argument that, rather than leading increased rates of growth in GDP, foreign investment tends to follow them. Thus, it is an economy which is already on a path of sustained high growth which is able to attract significant levels of direct investment. In 1988, for example, nearly

79 per cent of foreign direct investment was located in the developed countries; little more than 21 per cent went to the developing countries. Moreover, within the developing countries, just five – China, Indonesia, Malaysia, South Korea and Thailand – accounted for most of the FDI. The countries of attraction do of course vary from time to time, but the evidence is pretty clear: 'foreign investment tends to be attracted to the relatively better off and more rapidly growing countries. The poorer the country and the lower its rate of growth, the less likely it will be able to attract foreign capital – unless of course it happens to possess a rich source of raw materials.'[10] It is for these reasons that we believe that in sub-Saharan Africa, private foreign direct investment is more likely to be a consequence of a successful structural adjustment strategy than a cause of it.

## Domestic financing for investment-led adjustment: the private sector

Thus it is likely that the financing of an investment-led strategy of adjustment will come primarily from domestic resources. In this section we explore some possibilities for increasing private sector savings, including possibilities for financing investment by mobilizing surplus household labour. In the following section we will consider the role of the public sector.

Gross domestic savings in sub-Saharan Africa are a lower percentage of gross domestic product than in any other developing region of the world. Such a situation clearly is incompatible with an investment-led strategy of structural adjustment and measures to mobilize resources for capital accumulation therefore deserve high priority. There is no simple formula for increasing savings, but there are a few cases where rapid progress might be possible. Too often, however, these opportunities are overlooked because they fall slightly outside conventional ways of thinking. Let us consider four examples.[11]

First, in some instances a judicious and discriminating rise in expenditures conventionally classified as consumption would result in a rise in output. For instance, increased food consumption among the very poor and those suffering from malnutrition, more extensive preventive health measures and expenditure on certain types of training and education (discussed below) can result in greater energy and morale, fewer days lost from work as a result of illness and higher productivity as a result of greater skills. These expenditures should be regarded as forms of human capital formation rather than current consumption.

Second, it sometimes is possible to increase investment not only by reducing unproductive consumption but also by reducing the amount of idle or unproductive labour time. Often labour is poorly utilized and in some areas seasonal unemployment is severe. Thus low-skilled labour power is not scarce but instead is waiting to be mobilized for development.[12] Experience shows that this 'surplus' labour can be organized and that it can be used to 'finance' capital formation in rural areas. Indeed we discuss at some length below a guaranteed employment programme intended to accelerate investment. It is also important to recognize, however, that 'slack' labour at the household level can in principle be used to undertake small, labour intensive investment projects. Whether on large public works schemes or on small household projects, additional investment and faster growth can be achieved by working longer and harder, and this need not imply a reduction in current consumption.

Third, in many instances 'savings' depend on the profitability of investment and will increase readily when investment opportunities arise. It often is incorrect to assume that in sub-Saharan Africa household savings and investment are two separate decisions taken by separate groups in the community. Most simple models are based on the assumption that it is households which save and firms which invest, and these two independent decisions are reconciled by the capital market through variations in the rate of interest and level of income.

In many African countries, however, savings and investment are interdependent and there is no capital market, or only a rather rudimentary one, to bring the two groups together. In these conditions savings and investment become indistinguishable; they are the same thing. A small farmer accumulates capital in the form of livestock by not slaughtering as many of his animals as are born. A small businessman increases the size of his firm by diverting part of his cash flow into the purchase of equipment rather than spending it on consumption goods. In other words, many of those who save do so in order to invest, and in the absence of a desire to invest no savings would be forthcoming. This suggests that until credit markets are fully developed, one way of increasing saving is to increase incentives and opportunities to invest.

Finally, one must be careful not to assume that low-income households are unable to save because of their poverty and hence that policy makers should concentrate on medium and large enterprises and on the savings potential of upper-income groups. There are a number of studies, mostly from Asia, which show that in rural areas the distinction

between rich and poor households is less significant in explaining savings behaviour than the distinction between landless labourers and
cultivating households. A study in Haryana, India indicates that there
is no systematic relationship between the degree of inequality in rural
areas and the savings ratio.[13] Another study in the Indian Punjab and
in Haryana shows that there is no tendency for large farmers to save
proportionately more than medium and small farmers.[14] On the other
hand, numerous studies have shown that non-cultivating rural households save a negligible proportion of their income whereas cultivating
households, including secure tenants, save a significant amount. There
is a suggestion that in Indonesia the marginal and average savings ratio
varies positively with the proportion of total income originating from
owned land,[15] but most studies indicate that the savings rate of tenants
and small farmers are comparable with those of large farmers. Research
in Taiwan, for instance, reveals that the marginal savings rates of large
and small farmers are not significantly different.[16]

Experience in other parts of the world also demonstrates that small
farmers are able to achieve high rates of savings and investment. In
Colombia, for example, the coffee sector once dominated the economy
(until it was superseded by cocaine), employing a quarter of the agricultural workers and producing a similar proportion of agricultural output.[17] Coffee is grown by over 300 000 farmers, the vast majority of
whom are smallholders. Only 843 farms are larger than 50 hectares,
while nearly 110 000 farms are less than one hectare in size. The coffee
sector is completely and efficiently organized. Producers can market
their crop through their own Coffee Federation or through Federation-
supported cooperatives or by selling directly to private merchants. The
Federation maintains a support price for coffee, provides excellent
extension services and runs a research station. Credit is available
through the Banco Cafetero or the Caja Agrario. And the Federation
even owns ocean-going ships to export the crop worldwide. Colombia's
coffee commands a premium on the world market and the country's
small coffee farmers have no difficulty competing with coffee grown
on large plantations in Brazil, Guatemala, El Salvador, etc.

Africa, too, has relevant experience. Until the very end of the colonial period, African farmers in Kenya were prohibited from entering
cash crop export agriculture; their role under the colonial division of
labour was to grow food for domestic consumption; the lucrative crops
were reserved for large European (mostly British) farmers. When the
prohibition against coffee and tea cultivation was relaxed just before
independence, small African farmers quickly responded to the newly

created profit opportunities and almost overnight established a large, new sector of economic activity. Indeed between 1955 and 1964 the value of output from African smallholdings increased by 169 per cent.[18] Saving was not a constraint on development; when profitable investment opportunities were created, the production of coffee and tea increased dramatically. In Kenya, as elsewhere, the poor demonstrated that they are able to mobilize their own 'surplus' labour and to combine this with modest savings to undertake investment projects, provided of course that the structure of incentives is attractive.

## Domestic financing for investment-led adjustment: the public sector

Domestic private sector financing of investment-led adjustment, however, is only one part of the picture. Public sector financing of investment also has a large role to play in the adjustment process.[19] Indeed, public investment is essential for success because of the externalities and complementaries associated with it. There is much recent evidence that challenges the common assumption that public spending is competitive with or 'crowds out' private sector investment. Given the conditions that prevail in most of sub-Saharan Africa, the types of public expenditure we recommend are likely to be complementary to private sector investment, i.e. public expenditure is more likely to 'crowd in' than 'crowd out'.[20] This will be true of many forms of human capital investment (primary and secondary education, applied agricultural research, certain types of vocational training, and basic nutrition and health programmes) as well as investment in rural and urban infrastructure (power, water and drainage, and roads). These public expenditures are likely to enhance profitable opportunities for the private sector, and lead to higher rather than lower private sector 'savings'.

A separate issue from the size of the public sector investment programme is the debate about the appropriate size of the public sector as a whole. The conventional wisdom is that the public sector in Africa is too large, unwieldy, and should be reduced. This is not obvious from the basic facts on the size of the public sector, which are presented in Table 8.6. Two indicators are included in Table 8.6: total tax revenue as a percentage of GNP for 1980 and 1994 and total government expenditure as a percentage of GNP for 1980 and 1993. For those countries for which data are available, several things emerge. First, there is considerable variation within sub-Saharan Africa with regard to the size of the public sector. The range is from Uganda, where in 1980 tax

*Table 8.6*   Tax revenue and total central government expenditure (as a percentage of GNP)

| Country | Tax revenue | | Total expenditures | |
|---|---|---|---|---|
| | 1980 | 1994 | 1980 | 1993 |
| Angola | n.a. | n.a. | n.a. | n.a. |
| Benin | n.a. | n.a. | n.a. | n.a. |
| Botswana | 26.8 | 30.5 | 36.5 | 40.2 |
| Burkina Faso | 10.5 | 8.7 | 14.1 | n.a. |
| Burundi | 13.3 | n.a. | 21.7 | n.a. |
| Cameroon | 14.8 | 10.9 | 15.5 | 18.3 |
| Cape Verde | n.a. | n.a. | n.a. | n.a. |
| Central African Republic | 14.9 | n.a. | 21.9 | n.a. |
| Chad | n.a. | n.a. | n.a. | 32.0 |
| Comoros | n.a. | n.a. | n.a. | n.a. |
| Congo | 29.9 | n.a. | 54.6 | n.a. |
| Côte d'Ivoire | 22.2 | n.a. | 33.3 | n.a. |
| Djibouti | n.a. | n.a. | n.a. | n.a. |
| Equatorial Guinea | n.a. | n.a. | n.a. | n.a. |
| Eritrea | n.a. | n.a. | n.a. | n.a. |
| Ethiopia | 13.2 | 12.4 | n.a. | n.a. |
| Gabon | 26.1 | n.a. | 40.5 | 33.8 |
| Gambia | 21.0 | 22.1 | 33.7 | n.a. |
| Ghana | 6.4 | 13.1 | 10.9 | 21.0 |
| Guinea | n.a. | 12.6 | n.a. | 21.9 |
| Guinea-Bissau | n.a. | n.a. | n.a. | n.a. |
| Kenya | 19.8 | 22.4 | 26.1 | 28.9 |
| Lesotho | 14.7 | n.a. | 22.7 | 32.1 |
| Liberia | n.a. | n.a. | n.a. | n.a. |
| Madagascar | 13.1 | 8.5 | n.a. | 16.1 |
| Malawi | 18.1 | n.a. | 37.6 | n.a. |
| Mali | 9.6 | n.a. | 21.6 | n.a. |
| Mauritania | n.a. | n.a. | n.a. | n.a. |
| Mauritius | 18.5 | 20.0 | 27.4 | 22.2 |
| Mayotte | n.a. | n.a. | n.a. | n.a. |
| Mozambique | n.a. | n.a. | n.a. | n.a. |
| Namibia | n.a. | 30.7 | n.a. | 40.2 |
| Niger | 12.4 | n.a. | 18.7 | n.a. |
| Nigeria | n.a. | n.a. | n.a. | n.a. |
| Reunion | n.a. | n.a. | n.a. | n.a. |
| Rwanda | 11.0 | 11.6 | 14.3 | 31.9 |
| Sâo Tomé and Principe | n.a. | n.a. | n.a. | n.a. |
| Senegal | 21.5 | n.a. | 23.9 | n.a. |
| Seychelles | n.a. | n.a. | n.a. | n.a. |
| Sierra Leone | 15.2 | 15.2 | 29.8 | 23.0 |
| Somalia | n.a. | n.a. | n.a. | n.a. |
| South Africa | 21.4 | 24.7 | 23.1 | 32.6 |

*Table 8.6* (*Continued*)

| Country | Tax Revenue | | Total expenditures | |
|---------|------|------|------|------|
| | 1980 | 1994 | 1980 | 1993 |
| Sudan | n.a. | n.a. | n.a. | n.a. |
| Swaziland | n.a. | n.a. | n.a. | n.a. |
| Tanzania | 17.2 | n.a. | 28.8 | n.a. |
| Togo | 28.0 | n.a. | 31.9 | n.a. |
| Uganda | 3.0 | n.a. | 6.1 | n.a. |
| Zaire | n.a. | n.a. | n.a. | n.a. |
| Zambia | 25.0 | 10.6 | 40.0 | n.a. |
| Zimbabwe | 19.5 | n.a. | 35.3 | 36.2 |

*Source*: World Bank, *World Development Report*, New York: Oxford University Press, 1995 and 1996.

revenue and central government expenditures represented 3 and 6.1 per cent of GNP, respectively, to the Congo, where in the same year the figures are 29.9 and 54.6 per cent, respectively. Second, in virtually every country, tax revenues are significantly smaller than total government expenditures, and in Africa the gap appears to be larger than in many other developing countries and growing over time. This can be confirmed by examining Table 8.7, where similar data to those included in Table 8.6 are presented for several other developing and developed countries. The data in Tables 8.6 and 8.7 also permit a comparison of the relative size of the public sector in sub-Saharan Africa with other regions. The results of such a comparison are striking. For while on average the public sector in sub-Saharan Africa is larger than in most other developing regions, the difference is not very great. In neither 1980 nor 1994, the two years we are considering, did the average size of the public sector in sub-Saharan Africa exceed by more than 9 per cent the size of the public sector elsewhere.[21] This is true regardless of the indicator used, namely the tax/GNP ratio or the ratio of total central government expenditure to GNP. Moreover, on average the size of the public sector in the OECD countries is larger than in Africa, again regardless of the criterion used.

The data for the various regions as a whole are summarized in Table 8.8. It is evident that sub-Saharan Africa's public sector, although above average in size, is not markedly out of line with other developing areas, and is not large by OECD standards. A more instructive comparison would be between Africa today and some of the Asian countries during the period when they were laying the foundations for their rapid

*Table 8.7*    Tax revenue and total central government expenditure (as a percentage of GNP)

| Region or group | Tax revenue | | Total expenditures | |
|---|---|---|---|---|
| Country | 1980 | 1994 | 1980 | 1993 |
| Asia | | | | |
|   Indonesia | 21.1 | 16.3 | 23.1 | n.a. |
|   Korea, Republic of | 15.8 | 18.1 | 17.6 | 17.1 |
|   Malaysia | 24.4 | 22.5 | 29.6 | 26.7 |
|   Singapore | 18.2 | 17.1 | 20.8 | 19.7 |
|   Thailand | 13.3 | 17.0 | 19.0 | 16.3 |
| OECD | | | | |
|   Australia | 19.9 | 21.2 | 23.1 | 28.2 |
|   Austria | 32.2 | 33.7 | 37.7 | 39.7 |
|   Belgium | 42.1 | 42.8 | 51.3 | 50.9 |
|   Canada | 16.6 | 19.5 | 21.8 | 25.8 |
|   Denmark | 32.2 | 33.3 | 40.4 | 45.5 |
|   Finland | 25.5 | 29.6 | 28.6 | 44.5 |
|   France | 36.5 | 38.0 | 39.3 | 45.5 |
|   Germany | n.a. | 29.6 | n.a. | 33.6 |
|   Ireland | 31.8 | 39.2 | 46.5 | 47.0 |
|   Italy | 29.1 | 38.8 | 41.0 | 53.4 |
|   Japan | 11.0 | 17.8 | 18.4 | n.a. |
|   Netherlands | 44.0 | 44.7 | 52.7 | 53.9 |
|   New Zealand | 31.3 | 33.5 | 39.0 | 36.6 |
|   Norway | 38.6 | 37.0 | 39.2 | n.a. |
|   Portugal | 24.9 | 29.3 | 34.1 | 42.3 |
|   Spain | 22.4 | 30.1 | 27.0 | 35.1 |
|   Sweden | 30.2 | 31.7 | 39.5 | 53.9 |
|   Switzerland | 17.5 | 20.0 | 19.5 | n.a. |
|   United Kingdom | 30.6 | 31.7 | 38.2 | 43.4 |
|   United States | 18.3 | 18.5 | 21.7 | 23.8 |
| Central America | | | | |
|   Costa Rica | 17.6 | 22.8 | 26.3 | 26.7 |
|   El Salvador | 11.3 | 10.7 | 17.6 | 11.2 |
|   Guatemala | 8.8 | 6.8 | 14.4 | n.a. |
|   Honduras | 14.4 | n.a. | n.a. | n.a. |
|   Mexico | 14.8 | n.a. | 17.4 | n.a. |
|   Nicaragua | 21.6 | 28.8 | 32.3 | 39.5 |
|   Panama | 19.5 | 21.8 | 33.4 | 32.1 |
| South America | | | | |
|   Argentina | 10.5 | n.a. | 18.4 | n.a. |
|   Bolivia | n.a. | 12.1 | n.a. | 26.6 |
|   Brazil | 18.4 | 17.5 | 20.9 | 25.6 |
|   Chile | 26.6 | 19.1 | 29.1 | 22.6 |
|   Colombia | 10.4 | 14.4 | 13.5 | n.a. |
|   Ecuador | 12.9 | 14.9 | 15.0 | 15.4 |

*Table 8.7* (*Continued*)

| Region or group | Tax revenue | | Total expenditures | |
|---|---|---|---|---|
| Country | 1980 | 1994 | 1980 | 1993 |
| Paraguay | 9.7 | 9.0 | 9.8 | 13.0 |
| Peru | 16.5 | 13.7 | n.a. | n.a. |
| Uruguay | 21.8 | 31.7 | 22.7 | 29.2 |
| Venezuela | 18.9 | 15.4 | 18.7 | 19.2 |

*Source*: World Bank, *World Development Report*, New York: Oxford University Press, 1995 and 1996.

*Table 8.8* Regional averages for tax revenue and total central government expenditure (as a percentage of GNP)

| Region or group | Tax revenue | | Total expenditures | |
|---|---|---|---|---|
| | 1980 | 1994 | 1980 | 1993 |
| Sub-Saharan Africa | 17.3 | 16.9 | 26.8 | 28.7 |
| | (27) | (15) | (25) | (15) |
| Asia | 18.6 | 18.2 | 22.0 | 20.0 |
| | (5) | (5) | (5) | (4) |
| OECD | 28.1 | 31.0 | 34.7 | 41.4 |
| | (19) | (20) | (19) | (17) |
| Central America | 15.4 | 18.2 | 23.6 | 27.4 |
| | (7) | (5) | (6) | (4) |
| South America | 16.2 | 16.4 | 18.5 | 21.7 |
| | (9) | (9) | (8) | (7) |

*Note*: Values in parentheses represent the number of countries used in calculating the average.
*Source*: Authors' calculations based on World Bank, *World Development Report*, New York: Oxford University Press, 1995 and 1996.

growth, say Korea and Taiwan in the 1950s and 1960s.[22] In those countries a large, strong, development-promoting state in the early stages of expansion encouraged the growth of the private sector which ultimately resulted in a relative decline in the size of the public sector. A small state, in other words, was a consequence of rapid development, not a cause of it.

We thus call into question the notion that the African state is too large and is an obstacle to development. Next let us consider a more pressing issue, namely the composition of public spending. As we have noted, African nations are confronted by pervasive market failures that the private sector cannot overcome unaided. There is a need for the state to intervene to ensure that resources are allocated efficiently and in particular that investment in human and physical capital is directed towards areas which have the highest rates of return. In the context of education, for example, this implies that investment in primary education should be given priority over secondary and tertiary education, and rural education given higher priority than urban. Similarly for health, this implies a shift of investment in favour of preventative medicine and primary care, and away from curative medicine located in large urban hospitals. Similar considerations arise when considering allocations between categories, such as spending on the military as contrasted with social spending.

Finally, there is the question of the ability of the state in sub-Saharan Africa to design, implement and monitor an investment-led adjustment programme. Many assume that the state is incapable of managing such an investment programme for both narrow technical and broad political economy reasons. This view, however, may be too sweeping and too pessimistic. It is surely correct that a disintegrated state (Liberia, Somalia) or a rapidly decaying one (Zaire, Sudan) cannot possibly implement the development strategy we recommend, but it is equally true that such a state cannot implement an alternative strategy either, including *laissez-faire*. Cases of state disintegration or decay are the exception rather than the rule, however. Most states in sub-Saharan Africa are viable political entities with considerable development potential. Botswana, in fact, has achieved remarkable success by any standard. More generally, there is no *a priori* reason to assume that African states are fundamentally different from, say, the Korean or Taiwanese state and thus are incapable of adopting and successfully managing an investment-led development strategy.

## The informal sector

Since the pioneering study of the International Labour Office (ILO) on productive employment in Kenya, the importance of the informal sector to both enterprise development and economic growth has become widely acknowledged.[23] Indeed, a 1988 survey by the ILO in 17 sub-Saharan African countries indicated that, on average, the informal sector accounted for roughly 20 per cent of GDP in the countries studied, and was estimated to account for 59 per cent of sub-Saharan Africa's urban labour force.[24] No doubt the proportions are even higher today as a result of the 'informalization' of the economies of sub-Saharan

Africa. In both the urban and rural context, the informal sector has been simultaneously creative and diverse in its responses to the varied and changing economic environments of sub-Saharan Africa. Not surprisingly, this adaptability and dynamism of the informal sector is crucial to our understanding of the adjustment process. However, much of the analysis surrounding the informal sector has obfuscated both its heterogeneity and its position in the broader economic context. This has sometimes led not only to an inadequate understanding of its potentials and limitations, but more importantly to inappropriate policy recommendations. This is a pitfall we hope to avoid, both by clarifying several issues at the outset, as well as by illustrating our claims with empirical evidence.

### Heterogeneity and the definition of the informal sector

The first issue to address is the very definition of what constitutes 'informality', something we feel has invited much confusion. In addition to the standard dichotomy between those enterprises which participate in the prevalent legal and bureaucratic institutions and those that do not, enterprises and their activities have alternatively been designated as 'informal' based on such characteristics as size, individual incomes, and sectoral activity.[25] In the first instance, we find the dichotomous division of 'formal' versus 'informal' somewhat unhelpful in understanding the informal sector. Instead, we think it is more useful to conduct the analysis in terms of the *degree of participation* of firms in the established legal and bureaucratic institutions. Such an approach acknowledges the fact that there are heterogeneous and sometimes conflicting motives determining the participation of firms in these institutions, not simply the polar extremes that the dichotomous approach yields. Our approach also highlights the fact that varying degrees of participation in such institutions is ubiquitous across countries and firm sizes.[26] It is not a phenomenon restricted to the 'underdeveloped' economies or to fledgling, start-up enterprises. Thus, our approach induces a shift in focus which potentially allows a much richer understanding of firm behaviour.

Moreover, thinking about informality in terms of the degree of participation is not idle speculation on our part, as empirical evidence from both the developing and developed world reinforces our contention. For example, the ILO in its 1988 study of sub-Saharan Africa determined that more than 40 per cent of 'informal' firms in ten countries were paying registration fees and taxes, hardly the mark of a completely invisible and unregulated sector of the African economy.[27]

Similarly, Victor Tokman notes that the Ministry of Housing in Santiago, Chile reported that six out of ten new housing starts between 1984 and 1985 were unauthorized, i.e. they did not have the required formal permits. Most important though was the fact that this construction was largely centred in high-income areas of Santiago, and carried out by 'modern' firms which otherwise complied with labour laws and tax regulations.[28] Evidence from Bolivia also supports our contention that firms participate in varying degrees in the specific legal and bureaucratic institutions that confront them. As seen in Table 8.9, a significant number of 'informal' firms both registered with the tax authorities and (albeit fewer) paid their allotted taxes.

In the second instance, the income or size measures often used to identify 'informal' activities and firms are also problematic, as they are powerfully homogenizing, and often mask the rich, heterogeneous character of such activities or firms. For example, consider the question of markets. Within a particular sector, 'informal' producers or service providers of the same size operate in a variety of different markets, e.g. providing goods and services for a narrow, geographically contiguous area such as the neighbourhood, participating in city-wide or even regional markets, and producing intermediate goods in subcontracting or supply relations with other businesses. Paul Strassman's analysis of home-based enterprises, a specific issue to which we will return later, captures this heterogeneity with respect to markets.[29] Table 8.10 illustrates this point for Lima, Peru.

*Table 8.9*   Bolivian informal businesses registered in the RUC and number of taxpayer by city (1987)

| | Number of informal businesses | Number registered in the RUC | Percentage of total businesses | Number of taxpayers | Percentage of total businesses |
|---|---|---|---|---|---|
| Cochabamba | 43 328 | 22 785 | 52.50 | 3 578 | 19.04 |
| La Paz | 154 188 | 90 352 | 58.60 | 18 029 | 15.70 |
| Oruro | 21 401 | 15 315 | 71.56 | 2 985 | 19.95 |
| Potosí | 10 673 | 5 434 | 50.91 | 1 227 | 22.58 |
| Santa Cruz | 87 945 | 25 018 | 28.45 | 3 940 | 15.75 |
| Sucre | 9 974 | 4 685 | 46.97 | 978 | 20.88 |
| Tarija | 11 059 | 3 002 | 27.10 | 986 | 32.80 |
| Total | 338 638 | 166 591 | 49.19 | 31 723 | 19.04 |

*Note*: RUC (*Registro Nacional Unico de Contribuyentes*) is the Bolivian Single National Register of Taxpayers.
*Source*: Roberto Casanovas, 'Informality and Illegality, a False Identity: The Case of Bolivia', in Victor E. Tokman, *Beyond Regulation: The Informal Economy in Latin America*, Lynne Rienner Publishers, Boulder, 1992.

*Table 8.10* Market locations for home-based manufacturing, retail trade and food service, Lima, Peru, 1983

| Market location | Manufacturing | | | | | | Services | |
|---|---|---|---|---|---|---|---|---|
| | Food products, textiles and clothing | | Leather, wood, and metal products | | Other manufacturing | | Retail trade, restaurants and bars | |
| | No. of firms | % | No. of firms | % | No. of firms | % | No. of firms | % |
| In neighbourhood | 123 | 37.0 | 29 | 31.5 | 12 | 25.0 | 754 | 84.0 |
| City-wide | 169 | 50.9 | 39 | 42.4 | 25 | 52.1 | 144 | 16.0 |
| Sell to other businesses | 40 | 12.0 | 24 | 26.1 | 11 | 22.9 | – | – |
| Total | 332 | | 92 | | 48 | | 898 | |

*Note*: Percentages may not add up to 100 due to rounding.
*Source*: Authors' calculations based on Paul Strassman, 'Home-based Enterprises in Cities of Developing Countries', *Economic Development and Cultural Change*, Vol. 36, No. 1, 1987, Table 2.

Indeed, differences in markets such as those reported in Table 8.10 are only the beginning of the potentially important variations among firms which otherwise are identical in terms of size. For example, other characteristics such as choice of production technique, labour supply (e.g. household labour compared to hired wage workers), source of financing and input supply are all potentially important sources of heterogeneity, and yet are masked in a size-based measure. Thus, in addition to enriching our analysis of firm behaviour, drawing out these distinctions between otherwise similar firms allows us to differentiate between the various *individual* motives for economic activity, such as household survival strategies, income-supplementing activities or dynamic entrepreneurship.

### Role of the informal sector in the broader economic context

By highlighting heterogeneity along these multiple dimensions, we are also able to discuss a second major issue surrounding the informal sector, namely its position in the broader economic context. Specifically, there is much interest in the possibility of using the informal sector as an engine of growth for developing countries in general, and particularly for sub-Saharan Africa. Indeed, this interest only deepens when one considers the dynamic, entrepreneurial segment of the informal sector engaged in formal sector subcontracting and supply relations. While an exhaustive analysis is not possible here, two particular issues are worth highlighting. The first is the distinction between the 'informalization' of the processes of production and distribution and the decentralized and specialized production and distribution arrangements known as 'flexible specialization'.[30] While both address the dramatic restructuring of industrial relations in the developed and developing world, focusing on the search for increased flexibility and reduced costs on the part of the firm, several key elements distinguish the two perspectives. The second issue is the relationship between small and large businesses in the context of economic growth, and the very feasibility of a small-business-led growth strategy.

With regard to the restructuring of production relations, in the case of the 'informalization' approach, flexibility and cost reduction in the formal sector are thought to be obtained by utilizing unprotected workers in the informal sector, via outsourcing and subcontracting arrangements. Such arrangements often entail a substantial decrease in living standards and job security, as well as deskilling of formal sector workers pushed into informality.[31] For example, such an 'informalization' strategy can be seen in the context of Kano, Nigeria, where by October 1984, 34 firms surveyed by the Manufacturers' Association of Nigeria had together retrenched 5774 workers.[32] Adebayo Olukoshi, in his study of Kano, notes four ways in which manufacturers informalized the labour process. First, 17 per cent of the firms surveyed resorted to hiring in of daily paid casual workers, up from 3 per cent before the onset of the economic crisis in Nigeria. Second, trade unions were dissolved or forced out of 25 per cent of the firms surveyed, and union activists attempting to organize the new casual workers were also forced out. Third, managers attempted to establish patronage systems in 18 per cent of the firms, whereby certain shop floor workers and supervisors were recruited to monitor shop floor activities and suppress union organizing in exchange for extra bonuses.[33] Finally, ex-employees were sometimes rehired in subcontracting relations, often supplied with credit, machinery and inputs by their former employer.

This market interlinkage was also reported by Lourdes Benería in the context of the electrical appliance and electronics industry in Mexico.[34] There she documents the links between multinational corporations operating in Mexico City and 'informalized' work arrangements such as homework. She finds that such linkages are prevalent, and cites one example where a multinational subcontracts 70 per cent of its production, utilizing a list of 300 regular and 1500 occasional subcontractors.

Moreover, she finds that for the electrical appliances and electronics sector, the average wage of manual workers in the multinationals is 6.76 times higher than the wage received by homeworkers. Finally, it should be noted that such 'informalization' is not limited to times of economic crisis or restructuring. As Fortuna and Prates show for Uruguay, such a process may also be fostered by economic booms, although with different specific forces driving the 'informalization'.[35]

Contrasted to this process of marginalization and impoverishment, others see the restructuring of production relations as simultaneously promoting greater flexibility and specialization for firms and higher skill and income levels for workers. Under the general rubric of 'flexible specialization', restructuring is viewed as a movement away from mass production, with its dedicated capital equipment, large inventories, highly segmented work patterns and consistent emphasis on technical and technological solutions.[36] Instead, this method of industrial organization is seen as producing a constantly shifting mix of specialized products, by finding new uses for existing equipment and skills and relying on an increasingly general resource base. Economies of scale are achieved at much smaller absolute sizes, and flexibility in application of resources, be they physical or human resources, serves to create sizable economies of scope. Also central to this pattern of industrial organization is the relationship between firms, as these much smaller, more specialized concerns are often organized into dense networks of regionally clustered small-scale enterprises, known as industrial districts. The result of this clustering is an array of positive technological and skill externalities as well as large agglomeration effects. Most important, perhaps, is the fact that such a view of restructuring is not merely academic but has practical implications, as witnessed for example by the UNDP/UNIDO industrial strategy recommendations made to Cyprus in 1987.[37]

In the African context there are also several cases which lend support to this view. Consider the Kebuye industrial estate in Kisumu, Kenya, for example, where hundreds of small-scale metal workers, carpenters and furniture makers have chosen to locate. There a 1990 IFAD Mission reported producers benefiting from many of the aforementioned aspects of flexible specialization, such as the sharing of certain tools and equipment, the renting of larger capital goods such as lathes and welding equipment from one another, the ability to attract consumers more readily due to the high concentration of similar workshops, the sharing of technology and organizational techniques of production, and the ability to subcontract work to neighbouring producers when large orders were obtained.[38] Indeed, potential benefits from collective action, such as input quantity discounts and the coordination of 'joint' production lines or cell production, are even greater. Experiences similar to the Kisumu case are also found in Ghana, pre-civil war Rwanda and Tanzania.[39] These examples do not indicate an inexorable turn from mass production to flexible specialization in the developing economies, nor do they contradict the reality of 'informalization' that is taking place on a large scale in sub-Saharan Africa, but they do support the claim that restructuring of production relations does not necessarily result in a worsening of working conditions and living standards. Moreover, if an understanding can be obtained of the conditions which facilitate flexible specialization as opposed to 'informalization', there is a real possibility that public policy can be used to foster such conditions, improving living standards in the process.

This discussion of production restructuring leads naturally to the second major issue concerning the informal sector and the broader economic context, namely the relationship between small and large businesses in the context of economic growth, and the feasibility of a small-business-led growth strategy. The central concerns are the ability of very small enterprises to grow beyond a certain size and the possible linkages between large businesses and small.

Those who are pessimistic about the potential of the informal sector to play a key role in an investment-led adjustment strategy emphasize the financial, material, managerial and legal constraints faced by 'informal' producers and their relative inability to expand beyond a certain (usually very small) size. The picture in Kenya, for example, is depicted in Table 8.11. In Kenya between 1983 and 1987 there was very slow growth in employment in small-scale manufacturing combined with a decrease in the number of firms employing between 20 and 49 persons. Moreover the mid-sized small-scale enterprises employing 20–49 persons accounted for less than 18 per cent of employment in small-scale enterprises as a whole. This 'missing middle' of small and medium-sized enterprises is a critical weakness in Kenya which limits the role of the 'informal' sector in the context of a growth strategy.

The situation in Kenya, however, need not be inevitable. While it is obvious that many firms in sub-Saharan Africa have not been able to grow beyond a very small size, there is no reason to believe that they cannot grow and survive because of something inherent to small firms. In fact the inability of firms to survive and grow is more likely to reflect the constraints they face than anything specific to their size.

ble 8.11   'Modern' small-scale manufacturing establishments, Kenya, 1983–87

| tivity | No. of establishments 10–19 persons | | No. of establishments 20–49 persons | | Total employees 10–49 persons | | Employment change 1983–87 |
|---|---|---|---|---|---|---|---|
| | 1983 | 1987 | 1983 | 1987 | 1983 | 1987 | |
| earing apparel, ot footwear | 21 | 28 | 51 | 38 | 1 914 | 1 793 | −211 |
| ooden furniture | 14 | 20 | 29 | 24 | 2 271 | 902 | −1 369 |
| etal products | 49 | 34 | 67 | 40 | 1 891 | 1 715 | −176 |
| achinery | 22 | 28 | 30 | 26 | 1 239 | 1 293 | 54 |
| ilroad equipment | 16 | 21 | 33 | 30 | 1 248 | 1 239 | −9 |
| inting | 37 | 46 | 36 | 38 | 1 575 | 1 785 | 210 |
| wmills | 15 | 29 | 26 | 25 | 1 004 | 1 172 | 168 |
| hemicals, aints, etc. | 20 | 28 | 22 | 26 | 992 | 1 208 | 216 |
| keries | 12 | 19 | 7 | 12 | 410 | 623 | 213 |
| rain mill roducts | 2 | 2 | 5 | 2 | 198 | 95 | −101 |
| airy products | 8 | 0 | 4 | 1 | 200 | 46 | −154 |
| ther food reparation nd processing | 13 | 10 | 23 | 41 | 1 024 | 1 801 | 777 |
| ther | 41 | 64 | 59 | 73 | 2 532 | 3 560 | 1 028 |
| tal | 273 | 329 | 403 | 376 | 16 496 | 17 232 | 736 |

urce: Adapted from Ian Livingstone, 'A Reassessment of Kenya's Rural and Urban Informal
ctor', *World Development*, Vol. 19, No. 6, 1991, Table 12.

Indeed one of the purposes of the programmes discussed in the next
section is to alleviate the constraints on the expansion of small businesses. Those programmes, when combined with a general reorientation of policy favouring investment and macroeconomic growth,
should provide considerable indirect help to small enterprises by substantially reducing the risk of failure. Even so, failure rates among
small enterprises are bound to remain high and expansion for most
'informal' producers will remain elusive, but some small enterprises
*will* grow, and many *could* grow under the right conditions. The task of
policy is to create the right conditions and not give up in despair.

Finally, there are potential linkages between small and large firms in
industrial development and these linkages can help to foster growth in
the informal sector. The experience of the Asian 'late-industrializers' is
particularly informative.[40] In Japan and South Korea large corporate
conglomerates (*zaibatsus* and *chaebols*, respectively) emerged as the

leaders in industrialization, around whom smaller subcontractors and suppliers clustered. In Taiwan, in contrast, such large-scale conglomerates never emerged to lead the industrialization process and yet small enterprises flourished there too. In China, small and medium-sized enterprises, the so-called township and village enterprises, played a major role in transforming the countryside and industrializing the country as a whole. Thus there are several possible environments in which small and medium-sized enterprises can succeed. Perhaps the Taiwanese case, however, is most instructive for sub-Saharan Africa. As Alice Amsden points out, Taiwan's decentralized and relatively small-scale production structure 'emerged more out of the throes of political economy than the play of free market forces'.[41] Indeed, she notes that small and medium enterprises developed in the shadow of an industrial base dominated by large public and private enterprises: 56.4 per cent of manufacturing value added in 1973 came from firms employing 500 or more workers. By 1984, however, almost 50 per cent of value added came from firms with fewer than 300 workers and smaller firms were clearly ascendant. None the less, the linkages between the large and small businesses were tight during the period of industrial development, and the small firms often depended on large ones for working capital, skill and technology transfers, and for subcontracting and supply relations. Thus the East Asian experience demonstrates that there is more than one model of industrial development in which small and medium enterprises play a central role. The challenge facing sub-Saharan Africa is to design an investment and growth strategy that builds on the latent potential of small enterprises and the energy and talents of the African people. It is to that challenge that we now turn.

## Investment-led structural adjustment: programmatic elements

In this section we set forth several of the programmatic elements which should form part of an overall investment-led adjustment strategy. We recognize that some African governments will be unable to implement policies and programmes of the type we recommend, but it is equally unlikely that such governments would be able to implement more conventional structural adjustment programmes. Six issues will be treated in this section, each in the context of domestic resource mobilization and enterprise development. Specifically, we will discuss access to credit and the role of credit markets; targeted credit programmes; housing as a productive asset; education and technical training; guaranteed employment programmes; and finally, the commercialization of state enterprises.

## Access to credit and the role of credit markets

The public sector has a major role to play in providing national infrastructure, both for human and physical capital. In addition, the public sector must ensure that actual and potential entrepreneurs have access to credit for investment purposes. This follows logically from our focus on an investment-led adjustment process, as access to credit is a critical condition for increased investment. Moreover, it is even more critical when small enterprises and informal producers are central actors in a future growth strategy, a perspective encouraged in our discussion of the informal sector. Many of our recommendations throughout this chapter address non-financial constraints on enterprise development, such as low productivity and skill levels, as well as the absence of general profit-making opportunities. However, alleviating financial constraints also is crucial to enterprise development and therefore in this subsection we will clarify some of the issues surrounding the functioning of credit markets in developing countries.

First, it is important to recognize that financial and non-financial constraints are intertwined. Lack of working capital or dependable access to it can be as severe a brake on growth, once constraints such as absence of profit-making opportunities have been alleviated, as were the original constraints themselves. Unfortunately, financial constraints are pervasive in developing countries, and obtaining credit from formal institutions such as commercial banks has not proved to be easy for many firms, even in the face of profitable economic activities. For example, Brian Levy, in his study of small and medium-sized enterprises in Tanzania, found that 97 per cent of the firms in his survey ranked access to finance as their most severe constraint.[42] Similarly, the ILO found that 95 per cent of microenterprises surveyed in Guinea were either self-financed or secured financing from family and friends during their initial start-up.[43] Results from Bangladesh further support the contention that credit is constrained, where the Bangladesh Institute of Development Studies found that a mere 14 per cent of rural households were benefiting from institutional credit.[44]

Next, we must address the many reasons that have been set forth to explain this poor penetration of formal credit institutions in developing countries, especially where services for the poor are concerned. Chief among these is the question of transactions costs. It is argued that, especially in rural areas and poor communities, the costs of organizing and operating formal financial services are prohibitive. For example, distances from banking centres in the urban areas are great and rural transportation and communication infrastructure is poor. In addition, where the average size of loans is small, the ratio of administrative overhead costs to the loan portfolio can be large. There are many complementarities between the programmatic elements discussed later and the constraints on financial deepening, such as the public provision of infrastructure. Moreover, there is much evidence from Africa and elsewhere that calls into question the notion that it is impossible to provide credit in the form of small loans to poor or rural borrowers at positive real interest rates, with positive bank profits. Indeed, what many cases indicate is the crucial roles that institution design and sensitivity to social context play in successful lending.

Furthermore there are two points worth noting with regard to administrative costs. First, while it is true that many of the lending programmes we will discuss shortly do have higher overhead and administrative costs compared to formal commercial banks on either a per loan or per loan officer basis, they are not as much higher as one might imagine. Design considerations and institutional arrangements have helped to prevent overhead costs from increasing proportionately with an increase in loan officers or transactions. Second, these administrative costs depend in part on the qualities of potential borrowers, including their literacy, numeracy and managerial expertise. Hence many of the educational and technical training programmes which we advocate will also help to reduce administrative overheads. Finally, where overhead and administrative costs are indeed higher, this should be reflected in the interest rate charged to borrowers.

Other often cited impediments to financial deepening are the direct and indirect barriers faced by potential borrowers. In Mali, for example, married women are legally prohibited from participating in commercial activities without the explicit consent of their husbands, and although they possess the legal right of access to banking services, many banks refuse to grant credit without the husband's authorization.[45] Such lending practices directly exclude half the population from expanding profitable economic activities in which they are engaged. Not only are such practices ethically questionable, they are economically unwise because such artificial barriers distort credit markets and seriously misallocate loanable funds. This impedes the efficiency of financial intermediation and it also reduces economic growth. Social norms of discrimination not codified into law are even more prevalent and equally distorting. Moreover, several other less transparent practices may also distort financial markets in developing countries. For example, collateral requirements, a standard instrument in commercial banking, serve to exclude many landless peasants and urban squatters from commercial borrowing, even when they have profitable projects. Similarly, many bureaucratic and administrative procedures required to secure loans necessitate literacy and numeracy in the official language, often marginalizing some indigenous people and the illiterate. Where formal, informal or bureaucratic barriers exclude sizable portions of the population, there is potentially a positive role for the government to play. In fact there is much evidence that indicates that lending to women, the poor, and other disenfranchised groups, at competitive interest rates, can be self-sustaining and even profitable.

Another argument that explains the prevalence of shallow and fragmented formal financial markets in developing countries is that these markets are credit rationed. Indeed, many authors in recent years have attributed the failure of domestic capital markets explicitly to policies and programmes adopted by governments, from subsidized interest rates for agricultural inputs to targeted sectoral credit.[46] Moreover, they argue that removing government interventions and liberalizing credit markets will promote a rational allocation of loanable funds and increased efficiency of financial intermediation.

While we agree that many, if not most, developing countries experience credit rationing in their capital markets, it is doubtful on both theoretical and empirical grounds that in the absence of 'clumsy' state intervention credit markets would function efficiently and allocate loanable funds optimally. Empirically, recent evidence from both developed and developing countries has demonstrated that even in situations of relatively freely functioning capital markets, credit rationing is the norm rather than the exception. This is true even in countries which have introduced financial 'liberalization' programmes as part of structural adjustment.[47] These findings are not surprising, given the many recent theoretical insights on the functioning of credit markets. In particular, the work of Joseph Stiglitz and Andrew Weiss has focused attention on the role that information plays in the allocation of credit.[48] They have argued that where information concerning the creditworthiness of borrowers and the riskiness of their potential projects is incomplete or absent, serious deviations from both market clearing and efficient allocations may arise. Their explanation for credit rationing is divided into two effects induced by these informational asymmetries. First, interest rates may not rise in the face of excess demand for loanable funds if higher interest rates reduce the proportion of low-risk borrowers in the applicant pool. Second, they may not rise because higher interest rates will induce borrowers to adopt riskier techniques or projects. Not surprisingly, informational asymmetries such as these are prevalent in developing country credit markets, and some authors even consider them to be the principal explanation behind the failure of formal financial sector institutions to broaden their lending base.[49] However, many institutions have emerged in developing countries which seem to have overcome the information, incentive and cost problems, and credit programmes directed to women and the poor have proven to be successful in a variety of situations. It is to a more detailed understanding of these institutions and their broader context that we turn in the next section.

## Targeted credit programmes

In this section we will discuss several of the institutional and social factors which account for the success of certain targeted credit programmes in their efforts to reach women and the poor. We will concentrate primarily on the group lending mechanism. We will illustrate two successful credit programmes, and describe their efforts to overcome transactions costs, information asymmetries and incentive problems. We will also comment on the success of these programmes in terms of loan recovery rates, financial sustainability, income generation and equity, where possible. We will conclude with the policy implications from these experiences.

### Overcoming barriers to financial deepening

A fundamental change in credit markets in developing countries has occurred in recent years, as the delivery of financial services has spread to some of the world's poorest inhabitants. Conventional wisdom that neither women nor the poor can utilize credit productively or repay loans on time has been abandoned, as numerous microcredit programmes operating in vastly different social and institutional contexts have demonstrated exactly the opposite. Yet, despite these successes, there are many failures as well, and the need to understand how the successful credit programmes navigated the information, incentive and transaction cost barriers to credit provision is great. One mechanism is the utilization of what is known as group (or solidarity) lending. Under such an arrangement, loans are disbursed to groups (or individuals in groups) and the group is required to play a role in securing the repayment of the loan.[50] Benefits to both the borrowers and lenders from this joint liability arrangement are numerous. For example, from the borrower's perspective joint liability often serves to reduce or eliminate collateral requirements, as group members represent multiple guarantors on each loan, spreading risk among themselves rather than assuming it individually. This spreading of risk among borrowers, in turn, reduces lender risk, and often eases credit rationing. Spreading risk through joint liability helps to reduce interest rates faced by borrowers and increase the proportion of funding for entrepreneurial projects coming from the loan.[51] Similarly, joint liability may serve to increase repayment rates on outstanding loans, as groups can and often do impose penalties on members who default, penalties which are generally not available to lenders. These social sanctions serve as a powerful disincentive for defaulting, particularly in intimate social contexts such as rural villages.[52] Finally, joint liability can also be seen as a way of reducing the transactions and information costs faced by the lender. Specifically, when borrowers form their own group they often engage in screening of their fellow borrowers, assessing their likelihood of repayment. From the lenders' perspective, collecting this information represents a significant cost which they no longer have to bear.[53]

Many other non-financial considerations which have influenced the success of group lending programmes deserve mention. For example, Avishay Braverman and J. Luis Guasch emphasize the need for any successful group lending programme to be rooted in the community it is intended to serve. They note that this requires patience on the part of governments during what can be a long gestation period, but emphasize the benefits of a bottom-up approach.[54] Similar considerations apply to the management of group activities, where those groups directly involved in self-management perform much better than those that cede management decisions to outsiders such as extension workers or agents of the financial intermediary. Such self-management is also said to strengthen social cohesiveness and thus make it easier to exert pressure on potential defaulters.[55] In addition, the relationship between group members is a critical element in successful group lending. Specifically, a group which is homogeneous along several socially relevant dimensions such as sex or ethnicity is more likely to be able to impose social sanctions than a more heterogeneous one.[56] Group size also plays a significant role, as smaller groups tend to have closer social ties and enjoy less costly access to information concerning group members. Small size also facilitates the imposition of social sanctions should they become necessary. On the other hand, from the point of view of the lending institution, there are considerable advantages in having a sizable programme. The potential for economies of scale dramatically

increases the chance for long-term financial sustainability of the institution, and carries with it large benefits to borrowers otherwise forced
to resort to local moneylenders or to depleting personal savings.[57]
Braverman and Guasch also note that many successful group lending
programmes do much more than provide credit, as they support a wide
range of institutional and human development initiatives, such as
managerial training, general and technical education, and provision of
health services. A final recurring element in the experiences of the most
successful group lending programmes is the role played by mandatory
savings. In addition to contributing substantially to the long-term viability of the lending programmes, compulsory savings provide additional credibility to sanctions imposed by group members on potential
defaulters, as group members or the credit institutions often retain the
right to disburse individual savings when members go into default.

*Case studies*

Several of the points made above can perhaps best be illustrated through
case studies. Here we shall consider only two, the Grameen Bank in
Bangladesh and the Badan Kredit Kecamatan in Indonesia. Both institutions are examples of targeted credit programmes, but they operate
in rather different ways.

*Grameen Bank.*   Bangladesh's Grameen Bank, perhaps the most famous
group lending programme, grew out of an action research project initiated by Dr Muhammad Yunus in 1976.[58] The goal of the bank is to provide financial resources at reasonable terms to the rural poor, primarily
women. While there are many distinguishing features of the Grameen
Bank, three are of particular note. The first is the Grameen Bank's group
structure. Relatively homogeneous groups are formed consisting of five
persons of the same sex, from the same village and of similar economic
background.[59] This process of group formation screens members
through self-selection, and the small size of the group and its homogeneity also increase the effectiveness of social sanctions. Second,
group members participate in a multi-faceted mandatory savings programme, which mobilizes household savings. Moreover, group members are involved in the management of part of the savings, a process
which reinforces the strength of social sanctions as well as the commitment of members to the group. Third, bank members also participate
in the 'Sixteen Decisions' social programme, which strives to link education, discipline and unity to promote development. In practice this

programme has led to investments in housing and education by group members, as well as to better health and standards of living.

Several other characteristics of the Grameen Bank are attractive. For example, by 1991, the bank had spread its activities widely across the country, operating 880 branches covering 22046 villages and serving 932574 members.[60] Since its inception in 1976, the bank has enjoyed a very low default rate of only 4.09 per cent after the first year of a loan, and 1.48 per cent after the second year.[61] Despite this, the bank does not cover its full costs, but considerable progress has been made. In 1986 the cost of administration was 18.1 per cent of the total amount of loans, and the interest paid on external funds borrowed by the bank was 3.6 per cent; the interest rate charged by the bank was 16 per cent. The bank's operating deficit was covered by external funds. The administrative costs of mature branches, however, have fallen to roughly 9.3 per cent a year, and the interest rate charged to borrowers has been raised to 20 per cent. Provided the bank is able to continue to borrow at low interest rates, it should now be able to cover its full costs.[62] Finally, consider the bank's achievements in generating income and increasing equity. The Grameen Bank has generated new employment for roughly one-third of its members and helped raise incomes for 98 per cent of its borrowers. By 1985 the increase in income per person was 696.01 taka on average.[63] As regards equity, by 1985 the bank was directing 59.9 per cent of its funds to its target group of households owning less than half an acre of cultivable land and total assets not exceeding the value of one acre. Moreover, the proportion of females among borrowers is higher than that of males, reinforcing the conclusion that the bank has been successful in reducing female poverty.

*Badan Kredit Kecamatan (BKK).*    Indonesia's Badan Kredit Kecamatan (BKK) was launched with a loan from the central Java Regional Development Bank (BPD) in 1970 to promote small industry and the economic activities of the poor in central Java.[64] The bank lends to individuals, not groups, and targets the rural poor. Since its establishment it has gone through many stages, but we will focus on the period from 1981 onwards. BKK is notable for having overcome many of the barriers to lending to the poor. Four features of its operations are of particular note. First, BKK recruits its staff from the areas in which it operates. This reduces the transactions costs associated with screening potential borrowers and strengthens the social sanction against defaulting. Second, the BKK has a mandatory savings programme, which is equivalent to 6.5–20 per cent of the total loan, depending on the repayment schedule.[65] The mandatory savings programme recently has been supplemented by an additional voluntary programme. These programmes help mobilize rural savings and ensure the financial viability of the BKK. The third important feature contributing to the BKK's success is its determination to charge interest rates that cover fully all operating costs. In 1988 the interest rate was 36 per cent a year. Finally, and perhaps most important, the BKK has been very successful in taking advantage of economies of scale. In 1989, there were 499 units of the BKK in operation and they provided almost complete coverage of central Java's 492 subdistricts; in that year the BKK made 609 668 loans through its 3440 subunits, the *pos desas* (village posts).

The BKK also has been successful in keeping default rates low and covering its full costs. As regards defaults, in 1989 the BKK's long-term loss ratio was only 2.1 per cent and arrears accounted for only 7.4 per cent of outstanding debt.[66] Moreover, the BKK made substantial profits throughout the late 1980s, 1.7 billion rupiah in 1989 alone, 90 per cent of which was retained by the bank to finance expansion. Turning to equity and income generation, the average size of a loan was less than Rp 75 000 (US$42), and approximately 90 per cent of the loans were for amounts less than Rp 100 000 (US$56). Sixty per cent of the borrowers were women, and more than 60 per cent of the rural borrowers had either no formal schooling or had not completed primary schooling. Evidently the bank was able to reach the poor and the disadvantaged, and to make a profit while doing so.

*Policy implications*

As the above case studies illustrate, targeted credit programmes directed to women and the poor are not only sustainable but in some cases profitable. They have succeeded in greater or lesser degrees in meeting all four goals of high repayment rates, long-term sustainability, enhanced income generation and increased equity. In both cases these targeted programmes were conceived as institutions concerned with entrepreneurial development rather than the provision of welfare, and much attention was paid to cost recovery and long-term viability. It is apparent, however, that no single model captures all the institutional and design criteria needed for success. Attention to the specific social and cultural context in which peer group and other sanctions operate, the degree of homogeneity among group members and the particular mix of information, incentive and cost mitigating structures is crucial. Given the heterogeneity of the programmes highlighted above, one conclusion is that experimentation is not only possible, but advisable.

## Housing as a productive asset

It has long been recognized that housing in developing countries has multiple uses. In addition to shelter, dwellings provide space for workshops, retail outlets, restaurants, warehouse and storage, and a source of critical inputs such as electricity and water for many small and medium-size home-based enterprises (HBEs). Yet many of the opportunities that derive from these home-based enterprises have not been fully exploited and their potential contribution to long-term development remains underdeveloped. In what follows we will briefly explore the empirical character of HBEs, discuss several reasons why HBEs should be better integrated into a development strategy, and highlight the role that can be played by credit targeted at housing used as a productive asset.

The prevalence of HBEs, as well as their physical characteristics, qualities and economic activities, vary significantly across neighbourhoods, cities and regions. For example, in the periurban settlements of Lusaka, Zambia, 25 per cent of the dwellings are utilized in home-based economic activity, while in the metropolitan area of Lima, Peru, a mere 10.8 per cent of dwellings are HBEs.[67] Similarly, striking differences exist between two residential areas of Kumasi, Ghana, where 12.7 per cent of the dwellings in Asawase include space for HBEs, as contrasted with 40.2 per cent in Anloga.[68] As with informal activities as a whole, those undertaken by HBEs display significant heterogeneity, as can be seen in Table 8.12 for Lima, Peru. Moreover, the evidence on market niches in Table 8.10 shows the substantial variation that occurs even *within* the particular activities in which HBEs are engaged. Finally, there is variation in the physical dimensions of HBEs as well. This is illustrated, for example, by the fact that 73 per cent of HBEs in Lima had indoor piped water, while in Kalutara, Sri Lanka this was true for a mere 16 per cent of HBEs.[69]

Despite this heterogeneity, it is evident that informal production based on the home is present to a significant extent in most, if not all, developing countries. Moreover, if the programmes we recommend are adopted – such as public works projects for infrastructure and targeted credit – the importance of home-based enterprises will increase. Consider for example, two types of irregular settlements – the 'pirata' and invasion 'barrios' – in Medellin, Colombia.[70] The invasion 'barrios' are settlements where land possession is not recognized by a legal title, and conditions such as plot size and shape are uncoordinated and irregular, a function of the dynamic of the land invasion itself.

*Table 8.12*    Enterprise types among home-based enterprises, Lima, Peru, 1983

| Enterprise type | Number in survey | Percentage of total |
|---|---|---|
| Manufacturing | | |
| Food products, textiles, and clothing | 332 | 19.46 |
| Leather, wood and metal products | 92 | 5.39 |
| Other manufacturing | 48 | 2.81 |
| Services | | |
| Retail trade, restaurants, bars | 898 | 52.64 |
| Repairs | 59 | 3.46 |
| Medical services | 70 | 4.10 |
| Laundries and cleaning | 23 | 1.35 |
| Lodging | 71 | 4.16 |
| Miscellaneous | 113 | 6.62 |
| Total | 1706 | 100 |

*Source*: Adapted from W. Paul Strassman, 'Home-based Enterprises in Cities of Developing Countries', *Economic Development and Cultural Change*, Vol. 36, No. 1, 1987, Table 2.

'Pirata' settlements, in contrast, refer to settlements where landowners promote subdivided plots and self-built houses, intentionally ignoring planning regulations concerning plot dimensions and infrastructural connections. In the particular case of Medellin, the 'pirata' settlements are somewhat older than the invasion 'barrios' and they exhibit a much more consolidated pattern of land use than one finds in the invasion settlements. What is significant is that the 'pirata' settlements utilize 36 per cent of their dwellings for economic purposes, as compared with 21 per cent for the invasion settlements. Consolidation appears to have played a role in that it permits further subdivision of plots for economic activities and indirectly facilitates access to infrastructure such as roads, power and water.

Another example comes from Manila, Philippines, where a 'sites and services' development project was undertaken in the slums of metropolitan Manila in the early 1980s.[71] The Zonal Improvement Programme (ZIP) was designed to resolve land tenure problems and introduce basic amenities and social services, primarily through a process of 'reblocking', which implied a realignment of road networks and land allocations in the selected neighbourhoods. Much of the reblocking was physical in nature, involving improvements of the existing infrastructure and land quality, as well as realigning existing structures into the block plans. Sample studies were conducted before and after implementing the programme in 4 of the 13 ZIP sites with results similar to those in Medellin. In 1981, before the ZIP was implemented, 19 per cent of the dwellings contained HBEs, whereas in 1984 after the ZIP improvements were introduced, 35.55 per cent reported HBE activity. Moreover, the monthly household median income rose from US$71.29 to US$114.10, a 60.2 per cent increase. These findings are not at all surprising. W. Paul Strassman, for instance, noted in his study of Lusaka and Colombo that in those households where HBEs were present, reported incomes were significantly higher than those without, namely 10.7 and 10.3 per cent higher, respectively.[72]

These experiences indicate that if well conceived investment programmes are undertaken, there is likely to be an increase in HBEs. The provision of infrastructure and other services increases the profitability of home-based enterprises and economic activity consequently responds. Moreover, as the data from Manila, Lusaka and Colombo demonstrate, such activities are likely to increase household incomes as compared to those households which do not engage in home-based economic activity. Hence for these reasons housing as a productive asset should be incorporated into a long-term development strategy. Indeed, low-income housing is an attractive candidate for a targeted credit programme.

Additional reasons strengthen this conviction. First, home-based work is associated with low transport costs and a high degree of flexibility. This flexibility is one of the great virtues of HBEs, as domestic physical and human capital can be readily shifted into and out of a variety of uses. Moreover, the ability to reduce travel to and from work, as well as transporting goods to and from external storage, substantially reduces the real costs of operating microenterprises. No doubt this helps to explain why, judging from the responses from HBEs in Lima, home-based work is popular for so many people. Indeed, 71 per cent of those employed in HBEs in W. Paul Strassman's survey responded that in order to induce them to switch to formal sector work, wages would have to be 'much more' than they were earning at present, and only 5.7 per cent were considering moving their business from their dwelling.[73]

A second major reason why housing as a productive asset can play a central role in long-term development is that investment in housing provides substantial direct employment and income benefits and also generates large forward and backward linkages to the local economy. For instance, the direct employment and income benefits from housing come not just from the construction and improvement of homes, but also from the necessary investments in roads, sewers and other public infrastructural improvements. Indeed, there are many opportunities to provide 'sites and services' under the guaranteed employment programmes discussed below. Furthermore, housing and related investments will generate backward and forward linkages to construction materials, capital equipment and home furnishings. While this does not guarantee large employment effects, if small-scale, local, labour intensive techniques are favoured both backwards and forwards, the probability is high that much employment will be created.

Finally, an emphasis on housing as a productive asset confers an obvious direct benefit in the form of improved shelter for low-income families. There continues to be great interest, nationally and internationally, in affordable and adequate shelter, as witnessed for example by the United Nations Global Strategy for Shelter (GSS).[74] Investing in housing has the dual advantage of enhancing productive capacity while strengthening the provision of basic needs. Moreover, if a housing programme is carefully designed and implemented, it is likely to have a favourable impact on equity as well.

Thus there is much to be said in favour of housing as a productive asset. The potential benefits for developing countries are many, as are the complementarities between this and other programmatic elements discussed in this chapter. None the less, it must be recognized that a higher level of investment in housing and an improved composition in favour of low-income housing will not happen automatically under conventional structural adjustment programmes. As indicated above, credit markets in sub-Saharan Africa will continue to misallocate funds even after 'liberalization' and hence a targeted credit programme for housing merits careful consideration.

The informational asymmetries between borrowers and lenders are very great in the case of home-based enterprises and access to credit is further complicated by the fact that the income stream generated by HBEs often is ignored when decisions are taken about lending for housing. This occurs despite the fact that income generated by HBEs significantly increases the ability of borrowers to service a housing loan. W. Paul Strassman confirms this conclusion in his discussion of Lima, where he notes that of the 1706 HBEs surveyed, a mere 37 had received credit from the Banco Industrial del Peru (BIP), the official institution charged with such lending, and those few who did receive credit tended to be one-third larger in terms of housing floor space than those who did not. This suggests that providing collateral was a severe constraint.[75] As with all special financial programmes, a targeted credit programme for housing should be conceptualized as an entrepreneurial development programme: interest rates should be set to cover all costs fully and attention should be devoted to efficient targeting and screening. Where these elements of success are ignored, as the experience of Madhya Pradesh, India, illustrates, results will be disappointing.[76]

### Education and technical training

It has long been known that investment in human capital – and particularly expenditures on education and technical training – enjoy high rates of return,[77] indeed rates of return that are comparable to the returns on investment in physical capital.[78] The 'market' for human capital, however, does not operate efficiently, primarily because the benefits from investing in education and technical training are widely dispersed: they accrue partly to the individual receiving the education, partly to those who employ educated and well trained workers and partly to the society at large. In other words, investment in human capital is characterized by widespread positive externalities and this results in 'market failure' and underinvestment in education. The consequence of underinvestment, in turn, is a slower rate of growth than would otherwise be possible.

The problem of underinvestment in education and training is exacerbated by market failure in the credit markets. Low-income people wishing to invest in their education, or in the education of their children, are unable to finance educational expenditures out of their own resources because of their poverty, and they are unable to finance the expenditures with borrowed resources because investment in education, from the perspective of a bank, is very risky: collateral usually is not available; the income stream from investment in human capital, out of which the loan would be serviced, is uncertain; and the possibility of default is high. Thus investment in education usually can be neither self-financed nor bank-financed.

Employers evidently have no incentive to finance the general education of present and future workers. The ability of employees to read, write and calculate clearly is of benefit to employers, but they are unable to appropriate those benefits because, short of 'bonding' labour, there is no means to ensure that those whose education is financed by a particular enterprise will end up working for that enterprise or, if they do work for the enterprise, they will remain long enough for the employer to recover his outlay.

A similar problem arises in the case of employer-financed training programmes. Some apprenticeship schemes, in effect, are jointly financed by the employer and the apprentice, the latter by agreeing to accept a low wage and to spend many years working as an apprentice. Some training programmes are fully funded by the enterprise, but these programmes usually train workers in skills which are specific to the enterprise and hence are of little value to other potential employers. These training programmes, in other words, do not significantly increase the job mobility of workers outside the enterprise. Training programmes that do increase the mobility of workers – by providing skills that are in general demand in the market place – tend to be underfunded because of the difficulty of employers in recovering their costs.

Thus for a variety of reasons investment in human capital requires substantial financial support by the state, and in fact governments in sub-Saharan Africa have responded to the challenge by allocating a significant proportion of public expenditure to education. This relatively generous allocation, however, has yielded lower returns than anticipated because of a series of biases in the expenditures, namely biases in favour of tertiary education, biases in favour of urban residents, biases in favour of the formal sector and biases in favour of males.

The 'expenditure pyramid' in education typically concentrates resources on university and other tertiary education, where expenditure per student often is extraordinarily high; expenditure per student in secondary education is much lower while expenditure per student in primary education is lower still.[79] Yet the empirical evidence indicates that the returns to expenditure on education are highest at the primary level, declining at the secondary level and further still at the tertiary level. That is, the composition of expenditure is the opposite of what it should be if the objective is to achieve a rapid rate of growth. There is thus a strong case for reallocating expenditure away from tertiary education in favour of primary education.

There is a similar bias in favour of urban areas: most schools are located in the cities and large towns while the rural areas are neglected.[80] Yet most people live in the countryside and the agricultural sector usually is the largest source of employment and a major source of output. Moreover, there is considerable evidence that expenditure on rural education, extension services and agricultural research can generate high returns.[81] Equally, we now have evidence that there are substantial returns to education for informal sector workers and for women.[82] Hence there are significant gains to be reaped by eliminating the biases in educational expenditure and increasing allocations in favour of primary and secondary education, vocational training, the rural and informal sectors, and women. Such a reallocation of investment in human capital is especially important for the type of strategy recommended in this chapter, since our emphasis is on creating investment opportunities for the largest possible number of people by concentrating on the development of small enterprises, particularly in the informal sector.

If entrepreneurship is to flourish in sub-Saharan Africa, public expenditure on human capital must be substantial and efficiently allocated. Efficiency implies not only the elimination of the biases we have highlighted but also a concern with the quality of education that young people receive. Students must have access to books, classrooms should be properly equipped, teachers should be well trained and the pay structure should reward good teaching, etc. In some cases expenditure on raising the quality of education can yield as much as expenditure on increasing the quantity of education.[83]

Finally, expenditure on education and technical training should be seen within the context of a broad development strategy. The point has already been made that if domestic entrepreneurship and small business development are to be the engines of growth, then special attention must be paid to primary and secondary education. The expansion of small enterprises and the expansion of human capital are complementary: the returns to both activities taken together are much greater than the return to each taken separately.

Consider, for example, the credit market. Small entrepreneurs need access to credit and hence there is a strong case to be made for special credit schemes aimed at those currently excluded from the market: workers in the informal sector, small farmers, fishermen, artisans and women in general. Credit institutions, however, encounter high costs of lending to such people, in part because they are illiterate (and cannot, for example, read and complete loan application forms) and cannot make simple calculations or maintain accurate accounts. A universal programme of basic education, by increasing literacy and numeracy, would lower the costs of lending, increase the number of potential borrowers and raise the likelihood of success of credit programmes aimed at low-income people. Thus small enterprise development depends in part on the availability of credit and the availability of credit to small entrepreneurs depends in part on a minimum level of human capital. If either credit or education are provided in isolation, the returns may be disappointing, but if both are provided simultaneously, the strong complementarities between the two may ensure that the overall returns are high.

## Guaranteed employment programmes

Sub-Saharan Africa has long suffered from underutilization of labour in the form of seasonal unemployment in the countryside and open unemployment in the cities. The stabilization and structural adjust-ment policies adopted in recent years, however, have greatly aggra-vated the problem and the region now finds that its greatest asset, its labour power, is massively underemployed. At the same time there are very great needs for physical capital accumulation and there are many socially profitable investment projects which can be undertaken with labour intensive methods of production. An acute social and economic problem can be transformed into a development opportunity by mobi-lizing underemployed labour on capital construction projects.

The best way to do this is by organizing a guaranteed employment programme.[84] The purposes of the programme would be, first, to increase the overall rate of investment by launching nationwide pub-lic works projects and, second, to provide employment opportunities for all able-bodied workers willing to perform unskilled manual labour for a minimum wage. There have, of course, been public works projects in many countries, including sub-Saharan Africa,[85] but these have been largely emergency relief schemes introduced during periods of famine or severe distress rather than a component of a development strategy designed to accelerate investment and growth.

Several Asian countries, however, have viewed public works projects as an integral part of their long-term development policy and their experi-ence is relevant to sub-Saharan Africa. In Bangladesh, for example, there has been a large food-for-work programme for about three decades and by the second half of the 1980s it provided approximately 15 days of work per year (or three weeks) for all those households which owned less than 0.5 acre of land (i.e. for the landless and near-landless).[86] The expe-rience in China during the Maoist period was much more extensive and the mobilization of surplus labour within the commune system was a key mechanism for rural capital construction which succeeded in large part in transforming the countryside.[87] Indeed in 1960 (when decolo-nization began in Africa), per capita incomes in China were well below those in sub-Saharan Africa; today, China has caught up and in many cases exceeded the per capita income of countries in the region. One rea-son for this success was massive investment in labour intensive public works projects. Perhaps the most relevant example for sub-Saharan Africa, however, comes from India. The state of Maharashtra has imple-mented a successful employment guarantee scheme in the rural areas since 1975 and this has made a major contribution to reducing poverty.[88] The key to success of such schemes is wage policy.[89]

Any able-bodied person seeking employment and willing to do man-ual work should be guaranteed a job at a subsistence wage. The daily wage rate or piece rate should be set at a level which does not attract workers from other jobs, notably from the private sector, since the purpose of the scheme is to provide work to those who have no other source of gainful employment. In the rural areas this means that the wage should be set marginally below, say 5–10 per cent below, the wages received by hired workers in the lowest-income regions of the country. A similar principle should be applied in urban areas, i.e. the wage should be set fractionally below the going wage for unskilled workers. Such wages probably would reflect fairly closely the opportunity cost of labour and would ensure that the guaranteed employment scheme does not raise labour costs and damage employment prospects in other sectors of the economy.

Projects should be designed in such a way that labour costs account for a high proportion of the total. As a guideline, one might aim for projects in which the costs of employment represent about two-thirds or more of total project costs. The experience of Maharashtra indicates this is realistic. If, for any reason, work cannot be provided to those who seek it, and the government is in fact unable to guarantee employment, unemployment compensation should be paid at a rate equivalent to the daily wage rate on works projects. This will provide an incentive to government to design and implement useful projects since, if they do not, the workers will be entitled to a wage payment in any case.

Whenever feasible, the assets created by a guaranteed employment programme should become the property of the labourers who construct them.[90] If instead the assets are owned by the state and the services produced by the assets are provided free of charge, as is often the case, 'externalities' are generated and usually these are captured by property owners. For example, the benefits of a public highway or of soil conservation works or of drainage and irrigation facilities are reflected in part in a higher price of land and in part in higher returns to farmers and in higher rents received by landowners. Except where land is equally distributed among all rural households, public works programmes are likely to increase inequalities in the distribution of income and wealth.

On the other hand, in principle it would be possible in many cases to combine capital formation with progressive income redistribution by ensuring that the assets are constructed by the poor, e.g. the landless and near-landless, and that upon completion, ownership of the assets is transferred to a cooperative consisting solely of those who supplied their labour. The purpose of the cooperative would be to manage the assets and charge for their use, distributing part of the income to the members and retaining part to finance future capital accumulation. In this manner the productive base of the poorest households could be strengthened on a continuing basis. In addition, an institutional basis for small-scale entrepreneurship would be created and a mechanism for generating a steady flow of savings for financing new projects would be in place.

There are a great many projects which could be undertaken which could yield a permanent flow of income to organized groups of the rural poor. Examples include the reclamation of waterlogged or salinated land, the construction or rehabilitation of fish ponds and fish farms, the construction of irrigation facilities of various sorts, construction of bridges and roads, and the planting of timber forests, plantations and fruit orchards. Income from projects such as these would be derived from the sale of products (fish, fruit, timber), fees for services provided (irrigation water and drainage facilities) and tolls for the use of social infrastructure (roads, bridges). Reclaimed land could either become commercial property and cultivated under the authority of the cooperative (e.g. by renting it out) or sold and the proceeds reinvested in other activities. Similarly, the products produced by the cooperative could be sold on the market, distributed among the members for direct consumption or used to provide the major input into commercially run processing enterprises such as canneries, timber mills and fish processing plants.

Linking asset creation by the poor with asset ownership by institutions organized for the poor provides both a mechanism and an incentive for the works constructed under an employment guarantee programme to be maintained and improved. In this way the chronic problem of inadequate or non-existent maintenance could be overcome. Morever, some of the net income generated by the cooperatives of the poor could be set aside as savings for investment in other productive activities, thereby initiating a sustained if modest process of cumulative expansion. Public land could be leased by the cooperative and private land could either be bought by the cooperative from the landowner at the unimproved site value or rented, or the landowner could be offered a share of the output. Members would participate in the distribution of income generated by the cooperative in proportion to the number of days of work contributed. In these ways a guaranteed employment scheme could simultaneously increase investment, generate jobs, contribute to a steady flow of savings and raise incomes among the very poor.

## Commercialization of state enterprises

The conventional view is that the disposal of state-owned enterprises should be an integral part of any structural adjustment programme. This is said to be a universal principle, applicable alike in the United Kingdom, the ex-socialist countries and sub-Saharan Africa. Advocates of the 'privatization' of state enterprises usually cite three reasons. First, it is claimed that public ownership is incompatible with the operation of a market economy. Second, in practice state enterprises are said to be inefficient in their use of resources. Third, many state enterprises operate at a loss which has to be covered by the government; these losses, in effect, are negative savings which reduce the overall rate of investment and growth.

The first claim clearly is false and the last two must be carefully qualified. Economic theory provides no justification for the claim that a market economy requires a particular ownership regime. Owner-operators, partnerships, cooperatives, limited liability corporations and state ownership are all compatible with a market system and indeed most market economies contain examples of all of these forms of ownership. Mainstream theory provides no case for privatization of state enterprises.[91]

It is true that many state enterprises in sub-Saharan Africa, and elsewhere, are inefficient. This inefficiency, however, is not inherent in public ownership, but arises from macroeconomic and microeconomic policies. At the macroeconomic level, the strategy of development often has resulted in a structure of incentives that is highly distorted. Relative factor prices do not reflect opportunity costs (e.g. because of overvalued exchange rates and artificially low real rates of interest) and product prices (e.g. because of tariffs or other trade restrictions) do not reflect the country's comparative advantage. The solution to the problem in this case is not privatization but a change in the development strategy.

At the microeconomic level a problem may arise from the inability of the owners of the enterprise (the state) to ensure that management (the state's agent) operates the enterprise in the interests of the state (or of society as a whole). In sub-Saharan Africa this principal-agent problem takes several forms: plunder of the enterprise by its managers (corruption), interference in the day-to-day operation of the enterprise by politicians (political interference), and poor service to customers (exploitation of monopolistic advantages). In this case the solution is not privatization but rather the commercialization of state enterprises.

It is also true that many state enterprises fail to earn a profit. Rather than generating savings out of retained profits, they require heavy subsidies from the exchequer and these subsidies reduce national savings. This behaviour evidently is incompatible with an investment-led strategy of structural adjustment. What, then, should be done?

The first thing to do is to reform the state enterprises. Where they enjoy monopoly protection, their protection should be removed and they should be subjected to competition from other enterprises, domestic and foreign. Barriers to entry into industries dominated by state enterprises should be dismantled. Where state enterprises enjoy subsidies, these subsidies should be gradually reduced over a fixed time period and the firm's budget constraint continuously tightened. Decision making should be decentralized, management given greater autonomy in day-to-day decision making and ministerial and political interference terminated. Management should report to an independent board of directors (on which there may be ministerial representation) and be responsible to it. In other words, state enterprises should be commercialized and managed much like a large private corporation.

If despite organizational and economic reforms some state enterprises continue to operate at a loss, they should be declared bankrupt and closed down and their remaining assets sold. Subsidies should not be continued indefinitely except in those few cases where market prices do not reflect social benefits produced by the firm, i.e. except in cases where positive externalities exist. Normally, state enterprises should be expected to pay their way and produce a profit, part of which can be retained by the firm to finance its expansion and the rest paid to the state as owner. Government revenues from state enterprises can then be used to help finance the government's contribution to an investment-led structural adjustment strategy.

An alternative to the commercialization of state enterprises is privatization. Experience has shown, however, that privatization is neither necessary nor sufficient for a successful reform programme. In China, for example, privatization played almost no role in the reform process, yet structural adjustment and the transition from central planning to a market-guided economy have been highly successful.[92] In Russia, in contrast, privatization has occurred on a massive scale, yet the economy remains depressed, inefficiency is very widespread, and savings rates are low. Similarly in Mongolia, where privatization was put at the centre of the reform programme, the disposal of state enterprises (by giving vouchers to the entire population) has proved to be irrelevant to the reform process and the economy continues to be severely depressed.[93] Even in Eastern Europe, where the transition proceeded much more smoothly than in the former Soviet Union, privatization of large-scale state enterprises encountered serious difficulties.[94]

Sub-Saharan Africa can learn from these experiences. First, many state enterprises are monopolies. Hence successful privatization would have to be accompanied by a well conceived and implemented competition policy, including a liberal import policy, in order to prevent the newly privatized enterprises from exercising market power and engaging in uncompetitive behaviour. Implementation of an effective competition policy takes time and, in any case, should be done whether or not state enterprises are privatized. In the absence of anti-monopoly measures, however, privatization actually could result in greater inefficiency in the allocation of resources.

Second, short of giving the enterprises away, it is not obvious how the government can efficiently transfer state enterprises to the private sector when relative prices are subject to very large change, as they are during a structural adjustment programme. If state enterprises are given away or sold at bargain basement prices, the government will lose an opportunity to obtain revenue from the sale of assets, revenue which could be used to finance other public sector investments. Moreover, depending on how the privatized assets are given away, inequalities in the distribution of income and wealth probably will increase. This certainly will occur if the enterprises are transferred to the former state managers, as has often happened, e.g. in Russia.

If the government wants to avoid these consequences, state enterprises should be sold at their full market value. The problem then becomes how to determine full market value. Given the distorted prices that are present during structural adjustment, it is virtually impossible to know which state enterprises ultimately will be profitable and which are likely to operate at a loss, and hence should be allowed to become bankrupt.

Third, if state enterprises are sold during a period of falling per capita incomes, the market values of the enterprises are likely to be depressed, even if they reflect the current full market value. That is, the timing of privatization is important. Market values of state enterprises will be much higher at the end of the period of structural adjustment than at the beginning. Finally, if foreigners are allowed to bid for state enterprises, this could result in a welcome inflow of foreign capital, but the larger is the inflow of foreign capital, the larger will be the proportion of the stock of physical capital under the control of non-citizens. A market economy in which the large capitalists are mostly foreigners and the workers are local people may not be socially or politically attractive.

Thus for all these reasons privatization is more likely to be a distraction during the reform process rather than a source of recovery. Efforts should instead be concentrated on commercializing the state enterprises and creating an attractive environment in which new private enterprises can emerge and entrepreneurship flourish.

## Conclusions

Structural adjustment should be seen not as a resource reallocation strategy but as part of a long-term growth strategy. The key to successful structural adjustment in sub-Saharan Africa is an increase in investment in human, physical and natural capital and an improvement in the allocation of investment. This is also the key to an acceleration in the rate of growth.

Sub-Saharan Africa's dependence on foreign aid has not been helpful and its hopes of receiving substantial inflows of private foreign capital have not materialized. Official development assistance has indeed been exceptionally large, but foreign aid has not resulted in an acceleration of investment or an improvement in the effectiveness of investment. Foreign direct investment, despite economic liberalization, has not been forthcoming, providing support for the view that foreign investment is a consequence of growth rather than a cause of it.

The conventional approach to structural adjustment implicitly posits a sequence that begins with a change in the structure of incentives ('getting prices right') which then leads to an inflow of foreign direct investment (supplemented by foreign aid) which, in turn, results in an increase in the pace of economic expansion. We argue in this chapter, however, that the correct sequence should begin with an increase in the level of investment and an improvement in its composition; this would lead to structural change and to an acceleration of growth, which in turn would attract private foreign capital and further accelerate growth.

The financing of an investment-led strategy consequently will have to come from domestic resources. It does not follow from this, however, that the solution to Africa's problem is further belt tightening and a squeeze on consumption in an attempt to raise domestic savings. In many instances it should be possible to finance human capital accumulation merely by changing the composition of expenditures conventionally classified as current consumption, e.g. by reducing military expenditure while increasing expenditures on basic health programmes. It is also possible to undertake investment by mobilizing labour both at the household level (digging an irrigation ditch) and at the local or regional level (constructing a farm-to-market road). That is, small, labour intensive investment projects can be 'financed' not just by consuming less (saving) but by working longer (reducing unemployment).

In the absence of comprehensive and well functioning capital markets, saving largely depends upon the existence of profitable investment opportunities. That is, people save in order to invest and where there is no desire to invest, there will be no savings. Public policy should therefore concentrate on creating a favourable climate for private investment rather than attempt to raise savings directly. Moreover, the possession of wealth or assets (say, in the form of land or a house) often provides investment opportunities and a profitable outlet for savings. That is, the linkages run from asset ownership to investment opportunities and thence to savings behaviour. The policy implication is that government should encourage a wide ownership of productive resources and ready access to land, housing and credit because this will lead to greater investment and savings, and of course to a more equitable society.

There is no compelling evidence that the size of government in sub-Saharan Africa is too large and ought to be reduced. There is evidence, however, that the composition of government expenditure could be improved in order to contribute more to human development and capital accumulation. For example, a reallocation of expenditure from tertiary to primary education, from urban hospitals to rural health clinics, from airports to expanded and improved road networks would greatly increase the contribution of government to development. Moreover, a reallocation of expenditure within functional categories should be accompanied by a reallocation between categories. A switch of expenditure from armaments to public health, mentioned above, is an obvious example.

It is commonly argued that public investment 'squeezes out' private investment, i.e. that public and private investment are competitive. We believe this view is mistaken. Indeed it is much more likely that a well designed public investment programme in sub-Saharan Africa would be complementary to private investment rather than competitive with it. The reason for this is that public investment in physical infrastructure (transport, communications, power), in human capital (basic health services, nutrition, primary and secondary education, family planning services) and in many other areas (applied research, irrigation systems) creates investment opportunities for the private sector and strong incentives to save. A reduction in investment in the public sector could well lead to a reduction in savings in the private sector.

The private sector includes of course the informal sector. The informal sector, in turn, is very heterogeneous, but it does contain a dynamic, entrepreneurial segment that can make an important contribution to an investment-led strategy of adjustment. Indeed, microenterprises and small businesses have considerable potential for growth in their own right and, in addition, they can establish mutually advantageous linkages with medium and large businesses.

The development potential of small business, however, will be frustrated if entrepreneurs from small enterprises and informal producers generally do not have access to credit to help finance investment. Unfortunately, credit markets in sub-Saharan Africa, as elsewhere, do not function efficiently – they are prone to 'market failure' – and consequently government has an important role in improving the performance of capital markets.

There is now considerable evidence that targeted credit programmes – which facilitate group lending, or which are aimed specifically at women, small farmers or small business persons – can succeed in reaching the poor. Moreover, it is now clear that it is possible to design such programmes to cover their full costs while charging positive real rates of interest. That is, targeted credit programmes can be profitable and sustainable over the long term. Here again, however, there are complementarities which should be taken into account when constructing an overall strategy. For instance, the cost of lending depends in part on the literacy and numeracy of borrowers as well as upon the transportation and communication network. Hence investments in human capital and in physical infrastructure will affect the viability of the credit market and the access of poor people to finance capital.

The potential dynamism of the housing sector in sub-Saharan Africa has long been overlooked and investment in housing is widely regarded as unproductive. This is a serious mistake. Housing not only provides shelter (and thereby contributes directly to the well being of people), it also represents a productive asset which can create profitable investment opportunities. Home-based enterprises have been neglected, yet microenterprises centred on private housing are common throughout sub-Saharan Africa and they can contribute to long-term development. Government can encourage the growth of home-based enterprises by, for example, providing secure titles to homesteads and by providing 'sites and services' for low-income housing developments. In addition, investment in low-income housing is a good candidate for a specially designed targeted credit programme. Just as there are specialized mortgage lending institutions in most developed economies, so too there should be specialized institutions in Africa that finance investment in housing. The added dimension in sub-Saharan Africa, however, is that lending for house construction should be regarded, at least in part, as a microenterprise development programme.

The market for human capital, like the credit market, is prone to market failure. There are high rates of return on investment in education and training and other forms of human capital, but because of pervasive externalities these returns are hard to capture. As a result, there is underinvestment in human capital. Government thus has an important role to play in encouraging or directly financing investment in human capital, and particularly in education. Unfortunately, however, government expenditure on education has been biased in a number of ways, namely in favour of tertiary education, urban residents, the formal sector and males. Removal of these biases would greatly increase the contribution of educational expenditures to development while reducing inequality. Moreover, because of complementaries, greater and more efficient investment in human capital would promote a more rapid expansion of physical capital, and particularly more rapid growth of small enterprises.

A guaranteed employment programme represents yet another opportunity to mobilize domestic resources in support of an investment-led growth and adjustment strategy. Labour power is sub-Saharan Africa's greatest asset and unemployed labour power can be used to 'finance' physical capital accumulation in a wide range of activities, yet these opportunities sometimes are obscured by lumping them together under the label of public works projects. There is enormous scope for labour intensive investment in Africa: in the cities as well as in the countryside, in directly productive activities as well as in infrastructure, on small projects as well as large.

One suggestion we make is that asset creation by the poor should be linked with asset ownership by institutions organized for the poor. That is, the physical capital assets created under a guaranteed employment programme should, whenever possible, become the property of those who constructed them, namely the poor. Cooperatives could be formed which would own and manage the assets, and the income generated would partly be distributed to the members of the cooperative and partly be retained by the cooperative to finance future investment projects. In this way, underemployed, low-skilled, poor people gradually would be transformed into people who construct, maintain, manage and accumulate assets from which they obtain a modest but welcome addition to their income.

Finally, there is the vexed question whether state-owned enterprises should be reformed or privatized, i.e. their ownership transferred to the private sector. We recommend reform. The reforms we advocate would include the following: exposing state enterprises to competition from the private sector, gradually reducing the subsidies they receive from government, terminating political influence in the conduct of day-to-day affairs, decentralizing management while holding management accountable to an independent board of directors, and generally 'commercializing' state enterprises so that they behave much like private enterprise. The purpose of the reforms would be to increase the efficiency of state enterprises and ensure that they produce a profit, and thereby contribute to financing investment.

The mere transfer of ownership of large enterprises from the public to the private sector is unlikely to increase efficiency in the allocation of resources or to accelerate the rate of accumulation of capital. Privatization, in other words, is largely a distraction; with few exceptions, it is not relevant to the serious problems faced in sub-Saharan Africa. Rather than enlarging the private sector artificially by privatizing state-owned enterprises, efforts should be concentrated on creating opportunities for new, small-scale and medium-sized private enterprises to develop and prosper. If profitable investment opportunities are created, savings will be forthcoming to take advantage of those opportunities, and the foundations for an investment-led strategy of adjustment and growth would then be in place.

# Part III
# Case Studies

# 9
# Structural Adjustment and Macroeconomic Reform in Vietnam*

The economic reforms introduced in Vietnam after 1989 have been remarkably successful. Indeed of the 28 countries currently going through the transition from central planning to a more market-oriented regime, only China compares favourably with Vietnam.[1] All of the other 26 countries have performed much worse than Vietnam, including Poland, perhaps the most promising of this large residual group. Yet Vietnam's story is poorly understood and is not well known outside a small circle of specialists; it deserves to be told. In this essay we focus on the management of structural adjustment in Vietnam, concentrating on the macroeconomic reforms.

Vietnam is the poorest of the transition economies, even poorer than Mongolia, if one can believe the published data. Per capita income in 1994 was estimated to be about $200, the same as in Nepal, less than in Haiti, but more than in Chad. On the World Bank's list of 133 countries, Vietnam ranks 12, making it one of the poorest countries in the world. From such an impoverished starting point, Vietnam in recent years has achieved one of the fastest rates of growth in the world, well above the average for the developing countries as a whole and broadly comparable to the growth rates enjoyed in Indonesia, Thailand and Malaysia, neighbouring countries in South-east Asia.

The political history of modern Vietnam would not lead one to anticipate explosive economic growth. The country became a French colony towards the end of the nineteenth century. Independence was declared in 1945, very shortly after the Japanese surrendered at the end of the Second World War. The French government, however, did not recognize Vietnam's independence and tried to regain control of its former colony. War broke out in 1946. The French set up a puppet regime in the southern half of the country but were defeated in the north and finally withdrew in 1954. The country was divided in two parts. Civil war ensued. The United States became deeply involved in the conflict and especially after 1960 the intensity of war escalated dramatically. Eventually the Americans, too, were defeated and the country was reunified in 1975.

Three decades of warfare, however, had imposed heavy costs in the form of a huge loss of life, physical injury and psychological damage, demographic imbalance characterized by a relative scarcity of males and a large number of female-headed households, destruction of the country's infrastructure, and severe disruption of the economy. Indeed at the time of reunification Vietnam became one country with two economic systems, neither of which was well designed to achieve growth with equity and human development. A form of comprador capitalism had emerged in the south that was heavily distorted by the need to service a large foreign military force, while in the north a system of central planning emerged whose primary purpose was to mobilize resources for the war effort. The task after reunification was to transform these two incompatible economic systems into one and then redirect it so that it would serve developmental purposes. This was a formidable task and few would have predicted that it would be accomplished with such success.

Among the transition economies Vietnam is the third largest in terms of population. China is of course the largest, with 1.2 billion people. Next comes Russia, with 148 million, followed by Vietnam, with 72 million. These three countries account for nearly 85 per cent of the population of all 28 transition economies. Income per head is far higher in Russia than in China and Vietnam, but incomes have fallen steadily in Russia since the transition began whereas in Vietnam and China they have risen rapidly. The basic information is presented in Table 9.1.

Consider the period 1990–95. The current phase of economic reform in Vietnam began in 1989, although there were of course a series of reforms that go back to reunification in 1975, some of which, as we shall see, were important for our story. Most of the macroeconomic reforms, however, were introduced after 1989 and hence the data in Table 9.1 cover the first six years of macroeconomic reform in Vietnam. The same period coincides roughly with the beginnings of economic reform in Russia, initially while it was still the keystone of the USSR and subsequently, and more intensively, after the disintegration of the Soviet Union. The economic reforms in China, in contrast, began in 1979, a decade before the reforms in Vietnam and Russia, and hence the data in the table describe the situation in China in a later phase of the transition process.

*Table 9.1*  Vietnam, China and Russia compared

|  | Vietnam | China | Russia |
|---|---|---|---|
| 1. Population, 1994 (millions) | 72.0 | 1190.9 | 148.4 |
| 2. Population growth rate, 1991–94 (per cent per annum) | 2.1 | 1.2 | 0.0 |
| 3. GNP per capita, 1994 ($) | 200 | 530 | 2650 |
| 4. Growth of GDP, 1990–95 (per cent per annum) | 7.6 | 10.2 | −8.1 |
| 5. Growth of GDP per capita, 1990–95 (per cent per annum) | 5.4 | 8.9 | −8.1 |
| 6. Cumulative change in per capita income, 1989–95 (per cent) | 37.9 | 67.7 | −40.0 |

*Source*: Calculated from data in World Bank, *World Development Report 1996*, New York: Oxford University Press, 1996, Tables A.2 and A.4, pp. 173 and 175.

Gross domestic product (GDP) increased on average by 7.6 per cent a year in Vietnam. In China it increased by 10.2 per cent a year. Moreover, in both countries there was not a single year in which output failed to rise. In Russia, in contrast, GDP declined on average by 8.1 per cent a year and, furthermore, there was not a single year in which output failed to fall. The economic reforms in Vietnam and China, in other words, occurred within an expansionary environment and this made further reforms easier to introduce, whereas in Russia reforms occurred within a contractionary environment and this made it extremely difficult to sustain the reform process. The environment itself, however, was created by the policies introduced, and the sequence in which they were introduced. In Vietnam and China initial efforts were concentrated on sectors and activities in which output could be increased quickly, i.e. on sectors in which the elasticity of supply was high, and this enabled incomes, savings and investment to rise in a self-sustaining manner. In Russia initial efforts were concentrated on reallocating the existing stock of resources (price liberalization) and on changing the structure of property rights (privatization of state-owned enterprises) rather than on stimulating the growth of output and incomes.

The rise in income per head depends partly on the rate of growth of output and partly on the rate of growth of the population. In Vietnam the rate of growth of the population was relatively high (2.1 per cent per annum) and consequently the growth of per capita income was reduced to 5.5 per cent a year. The population growth rate in China was much lower (1.2 per cent a year) and hence per capita incomes rose much more rapidly than in Vietnam, namely by 9.0 per cent a year.

In Russia there was a demographic collapse. The hardships associated with the transition led to a rise in mortality rates, a sharp decline in life expectancy from 68.8 years in 1981–90 to 64 years in 1994, a rise in the divorce rate, a fall in the marriage rate, a very steep fall in the birth rate and, consequently, to a zero population growth rate. Per capita incomes declined at the same rate as output, namely 8.1 per cent a year.

The cumulative change in average incomes over the period differed considerably among the three countries. In Vietnam per capita income increased 37.9 per cent from 1990 to 1995. In China, during the same six-year period, the rise was 67.7 per cent. In Russia, the cumulative fall in average incomes was 40 per cent. Vietnam and China prospered while Russia became impoverished. The difference in outcomes reflects differences in policies, particularly macroeconomic policies.

## Structural change

Having placed the country in a wider global context, let us now concentrate exclusively on structural change and economic policy within Vietnam itself. The rapid growth in overall output was accompanied by a remarkable change in the composition of output. The essence of this transformation can be seen in Table 9.2 where GDP is disaggregated into three broad sectors.

In just four years, between 1991 and 1995, the share of agriculture in total output declined from 40.5 to 27.5 per cent. That is, the share of agriculture fell by nearly a third. There was a corresponding rise in the share of industrial output in GDP from 23.8 per cent in 1991 to

*Table 9.2*  The composition of output, 1991 and 1995 (per cent of GDP and per cent change over the entire period)

|  | *1991* | *1995* | *Percentage change in output* |
|---|---|---|---|
| Agriculture, forestry and fishing | 40.5 | 27.5 | 21.0 |
| Industry and construction | 23.8 | 30.1 | 67.6 |
| Services | 35.7 | 42.4 | 42.8 |

*Note*: The percentage composition of GDP in 1991 and 1995 is measured in current prices of the respective years; the percentage change in output over the period is measured in constant prices of 1989.
*Source*: Government of Vietnam, General Statistical Office, *Statistical Yearbook 1995*, Hanoi: Statistical Publishing House, 1996, Table 4.2, p. 58 and Table 4.3, p. 59.

30.1 per cent in 1992. This represents an increase in the share of industry by more than a quarter. Services also increased in relative importance, their share rising by less than a fifth, from 35.7 to 42.4 per cent of GDP. Vietnam today is an industrial and service economy, not an agricultural economy, and this transformation occurred in only four years. As late as 1991 the agricultural sector was larger than either industry or services; by 1994 it was smaller than both.

This dramatic and rapid shift in the composition of output occurred despite exceptionally rapid growth in the agricultural sector. As can be seen in the last column of Table 9.2, agricultural output increased in real terms by 21 per cent between 1991 and 1995, that is, by more than 5 per cent a year. Of course industrial output and the output of the services sector increased more rapidly still, namely by 67.6 and 42.8 per cent, respectively, over the four-year period. The important point to understand, however, is that structural change did not consist of a reallocation of an existing volume of resources (implying a contraction of some activities and an expansion of others) but of rapid (but different) rates of growth of all three sectors.

In most countries industrialization and the growth of the services sector are accompanied by urbanization. This apparently has not happened in Vietnam, or at least not yet. The transition to a more market-oriented economy, and the radical shifts in the composition of output that transition policies have encouraged, have not resulted in rapid rural-to-urban migration. Vietnam remains a predominantly rural society. Indeed in 1991, official data indicate that 79.6 per cent of the (registered) population lived in the countryside and 20.4 per cent in the cities. By 1995, according to official data, the proportion in urban areas had risen only 0.1 per cent and the proportion in rural areas had fallen by the same amount, to 79.5 per cent. In other words, there has not been a structural change in the location of the population. The official data, however, almost certainly understate the shift in the population that has occurred, primarily because the permanent 'floating' or unregistered population in the cities is ignored. Even so, the degree of urbanization in Vietnam is lower than in other broadly comparable Asian countries.

## The accumulation of capital

Rapid growth requires high levels of investment in physical assets. A high rate of accumulation of capital is not sufficient to achieve sustained rapid growth but it is necessary. Also necessary are investments in human capital (education, health, nutrition) and measures to preserve and enhance the stock of natural capital (land, fresh water supplies, coastal waterways, etc.). Equally important are policies that ensure that investment is allocated efficiently, i.e. to projects with the highest social rates of return.

The official data on investment are reproduced in Table 9.3 below. As can be seen, the data indicate that gross investment has increased steadily, from 14.3 per cent of GDP in 1991 to 25.1 per cent in 1995. This represents a relative increase in the share of investment of 43 per cent in just four years, an impressive achievement. The average rate of investment during the entire period, however, was only 20.5 per cent of GDP, a rather modest rate compared to many other developing countries and well below the investment rates achieved in rapidly growing economies such as China, Thailand, Malaysia and Indonesia.

Indeed the puzzle is how Vietnam managed to achieve such a rapid rate of growth during the transition period with such a modest rate of accumulation of capital. There are four plausible possibilities. First, it could be argued that the rise in total output had little to do with the rate of investment but instead reflects a more efficient allocation of resources in response to price liberalization. The implication is that the benefits achieved so far during the reform process are once-for-all gains which cannot be repeated. Given the rapid growth that occurred in all sectors of the economy, however, it seems unlikely that the large cumulative gains in per capita income are due primarily to an increase in static allocative efficiency. Something else must be going on apart from the magic of the market.

A second possibility is that Vietnam has been unusually successful in allocating investment to projects with extraordinarily high rates of return on capital. This is reflected in exceptionally low incremental capital–output ratios, which vary between less than three (with no gestation lag) and less than two (with a one-year lag). Given the general

*Table 9.3* Gross capital formation, 1991–95 (per cent of GDP)

| | |
|---|---|
| 1991 | 14.3 |
| 1992 | 17.0 |
| 1993 | 22.6 |
| 1994 | 23.5 |
| 1995 | 25.1 |
| Average | 20.5 |

*Source*: Government of Vietnam, General Statistical Office, *Statistical Yearbook 1995*, Hanoi, Statistical Publishing House, 1996, Table 4.7, p. 63.

scarcity of capital in the country and the damage to the existing stock of capital that occurred during decades of war, it is conceivable that returns on the margin to capital accumulation are remarkably high. It is harder to believe, however, that capital markets were able to achieve a high degree of efficiency in allocating investment funds. Indeed it is widely known that the banking system is inefficient and in need of reform, that state-owned enterprises have privileged access to credit at low interest rates, that many people (women, the poor in general, the urban informal sector, small farmers) have virtually no access to formal sector credit, etc. Most domestic investment is self-financed or financed through informal credit arrangements; the capital market is under-developed and the commercial banking system plays a minor role in financial intermediation. It is thus unlikely that efficiency in investment allocation is the answer to the puzzle.

A third possibility is that Vietnam in the 1990s is reaping the benefits of investment in the 1980s. That is, paradoxically, that gestation periods have been exceptionally long. Those who put forward this explanation point to large investment projects financed by foreign aid (usually from the Soviet Union) that happened to come to maturity around the time 'doi moi' was first implemented and the Soviet Union collapsed. These projects include hydro-electric dams, crude oil, coffee and rubber (all financed by the Soviet Union), as well as cement and paper (financed by Sweden). The argument is that not only did these particular sectors enjoy very rapid growth in the 1990s but that in the cases of electricity and petroleum, expansion in these sectors also allowed other sectors to expand and increase their degree of capacity utilization. Thus growth as a whole accelerated. This argument implicitly plays down the importance of the economic reforms and domestic initiatives while attaching great importance to foreign aid in the pre-reform period. This may be part of the answer to the puzzle, but it relies too much on a happy coincidence to be persuasive.

The fourth and most likely explanation is that investment has been underestimated. The statistical system is able to estimate accurately government investment (whether financed by tax revenues or foreign aid) and investment by state enterprises. It is also able to measure direct foreign investment, almost all of which is in the form of joint ventures with state enterprises. Private domestic investment in relatively large enterprises presumably also is accurately measured. Much of the rest, however, may be missed, namely private investment in urban small and medium enterprises, urban informal sector investments in service activities and workshops, investments by small farmers in land improvements, many investments in small-scale non-agricultural rural activities, and most investments which require an expenditure of labour effort rather than the purchase of equipment and materials. It is impossible to ascertain the extent of underestimation of total investment, but it could be considerable.

This suspicion is reinforced by the very low estimates of domestic savings and the consequent high dependence on external resources (foreign aid and private foreign capital) to finance investment. In 1994, for example, domestic savings were only 13 per cent of GDP and Vietnam apparently had to rely on foreign savings to finance nearly 45 per cent of total investment. It is quite possible that the large inflows of aid and other forms of foreign capital have facilitated an expansion of consumption and thereby lowered domestic savings – empirical evidence from many other countries shows that this frequently has occurred[2] – but the primary explanation for the low rate of savings in Vietnam is that savings (and investment) have been seriously underestimated and dependence on foreign capital greatly exaggerated.

## Are the data credible?

Having questioned the accuracy of official estimates of investment and domestic savings, let us consider more generally the credibility of macroeconomic data and the possible biases introduced by inaccurate estimates. First, it is likely that the level of output is understated in some sectors. Agricultural production, certainly for the main crops, probably is estimated as accurately as in other developing countries of Asia. The data on production of goods and services by state-owned enterprises is reliable. Estimates of services produced in the private sector, however, are likely to be poor and output in this sector probably is substantially higher than the amount recorded in the national accounts. By extension, output in the private non-agricultural sector as a whole, including the output of small-scale industrial enterprises, probably is greatly underestimated. The growth of the informal sector almost certainly is not fully reflected in official data.

The implication of this is that gross domestic product is higher than the official data suggest. Indeed this is recognized by the government itself which states that the official estimate 'no doubt considerably understates the GDP, since there is a large informal economy'.[3] This, in turn, implies that the level of per capita income is higher than is widely believed and that the proportion of the population living in poverty is lower. In other words, the people of Vietnam are better off than the published statistical information suggests.

Second, this impression is strengthened by an abundance of anecdotal evidence that indicates aggregate expenditure is underestimated. It was argued above that private investment (and private savings) are higher than reported and hence that total investment is greater than the official figures suggest. Private consumption, which is estimated as a residual by subtracting public consumption and total investment from GDP, also is underestimated. We know for example that unrecorded imports are substantial and that much of this consists of smuggled consumer goods from China. We know, too, that some exports are unrecorded, although the underestimation of exports probably is rather modest. The implication is that investment (and savings), exports (and imports) and private consumption are understated in the official data and hence GDP as measured by aggregate expenditure is larger than reported in the national accounts.

In other words, whether one examines aggregate production or aggregate expenditure, the conclusion seems to be that gross domestic product is higher than the official data suggest. Finally, what about the rate of growth? Is that also underestimated?

The answer largely turns on whether the underestimation of investment is greater than the underestimation of total output. That is, if the proportion of total output that is invested is higher than the proportion recorded in the national accounts, it is likely that the rate of growth of total output also is higher than the rate implicit in the national accounts. One unpleasant implication of this is that the national accounts are becoming increasingly unreliable.

One cannot be certain whether the rate of investment (as opposed to the level of investment) has been biased downwards in the official data, but it is quite possible that it has. That is, the errors made in estimating total investment may well be proportionately greater than the errors made in estimating total product. The investment accounts, in our judgement, are likely to be less accurate than the production accounts. If this view turns out to be correct, the rate of accumulation of capital, and hence the growth rate, may be faster than most analysts believe.

A hint that something is seriously wrong in the national accounts comes from an inspection of the data on the structure of ownership. One would expect that in an economy moving towards greater reliance on the market mechanism and creating more opportunities for private initiative the share of state ownership would decline. The official statistics, however, report the opposite: the proportion of output originating in state-owned enterprises (including joint ventures between state enterprises and foreign investors) is said to have risen. In 1990, for instance, 32.5 per cent of output in Vietnam was generated in state-owned enterprises or by the state itself whereas in 1995 the share of state ownership had risen to 42.2 per cent. That is, the share of state ownership increased by nearly 30 per cent in only five years. This is not plausible and the likely explanation is that the increase in output in the non-state sector is hugely underestimated. In other words, the growth of the non-state sector has in fact been much more rapid than the data indicate.

If this is true, gross domestic product as a whole must have been rising faster than the official statistics would have us believe. Indeed the material well being of the people of Vietnam may be increasing more rapidly than the available data indicate. Restructuring and the economic reforms have been even more successful than they appear in the official data.

## The nature and sequence of policy reforms

The question that now arises is how these remarkable accomplishments were achieved. Two important points need to be made at the start. First, the 'initial conditions' were favourable. Vietnam inherited from the socialist period – or the period of central planning – a fairly equal distribution of wealth, particularly landed wealth. Collective agriculture in the north and land reforms in the south after reunification ensured that when a more market-oriented economic system was created, great inequalities in income and wealth did not swiftly emerge. The degree of equality was greater in the north than in the south, but in neither region were there extreme forms of inequality. In addition, Vietnam also inherited from the socialist period a fairly equal distribution of human capital. Literacy was widespread, most people had at least a few years of formal education and the great majority of the population had access to primary health care. As a result, Vietnam possessed at the outset of the reforms a skilled and healthy labour force that was able to respond quickly to economic opportunities.

Second, the reforms were introduced quickly but in sequence over a series of years. There was no 'big bang' when an attempt was made to introduce many fundamental changes simultaneously. 'Doi moi' (or renovation) took off in 1989 and the reform process conventionally is dated from that year, but 'doi moi' was announced in 1986 and several important policy changes or policy experiments were introduced several years before that. The reform process has been pragmatic, experimental and cautious – in short, well managed – and the authorities have been able to tolerate during the transition inconsistencies, half measures and ambiguities that would be unacceptable to an ideologically motivated transformation.

The acceleration of economic reform in Vietnam after 1989 was precipitated by an economic crisis caused in part by a severe drought but mostly by the collapse of the Soviet Union, the break-up of the Soviet trading bloc (CMEA) and the sharp fall in Soviet aid. The foundations of economic reform, however, had been constructed much earlier. A calendar of the basic reforms would include the following:

1979–85:    improvement in agricultural incentives and the introduction of the output contract system; abolition of agricultural collectives; state enterprises allowed to sell in the market any above-quota output

1987:       internal trade liberalized; rationing system abolished for many commodities and market determined prices for non-essential goods introduced; the dual price system was modified to reduce price differentials

1988:       in agriculture, land tenure (user) rights set at 15 years (increased to 20–50 years in 1993); greater autonomy given to managers of state-owned enterprises

1989:       foreign trade liberalized; foreign exchange rate devalued and set close to the market rate; dual price system abolished; positive real rates of interest introduced; tax reforms introduced

1990:       restructuring of state enterprises begun, largely through mergers and consolidations

1992:       tight monetary policy introduced in order to control inflation; restructuring of state enterprises intensified

In Vietnam, as in China, reforms began in agriculture. This was the largest sector of the economy; it was also the sector which accounted for most of the employment; equally important, it was the sector where most of the poor were concentrated. The benefits of the initial reforms were therefore very widespread. They reached the great majority of the population and created a favourable political environment for subsequent reforms. Moreover, because the reforms benefited the poor disproportionately, the first phase of the reform process probably reduced inequality in the distribution of income. Later phases, centred on foreign aid and foreign direct investment, helped increase urban incomes disproportionately and probably increased inequality in the distribution of income.

A key feature of the reform process is that efforts were concentrated where output could respond quickly, i.e. where supply elasticities were high. In agriculture initially this was in rice farming, but other natural resource-based activities soon followed and as a result Vietnam enjoyed an export boom in rice, marine products, coffee, cashew nuts, i.e. in labour intensive products produced by relatively low-income people. The liberalization of internal trade and the creation of space for the private sector was met by a rapid supply response from the informal sector and from small-scale private sector service and manufacturing activities. More recently, labour intensive, export-oriented industries have begun to emerge, notably footwear and garments. Finally, Vietnam is experiencing rapid growth in the tourist industry – another labour intensive activity – and establishing close links with overseas Vietnamese.

It was important to concentrate on sectors where supply elasticities are high in order to ensure that growth was maintained and preferably accelerated during the transition process. Rapid growth makes it easier to effect radical changes in the composition of output because it provides an environment favourable to high rates of investment and savings. In transition economies where growth was allowed to falter, investment, output and incomes usually collapsed and the entire transition process encountered serious difficulties. Vietnam skilfully avoided that trap.

Foreign trade liberalization, introduced after the liberalization of internal trade, led to the creation of an open economy in Vietnam. The speed with which this occurred is remarkable because the country simultaneously had, first, to find new trading partners (as it happens in South-east and East Asia primarily) when its former partner (the Soviet Union) no longer could supply imports or provide an outlet for exports and, second, to create a structure of incentives that enabled Vietnam to trade at competitive world prices.

The transformation of the international trade regime has been a great success. Exports have grown at an explosive pace, far more rapidly than GDP, and as a result, the proportion of total output exported has increased dramatically. Moreover, openness to trade has been accompanied by openness to foreign investment. There seems, however, to have been an expectation that foreign direct investment would be a major source of growth, and when this failed to materialize to the extent desired, some disappointment appears to have occurred. The experience of Vietnam, however, is consistent with that of many other countries, namely that foreign investment is more often a consequence of rapid economic growth than a cause of it. If economic policies continue to be successful and growth remains rapid, foreign investment is likely to be attracted to the country in considerable volume, but if economic performance should deteriorate for any reason, foreign capital is likely to stay away. The lesson to be drawn from this experience is not that foreign capital has no contribution to make – surely it does – but rather that it would be imprudent to rely on foreign capital to be an engine of growth.

Finally, Vietnam has been successful in maintaining a reasonable degree of macroeconomic stability. This is important during the transition from central planning to a more market-oriented economic system because the price mechanism conveys signals through changes in relative prices. If there is rapid inflation, i.e. if the general level of prices is rising rapidly, it is difficult for buyers and sellers to detect changes in relative prices and hence to alter their production, investment and purchasing decisions in an efficient manner. The price mechanism ceases to function effectively when inflation becomes excessive. Unfortunately, it is impossible to know when the rate of inflation begins to become 'excessive' and consequently it is wise to err on the side of caution.

The rate of inflation reached a peak of 774 per cent a year at one point during 1986, the year 'doi moi' was announced. Price increases moderated somewhat in 1987 and 1988 although they remained very high. Sustained inflation of about 70 per cent a year occurred during 1989–91 as a consequence of the economic disruption caused in Vietnam by the disintegration of the Soviet Union. However, the authorities responded by introducing tight monetary and credit policies in 1992 and they have been maintained ever since.

As can be seen in Table 9.4, the rate of inflation was brought down to an annual rate of 17.5 per cent in 1992 and in no year since then has it exceeded 20 per cent a year, a possible threshold figure beyond

*Table 9.4*  Changes in consumer prices, 1985–95 (per cent per annum)

| 1985 | 192  | 1991 | 67.5 |
|------|------|------|------|
| 1986 | 487  | 1992 | 17.5 |
| 1987 | 317  | 1993 | 5.2  |
| 1988 | 311  | 1994 | 14.4 |
| 1989 | 76   | 1995 | 12.7 |
| 1990 | 67.1 |      |      |

*Sources*: 1985–89: World Bank, *Vietnam: Transition to the Market*, Washington, DC, 15 September 1993, Table 2.1, p. 235. 1990–95: Government of Vietnam, General Statistical Office, *Statistical Yearbook 1995*, Hanoi, Statistical Publishing House, 1996, Table 8.5, p. 247. Note that the price changes in the second period are from December of one year to December of the next.

which inflation hampers allocative efficiency. Indeed the rate of inflation appears to be falling and by the end of this year (1997) it is likely to be in single figures. Tight monetary policies have been supplemented by tax reforms (which have increased government revenue) and by imposing a hard budget constraint on state-owned enterprises (which has made it possible to terminate government subsidies to finance enterprise deficits). Thus fiscal and monetary policies have worked in harmony to maintain macroeconomic balance and this, in turn, has made it possible to stabilize the exchange rate (and thereby avoid inflation caused by devaluation).

In summary, macroeconomic management has been skilful and has created a favourable environment for the structural reforms that have been introduced. Vietnam has transformed its economic system, restructured output and maintained reasonable stability while accelerating the rate of growth. In the process, the average standard of living has improved considerably and poverty has been reduced. It is a remarkable record from which other countries can learn.

# 10
# Employment, Poverty and Social Protection in Kazakhstan*

The people of Kazakhstan have experienced severe hardship since the country became independent in 1991 following the disintegration of the Soviet Union. Six years of economic decline and rising social distress are leading the government to reassess the situation and formulate a new strategy for development. The purpose of this study is to contribute to the reassessment and to suggest policies that could reverse the decline and help to improve the general well being of the population. We shall be particularly concerned with employment policies and social protection and the way they are inserted into a coherent overall strategy of development.

We begin with a discussion of the broad objectives of development, drawing attention to the difficulties often encountered in distinguishing between ends and means and the multiple purposes of policies intended to create employment. We then consider the systemic reform in Kazakhstan and the policies adopted to effect a transition from a centrally planned economic system to a more market-oriented economy. This is followed by an analysis of the policies pursued, the choice of priorities and the undesired consequences of the strategy adopted. Finally, we outline an alternative strategy that is pro-growth, pro-employment and pro-poor.

## Objectives of development

It is now widely accepted that the objective of development is to increase the capabilities of people to pursue a life of their choice.[1] The central ideas here are 'capabilities' and 'choice'. The ultimate purpose of development, and of development policy, is to enable people to lead a long life, to have access to the world's stock of knowledge and

251

information, to be able to participate in the life of the community, to be capable of moving about from place to place, to have sufficient material possessions so that they can live without shame, and so on. Development, then, is a process that increases people's abilities to achieve their potential; whether or not they actually choose to achieve their potential is an important but secondary matter.

The element of individual choice is what is most important. It is one thing to go hungry because one is incapable of acquiring the means of sustenance; it is quite another thing, having the capability to acquire adequate food, to choose to go hungry, for example, by engaging in a hunger strike to make a political point. Hunger is present in both cases but the significance of hunger is quite different, since in the first case the individual had no choice in the matter whereas in the second case hunger was freely chosen. Similarly, it is one thing to stay at home out of choice; it is quite another thing to be confined to an isolated region because lack of transport severely reduces one's mobility. Development expands the range of choice: it increases people's freedom to be what they like and to do what they wish. Indeed, it can be argued that development ultimately is about freedom, in two senses.[2]

First, there are the negative freedoms, e.g. freedom from hunger, from avoidable illnesses, from insecurity in old age. Development increases these freedoms by increasing the capability of people to acquire adequate nutrition, to obtain health services, to save for a pension, etc. Second, there are the positive freedoms, e.g. the freedom to travel, to study at high school or university, to play a violin. Development increases some of these positive freedoms by providing the resources necessary for travel by train, by making it possible to allocate time to intellectual pursuits, by providing the income needed to purchase a musical instrument and hire a tutor. Capabilities and choice thus go together to enhance freedom and hence development and freedom, while not the same thing, are in many instances closely connected.

This conception of development differs from the older view which regards development as virtually synonymous with an increase in output per head. That is, the older view was a commodity-centred view of development which gave priority to the production of goods and services whereas the new view is a people-centred view of development which gives priority to the enhancement of individual capabilities. The new view is commonly known as the human development approach.[3] Governments, including Kazakhstan's, have accepted the new view in principle, but policy-making bodies, including the Strategic Planning

Agency, have found it difficult to grasp the full implications of the new view and to put them into practice.

The human development approach represents a shift away from a commodity-centred view of development, but it does not deny the important role played by increased production in enhancing human capabilities. Instead it transforms increased production from an end in itself into a means to increase human capabilities. That is, the enhancement of capabilities is the end and an increased output of goods and services is one of the means.

This shift of emphasis and the transformation of material production from an end to a means has led to a reconsideration of development policy and, in particular, to a more modest role being given to 'economic policy' and correspondingly greater importance being attached to 'social policy'. The former once occupied the centre of the stage, since economic policy focuses on macroeconomic balance, investment in physical assets and the growth of domestic product, i.e. the central preoccupations of a commodity-centred view of development. Social policy, on the other hand, was relegated to the margins, since its role was to provide assistance (in the form of transfer payments and social services) to those who failed to benefit from the growth of output, such as the elderly, the handicapped and perhaps widows and orphans. Under the human development approach, in contrast, social policy becomes a major component of overall development policy, in part because social policy is directly concerned with the enhancement of human capabilities and in part because social expenditure has come to be viewed as an 'investment in people' with a potentially high rate of return. That is, social expenditure may help to increase the output of goods and services and this increased output, in turn, may contribute to the enhancement of people's capabilities. Thus social expenditure can be simultaneously an end (directly increasing human development) and a means (increasing material output which indirectly increases human development). Some analysts, in fact, regard the distinction between 'social development' and 'economic development' as obsolete and the distinction between social policy and economic policy as misleading.[4] Both are parts of development policy and the objective of development policy is to promote human development.

Public expenditure on such things as primary and secondary education, basic health care, child nutrition and family planning services are somewhat analogous to expenditures on plant and equipment. These investments in 'human capital' help to increase output and thereby contribute to the growth of domestic product.[5] Indeed it has been shown in a number of cases that the rate of return on investments in human capital is at least as high and sometimes is higher than the rate of return on investments in physical capital.[6] Moreover, some investments in human capital can have a multiplicity of desirable consequences. For example, increased education for women has been shown to raise the productivity of female labour (and thereby increase aggregate output), reduce the average number of births per woman (and thereby lower the rate of growth of the population and increase the rate of growth of income per capita), improve the nutritional and health status of children (and thereby raise the productivity of the next generation of workers) and increase the likelihood that their children in turn will receive an education (thereby completing a virtuous circle).

Empirical findings such as these have helped to transform what was once classified as 'social expenditure' into 'human capital formation'. Notice, however, that in this formulation social expenditure is treated as a means to an end, namely an input (human capital) into a production process which results in a higher output of goods and services. This formulation, in other words, while a great advance over the earlier view that social expenditure is unproductive, still falls squarely within a commodity-centred view of development.

The human development approach, in contrast, helps us to see that social expenditure can be simultaneously an end in itself as well as a means to some other end. Expenditure on primary health care, for instance, directly contributes to human development and is therefore an end in itself, but it also helps to increase the productivity of labour and thus indirectly contributes to human development by increasing the volume of goods and services produced. The provision of family planning services has a direct impact on the capabilities of women to pursue a life of their choice. It may also have an indirect impact on human development through its effects on fertility and the growth of income per capita. It is important not to lose sight of the fact that public spending on social services is not just a form of human capital formation, it is also an end in itself, an important aspect of human development.[7] Hence a development strategy that reduces social expenditure, whatever its other virtues may be, runs a serious risk of reducing the level of human development and undermining the objective it seeks to promote.

Employment, like social expenditure, has multiple facets. First, it contributes to the output of goods and services; it is a productive input in the process of production and a source of economic growth. Second, employment provides people with a source of income. Indeed, for most people it is the work that they perform which establishes their claim to a share of the economy's income. In many cases the production and income aspects of employment coincide but they need not do so. For example, in some state enterprises there may be 'surplus' labour in the sense that the volume of employment is substantially larger than is necessary given the firm's volume of production. In such cases employment (on the margin) does not contribute to output but it does none the less provide a source of income to the employed workers. Third, quite apart from its effect on production and the distribution of income, employment gives workers a sense of dignity by enabling them to participate in the activities of the community and contribute something of value. Absence of employment, in contrast, often is demoralizing and can lead to self-destructive and anti-social behaviour: drug and alcohol addiction, ill health, depression and other mental disorders, crime and vandalism, and even suicide. Lack of employment, in other words, can have heavy social costs, some of which are borne by the individual and some by the society at large. Finally, employment is the vehicle which makes it possible to reap the benefits of investment in human capital. The returns to human development expenditure will fall dramatically if those who embody human capital are unable to put their energy, skills, knowledge and initiative to productive use. Since in most instances human capital cannot be separated from the human beings who incorporate it, failure to provide employment to all who seek it will result in failure to exploit fully the economy's stock of human capital.[8]

## Systemic reform in Kazakhstan

Given the development objectives discussed above, let us turn now to a consideration of the strategy adopted by Kazakhstan to effect a transition from a centrally planned to a more market-oriented economy. In fact in retrospect the strategy was remarkably simple and rested on two pillars: price liberalization and privatization of state-owned enterprises. Both sets of policies were intended to be implemented quickly and thus Kazakhstan is a classic case of what is known popularly as 'shock therapy'.

The justification for giving high priority to price liberalization is obvious. A market economy responds to price signals, i.e. to changes in relative prices of goods and services, raw materials, labour, finance capital and foreign exchange. In order for a market economy to function efficiently, prices must reflect the real costs of production. Under a centrally planned system, however, prices are administratively set, do not reflect real costs and perform no allocative function. It is therefore desirable, according to this argument, to create an efficient structure of incentives as quickly as possible by liberalizing prices instantaneously in a 'big bang'.

This argument is valid, however, only under certain assumptions. First, there must be macroeconomic balance and in particular the rate of inflation must be moderate. If the general level of prices is rising rapidly, it will be difficult for investors, producers and consumers to detect small changes in relative prices and profit incentives – particularly if the participants in the market are unfamiliar with market processes – and hence the allocative function of the price system will perform poorly. Second, the responsiveness of supply and demand to price changes must be significant – that is, elasticities must be relatively high – otherwise changes in relative prices will have little effect on the composition of output and the pattern of consumption. Third, the level of employment and the degree of capacity utilization must be high. The reason for this is that the responsiveness of output to changes in relative prices depends on the rate of investment and investment, in turn, is strongly influenced by the tempo of economic activity. If the economy is depressed, investment will be low, and if investment is low, the pace of structural adjustment in the composition of output will be impaired.

Unfortunately, none of these conditions for the success of price liberalization were present in Kazakhstan. Prior to independence, Kazakhstan received very large transfers from the Soviet Union which were used to finance a very substantial part of total government expenditure. In the late 1980s these transfers were equivalent to more than 9 per cent of domestic product. After independence these transfers ceased abruptly and the government faced a huge deficit. Rather than restore macroeconomic balance by raising tax revenues and reducing expenditure, the government chose to monetize the deficit.[9] As we shall see below, this resulted in hyper-inflation and destroyed any possibility that rapid price liberalization would succeed.

The problem was exacerbated by the low supply elasticities in response to price liberalization. The market could not replace the planning system instantaneously and the collapse of trading arrangements with the Soviet Union and the rest of the CMEA meant that Kazakhstan lost the market for its exports. It proved impossible to switch supply to other markets quickly and as a result output fell. The economy entered a deep depression. The state-owned industrial enterprises in particular were severely affected because of the tight integration of state enterprises under a planning regime with their suppliers and buyers, many of whom were located in other republics of the USSR. The depression, in turn, led to a sharp fall in investment, which further reduced the ability of the economy to increase supplies in response to price signals.

Given the magnitude of the external 'shocks' to the economy – the loss of large transfers from the Soviet Union and the loss of export markets and of sources of imports – severe disruption was unavoidable, but the policies adopted by the government made a bad situation even worse. The alternative was to follow the Chinese example by (i) not allowing inflation to become rapid and (ii) liberalizing gradually, initially allowing only above-quota output to be sold at market prices while maintaining fixed prices for deliveries under quota. Such a 'dual price' system does not produce 'equilibrium' or market clearing prices and it creates opportunities for corruption through illegal arbitrage and hence cannot be sustained indefinitely, but it proved to be an effective way to introduce market mechanisms into a centrally planned economy.[10]

Let us now turn to the second pillar on which the transition strategy rests, namely privatization. It is widely believed that private ownership of the means of production is a precondition for an efficient market economy, but this is not true. A market economy is compatible with many forms of ownership – owner-operators, partnerships, limited liability corporations, cooperatives and state-owned enterprises. There is no basis in economic theory for making privatization of state-owned enterprises a top priority in transition economies, and indeed in Kazakhstan it is said that 'political and social motivations' were the basis for the privatization programme.[11] Be that as it may, privatization proceeded quickly, beginning in 1992 with small enterprises. By May 1997, more than 18 500 enterprises had been privatized, including nearly 3000 large and medium enterprises.[12] Ownership of state enterprises was transferred to the private sector in a variety of ways: through vouchers, by auction, through direct sale (e.g. to foreign enterprises or to the managers and workers of the enterprise) and through sale of shares. The net result, however, has been disappointing. Privatization has not been popular with the public. Moreover the 'privatisation process was not successful and in 1996 the government discontinued it' for five months, turning instead to establishing management contracts with outside enterprises to operate state-owned companies, particularly in the mining and metallurgical sectors.[13]

No doubt there are many reasons for the lack of success of the privatization programme, but even had it been a success on its own terms, it still would have been a strategic error, an example of wrong priorities. There are two reasons for saying this. First, the problem of the state enterprises could not be remedied by a mere transfer of ownership. They needed to be reorganized; they required reform of their system of management and modernization of their plant and equipment. State firms which had responsibilities for providing social services to their employees should have been relieved of these responsibilities so that they could compete effectively with privately owned enterprises, but obviously this could not be done until government had reformed the system of social provisioning. Similarly, tax reform should occur before privatization so that a transfer of ownership (particularly of small enterprises) does not result in a loss of government revenue, a larger budget deficit and faster inflation.[14] A system of commercial law should be in place before privatization occurs so that 'mafia capitalism' does not discredit the idea of a market economy and undermine public support for the reform process as a whole. And in Kazakhstan, where state enterprises often are monopolies and many towns have a single state enterprise as a dominant employer, a regulatory framework should be in place before enterprises are privatized. In other words, privatization should be the last step in a sequence of reforms rather than the first.

Second, rather than privatizing existing enterprises, high priority during the transition period should be given to creating new private enterprises, especially small and medium size enterprises. Such enterprises tend to economize on capital; they are employment intensive; they are flexible and highly responsive to market signals. They add dynamism to the economy and can make a substantial contribution to accelerating growth. Once again, the Chinese example is instructive.[15] There has been virtually no privatization of state enterprises in China, although some have been transformed into collective enterprises. Instead effort has been directed towards creating an environment in which new, small private enterprises can emerge and flourish. The result has been a rapidly expanding private sector. The state sector has grown too but the private sector has grown faster and is now considerably larger than the state sector. In other words, China created a large and strong private sector through a process of growth rather than by contracting the state sector through a process of privatization. Vietnam has adopted a similar strategy and there too it seems to be working.[16]

With the benefit of hindsight and the successful examples of China and Vietnam in front of us, it appears that Kazakhstan adopted the wrong strategy to create a market economy. The economic and social consequences, as we shall see, have been disastrous.

## The outcome of the reform process

The initial conditions at the time of independence were not bad. The population of Kazakhstan was well educated, healthy and enjoyed a long life. Income inequality was low, there was a wide range of social services and access to these services was equitable. The country enjoyed an abundance of natural capital, much of which had not been exploited. True, the growth rate had been falling since the 1970s (see Table 10.1) and the country faced severe environmental problems including rapid desiccation of the Aral Sea, the rising water level of the Caspian Sea, radioactive contamination from nuclear tests and heavy industrial pollution in many urban centres. Even so, the development prospects for Kazakhstan were rather favourable compared to other landlocked countries in central Asia.

The transition strategy, however, concentrating on price liberalization and privatization of state-owned enterprises, was narrow in its focus and addressed the wrong issues. As a result, the country could not respond to the loss of the financial subsidy from the Soviet Union, the collapse of the CMEA trading arrangements and the exodus of large numbers of skilled managerial and technical personnel. The top priorities were to stabilize the economy in response to large external shocks and maintain output and incomes and, if possible, a positive rate of growth. These priorities were neglected.

As can be seen in Table 10.1, the price level exploded. In 1990, the rate of inflation was only 4.2 per cent a year. At its peak in 1994, the rate of inflation was 1980 per cent a year. The government, to its credit, responded promptly and since then the rate of inflation has declined sharply and the situation may at last be under control. The hyper-inflation, however, coincided with the period of price liberalization and destroyed the possibility of a smooth transition to an efficient market economy. A 'hard landing' became inevitable.

The external shocks, the hyper-inflation and the emigration of skilled people led to an enormous contraction of output. Between 1990 and 1995 the rate of growth of domestic product was negative and the rate of decline accelerated rapidly during the first five years of this period. The data in Table 10.1 imply that from 1990 to 1995 there was a cumulative fall in output of 54.5 per cent. In other words, output today is almost certainly less than half what it was at the beginning of

*Table 10.1*  Inflation and economic growth in Kazakhstan, 1971–96 (per cent per annum)

| Years | Growth of GDP | Rate of inflation (% per year) |
|-------|---------------|-------------------------------|
| 1971–80 | 4.4 | – |
| 1981–89 | 2.0 | – |
| 1990 | −4.6 | 4.2 |
| 1991 | −6.8 | 91.0 |
| 1992 | −13.0 | 1610.0 |
| 1993 | −15.6 | 1760.0 |
| 1994 | −25.0 | 1980.0 |
| 1995 | −9.0 | 180.0 |
| 1996 | 1.1 | 39.7 |

*Sources*: 1971–95: World Bank, *From Plan to Market, World Development Report*, New York: Oxford University Press, 1996; 1996: International Monetary Fund, *Republic of Kazakhstan: Recent Economic Developments*, 4 June 1997, processed, Appendix Table 1, p. 87 and Government of Kazakhstan, Centre for Economic Reforms, *Kazakhstan Economic Trends*, Almaty, May 1997.

the decade. Fortunately, recovery from the deep depression may have begun since output appears to have increased in 1996 and the first quarter of 1997. The rate of growth is, however, still very low and a sustained effort will have to be made to ensure that growth continues, and at a much quicker pace.

Growth is estimated to have been 1.1 per cent in 1996. Most of the increased output, however, originated in one sector, namely trade and catering, which grew by 16.9 per cent. If one excludes trade and catering from GDP, then output actually declined by 1.3 per cent. In other words, growth in 1996 was narrowly based and the economy remains very fragile. The output of the construction sector, for instance, which is closely associated with the level of investment, declined by 22.9 per cent, again indicating that the sustainability of growth is uncertain.

The collapse of output was of course accompanied by a collapse of incomes. The entire population of Kazakhstan became impoverished. At the same time, inequality in the distribution of income appears to have increased: the Gini coefficient is reported to have risen from 0.297 in 1990 to 0.327 in 1993, a rise of just over 10 per cent.[17]

Data on the distribution of personal income by quintiles are presented in Table 10.2. If one compares 1989 (prior to the beginning of the transition period) with 1993 and 1994 (the two years of most severe decline), it is evident that the economic depression affected disproportionately the lowest 60 per cent of income recipients. In fact the

*Table 10.2* The distribution of personal income in Kazakhstan, 1989–94 (percentage shares)

| Quintiles | 1989 | 1993 | 1994 |
|---|---|---|---|
| Poorest | 9.6 | 5.7 | 6.3 |
| 2 | 13.7 | 11.0 | 12.4 |
| 3 | 18.2 | 16.2 | 17.8 |
| 4 | 24.0 | 25.7 | 29.5 |
| Richest | 34.5 | 41.4 | 34.0 |

*Source:* UNDP, *Kazakhstan Human Development Report 1996*, Almaty: UNDP, Table 4.1, p. 52.

*Table 10.3* The change in real personal income in Kazakhstan between 1989 and 1994 (percentages)

| Quintiles | Change in real income |
|---|---|
| Poorest | −67.9 |
| 2 | −55.8 |
| 3 | −53.7 |
| 4 | −39.9 |
| Richest | −51.8 |

*Source:* Author's calculations.

poorest quintile experienced the greatest fall in its share of income: between 1989 and 1994, for example, the share of the bottom quintile fell by more than 34 per cent. The poor were thus doubly harmed: they, along with others, experienced the fall in average incomes and, in addition, they suffered a fall in their share of income. The lowest-income people were reduced to destitution.

If one combines the data in Tables 10.1 and 10.2 and assumes, per-haps unrealistically, that on average personal income declined at the same rate as gross domestic product, it is possible to obtain a rough estimate of the extent of the fall in real income of each quintile group between 1989 and 1994. These estimates are presented in Table 10.3. The effects of declining average income combined with the worsening of the distribution of income can be clearly seen. The poorest group suffered the most: their real income fell by nearly 68 per cent. The next two quintiles also experienced substantial falls of between 54 per cent (quintile 3) and 56 per cent (quintile 2). The fourth quintile was able to cushion the fall in average incomes by increasing its share of total income and, as a result, its real income declined the least, namely by about 40 per cent. The richest 20 per cent of the population maintained a nearly constant share of total income and hence their real income fell in line with the average, i.e. by 51.8 per cent.

When one remembers that average incomes continued to fall in 1995, the scale of the calamity becomes truly appalling. This is reflected in the demographic statistics. The death rate rose from 7.6 per thousand in 1989 to 10.1 in 1995, a rise of 32.9 per cent in just six years. The birth rate fell from 23 per thousand in 1989 to 16.6 in 1995, a fall of 27.9 per cent and then fell further to 15.3 per cent in 1996. These two tendencies combined to cut the natural rate of growth of the population by well over half, from 1.5 per cent a year in 1989 to 0.7 per cent in 1995. In addition, between 1989 and 1995, about 1.3 million people emigrated, out of a total population of 16.6 million.[18] As a result, the population actually declined during 1993–97,[19] and the projected rate of growth of the population is only 0.1 per cent a year.

The decline in life expectancy from 68.6 years in 1990 to 64.9 years in 1995 provides further evidence of acute distress.[20] The infant mortality rate in urban areas rose sharply from a low of 26.1 per thousand births in 1992 to 29.4 in 1995, although in rural areas it increased only 0.3 per thousand from the same initial base.[21] The marriage rate has declined by 38 per cent (1989–96), presumably in response to the deterioration in economic and social conditions. Included among the deteriorating conditions is the outlook for employment. Although it is impossible to obtain accurate estimates of the underutilization of labour, it is evident that there is a great deal of slack in the labour market. The official unemployment rate (4.1 per cent), although still low, has increased sharply. More important is the large volume of part-time work and involuntary leaves from jobs, most of which are unpaid. Others, discouraged by the lack of employment prospects, have withdrawn from the labour force entirely and the economically inactive portion of the population has risen dramatically. Women have been disproportionately affected.[22] The total number of workers fell by 15.6 per cent between 1991 and 1996. To get back to something approximating full employment, the economy needs to create an extra 1.0–1.2 million jobs.

Virtually all the indicators tell a similar story. Systemic reform in Kazakhstan has been an economic, social and demographic disaster. The general well being of the population has declined precipitously. All have suffered. The poor have suffered more than average and women have suffered more than men. Human development has gone into reverse. The question now facing policy makers is what is to be done.

Is there a revised strategy that promises a more hopeful outcome? It is to this question that we now turn.

## Elements of a revised strategy

A revised strategy has six elements, each of which is essential because each contributes to the success of the others. The six elements are the following: (i) macroeconomic stabilization; (ii) the resumption of growth of output per head by increasing the rate of investment in natural, physical and human capital; (iii) the creation of an incentive structure in which 'key' prices reflect real costs; (iv) the promotion of small and medium size private enterprises; (v) the creation of an employment intensive pattern of growth, in part through a guaranteed jobs scheme on a public investment programme; and (vi) the provision of social protection services in order to cope with residual poverty. Let us consider each of these elements briefly in turn.

### Macroeconomic stabilization

After a long struggle price stabilization now is in sight. Inflation rates are falling and in the first quarter of 1997 the increase in consumer prices was 4.9 per cent, substantially less than in previous years. As explained above, radical changes in *relative* prices are more likely to be successful if there is general stability in the overall *level* of prices. That is, macroeconomic stabilization is a prerequisite for successful price liberalization. Hence it is important for the stabilization effort to continue.

This does not imply that the government should aim for a zero rate of inflation, or any other specific inflation target. But the empirical evidence from other countries suggests that once the annual rate of inflation exceeds 20 per cent, the price mechanism begins to function less efficiently and inflation begins to reduce the rate of economic growth.[23] The government should therefore be encouraged to pursue its plans and attempt to bring the rate of inflation down to a 'low' level – somewhere in a range of 5–20 per cent a year – and keep it there.

### Investment-led growth

The next priority is to stimulate long run growth. This will require a sharp increase in the rate of investment in physical, natural and human capital. Consider what has happened to the rate of accumulation of physical capital. According to the World Bank, gross domestic investment in 1990 was 42.6 per cent of gross domestic product; four years later, in 1994, it was only 24 per cent.[24] That is, the *rate* of investment fell by 43.7 per cent. At the same time, however, the level of GDP was falling, as we have seen. So investment became a smaller share of a smaller domestic product. The consequence was that the *level* of investment fell by 72.8 per cent. In many sectors of the economy, net investment must have been negative. The IMF has reached similar conclusions. In its latest report it estimates that investment in constant prices declined by 89.8 per cent between 1991 and 1996.[25] Here again, the implication is inescapable: net investment in Kazakhstan must have been negative in many sectors and perhaps was negative overall. Obviously, this cannot continue if Kazakhstan is to reverse its decline. It will not be possible to provide productive employment at rising real wages if material output fails to grow; and unless there is a rise in average incomes, it will not be possible to reduce poverty and provide social protection to those in need. Faster growth is essential.

In the long run – perhaps a generation from now – Kazakhstan can look forward to greater prosperity based on the exploitation of its natural capital in minerals, petroleum and gas. The difficulties of basing development on foreign direct investment should not however be underestimated. The process is likely to be much slower than many policy makers appear to believe.[26] Meanwhile, there are things that can be done now, and in particular the country could make use of its abundant stock of land. The way to do this is to create a market in land, so that land can be used as collateral to obtain finance capital which, in turn, can be used to increase investment in physical capital and in the land itself.

Creating a market in land does not necessarily imply the privatization of land. It is possible for the state to retain ownership of the land and allow individuals, private companies and state enterprises to use the land under lease contracts. Provided the lease contracts are of sufficient duration to permit investors to recover their capital outlay, and provided leasehold tenure is secure and use-rights are enforced by the courts, and provided also that leases can be freely traded in the market, a system of land tenure based on leaseholds with state ownership of land can be very efficient. Private ownership of land is not necessary. All that is necessary is that the land be 'commercialized'. This will ensure that it will be allocated efficiently and that there will be an incentive to invest in it.

The 'commercialization' of land will cost the state nothing and yet it will greatly stimulate investment in natural and physical capital.

Indeed if the state retains ultimate ownership of the land, it will obtain a steady flow of revenues from leaseholders, revenues which can be used to finance investment and improve social services. Thus a land reform of the type recommended has many advantages: it will lead to a better allocation of land, it will stimulate investment and growth and it will increase government revenues which, if used wisely, can provide a further stimulus to growth.

It is equally important to increase the rate of human capital formation. This is desirable in its own right because, as explained above, investment in people is an objective of development as well as a means of achieving development. Like physical capital formation, investment in people in Kazakhstan has collapsed. One indicator of the collapse is the fact that between 1991 and 1996 the number of students enrolled in schools declined by 39 per cent.[27] The implication is that the present generation of children is likely to be less well educated and less well trained than their parents, and consequently poorly equipped to obtain highly productive and well paid jobs.

State expenditure in this area should aim to increase the quality of the labour force and promote human development of the population as a whole. It is sometimes argued in Kazakhstan that because of its small population, low population density and the absolute decline in the size of the population in recent years, priority should be given instead to increasing the rate of growth of the population. That is, public resources should be used to finance a pro-natalist policy. The implication of this view is that the government believes that a larger quantity of people is more desirable than a smaller population of higher quality.

The alternative approach is one of neutrality towards the desired size of family. That is, the decision about how many children to have should be left to the mother and her choice should not be influenced in either direction by state-financed incentives, apart from child allowances which may well form part of an anti-poverty strategy. There are several arguments against a pro-natalist policy. First, to the extent that it is motivated by the current 'demographic crisis', it is unnecessary. Once development resumes, mortality rates will fall, life expectancy will rise, marriage rates will increase, and the population growth rate will cease to be negative. The problem will be corrected automatically and there will be no need for the government to allocate its scarce resources to create incentives to increase the birth rate.

Second, given the scarcity of employment opportunities, the high degree of structural unemployment and the need to create at least a million extra jobs, a faster rate of growth of the population – and the subsequent increase in the supply of labour – will do nothing to increase the rate of growth of output. The most likely outcome is that the rate of growth of per capita income will decline below what it otherwise would have been. Surplus labour in various forms will increase, the incidence of poverty will rise and the distribution of income will become more unequal. Third, resources used to support a pro-natalist policy have a high opportunity cost. Money spent on pro-natalist policies is money that is not available for spending on other priority activities such as financing investment to accelerate growth, increasing expenditure on human capital formation, funding public works programmes to generate productive employment and providing a social safety net to reduce poverty.

The thrust of policy should be to promote growth by accelerating investment in all its forms. Expenditures on pro-natalist programmes would be anti-growth, anti-employment and anti-poor.[28]

### Key prices and the incentive structure

Once the revenues from an expanding petroleum sector come onstream, the government will be in a good position to finance a development strategy led by public sector investment. Kazakhstan can then aspire to a savings rate similar to the savings rates achieved in the rapidly growing economies of East and South-east Asia, including of course the two transition economies in China and Vietnam. A savings rate of 30 per cent of GDP or more should certainly be feasible. Meanwhile, savings are likely to be much lower and it is vital that they be allocated efficiently so that the return on investment is maximized and the contribution of capital formation to growth is as large as possible.

An efficient allocation of investment depends upon the incentive structure, i.e. the set of relative prices, the degree of access of economic agents (buyers, sellers, borrowers, lenders) to all markets and the intensity of competition. Some prices, however, are more important than others because these prices affect all or nearly all sectors of the economy and hence have a pervasive influence on the composition of investment and the allocation of scarce resources. These prices are called key prices. In the specific case of Kazakhstan three key prices can be singled out for comment.

First, there is the price of low-skilled labour. The alternative transition strategy being proposed here centres on the creation of productive employment. It is therefore essential to the success of the strategy that there be no market disincentive to wage employment. That is, the wage rate should reflect the opportunity cost of labour in different regions of the country. In current conditions, where there is a huge amount of unemployed and underemployed labour, the opportunity cost of low-skilled labour is very low and hence market-determined wages are likely to be low.

The government may be tempted as part of an anti-poverty pro- gramme to intervene in the labour market and impose a legal minimum wage. Indeed there already is a 'minimum salary' that all employers are required to pay. This requirement should be withdrawn. A legal mini- mum wage, in so far as it is effective, does not address the problems faced by workers in Kazakhstan. Those who have jobs suffer not so much from a low real wage as the failure of employers, particularly in state enterprises, to pay their workers on time. There is a massive prob- lem of arrears in the payment of wages – a lag of six months is not uncommon – and the government priority should be to clear these arrears as quickly as possible. Legislating a minimum wage is an irrele- vance to those who are employed. For those who are unemployed or who have withdrawn from the labour market because they despair of ever finding a job, a minimum wage makes their situation slightly more difficult by reducing the incentive of potential employers to hire labour. The unemployed need jobs, not legal minimum wages.

In any case, the government is a dominant employer and the wage rate paid by the government to its own employees is bound to have a strong influence on wages in the private sector. That is, the govern- ment is a 'wage leader' and hence minimum wage legislation is unnec- essary as well as undesirable. Foreign enterprises almost always pay above the market wage, in part in order to attract high-quality workers, and hence a legal minimum wage would have very little impact on them. The largest group affected would be domestic employers in the private sector and it is from this group that most of the growth in employment could originate. Legal obstacles to job creation should not be put in their way.

Once the economy recovers and conditions in the labour market improve, the government may wish to reconsider the situation. The rea- son for this is that Kazakhstan possesses an unusually large number of 'company towns', i.e. localities in which there is only one employer. Unless there is an exceptionally high degree of labour mobility from one region to another, the local employer in the company town – whether a privatized firm or a 'commercialized' state enterprise – will enjoy monopsony power in the labour market and will use this power to depress wages and reduce the volume of employment. In such circumstances a legal minimum wage actually would result in increased employment as well as in a higher real wage. At the moment, however, this is more a theoretical possibility than a practical consideration, but in future it could provide a strong reason to introduce minimum wage legislation.

The second key price to consider is the real rate of interest. Here again, the objective should be to create a structure of incentives which encourages employment. This can be done by ensuring that in an inflationary environment financial institutions provide capital to borrowers at positive real rates of interest. This will create an incentive to economize on capital, which is very scarce, to spread it thinly across sectors and where possible to substitute labour for capital equipment. These responses, in turn, will ensure that the return on investment is high and that investment makes a major contribution to an acceleration of growth and the creation of employment.

Policy should focus on borrowing rates of interest. It is also desirable, however, that deposit rates of interest should be positive. This will provide a small incentive to increase savings. More important, it will provide incentives to savers to deposit their funds in financial institutions rather than hoard cash in a sock or accumulate foreign currency, and this too should help to improve the allocation of investment. This second role of a positive rate of interest on deposits is especially important in Kazakhstan because of the need to rebuild public confidence in the banking system after so many episodes of instability when depositors lost their money or had difficulty withdrawing their funds.

Unfortunately, real interest rates in Kazakhstan were negative until 1996. Since then they have been positive but rather low. They should not be allowed to fall any lower and, in general, an average borrowing rate in real terms of about 10 per cent a year should be consistent with the development potential of the country. Of course as the rate of inflation continues to fall, nominal rates of interest should be lowered in order to maintain constant real rates of interest. Unfortunately, in many countries undergoing stabilization programmes, real rates of interest have been allowed to soar when the rate of inflation falls, and this has had serious consequences for investment and output just when the economy was poised for growth. It is important for the authorities to be alert to this danger and for the National Bank to take steps to avoid it.

It will be objected that many borrowers – small businessmen, women, microenterprises – cannot afford to pay a real interest rate of

10 per cent a year and that they should be offered preferential rates. This amounts to subsidizing selected groups (which costs the government money which in principle could be used to pursue other desired objectives) and, moreover, doing so in such a way that employment is discouraged. Such policies normally should be avoided.

The problem facing small businesses and microenterprises is not the price of credit but access to credit. Many people are unable to obtain credit at any price because they are not regarded as suitable borrowers by the banking system. This may be the case because of lack of collateral and, if so, our proposal to 'commercialize' land and create an active land market will help. A more important problem is that the banks strongly discriminate in favour of selected clients and exclude other would-be borrowers from the capital market. Specifically, state banks are biased in favour of state enterprises.

One solution to the problem would be to privatize fully the banking system so that commercial criteria determine the allocation of funds. Another solution would be to reform the state banks, in effect to 'commercialize' them, so that they are subjected to competition and have an incentive to behave in a more market-oriented way. A third solution would be to create specialized lending institutions that would serve specific sectors (housing, agriculture) or specific types of enterprises (small and medium size firms, microenterprises) or specific groups (women). The three approaches are not mutually exclusive and a solution which combines all three is feasible, but whichever alternative is adopted, the objective should be to create equal access to the banking system and not to provide subsidized credit.

Banking reform would cost the government almost nothing and would lead to a more efficient allocation of investment and faster growth. Credit subsidies would have to be large to have an impact and would therefore be costly to the government. Their impact on growth would be negligible if not negative.

The third key price is the exchange rate. In a small open economy such as Kazakhstan's, where exports account for about 30 per cent of GDP, the overall performance of the economy is strongly influenced by the performance of the foreign trade sector. The price of foreign exchange not only affects incentives to produce for the domestic or foreign markets, it also affects the structure of costs throughout the economy through the price of imported raw materials and capital equipment. Government may be tempted to emulate the success of export-led growth in some Asian countries by deliberately undervaluing the exchange rate and running an export surplus. The danger of such a policy, however, is that it creates an incentive to shift capital and other resources away from the domestic and into the export sector and therefore hampers the development of many small enterprises satisfying local demand.

The opposite danger, especially in an inflationary environment, is that the exchange rate will become overvalued. This has a short run advantage in that it temporarily moderates the rate of inflation, but it creates serious problems in the long run by discouraging investment in the export sector, encouraging an unsustainable inflow of imports and subjecting domestic import competing industries to severe competition. The result is to reduce the level of investment in plant and equipment and lower the rate of growth.

The best policy, therefore, is to adopt an exchange rate which is neutral, neither biased in favour of exports nor biased against them. This can best be achieved for the time being by allowing market forces to determine the exchange rate and limiting interventions by the National Bank to smoothing short-term or seasonal fluctuations. It must be recognized, however, that large inflows of foreign direct investment and foreign aid will tend to cause the exchange rate to appreciate and this will create a disincentive to invest in the export sector, since to domestic investors the exchange rate will appear to be overvalued. Unless these inflows of foreign capital are thought likely to continue on a semi-permanent basis, the authorities may wish to intervene in the foreign exchange market to prevent an appreciation of the exchange rate and a distortion of investment incentives.

A similar problem will arise when petroleum and other mineral exports occur in very large volumes. This will lead to an appreciation of the exchange rate, cheapen the domestic cost of foreign imports and discourage investment in the non-oil export sector and in the import competing sector. If the authorities do not wish this to happen, they will have to intervene in the foreign exchange market, e.g. by introducing a dual exchange rate system in which one exchange rate applies to oil and other mineral exports and the other to all other international transactions. This issue will not arise for several years, but it underlines the difficulty of designing and implementing a sensible exchange rate policy and suggests that it is not too soon to begin to think how best to manage this key price.

### Small and medium enterprises

It is widely recognized that small and medium-sized private enterprises have enormous potential in Kazakhstan. They can be highly responsive to market opportunities. They economize on capital. They can generate a great deal of employment and they can make a large contribution to reducing poverty. Yet the small and medium enterprise sector has not developed and flourished. Why? Many explanations have been put forward, for example, that the people of Kazakhstan lack entrepreneurial initiative and are risk averse because they are accustomed to secure employment in state enterprises, that they lack management skills and knowledge in profit and loss accounting, that the market is depressed because of the steep fall in average incomes and hence there are few profit opportunities.

The government has passed many decrees and launched numerous programmes to help the sector and foreign donors have financed a large number of projects and provided much technical assistance. The decrees, however, have had little impact, the programmes have been ineffective and foreign-funded activities have failed. The reason, I believe, is that the diagnosis of the problem has been incorrect.

The problem is not that the people of Kazakhstan lack initiative or information or training; the problem is that government has failed to remove the obstacles that prevent people from exercising initiative and applying their talents. The solution is to change government policy, not the people. The central obstacle is that small private investors do not have access to the resources they need to create and expand a business. They do not have access to land, building sites or premises and when they do obtain access their tenure is not secure and enforced by the courts. This is one reason why the 'commercialization' of land is so important. Potential investors have difficulty obtaining supplies and raw materials because marketing channels are monopolized by state enterprises which do not allow potential competitors to emerge. Small businesses do not have access to credit because state banks channel their credit to state enterprises. The credit is used by the state enterprises to stay afloat, to avoid bankruptcy, and not to invest in new activities which create permanent jobs and contribute to economic growth. This is one reason why the reform of the banking system is so important.

The irony is that the government in its transition strategy gave high priority to price liberalization but it failed to create the legal framework and undertake the institutional reforms that are necessary for a market economy to function properly. And then, when a private sector failed to emerge, fault was found with the people rather than with their government.

The people do not need training; they do not need market information; they do not need subsidized interest rates; they do not need special tax advantages. What they need are open markets for land, raw materials and finance capital and the elimination of burdens in the form of licences, permits and controls. Given access to markets, private investors will do the rest: if there is money to be made, they will find a way to make it. The implication is that an effective programme to encourage the small and medium enterprise sector will cost government nothing, although it will require a great deal of effort to dismantle obstacles inherited from the pre-independence period. The construction of the right policy framework will have a very large pay-off in terms of rapid growth of small private enterprise. Absent an appropriate policy framework, no amount of public expenditure will produce a vibrant and dynamic private sector.

### Employment creation on public works

One of the country's most valuable assets is its labour force, its stock of literate, skilled and experienced workers. This asset currently is greatly underutilized as evidenced by the large amount of slack in the labour market. Hence the attraction of an employment intensive pattern of growth.

A policy framework designed to promote development through the creation of employment should have three major components. First, the structure of incentives should encourage the efficient use of labour in all sectors of the economy and in particular it should encourage a pattern of investment which combines scarce capital with temporarily abundant labour in the most advantageous proportions. This is the function of the set of key prices discussed above. Second, a special effort should be made to create an institutional environment which encourages the rapid growth of small and medium-sized private enterprises. Compared to other successful East and South-east Asian countries, Kazakhstan is conspicuous for the underdevelopment of this sector. A major opportunity is waiting to be grasped, at virtually no cost to the government.

The third component of an employment strategy should be the organization of a nationwide programme of public investment. The purposes of this programme are (i) to create employment for those who have become impoverished during the period of transition and (ii) to undertake capital construction projects which will contribute to the acceleration of economic growth. These capital construction projects should be carefully selected so that they become permanent physical assets which this generation hands on to the next. Some of the projects may be of national importance, such as the building of infrastructure, housing and office accommodation in the new capital at Akmola, whereas other projects may be primarily of regional interest, such as the construction of local roads, the repair and extension of irrigation facilities, reforestation and small-scale water management projects, construction of civic buildings, schools, medical clinics, etc.

Public investment schemes of the type envisaged have made significant contributions to development in countries which differ widely in other respects: the United States during the depression of the 1930s, Germany in the period after reunification, China during the Maoist period, Bangladesh after independence, Cambodia after the fall of Pol Pot's regime and, perhaps most famous of all, in the state of Maharashtra, India since the middle of the 1970s. The organization of the schemes has of course varied from country to country and the details of a large public works programme in Kazakhstan will have to be carefully considered so that the specific conditions that prevail in this country are fully taken into account. Some general principles, however, can be proposed.[29]

First, the state should act as the employer of last resort. All those seeking work should be guaranteed a job on a public investment project and this job guarantee should replace unemployment compensation. Only if the state is unable to honour its guarantee should the jobless be offered unemployment compensation. Second, public works projects should not be seen as a disguised form of welfare or as outdoor relief. Their central purpose is to increase investment in physical assets by mobilizing labour of low opportunity cost. Third, the wage rate on public works projects should not compete with wages offered in the private sector or in the public administration. The purpose of the scheme is not to attract workers from other activities but to create additional jobs. In practice this implies that wages on public works projects should be slightly lower than the market wage.

Fourth, the projects to be undertaken should be selected by local government, presumably at the *oblast* level, and preferably advised by various local civil organizations that can identify local priorities. Fifth, the implementation of projects should be the responsibility of local private contractors. Indeed, a nationwide public investment scheme should provide a stimulus to the development of small and medium enterprises throughout the country. Moreover, the construction projects will create additional opportunities for small businesses linked to the public works programme. Examples include suppliers of construction materials (bricks, cement, gravel), producers of construction tools (picks, shovels, rollers) and those engaged in truck transport. These activities, in turn, will increase incomes at the local level and this higher purchasing power will have multiplier effects, generating demand for a wide range of products and thereby creating numerous profit opportunities. The public works scheme should therefore be seen as complementary to the efforts discussed above to encourage small and medium enterprises.

Sixth, the central government should be responsible for monitoring progress. Financial audits would be essential to ensure that funds are spent for the purposes intended and not allowed to 'disappear into the sands', as sometimes has happened. There should also be systematic evaluations of the results to ensure that minimum quality standards are maintained by contractors, that *oblasts* have made adequate provision for the repair and maintenance of assets after they have been constructed and that project selection does indeed reflect the development needs of the country.

Such a programme would be ambitious, and would produce a number of exceptionally large benefits. It would prevent open unemployment from increasing to its projected rate of 6.7 per cent in 1999. It would allow state enterprises and newly privatized enterprises to continue to shed redundant workers, secure in the knowledge that their employees would be able to find a job, even as a last resort and at a very low wage, on the public works programme. It would allow those who have withdrawn from the labour force to re-enter the labour market and contribute to their own well being (and that of their family) while helping to build their country. It would lead to explosive growth of small and medium enterprises and spread the benefits of growth widely throughout the country. It would make a major contribution to the reduction of poverty. And it would lead directly to increased investment in a large variety of projects which would accelerate the pace of economic expansion.

Financing of a large public investment programme might come from several sources. First, the central government could use funds presently allocated for unemployment compensation to finance instead a job creation programme. Second, part of the funds allocated for the construction of the new capital at Akmola could be channelled through the public works programme. Beyond this, third, some additional funding from domestic resources will have to be found by altering spending priorities and raising revenues. Finally, assuming the programme is well designed and viable administrative arrangements are in place, it should be possible to obtain international financing from institutions such as the World Bank, the Asian Development Bank and the European Bank for Reconstruction and Development.

## Social protection and residual poverty

The traditional method of responding to social needs and poverty in Kazakhstan has been through a system of entitlements, most of which consist of earmarked transfers such as child allowances, maternity allowances, sick pay and housing allowances. There are in fact about 220 different allowances. This system has broken down because of the dramatic increase in poverty and decline in government revenues. The real value of grants now is minuscule, there are in any case large arrears in the payment of grants and many grants benefit the non-poor as well as the poor. It is fairly obvious that under current conditions a system of direct transfers cannot provide social protection for the population let alone eliminate poverty and create a more equal society. Fresh thinking is needed.

Depending on the source, the standard used and the time the survey was taken, the incidence of poverty in Kazakhstan can be 20 per cent (Ministry of Labour), 31 per cent (World Bank) or 76 per cent (Red Cross). Only about 10 per cent of the population actually receive assistance, however. Assume for the sake of illustration that 31 per cent is the 'correct' estimate. This implies that for every person in poverty, there are only two persons who can be taxed by the government in order to finance anti-poverty transfers. Moreover, those two non-poor persons have themselves experienced a steep decline in their standard of living. In such circumstances a tax-and-transfer social security system is not likely to be politically feasible or administratively easy to operate.

What is needed is a system of social protection that simultaneously provides more support for those most in need while helping to eliminate the causes of need. Ideally, the system should be transparent so that the general public can understand the principles involved and endorse them. The scheme outlined below meets these criteria and perhaps merits serious consideration.

The centrepiece of the proposed system of social protection and poverty reduction is the creation of employment. Most of the poor are adults and youths of working age who lack full-time jobs. An employment intensive growth strategy of the type discussed above would provide immediate assistance to many low-income households and, through its contribution to increased production, reduce the number of low-income families in future. Employment creation is a better remedy for poverty than unemployment compensation. If job losses were temporary and reversible, say, the result of a cyclical downturn in production, unemployment compensation would be effective, but where lack of employment is structural, arising from systemic transformation, as in Kazakhstan, more active measures are required.

The second component of an anti-poverty strategy is improved provision of basic health services. This is necessary in any case to combat the demographic crisis, but improved health and nutrition would also reduce poverty by increasing productivity per work day, reducing absenteeism and days lost from work because of sickness, and generally raising the morale and intensity of work of the labour force. Better health would not only contribute to human development directly, it would also contribute indirectly in raising the output of goods and services.

Not all the poor, however, are unemployed or sick; some are elderly and have withdrawn from the labour force. A basic pension to which everyone is entitled should be the third component in a comprehensive programme to provide social protection and reduce poverty. Kazakhstan recently has reformed the pension system and the new arrangements will come into effect on 1 January 1998. It is too early to know whether the reformed pension system will, as hoped, provide security in old age while creating an additional incentive to save during one's working years. Time will tell.

A consolidated child allowance should be the fourth component. The probability of a family falling into poverty increases with the number of children in the household. There is therefore a strong case for Kazakhstan to retain child benefits, but the system could be improved by consolidating the means-tested child allowances with 'other child allowances' (which are largely for single mothers) to produce a single entitlement payable to the mother. At present, because of the acute scarcity of resources, it may be necessary to continue to target poor households through a means test, but in the long run it is worth considering whether child benefits should be universal. This would help to ensure that non-poor tax-paying households in a democracy will continue to provide political support for this important component of an anti-poverty strategy. Targeted benefits can be attractive in the short run because they appear to be cost effective, but if the majority of the population is excluded from a programme, it runs the risk of losing public support and a short-term gain can be transformed into a permanent loss.

Finally, provision should be made for a small transfer programme to respond to residual poverty not addressed by any of the four national programmes itemized above, namely employment creation, provision of basic health and nutrition services, an old age pension and a child allowance. The transfer scheme should be modest in size, flexible in administration and quick to respond to unforeseen or emergency situations in a household. The funds should be allocated by the central government but administered by local government (advised by citizens' groups) where knowledge of local conditions and of the most urgent needs is greatest. Transfers would be discretionary – and hence in a sense means tested – but because the implementation of the scheme would be at the local level, its operation would be open to public scrutiny. This would ensure a degree of transparency and, hopefully, public support. The central government would of course have to audit the accounts periodically to ensure that taxpayers' funds were properly used.

If some variant of the five-component scheme for social protection outlined above were adopted, it would be possible to abolish all other entitlements, e.g. birth allowances, funeral allowances, sanatoria vouchers, housing allowances, unemployment compensation, sick pay. The funds saved could be used to strengthen the remaining programme, e.g. child allowances and local government transfer payments. It will be objected that individuals who have entitlements under the old system will resist change and hence that reform is politically impossible. The old entitlements, however, are more hypothetical than real since they are seldom paid, there are large arrears and the monetary value is low. Surely it would be better to have a small number of good programmes that actually succeed in helping the poor than a large number of bad programmes that so far have done nothing to stem the tide of rising impoverishment. A transformation of the system of social protection is a vital element in a new strategy to complete the transition.

## Appendix: a note on poverty concepts and poverty lines in Kazakhstan

There is great confusion and debate in Kazakhstan about the appropriate concept of poverty to use, where to draw the poverty line and indeed the purpose of measuring the extent of poverty.

As regards the purpose of measuring poverty, there are several possibilities:

(i) to provide accurate information to the government so that it can monitor the performance of the economy as a whole and formulate corrective policies;

(ii) to assist the government to identify the characteristics of the poor – the specific groups that are most vulnerable – so that appropriate social protection policies can be designed;

(iii) to provide information to the general public in order to facilitate informed debate on public policy issues; and

(iv) to provide a standard of reference to which state transfer payments are linked.

The first three purposes are straightforward and clearly desirable. Difficulties can arise, however, in linking the measurement of the extent of poverty to the disbursement of public funds. There is a temptation to define the number of poor in terms of the volume of resources available to assist them. Thus if budget allocations decline, the number of poor is adjusted downwards. There are advocates of this approach in Kazakhstan.

This is a dangerous practice and should be avoided. Taken to an extreme, it implies that if budget allocations to combat poverty were reduced to zero, poverty would disappear! The definition of poverty should be sharply separated from fiscal considerations. Otherwise it will be impossible for the measurement of poverty to play its *informational* role.

Let us turn next to the appropriate concept of poverty. Here again there are several possibilities:[30]

(i) income poverty, in which poverty is conceived as a relationship of a person to a bundle of commodities, e.g. a food basket necessary for adequate nutrition, or a set of 'basic needs' or a minimum living standard;

(ii) capability poverty, in which poverty is conceived as a relationship of a person to a set of 'functionings' or 'capabilities', such as the ability to read and write, to enjoy good health, or to have access to public transportation; and

(iii) social deprivation, in which poverty is conceived as a relationship between one person and another, e.g. when a person's income is less than one-half the median income.

In Kazakhstan poverty tends to be conceptualized as a physiological phenomenon. The poor are those whose diet is inadequate in some sense. The first approach adopted is to calculate a subsistence minimum food basket based on norms established by the Institute of Nutrition. The poor are those whose consumption of one or more of the various items in the normative food basket is less than the recommended level. The problem is that the recommended food basket is purely normative and is not based on observed food preferences of the population. It is conceivable, although far fetched, that no one in Kazakhstan would choose the Institute of Nutrition's food basket no matter how high their income, and thus everyone would be classified as poor!

A second approach, used by the Ministry of Labour, is to estimate the cost of a minimum food basket by observing the actual food prefer- ences of 'low-income' households. This method produces a food basket that costs about 20 per cent less than the basket recommended by the Institute of Nutrition.

A problem with both approaches is that the food basket is fixed either permanently (Institute of Nutrition) or in the base year of the household survey (Ministry of Labour) and there is no possibility of adjusting a household's diet in response to changes in relative food prices. For example, if the price of milk falls relative to the price of meat, one would expect households to respond by buying more milk and less meat, but this possibility is excluded by the food basket approach and consequently there is a danger that some households will be classified as poor merely because they changed the composition of food consumption in response to price signals.

This problem can be overcome by defining the poverty threshold not in terms of a specific food basket but in terms of the total number of kilocalories consumed per day. That is, food items are converted into calorie equivalents and households are ranked in terms of a single indi- cator of calories consumed. This simplifies matters considerably and makes allowance for substitution among foodstuffs; it does, however, ignore the possibility that households that consume a nutritionally adequate number of calories (and hence are classified as not poor) none the less are lacking in some other nutrient (e.g. proteins). Despite this last disadvantage, most countries that define poverty in terms of nutritional adequacy use calorie consumption as a proxy for the nutri- tional status of a household.

In Kazakhstan the cost of a food basket is then inflated by 30 per cent to make some provision for non-food items of expenditure. The cost of the Ministry of Labour's food basket plus 30 per cent is called the minimum living standard. If this estimated minimum living stan- dard is viewed as the poverty line, then according to the World Bank sponsored Kazakhstan Living Standards Survey of July 1996, the pro- portion of the population living in poverty is 30.9 per cent.

There is, however, a third approach that is used to estimate the extent of poverty. The Ministry of Labour has a national allowance or entitlement which is granted to help support families with children. (In practice the grant often is not paid because of lack of funds.) As a rule of thumb, those with an income less than twice the value of this grant are regarded as poor. By this criterion, about 20 per cent of the population of Kazakhstan were poor in July 1997.

The problem with this third approach is that the concept of poverty itself is mixed up with the size of the national grant (or 'calculation-base index' as it is called) that is intended to alleviate poverty. The approach leads to great confusion and it would be sensible to abandon it.

# 11

# Poverty Reduction in China

*with Azizur Rahman Khan*

## The nature and causes of China's poverty problem

In the years following the beginning of economic reforms in 1978, China enjoyed remarkable growth of output and income per head, and this rapid growth was accompanied by an equally remarkable reduction in poverty, where poverty is measured as the proportion of the population living below some minimum acceptable standard of living. In practice the minimum acceptable standard of living is measured in money terms adjusted for changes over time in the cost of living. This coincidence of rapid growth and a sharp fall in the incidence of poverty was particularly dramatic during the first seven or eight years of the reform process.

During the decade beginning in the mid-1980s, however, the pattern changed. China's economic growth continued to be very rapid, but progress in reducing poverty slowed substantially. There is widespread agreement about this among official Chinese agencies, international development institutions and independent scholars, even if the details of quantitative estimates vary. Official Chinese estimates point to a continued significant reduction in poverty in both rural and urban areas, although at a slower pace than before.[1] World Bank estimates suggest there was a sharp decline in the incidence of rural and urban poverty until 1984 and then virtual constancy in the incidence of poverty for the rest of the decade.[2] A recent independent study with which we are associated, based on more detailed data and a more comprehensive definition of income than is used in official and World Bank estimates, has found that the rate of poverty reduction in the late 1980s and the early 1990s was much slower than before in rural China and poverty ceased to fall and perhaps even increased slightly in urban China.[3]

Analysis of change in poverty is complicated by the fact that some components of personal income are excluded from official estimates of personal income. These omissions have been declining in importance over time, and as a result, official estimates of the rate of growth of personal income overstate the true rate of growth. This is especially true of official estimates of personal income in urban areas. The consequence of this and other minor biases in the official data is that the official estimates of poverty do not accurately reflect the full magnitude of the problem. The independent study mentioned above, although not without weaknesses of its own, better reflects the existing state of affairs. This study indicates that since the mid-1980s the rate of decline of poverty in rural China slowed dramatically while in urban China the incidence of poverty at best remained unchanged and, if the 'floating population' had been included, urban poverty undoubtedly would have increased (Table 11.1).[4]

These findings about poverty, especially the decline in poverty in rural areas, would not be regarded as unsatisfactory in a country with a slow rate of growth. What makes the findings disappointing in China, especially the failure of urban poverty to decline, is that China experienced a historically unprecedented rate of growth of per capita GDP of more than 8 per cent a year during this period. What are the factors that prevented the poor in China from benefiting more from this remarkable growth?

The first important factor is that growth in per capita personal income lagged far behind the growth in per capita GDP. While the latter increased 8.1 per cent a year between 1988 and 1995, the annual growth in per capita personal income was much lower, namely 4.71 per cent in rural China and 4.48 per cent in urban China. Since poverty thresholds in China, as elsewhere, are measured in terms of per capita personal income, not per capita GDP, the low response of personal income to a rise in GDP made it much more likely that an increase in inequality

*Table 11.1*   The proportion of the population in poverty, 1988 and 1995 (percentages)

|  | *1988* | *1995* | *Percentage change* |
|---|---|---|---|
| Rural population | 35.1 | 28.6 | − 18.5 |
| Urban population | 8.2 | 8.0 | − 2.4 |

*Source*: Azizur Rahman Khan, *Poverty in China in the Period of Globalization: New Evidence on Trend and Pattern*, ILO, Issues in Development Discussion Paper No. 22, 1998, Table 6, p. 13 and Table 10, p. 19.

could offset the positive effects on poverty of an increase in personal income. This is what happened in urban China and nearly happened in rural China during this period. Had personal income grown say, 80 per cent as fast as GDP rather than the actual 60 per cent, it would have been much easier to absorb the effect of increased inequality in China, and the consequences for poverty would have been much more favourable.

China's published macroeconomic accounts are not sufficiently detailed to enable one to document the precise mechanism that created the large wedge between growth of GDP and growth of personal income. It is likely, however, that the wedge is largely a consequence of China's unrelenting drive for higher rates of saving and investment, a drive that required a redistribution of income away from households in favour of 'the business sector', public and private. The period of rapid reduction in poverty – 1978 to 1984 – witnessed a growth in personal income in excess of the growth in GDP and a reduction in the domestic saving rate from 34 per cent of GDP to 32 per cent.[5] During the period under review – 1988 to 1995 – when performance in alleviating poverty deteriorated and there was a slower growth in personal income than in GDP, the saving rate rose from 32 per cent of GDP to a staggering 42 per cent in just nine years.[6]

Although per capita personal income increased at a much slower rate than GDP, growth nevertheless would have had a strong impact on poverty were it not for the sharp increase in income inequality. A simulation exercise shows that, given the actual increase in per capita personal income from 1988 to 1995, the proportion of the rural population in poverty at the end of the period would have been only half as high as it actually was and the proportion of the urban population in poverty would have been close to zero if inequality in the distributions of income in the two sectors had remained unchanged over the period. Unfortunately, however, the Gini ratio of income distribution increased from 0.34 to 0.42 in rural China and from 0.23 to 0.33 in urban China during the period. That is, rural inequality increased by more than 23 per cent and urban inequality increased by more than 43 per cent. In China as a whole, the Gini ratio increased from 0.38 in 1988 to 0.45 in 1995, a rise of more than 18 per cent.

Given that the increase in inequality was proportionately smaller in rural China than in urban China, and as noted above, the increase in personal income was faster in rural China than in urban China, it is not surprising that the poverty outcome was less unfavourable in rural than in urban areas. Even so, increased inequality in rural China reduced by half the fall in poverty reduction that would have resulted from the actual growth in income.

Why did inequality increase in rural areas? One possibility is that the agrarian reforms resulted in an unequal access of households to land. Indeed many analysts expected that decollectivization would lead to great inequalities in land distribution, but this clearly has not happened. Not only was the pre-existing equality of land distribution preserved, the degree of equality in access to land actually increased. That is, between 1988 and 1995, China created a small peasant farming system in which access of different income groups to land became more equal, not less.[7]

The source of increased rural inequality is to be found in changes in the composition of rural incomes. During the period from 1988 to 1995, household income from farming, as a proportion of total rural personal income, fell sharply, whereas other sources of income rose in importance. Because of the equality of access to land, farm income is much more equalizing than other sources of income in the countryside. The relative fall in farm income therefore contributed significantly to a rise in overall inequality in rural areas.

What caused the relative fall in farm income? The answer is a fairly sharp decline in the rate of growth of agricultural output which, in turn, was caused by a fall in public investment in agriculture and weaker incentives for producers. The improvement in agriculture's terms of trade, which was pivotal in explaining agricultural growth in the early years of the reforms, came to a halt and was reversed after the mid-1980s. It was only in 1994 that agriculture's terms of trade improved again, and this helped to end the agricultural stagnation that had lasted nearly a decade. Were it not for this change in relative prices, the extent of poverty in rural China in the mid-1990s would have been greater than it was.

Coinciding with the decline in the share of farm income in total rural income were increased shares of wages and of non-farm entrepreneurial income. Both these sources of rural income have been highly disequalizing. The reason for this has much to do with regional inequalities. Wage employment, especially in non-farm rural activities, as well as non-farm entrepreneurial activities are concentrated in the richer provinces and regions. During the mid-1980s onwards China became increasingly integrated into the global economy and much of the impetus for growth came from exports and foreign direct investment, both of which have been concentrated in the richer 'coastal provinces'. Income from wages and non-farm entrepreneurship have been very disequalizing precisely because they have been located primarily in the rich coastal provinces and, within these provinces, in the more prosperous counties and regions.

Public finance has been another source of increased inequality in the countryside. Rural Chinese households have only two-fifths of the per capita income of urban Chinese households yet they pay more in taxes than they receive in transfers while urban households receive a significant net subsidy. Moreover, fiscal inequity in China is not limited to inequity between rural and urban areas. Within the rural areas, net taxes are highly regressive: the top decile of the rural population appropriates 133 per cent of all net subsidies while the two poorest deciles pay nearly half of all net taxes.

In urban China the increase in inequality outweighed the potential poverty-alleviating effect of the growth in personal income.[8] During the period under review the distribution of urban wages became more unequal as an undifferentiated wage structure was gradually replaced by a more differentiated structure. This was essential in order to improve incentives and on balance was desirable. The disequalizing effect of this change in the wage structure could have been offset by a reform in the distribution of net subsidies and transfers to households. Between 1988 and 1995, subsidies declined from 39 per cent to only 11 per cent of household income, but the subsidies that were retained (notably, housing subsidies) were far more unequally distributed than the subsidies that were abolished (e.g. food subsidies). During this period, there was a major change in the housing market: private ownership of housing expanded greatly and public provision of housing declined. Unfortunately, however, the housing reform in urban China created a very unequal distribution of ownership of housing, and this contributed to increased income inequality in urban areas.

There were three further sources of increased urban inequality: a sharply lower output elasticity of employment in industry, particularly in state-owned enterprises; increased regional inequality; and the denial of official resident status to the 'floating population', mostly migrants from rural areas. China's integration into the global economy should have led to a restructuring of industries on the basis of comparative advantage and a rapid expansion of demand for labour, its abundant factor of production. Instead, the rate of growth of employment in industry was extraordinarily low. The output elasticity of employment in urban industries was only 0.037. The likely explanation is that increased competitive pressures associated with globalization combined with competition from the emerging private sector and other non-state forms of ownership forced China's state and collective enterprises to reduce the hidden unemployment that they had maintained in the past under the policy of guaranteed employment. The observed low output elasticity of employment is actually the net outcome of two very different trends: a relatively high output elasticity of employment at a given intensity of effort per worker and a rise in the intensity of effort per worker due to a reduction in the concealed unemployment in state and collective enterprises. Ultimately these forces will make China's state and collective industries more efficient and, once the transitional period of shedding concealed unemployment is over, the output elasticity of employment should increase. But meanwhile the growth of industrial employment continues to be very slow and this prevents the benefits of rapid growth from spreading widely to the urban population as a whole.

As in rural China, the period of integration into the global economy has meant a greater concentration of the benefits of exports and foreign direct investment in the rich coastal provinces. This has exacerbated urban inequality.

During the last decade China has become more tolerant of the presence of unauthorized migrants in urban areas. This has almost certainly helped to reduce overall poverty in China. The problem of poverty in rural China would have been more severe if rural-to-urban migration had been lower. First, there would have been more competition in the countryside for the limited number of rural employment opportunities and, second, there would have been a smaller flow of remittances from the urban to the rural areas. But the migrants are confined to marginal jobs, with long hours of work, low cash wages and few benefits; they are also denied access to basic urban services and proper housing.[9] As a result, it has been hard for migrants to rise above the poverty line. Indeed most migrants do not remain permanently in urban areas, but instead engage in circular migration, returning to their homes in the countryside after a period of time. Without doubt estimates of urban poverty would be even higher if the migrants, now estimated to exceed 20 per cent of the official urban population, were included in the estimates of poverty.[10]

## China's poverty reduction strategy

Government policies for poverty reduction in China are completely separate from overall economic policy. As a result, the strategy for poverty reduction is narrowly focused and ignores the effects of broader economic policies, such as those discussed above, on the level of poverty and the well being of the poor. Official anti-poverty policies have a strong geographical orientation and, in addition, are based on an assumption that poverty is primarily a rural problem. The government has identified 592 rural counties which are designated as poor on the basis of their average income per head. Policy has focused attention on these counties and the objective of policy has been to raise average incomes in these counties through a variety of microeconomic interventions. In other words, anti-poverty policies in China are in essence regional development policies.

In January 1994 the State Council adopted a National 8-7 Plan for poverty reduction, the objective of which was to lift the officially estimated 80 million rural poor above the poverty level in a seven-year period between 1994 and the end of the millennium. The goal was to raise the average real income in these poor counties, and by implication the average income of most households, to 500 yuan or more at 1990 prices. In addition, the plan set goals for infrastructure development, education, vocational and technical training, sanitation and family planning in the 592 counties. Support for individual poor households, however, is not part of the strategy.

The state provides resources for poverty reduction activities through the Ministry of Finance, the State Development Planning Commission and the Agricultural Development Bank. The largest part of the funds is provided by the Agricultural Development Bank in the form of low-interest loans for a variety of production activities. The funds of the Planning Commission are used to finance Food-For-Work programmes, mostly construction of infrastructure projects using local labour. Funds from the Ministry of Finance are used for training purposes.

In addition, all government departments are asked to allocate a part of their budget for the development of the designated counties. International agencies (e.g. the United Nations Development Programme and the World Bank) and NGOs have their own programmes for poverty reduction in some of the 592 designated poor counties.

Official sources claim that the programme has enjoyed considerable success in lifting 5 million rural poor people above the poverty threshold each year during the first two years of the programme. Little is known about how these estimates were made and no independent evaluation of the programme is available. There are, however, three serious and rather obvious inadequacies of the strategy that suggest a reappraisal would be desirable. The first is that the strategy excludes from its scope two large groups of poor people in China, namely the rural poor who live outside the designated counties and all of the urban poor. The State Statistical Bureau estimates that a third of the rural poor live outside the 592 designated poor counties while some independent studies suggest that half the rural poor live outside poor counties.[11] The urban poor, the other group excluded from the scope of the strategy, has been the most rapidly growing group of poor people in China in recent years. Indeed our estimate is that the number of urban poor increased by nearly 20 million between 1988 and 1995. Thus the anti-poverty programme ignores a significant part of the poverty problem.

The second major inadequacy of the programme is its failure to focus directly on poor households. Instead it focuses on uplifting poor counties as a whole, no doubt hoping that this will benefit the poor indirectly. Often, however, anti-poverty activities conducted under the programme are designed and led by the non-poor who thereby contrive to appropriate most of the benefits of the programme for themselves. Greater participation by the poor at the local level would be highly desirable. The programme has avoided targeted support to the poor even when such targeting might be possible. No doubt the aversion to targeted support reflects a wish to avoid dependency, permanent subsidies and the excesses of the 'iron rice bowl', but the complete rejection of this approach results in a huge leakage of benefits to the non-poor.

The third and perhaps most serious limitation of the present anti-poverty strategy is that it is completely segregated and isolated from overall economic policies, both microeconomic and macroeconomic. The general economic policies pursued by the government have fostered growth by shifting resources away from the poor while the specific interventions under the poverty reduction programme have tried to return to the poor some of the resources originally taken from them. It would be far better to design an overall economic strategy which simultaneously takes into account the effects of policy on growth, poverty and the distribution of income. In other words, poverty reduction should become an integral part of China's overall economic strategy.

## Restructuring China's poverty reduction strategy

The analysis above implies there is some urgency to restructure China's strategy for poverty reduction. The analysis also suggests what the elements of such a strategy should be. In what follows below the principal elements of a revised strategy are outlined.

## The need for a comprehensive strategy

China's poverty reduction strategy should be brought out of the shadows and become an integral part of overall economic policy. Unless this occurs the conflicting outcomes of general economic policy and specific poverty interventions are likely to continue. For example, if the incentives now favouring regional concentration in the coastal areas were altered, more resources could be attracted to poor areas and their development accelerated. Indeed it is likely that a change in incentives would be more effective in promoting development than directly targeting funds to poor areas when the overall structure of incentives is biased against them. Similarly, as will be argued below, incomes in poor areas could be increased significantly if pricing policies which discriminate against poor areas were abandoned.

## Economic growth

The maintenance of a high rate of growth is a critical component of any strategy to reduce poverty. Despite the crises in other parts of Asia, China's growth performance has been extremely good so far, although the rate of growth has declined slightly. Macroeconomic stability has been maintained. China did not suffer from massive capital flight, a foreign debt problem, or a large trade imbalance and it continued to attract foreign direct investment. Growth so far has been maintained. Two things in particular are essential in order to continue to preserve a rapid rate of growth. First, while China has become much more integrated into the world economy, unlike the rest of Asia, China has not liberalized international capital flows. While being open to foreign direct investment, China has not become dependent on foreign capital to finance its high rate of investment. Indeed, despite the very large inflow of foreign capital, domestic savings in China continue to exceed domestic investment. In effect, the inflow of foreign capital has been used to increase the already large volume of international reserves. The large reserves have given China substantial protection against the volatile currency movements that have afflicted other Asian countries from Indonesia to Thailand.

Moreover, while trade has been liberalized in China, and the ratio of exports (and imports) to GDP has risen dramatically, China has retained the right to support infant industries and pursue its dynamic comparative advantage. It is entirely appropriate that it should do so. Indeed, while China continues to become more closely integrated into the world economy, it should retain its trade, investment and foreign reserve policies which have served the country well and enabled it to sustain rapid growth even in the face of an external financial crisis.

The second important issue concerns exports. The share of exports in GDP increased from 6 per cent in 1980 to 21 per cent in 1996. The demand for exports, however, will almost certainly be a less important source of growth in future than it has been in the recent past. Without turning away from global integration, China should compensate for the likely slower growth of external demand by giving higher priority to sources of domestic demand that have the potential to promote rapid growth. As will be argued below, such a shift in strategy may make it easier to combine rapid growth with a substantial reduction and perhaps even elimination of poverty.

If one compares the pattern of growth in the 1980s with the pattern of the 1990s, it becomes clear that growth in China has become increasingly unbalanced. Agricultural output in China grew 5.9 per cent a year from 1980 to 1990; the growth rate in agriculture then declined to 4.4 per cent a year during the period 1990 to 1996. That is, the rate of growth of agricultural output fell by 25 per cent. The opposite happened in industry. The rate of growth of industrial output accelerated from 11.1 per cent a year during the period 1980–90 to 17.3 per cent a year from 1990 to 1996. That is, the growth rate of industrial output increased by nearly 56 per cent. In the first period, industrial growth was 1.9 times faster than agricultural growth; in the second period it was 3.9 times faster. This pattern of growth, and specifically the relative neglect of agriculture, helps to account for the weaker impact of overall growth on the reduction in poverty in the 1990s.

## Distributing the benefits of growth to households

Poverty cannot be eliminated if households do not participate fully in the benefits of growth. There is a strong case in favour of at least reducing the difference between the rate of growth of GDP and the growth of personal income. This does not imply that the average savings rate should be reduced, but it does imply that efforts to increase the already high savings rate should be avoided. Even if one adjusts upwards the estimates of national income in China, as we believe would be appropriate, China would still have one of the highest saving rates in the world. Rather than increase saving and investment further, priority should be given to increasing the productivity of investment. A redirection of demand to domestic sources and an expansion of public investment in essential infrastructure would almost certainly raise the return on investment. Furthermore, policies which lead to a more rapid increase in personal incomes would also lead to a more rapid expansion of the domestic market, and this would constitute a source for future growth.

## Growth of the rural economy

While poverty in the recent past has declined more rapidly in rural China than in urban China, most of China's poor still reside in rural areas. The remarkably rapid reduction in poverty during the period 1978–84 was associated with a sharp fall in rural–urban inequality. This pattern then went into reverse and the ratio of per capita urban income to per capita rural income rose rapidly after 1984 as the momentum behind poverty reduction diminished. If the ratio of urban to rural incomes had not fallen in 1994, and the widening inequalities between the cities and the countryside halted, the reported decline in rural poverty between 1988 and 1995 would have been much smaller. Moreover, within the rural areas, as noted above, farming is a highly equalizing source of income. These two considerations imply that greater emphasis on the farm economy – improved incentives and additional resources – would go a long way towards eliminating rural poverty.

The reduction in the rate of growth of agricultural output since the mid-1980s was due in part to reduced public resources for agriculture and in part to a slight deterioration of the terms of trade for agriculture. The terms of trade could be improved by allowing market forces, rather than arbitrary public intervention, to determine agricultural prices. Most agricultural prices are now determined by market forces, but the prices of grains are still subject to government control. The elimination of these controls would both improve agriculture's general terms of trade and also raise incomes in the poor central and western provinces that specialize in grain production.[12]

It is important that agricultural growth in China continue to be based on equality of access to land. This has been the principal reason why farm income has been distributed so evenly. Land use rights are now quite secure, although some improvements may be necessary to encourage efficiency and investment. Further tenure reforms, however, should take into account the need to maintain flexibility in allocating land to households. Changing demographic and economic conditions require a continuous reallocation of land and China's present arrangements have demonstrated their worth for two decades.

Rural non-farm activities have been an important source of growth in China. They have also been a source of increased inequality in rural areas. The reason for this is that non-farm rural activities have been regionally concentrated and hence the incomes generated in this dynamic sector have accentuated inequality. Greater effort is needed to ensure that in future non-farm activities are distributed more evenly among regions. A renewed emphasis on public investment in transport, power, communications and irrigation, particularly in the interior provinces, would help considerably.

Another reason for concentrating on accelerating the growth of the rural economy is that it would reduce the incentive of people to migrate to the urban areas. Rural development, rather than administrative controls over granting official residence permits, is a more equitable and effective way to reduce the rate of increase in floating migrants in the cities.

There has been much discussion in recent years about removing the bias against agriculture and the rural economy. It is therefore of some concern that increased rural–urban inequality is an explicit objective of development plans. In his report on the Ninth Five-Year Plan to the National People's Congress on 5 March 1996 the then Prime Minister Li Peng says, 'During the Ninth Five-Year Plan period, the urban residents' per capita income spent on living expenses after allowing for price rises is expected to increase by about 5 per cent annually and the per capita net income of the peasants is expected to increase by about 4 per cent annually.' In other words, average incomes in the cities are intended (or expected) to grow 25 per cent faster than average incomes in the countryside. If this actually occurs, it would lead to a dramatic increase in rural–urban inequality, an acceleration in the pace of rural-to-urban migration, more unemployment in urban areas and a severe weakening of other policies intended to reduce poverty.

### Reducing the regional imbalance in development

Unequal growth between the rapidly growing eastern provinces on the coast and the slow-growing central and western provinces has been the most important source of regional inequality in China during the period under review.[13] Slow growth of the central and western regions has been a serious obstacle to reducing poverty in these poor provinces, where much of China's poverty is concentrated. Increasing regional income disparities do not simply reflect higher factor productivity in the eastern provinces. Many of the disparities arise from policies that are biased against the poor provinces. For example, special privileges concerning tax concessions and the repatriation of profits, privileges that were designed to attract foreign direct investment, were long limited to the rich coastal provinces. Artificial administrative obstacles, rather than competitive disadvantage, prevented backward regions from competing on equal terms for investment. The artificial depression of producer prices for grain hampered the development of the central and western provinces. Similarly, poor regions often received an unfavourable price for their natural resources. For instance, the low price paid for coal produced in the poor areas of Shanxi hampered development there. Both efficiency and equity would be increased if discriminatory policies such as these were eliminated.

Unfortunately the comparative backwardness of the poorer regions is now so great that merely eliminating existing discrimination is unlikely to be enough to raise them to prosperity. Positive measures, e.g. directed credit to support 'infant' activities in poor regions and the redirection of public investment in infrastructure, almost certainly are needed to help these regions overcome their economic backwardness.

### Ending fiscal inequity

The taxes and subsidies which apply to households in China are a source of increased inequality and aggravated poverty. An average household in rural China is subjected to a net tax while an average household in urban China receives a net subsidy, although urban households are much richer than rural households. Furthermore, net taxes in rural China are highly regressive whereas net subsidies in urban China are highly progressive. Thus the tax-cum-subsidy system accentuates poverty and inequality in both rural and urban areas. Of particular concern is the highly unequal distribution of urban net subsidies. Had these subsidies been evenly distributed among all households in 1995, 94 per cent of the increase in the Gini ratio of urban income distribution between 1988 and 1995 would have been avoided.[14] An even distribution of urban subsidies would also have helped reduce urban poverty quite significantly. Reform of the fiscal system could therefore make a major contribution towards reducing poverty. If the large net subsidies received by high-income households in urban areas were eliminated, more resources would be available to support the poor.

### Coping with urban unemployment

The very strong bias against employment creation in the urban industrial sector has been a major source of inequality and poverty in urban China in the 1990s. This, together with the sharp influx of migrants, has resulted in a disproportionate increase of low-wage and low-productivity urban employment. It has also led to an increase in unemployment. Unless action is taken to protect unemployed and laid-off workers, the problem is certain to become worse during the foreseeable future.

One possible solution would be to introduce a system of unemployment insurance. After all, workers received such benefits indirectly for years, often decades, in state and collective enterprises which had large numbers of surplus employees. The costs to the enterprise were covered by providing public funds in the form of subsidies or bank loans. Replacing this concealed and inefficient system of unemployment compensation by an open and transparent one would not necessarily require an inordinate increase in resources.

A second possible solution would be a large urban public works programme designed to improve the infrastructure in poorer localities and neighbourhoods. This would help to create domestic demand and compensate for the expected slower growth of export demand while also helping to reduce the competitive disadvantage of the poorer urban locations. A third possible solution would be to encourage the development of micro-enterprises and self-employment through the public provision of credit, technology and training. These programmes would have to be carefully designed to minimize the subsidy element. Otherwise the burden on public resources could become rather high and the incentive to migrate to urban areas could increase.

In recent years a number of projects similar to those advocated have been launched in China. The task now is to learn from that experience and expand the most promising programmes so that they can satisfy the country's needs.

### Mobility of labour

One feature of the reform process in China has been a relaxation of many of the controls regulating the mobility of labour. Movement away from the most densely populated poor rural areas has been encouraged, although policy makers have shown a strong preference in favour of migration to other rural areas and small towns rather than to the large metropolitan areas. Public policy has also been tolerant of the floating migrants. They have not been evicted from the cities. As a result, China is much more urbanized today than it was two decades ago. By 1996, 31 per cent of its population was officially classified as urban. The unofficial urban population obviously is higher, because of unregistered migrants.

Migrants have been allowed to seek employment outside the state sector. They have, however, been denied official resident status and access to public services. The result has been the emergence of a segmented urban labour market in which migrants are condemned to earn a living in less formal employment and in low-income self-employment. China's reluctance to grant migrants official residence status is understandable because it would risk opening the floodgates to migration from rural areas. Yet the existing policy of denying residence status to migrants cannot be a long-term solution. Indeed continued discrimination is likely eventually to provoke social discontent in the cities and a heightened sense of grievance; it will also perpetuate urban poverty and allocative inefficiency. The solution is to tackle the root cause of the problem by raising incomes in the countryside and by reducing the (often subsidized) privileges associated with urban employment and formal residence.

### Improved targeting of the poverty reduction programme

China's rejection of targeted direct support to the poor stands in sharp contrast to the large subsidies given to the upper-income groups. The memory of the excesses of the 'iron rice bowl' policy of the past appears to have led policy makers to go to the other extreme and avoid all subsidies to poor and vulnerable households. This is regrettable because some poor households, probably only a minority, e.g. those with a low labour endowment, cannot benefit from the existing poverty reduction programmes. The only way to address their poverty is through direct income transfers.

Targeted interventions can also help increase access of poor households to basic education and health services. These services once were provided collectively and China was widely admired for the health, longevity and literacy of its population. One consequence of the economic reforms, however, was to weaken the social services, particularly in rural areas. The rural poor have been the most adversely affected. Happily, the government is beginning to respond, for example by establishing a rural cooperative medical insurance scheme that is broadly similar to the health care system that existed in the collective era. This new scheme, if it is successful, will improve access of the rural population, and especially poor households, to basic health services. The intention is to cover 80 per cent of the rural population by the year 2010.

## Conclusion

The implementation of something approximating the above package of measures will ensure that in future China's growth is far more effective in reducing poverty than it has been in the past. A programme of targeted support to poor locations and poor households, combined with a reorientation of general development policy, should enable China to overcome the incongruity of continued poverty after years of rapid economic growth.

Is there a danger that the package of measures advocated will reduce the rate of growth? This seems very unlikely. The policies recommended have been carefully chosen to avoid the need for large expenditures on non-investment programmes. A reduction in the average saving rate has been rejected. Strict limits on the commitment of public resources to finance subsidies and transfers have been urged. Improved terms of trade for agriculture have been recommended, but this should occur not through expensive price support programmes but by allowing market forces to operate more freely. A reduction in urban subsidies channelled to the higher-income groups has been advocated, and if implemented, this would result in a substantial saving of public resources. Rapid growth could be sustained, and perhaps even accelerated, if China would concentrate more on increasing the efficiency of investment rather than increasing the already high level of investment. Such efforts would cost little but yield high returns. Similarly, a shift in favour of the domestic economy and less reliance on exports to stimulate growth would help to reduce poverty. Such a reorientation of development strategy probably also is essential in order to sustain rapid growth, since the expansion of exports is unlikely to be as strong a stimulus in future as it has been in the recent past.

# Notes

## 1 Introduction

1 Compare the topics covered in the last edition of Gerald Meier's famous textbook with those discussed in this volume. Gerald M. Meier, *Leading Issues in Economic Development*, sixth edn, New York: Oxford University Press, 1995.

2 For an attempt to analyse the multi-dimensional nature of globalization, see David Held and Anthony McGrew, David Goldblatt and Jonathan Perraton, *Global Transformations: Politics, Economics and Culture*, Stanford, California: Stanford University Press, 1999.

3 One sign of malnutrition is the proportion of children who are underweight. In sub-Saharan Africa the figure is just over 30 per cent and in South Asia it is 51 per cent (see UNICEF, *Malnutrition in South Asia: A Regional Profile*, Regional Office for South Asia, November 1997). The Human Development Index for sub-Saharan Africa in 1995 was 0.378 and in South Asia it was 0.452. This is 40 and 28 per cent, respectively, below the average HDI for developing countries of 0.630 (see UNDP, *Human Development Report 1998*, New York: Oxford University Press, 1998).

4 Jeffrey Sachs, an ardent advocate of shock therapy, asserted at a conference on the transition economies in San Francisco on 7–8 May 1993 that the reform of the Chinese state economic enterprises 'has been a real fiasco' and that China would not have any state enterprises in 15 years, i.e. in 2008.

## 2 Culture, Human Development and Economic Growth

\* Original version published in the UNRISD/UNESCO Occasional Paper Series on Culture and Development, No. 3, Geneva and Paris, 1997. I am grateful to Steven Helfand, Azizur Rahman Khan, Prasanta Pattanaik and Jan Nederveen Pieterse for helpful comments on an earlier version of this essay.

1 For statements of the human development approach see Amartya Sen, 'Development as Capability Expansion', in Keith Griffin and John Knight, eds, *Human Development and the International Development Strategy for the 1990's*, London: Macmillan, 1990 and United Nations Development Programme, *Human Development Report 1990*, New York: Oxford University Press, 1990, Ch. 1.

2 Indeed UNDP has devoted the *Human Development Report 1996* to the controversy. See UNDP, *Human Development Report 1996*, New York: Oxford University Press, 1996.

3 See the report of the World Commission on Culture and Development, *Our Creative Diversity*, Paris: UNESCO, 1995. Also see UNESCO, *World Culture Report 1998*, Paris: UNESCO, 1998.

4  For an attempt to link human development, social development and culture in a specific country context see Keith Griffin, ed., *Social Policy and Economic Transformation in Uzbekistan*, Geneva: International Labour Organization, 1996, Ch. 1.

5  The rise in relative prices will of course ration demand and reduce the rate of consumption. It is therefore unlikely that we will literally run out of resources, but the sharp increase in the relative price of natural resources could have serious implications for the rate of growth of average incomes.

6  Most non-Marxian theories of economic growth take as their point of departure the work of Roy Harrod or Robert Solow. See R.F. Harrod, 'An Essay in Dynamic Theory', *Economic Journal*, April 1939 and Robert Solow, 'A Contribution to the Theory of Economic Growth', *Quarterly Journal of Economics*, February 1956.

7  See Amartya Sen, 'Development: Which Way Now?', *Economic Journal*, Vol. 93, No. 372, December 1983.

8  Perhaps the most important case is the Soviet Union, where high rates of investment in physical capital were largely offset by sharply diminishing returns to capital. See William Easterly and Stanley Fischer, 'The Soviet Economic Decline', *World Bank Economic Review*, Vol. 9, No. 3, September 1995.

9  See, for example, UNDP, *Human Development Report 1996*, New York: Oxford University Press, 1996.

10  In fact real gross domestic product (GDP) per capita (expressed in purchasing power parity terms) was incorporated into the Human Development Index (HDI) and given a weight of one-third. The inclusion of GDP in the HDI can be understood as implying that it contributes directly to human development or that it is acting as a proxy for capabilities other than longevity and literacy (which are included in the HDI), or both.

11  For an early survey of the evidence see George Psacharopoulos, 'Education and Development: A Review', *World Bank Research Observer*, Vol. 3, No. 1, January 1988. For recent evidence see George Psacharopoulos, 'Returns to Investment in Education: A Global Update', *World Development*, Vol. 22, 1994 and Rati Ram, 'Level of Development and Rates of Return to Schooling: Some Estimates from Multicountry Data', *Economic Development and Cultural Change*, Vol. 44, No. 4, July 1996. Also see John Strauss and Duncan Thomas, 'Health, Nutrition and Economic Development', *Journal of Economic Literature*, Vol. XXXVI, No. 2, June 1998.

12  People's willingness to cooperate and make sacrifices for the common good depends partly on cultural variables, as we shall see in the final section.

13  This does not imply that better information is sufficient to produce growth-enhancing policies – vested interests, pressure groups and conflicting political priorities also are relevant, but strong and clear 'voices' also have a role to play.

14  Jean Drèze and Amartya Sen, *Hunger and Public Action*, Oxford: Clarendon Press, 1989. Also see N. Ram, 'An Independent Press and Anti-Hunger Strategies: The Indian Experience', in Jean Drèze, Amartya Sen and Athar Hussain, eds, *The Political Economy of Hunger*, Oxford: Oxford University Press, 1995.

15  See, for instance, Amartya Sen, 'Economic Development and Social Change: India and China in Comparative Perspectives', Development Economics Research Programme, Suntory Centre, London School of Economics and Political Science, DEP No. 67, December 1995.

16  Arthur Okun, *Equality and Efficiency: The Big Tradeoff*, Washington, DC: Brookings Institution, 1975.

17  Nicholas Kaldor, 'Capital Accumulation and Economic Growth', in Nicholas Kaldor, ed., *Further Essays on Economic Theory*, New York: Holmes and Meier, 1978.

18  Mahbub ul Haq, *The Strategy of Economic Planning*, Karachi: Oxford University Press, 1963.

19  The phrase 'imagined communities' is borrowed from B. Anderson, *Imagined Communities: Reflections on the Origin and Spread of Nationalism*, London: Verso, 1983.

20  See, for example, Albert Berry and William Cline, *Agrarian Structure and Productivity in Developing Countries*, Baltimore: Johns Hopkins University Press, 1979 and Keith Griffin, *The Political Economy of Agrarian Change*, London: Macmillan, 1974.

21  John Fei, Gustav Ranis and Shirley Kuo, *Growth with Equity: The Taiwan Case*, Oxford: Oxford University Press, 1979.

22  See, for instance, Nancy Birdsall, David Ross and Richard Sabot, 'Inequality and Growth Reconsidered: Lessons from East Asia', *World Bank Economic Review*, Vol. 9, Nov. 3, September 1995.

23  A great deal of evidence is assembled in UNDP, *Human Development Report 1995*, New York: Oxford University Press, 1995.

24  This idea is nicely captured in Joseph Schumpeter's statement that 'add successively as many mail coaches as you please, you will never get a railway thereby'. (Joseph A. Schumpeter, *The Theory of Economic Development*, Cambridge: Harvard University Press, 1959, p. 64, n. 1.)

25  Indeed it can be argued that European culture was constituted historically by non-European (namely Asian and African) influences and is a product of cultural mixing that goes back at least to ancient Egypt. See, for example, Jan Nederveen Pieterse, 'Unpacking the West: How European is Europe?', in Ali Rattansi and Sallie Westwood, eds, *Racism, Modernity and Identity: On the Western Front*, Cambridge: Polity Press, 1994.

26  See Jan Nederveen Pieterse, 'Globalisation as Hybridisation', *International Sociology*, Vol. 9, No. 2, June 1994.

27  See Hugh Thomas, *The Slave Trade*, New York: Simon and Schuster, 1997.

28  Hartmut Elsenhans, *Development and Underdevelopment: The History, Economics and Politics of North–South Relations*, New Delhi: Sage Publications, 1991.

29  For an analysis of how scientific and technological achievement became a measure of the value of a civilization in the eighteenth century, justifying the right to 'civilize' inferior 'races' and to dominate the world, see Michael Adas, *Machines as the Measure of Men*, Ithaca: Cornell University Press, 1989.

30  For a study of how this continues today in the Amazon, see Norman Lewis, *The Missionaries*, London: Secker and Warburg, 1988.

31  The phrase is borrowed from Alan Moorehead, *The Fatal Impact: An Account of the Invasion of the South Pacific, 1767–1840*, London: Hamish Hamilton, 1966.

32  The impact effects of European expansion and the 'development of under-development' are discussed in Keith Griffin, *Underdevelopment in Spanish America*, London: Allen and Unwin, 1969, Ch.1 and Andre Gunder Frank, 'The Development of Underdevelopment', *Monthly Review*, Vol. 18, No. 4, September 1966.

33  See the multi-volume study by Joseph Needham, *Science and Civilisation in China*, Cambridge: Cambridge University Press, various years.

34  David Landes, *The Wealth and Poverty of Nations*, New York: W.W. Norton, 1998, p. 54.

35  Ibid.

36  Ibid., p. 401.

37  In the late 1960s to the early 1980s some analysts advocated policies of semi-autarky and 'delinking' underdeveloped countries from the global economy. (See, for instance, Samir Amin, 'Crisis, Nationalism and Socialism', in S. Amin, G. Arrighi, A.G. Frank and I. Wallerstein, eds, *Dynamics of Global Crisis*, New York: Monthly Review Press, 1982.) It is obvious today, how-ever, that neither involuntary delinking (as in Iraq and North Korea) nor voluntary delinking (as in Myanmar and Pol Pot's Cambodia) are promising avenues for economic growth or human development. (See Jan Nederveen Pieterse, 'Delinking or Globalisation?', *Economic and Political Weekly*, 29 January 1994.)

38  Jan Nederveen Pieterse, 'The Cultural Turn in Development: Questions of Power', *European Journal of Development Research*, Vol. 7, No. 1, 1995, p. 185.

39  Samuel Huntington has argued that in future the 'principal conflicts of global politics' will be dominated by the clash of civilizations or cultures. See Samuel P. Huntington, 'The Clash of Civilizations?', *Foreign Affairs*, Vol. 72, No. 3, Summer 1993.

40  See T. Banuri, 'Modernization and its Discontents: a Cultural Perspective on Theories of Development', in F. Appfel Marglin and Stephen A. Marglin, eds, *Dominating Knowledge*, Oxford: Clarendon Press, 1990.

41  Jan Nederveen Pieterse, 'Globalisation as Hybridisation', p. 177.

## 3   Globalization and the Shape of Things to Come

*   Keynote address at the Macalester International Round Table on 'Globalization and Economic Space', Macalester College, St Paul, Minnesota, 8–10 October 1998. The original, longer version was published in *Macalester International*, Vol. 5, Spring 1999.

1  This point is emphasized by Dharam Ghai in his 'Globalization and Competitiveness: Implications for Human Security and Development Thinking', in Louis Emmerij, ed., *Economic and Social Development into the XXI Century*, Washington, DC: Johns Hopkins University Press for the Inter-American Development Bank, 1997, p. 168.

2  Susan B. Carter and Richard Sutch, 'Historical Perspectives on the Economic Consequences of Immigration into the United States', in Joshua DeWind, Charles Hirschman and Philip Kasinitz, eds, *Becoming American/America Becoming: International Migration to the United States*, forthcoming.

3  The growth estimates were compiled from data in World Bank, *World Development Indicators 1998*, Washington, DC: World Bank, 1998.

4  Angus Maddison, 'Economic Policy and Performance in Capitalist Europe', in Louis Emmerij, ed., op. cit., Table 3.12, p. 295.

5  The UNDP comes to the opposite conclusion in a study covering the period 1960 to 1989. See UNDP, *Human Development Report 1992*, New York: Oxford University Press, 1992, Ch. 3.

6  The contrast between the Chinese and Soviet experiences is highlighted in Keith Griffin and Azizur Rahman Khan, 'The Transition to Market Guided Economies: Lessons for Russia and Eastern Europe from the Chinese Experience', in Bernd Magnus and Stephen Cullenberg, eds, *Whither Marxism? Global Crises in International Perspective*, New York and London: Routledge, 1995.

7  For a short statement of how East Asia's development strategy differed from the liberalization strategy of the 'Washington consensus' see Frances Stewart, 'John Williamson and the Washington Consensus Revisited', in Louis Emmerij, ed., op. cit., pp. 64–7.

8  See Overseas Development Institute, *Foreign Direct Investment Flows to Low-income Countries: a Review of the Evidence*, Briefing Paper, September 1997, Table 1, p. 2.

9  H. Singh and K.W. Jun, *Some New Evidence on Determinants of Foreign Direct Investment in Developing Countries*, Policy Research Working Paper No. 1531, Washington, DC: World Bank, 1995.

10  See, for example, A. Bhattacharya, P.J. Montiel and S. Sharma, 'Private Capital Flows to Sub-Saharan Africa: an Overview of Trends and Determinants', unpublished paper, World Bank, Washington, DC, 1996.

11  The argument that follows was first presented in Keith Griffin and Azizur Rahman Khan, *Globalization and the Developing World*, Geneva: UNRISD, 1992, Ch. 8.

12  These points are discussed at greater length in Keith Griffin, 'Globalization and Development Cooperation: A Reformer's Agenda', in Albert Berry, Roy Culpeper and Frances Stewart, eds, *Global Governance and Development Fifty Years after Bretton Woods*, London: Macmillan, 1997.

13  Graciela Chichilnisky has suggested creating an International Bank for Environmental Settlements that would be responsible for creating a global market in emissions permits (including loans of emissions permits and derivative instruments associated with them) and monitoring the results. See her *Development and Global Finance: the Case for an International Bank for Environmental Settlements*, UNDP, Office of Development Studies, Discussion Paper No. 10, 1997.

14  The argument that follows is developed at greater length in Chapter 2.

# 4  Human Development: Origins, Evolution and Impact

*  This was originally presented as the keynote address at the tenth anniversary conference of HEGOA: Institute for the Study of Development and the International Economy, Bilbao, Spain, 18–20 February 1999.

1  See, for example, Paul Rosenstein-Rodan, 'Industrialisation in Eastern and South Eastern Europe', *Economic Journal*, Vol. 53, 1943.

2  A number of different approaches are analysed in Keith Griffin, *Alternative Strategies for Economic Development*, London: Macmillan, 1989.

3  Amartya Sen, 'Development as Capability Expansion', in Keith Griffin and John Knight, eds, *Human Development and the International Development Strategy for the 1990s*, London: Macmillan, 1990.

4  Amartya Sen, *Inequality Reexamined*, New York: Oxford University Press, 1992.

5  T.W. Schultz, 'Capital Formation by Education', *Journal of Political Economy*, December 1960 and T.W. Schultz, 'Investment in Human Capital', *American Economic Review*, March 1961.

6  See, for example, George Psacharopoulos, 'Education and Development: a Review', *World Bank Research Observer*, Vol. 3, No. 1, 1988; George Psacharopoulos, 'Returns to Investment in Education: a Global Update', *World Development*, Vol. 22, 1994; Rati Ram, 'Level of Development and Returns to Schooling: Some Estimates from Multicountry Data', *Economic Development and Cultural Change*, Vol. 44, No. 4, 1996.

7  For a survey of the benefits of investing in health and nutrition see John Strauss and Duncan Thomas, 'Health, Nutrition and Economic Development', *Journal of Economic Literature*, Vol. XXXVI, No. 2, June 1998.

8  See Hollis Chenery, Montek S. Ahluwalia, C.L.G. Bell, John H. Duloy and Richard Jolly, *Redistribution with Growth*, London: Oxford University Press, 1974.

9  International Labour Organization, *Employment, Growth and Basic Needs: A One-World Problem*, Geneva: ILO, 1976.

10  Giovanni Andrea Cornia, Richard Jolly and Frances Stewart, eds, *Adjustment with a Human Face*, Oxford: Clarendon Press, 1987.

11  Keith Griffin and John Knight, eds, op. cit.

12  Committee for Development Planning, *Human Resources Development: a Neglected Dimension of Development Strategy*, New York: United Nations, 1988, Chapter III.

13  See Mahbub ul Haq, *Reflections on Human Development*, New York: Oxford University Press, 1995.

14  Keith Griffin and Terry McKinley, *Implementing a Human Development Strategy*, London: Macmillan, 1994.

15  See Keith Griffin, ed., *Poverty and the Transition to a Market Economy in Mongolia*, London: Macmillan, 1995; Keith Griffin, ed., *Social Policy and Economic Transformation in Uzbekistan*, Geneva: International Labour Office, 1996; Keith Griffin, ed., *Economic Reform in Vietnam*, London: Macmillan, 1998.

16  A.C. Pigou, *The Economics of Welfare*, London: Macmillan, 1920.

17  M.D. Morris, *Measuring the Condition of the World's Poor: the Physical Quality of Life Index*, Oxford: Pergamon Press, 1979.

18  For the most recent methods used in computing the HDI see UNDP, *Human Development Report 1997*, New York: Oxford University Press, 1997, Technical Note 2, p. 122.

19  UNDP, *Human Development Report 1996*, New York: Oxford University Press, 1996.

20  Terry McKinley, 'Capability Poverty in Vietnam', in Keith Griffin, ed., *Economic Reform in Vietnam*.

21  The gender-sensitive HDI is obtained by multiplying the overall HDI by the ratio of the female-to-male HDI: $HDI_{gs} = HDI \times \dfrac{HDI_f}{HDI_m}$

22  See, for example, Chapter 6.

23 See Chapter 5. Also see Louis Putterman, John E. Roemer and Joaquim Silvestre, 'Does Egalitarianism Have a Future?' *Journal of Economic Literature*, Vol. XXXVI, No. 2, June 1998.

# 5 The Distribution of Wealth and the Pace of Development

* Original version published by UNDP, Social Development and Poverty Elimination Division, Working Paper Series, WP3, November 1997.

1  Simon Kuznets, 'Economic Growth and Income Inequality', *American Economic Review*, Vol. 45, 1955, pp. 1–28.

2  Arthur Okun, *Equality and Efficiency: the Big Tradeoff*, Washington, DC: Brookings Institution, 1975.

3  Simon Kuznets, 'Quantitative Aspects of the Economic Growth of Nations: VIII, Distribution of Income by Size', *Economic Development and Cultural Change*, Vol. 11, No. 2, 1963, p. 69.

4.  Irma Adelman and Cynthia Taft Morris, 'An Anatomy of Patterns of Income Distribution in Developing Nations', Part II of *Final Report*, Grant AID/csd-2236: Northwestern University, 1971.

5  Felix Paukert, 'Income Distribution at Different Levels of Development: a Survey of Evidence', *International Labour Review*, Vol. 108, 1973, p. 120.

6  Montek S. Ahluwalia, 'Inequality, Poverty and Development', *Journal of Development Economics*, Vol. 3, 1976, pp. 307–42.

7  Sherman Robinson, 'A Note on the U-Hypothesis', *American Economic Review*, Vol. 66, No. 3, 1976, p. 437.

8  Simon Kuznets, 'Underdeveloped Countries and the Pre-industrial Phase in the Advanced Countries', in A.N. Agarwala and P.S. Singh, eds, *The Economics of Underdevelopment*, New York: Oxford University Press, 1967, p. 153.

9  Ashwani Saith, 'Development and Distribution: a Critique of the Cross-Country U-Hypothesis', *Journal of Development Economics*, Vol. 13, 1983, p. 378.

10  Shail Jain, *Size Distribution of Income: A Compilation of Data*, Washington, DC: World Bank, 1975.

11  Klaus Deininger and Lyn Squire, 'New Ways of Looking at Old Issues: Inequality and Growth', mimeo, 1996.

12  Torsten Persson and Guido Tabellini, 'Is Inequality Harmful for Growth?', *American Economic Review*, Vol. 84, No. 3, 1994, p. 601.

13  Gary Fields, 'Changes in Poverty and Inequality in Developing Countries', *World Bank Research Observer*, Vol. 4, 1989, pp. 167–86.

14  Alberto Alesina and Dani Rodrik, 'Distributive Politics and Economic Growth', *Quarterly Journal of Economics*, Vol. 108, 1994, p. 481.

15  G.R.G. Clarke, 'More Evidence on Income Distribution and Growth', *Journal of Development Economics*, Vol. 47, No. 2, p. 422.

16  Klaus Deininger and Lyn Squire, 'A New Data Set Measuring Income Inequality', *World Bank Economic Review*, Vol. 10, No. 3, 1996, p. 573.

17  Roberto Perotti, 'Income Distribution, Politics and Growth: Theory and Evidence', Columbia University, mimeo, 1991.

18    Deininger and Squire, 'New Ways', p. 7.
19    A. Deaton, 'Data and Econometric Tools for Development Analysis', in Jere Behrman and T.N. Srinivasan, eds, *Handbook of Development Economics*, Vol. IIIa, New York: Elsevier Science B.V., 1995, p. 1803.
20    Deininger and Squire, 'A New Data Set', p. 573.
21    Deininger and Squire, 'New Ways', p. 13.
22    Ibid., p. 7.
23    Ibid., p. 8.
24    See United Nations Development Programme, *Human Development Report 1996*, New York: Oxford University Press, 1996 and Asian Development Bank, *Emerging Asia: Changes and Challenges*, Manila: Asian Development Bank, 1997.
25    Robert J. Barro, 'Economic Growth in a Cross Section of Countries', *Quarterly Journal of Economics*, Vol. 106, May 1991, pp. 407–43.
26    Rati Ram, 'Level of Development and Returns to Schooling: Some Estimates from Multicountry Data', *Economic Development and Cultural Change*, Vol. 44, No. 4, 1996, p. 848.
27    George Psacharopoulos, 'Education and Development: a Review', *World Bank Research Observer*, Vol. 3, No. 1, 1988, p. 101.
28    George Psacharopoulos, 'Returns to Investment in Education: a Global Update', *World Development*, Vol. 22, 1994, pp. 1325–43.
29    Asian Development Bank, op. cit., p. 80.
30    Persson and Tabellini, op. cit., p. 604.
31    Alberto Alesina and Roberto Perotti, 'The Political Economy of Growth: a Critical Survey of the Literature', *World Bank Economic Review*, Vol. 8, No. 3, 1994, p. 361.
32    Guiseppe Bertola, 'Factor Shares and Savings in Endogenous Growth', *American Economic Review*, Vol. 83, No. 5, 1993, pp. 1184–98.
33    Alesina and Rodrik, op. cit., p. 481.
34    Ibid., p. 483.
35    Keith Griffin, *Studies in Globalization and Economic Transitions*, London: Macmillan, 1996, p. 144.
36    Samuel Bowles and Herbert Gintis, 'Escaping the Efficiency–Equity Trade-off: Productivity-enhancing Asset Redistributions', in Gerald A. Epstein and Herbert M. Gintis, eds, *Macroeconomic Policy after the Conservative Era*, New York: Cambridge University Press, 1995, p. 411.
37    Griffin, *Studies in Globalization*, p. 144.
38    Joseph Stiglitz and Andrew Weiss, 'Credit Rationing in Markets with Imperfect Information', *American Economic Review*, Vol. 71, 1981, pp. 393–409.
39    G.C. Loury, 'Intergenerational Transfers and the Distribution of Earnings', *Econometrica*, Vol. 49, 1981, pp. 843–67.
40    Deininger and Squire, 'New Ways', p. 10.
41    Nancy Birdsall, David Ross and Richard Sabot, 'Inequality as a Constraint on Growth in Latin America', Washington DC: Inter-American Development Bank, mimeo, 1994, p. 10.
42    Bowles and Gintis, op. cit., p. 412.
43    Nicholas Kaldor, 'Capital Accumulation and Economic Growth', in Nicholas Kaldor, ed., *Further Essays on Economic Theory*, New York: Holmes and Meier, 1978.

44 See Keith Griffin, *The Political Economy of Agrarian Change*, London: Macmillan, 1974 and Keith Griffin and Azizur Rahman Khan, *Growth and Inequality in Pakistan*, London: Macmillan, 1972.
45 P.G.K. Panikar, 'Rural Savings in India', *Economic Development and Cultural Change*, Vol. 10, No. 1, 1961.
46 A. Bergan, 'Personal Income Distribution and Personal Savings in Pakistan, 1963/64', *Pakistan Development Review*, Vol. VII, No. 2, 1967.
47 A.S. Kahlon and Harbhajan Singh, *Factors Associated with Farm and Farm Family Investment Pattern in Ludhiana (Punjab) and Hissar (Haryana) Districts: (1966–67 through 1969–70)*, Department of Economics and Sociology, Punjab Agricultural University, Ludhiana, n.d.
48 Keith Griffin and Terry McKinley, *Implementing a Human Development Strategy*, London: Macmillan, 1994, p. 81.
49 John C.H. Fei, Gustav Ranis and Shirley W.Y. Kuo, *Growth and Equity: the Taiwan Case*, New York: Oxford University Press, 1979.
50 Tibor Scitovsky, 'Economic Development in Taiwan and South Korea', *Food Research Institute Studies*, Vol. XIX, No. 4, 1985, pp. 215–64.
51 Birdsall *et al.*, 'Inequality as a Constraint', p. 2.
52 Ibid., p. 7.
53 United Nations Development Programme, *Human Development Report 1990*, New York: Oxford University Press, 1990 and United Nations Development Programme, *Human Development 1996*, New York: Oxford University Press, 1996.
54 Birdsall *et al.*, Inequality as a Constraint'.
55 Jeffrey G. Williamson, 'Human Capital Deepening, Inequality and Demographic Events along the Asia-Pacific Rim', in Naohiro Agawa, Gavin W. Jones and Jeffrey G. Williamson, eds, *Human Resources in Development along the Asia-Pacific Rim*, New York: Oxford University Press, 1993.
56 Nancy Birdsall, David Ross and Richard Sabot, 'Inequality and Growth Reconsidered: Lessons for East Asia', *World Bank Economic Review*, Vol. 9, No. 3, 1995, p. 482.
57 Birdsall *et al.*, 'Inequality as a Constraint', p. 12.
58 Scitovsky, op. cit.
59 John Mellor, *Agriculture on the Road to Industrialization*, Baltimore: Johns Hopkins University Press, 1995, p. 322.
60 Juha Honkkila, *Privatization, Asset Distribution and Equity in Transitional Economies*, United Nations University, World Institute for Development Economics Research, Working Paper No. 125, 1997.
61 Griffin, *Studies in Globalization*, p. 140.
62 Deininger and Squire, 'New Ways', p. 25.
63 William R. Cline, *Potential Effects of Income Redistribution on Economic Growth: Latin American Cases*, New York: Praeger, 1972.

# 6 Economic Policy during the Transition to a Market-Oriented Economy

\* Paper presented at a UNDP sponsored conference on 'Central Asia, 2010' in Almaty, Kazakhstan, 20–22 July 1998.

1  As will be indicated in Table 6.4 the fall in GDP during the transition was 24.3 per cent in Central and Eastern Europe, 46.7 per cent in the Baltic States and 45.4 per cent in the former Soviet Union. In contrast, between 1929 and the lowest point in the 1930s, GDP declined by 5.1 per cent in the UK, 8.9 per cent in Sweden, 7 per cent in Italy, 9.4 per cent in Australia, 23.5 per cent in Germany, 30.1 per cent in Canada and 29.7 per cent in the USA. (See Jacek Rostowski, 'Comparing Two Great Depressions: 1929–33 to 1989–93', in Salvatore Zecchini, ed., *Lessons from the Economic Transition: Central and Eastern Europe in the 1990s*, Dordrecht: Kluwer Academic Publishers, 1997, p. 226.)
2  For an analysis of the economic transition in Mongolia see Keith Griffin, ed., *Poverty and the Transition to a Market Economy in Mongolia*, London: Macmillan, 1995.
3  See Keith Griffin and Azizur Rahman Khan, 'The Transition to Market Guided Economies: Lessons for Russia and Eastern Europe from the Chinese Experience', in Bernd Magnus and Stephen Cullenberg, eds, *Whither Marxism? Global Crises in International Perspective*, New York and London: Routledge, 1995.
4  See Chapter 9.
5  See Chapter 10.
6  See Keith Griffin and Zhao Renwei, eds, *The Distribution of Income in China*, London: Macmillan, 1993.
7  See Azizur Rahman Khan and Carl Riskin, 'Income and Inequality in China: Composition, Distribution and Growth of Household Income, 1988 to 1995', *China Quarterly*, June 1998.
8  United Nations Development Programme, *Human Development Report 1997*, New York: Oxford University Press, 1997, p. 34.
9  Ibid., Figure 2.11b, p. 35.
10  Axel Leijonhufvud and Christof Rühl, 'Russian Dilemmas', *American Economic Review*, May 1997, p. 344.
11  Albert O. Hirschman was the first to use journeys as a metaphor for the process of transition and to coin the word 'reformmongering' to describe the sequence of policies which constitute the journey. See his *Journeys Toward Progress: Studies of Economic Policy-Making in Latin America*, New York: Twentieth Century Fund, 1963.
12  See UNDP, *The Shrinking State: Governance and Sustainable Human Development*, New York: UNDP, 1997.
13  Stephen Parker, Gavin Tritt and Wing Thye Woo, 'Some Lessons Learned from the Comparison of Transitions in Asia and Eastern Europe', in Wing Thye Woo, Stephen Parker and Jeffrey D. Sachs, eds, *Economies in Transition: Comparing Asia and Eastern Europe*, Cambridge: MIT Press, 1997, p. 15.
14  Ibid.
15  Ibid., p. 6.
16  Ibid., p. 7.
17  Lázló Szamuely, 'Privatization in a Transforming Central and Eastern Europe', in UNCTAD, *Privatization in the Transition Process: Recent Experiences in Eastern Europe*, New York: United Nations, 1994, p. 32.
18  Sunita Kikeri, John Nellis and Mary Shirley, *Privatization: Lessons of Experience*, Washington, DC: World Bank, 1992, p. 73.

19  See Chapter 10.

20  Jeremy Swift, 'Rural Development: The Livestock Sector', in Keith Griffin, ed., *Poverty and the Transition to a Market Economy in Mongolia*, London: Macmillan, 1995.

21  The case for gradual reform is presented in Gérard Roland, 'On the Speed and Sequencing of Privatization and Restructuring', *Economic Journal*, Vol. 104, No. 426, September 1994. The case for the big bang is presented in D. Lipton and J. Sachs, 'Privatization in Eastern Europe: the Case of Poland', *Brookings Papers in Economic Activity*, No. 2, 1990.

22  World Bank, *World Development Report 1996*, New York: Oxford University Press, 1996, p. 51.

23  Yuan Zheng Cao, Gang Fan and Wing Thye Woo, 'Chinese Economic Reforms: Past Successes and Future Challenges', in Woo, Parker and Sachs, eds, op. cit., pp. 22–5.

24  Yilmaz Akyüz, 'Reform and Crisis in the Transition Economies', in UNCTAD, op. cit., p. 6. Also see Wlodzimierz Brus, 'General Problems of Privatization in the Process of Transformation of the Post-Communist Economies', in UNCTAD, op. cit. pp. 47–59.

25  Akyüz, op. cit., p. 8.

26  Peter Boone and Boris Fedorov, 'The Ups and Downs of Russian Economic Reforms', in Woo, Parker and Sachs, eds, op. cit., p. 180.

27  Wing Thye Woo, 'Improving Enterprise Performance in Transition Economies', in Woo, Parker and Sachs, eds, op. cit., p. 313.

28  Ibid.

29  Philippe Aghion and Wendy Carlin, 'Restructuring Outcomes and the Evolution of Ownership Patterns in Central and Eastern Europe', in Salvatore Zecchini, ed., *Lessons from the Economic Transition: Central and Eastern Europe in the 1990s*, Dordrecht: Kluwer Academic Publishers, 1997, p. 243.

30  Gábor Hunya, 'Large Privatisation, Restructuring and Foreign Direct Investment', in Zecchini, ed., op. cit., p. 282.

31  UNDP, *Human Development Report 1997*, New York: Oxford University Press, Table 2.13, p. 47.

## 7  Macroeconomic Reform and Employment: an Investment-Led Strategy of Structural Adjustment in Sub-Saharan Africa

*    The essay was first published by the International Labour Office in Issues in Development, Discussion Paper 16, 1996. I am grateful to Samir Radwan, Rolph van der Hoeven, Frank Lisk, Steven Miller and Roberto Zachmann for stimulating discussions which influenced my views. Neither they nor the International Labour Office are responsible for any of the opinions expressed in this essay.

1  In the World Bank, *World Development Report 1996* (New York: Oxford University Press, 1996) 50 countries are listed. The UNDP, *Human Development Report 1996* (New York: Oxford University Press, 1996) contains 44 countries on its list. The six countries in the World Bank's list but not on

the UNDP's list are Djibouti, Eritrea, Mayotte, Reunion, Somalia and Sudan. This study will use the World Bank's list.

2 We have used a simple average rather than an average weighted by size of population because we want to give each country's development experience equal weight in assessing macroeconomic performance. Thus our growth rates do not measure the performance of sub-Saharan Africa seen as a whole but the average performance of the countries that comprise sub-Saharan Africa.

3 The World Bank, op. cit., reports that GNP per capita in sub-Saharan Africa declined 1.2 per cent a year during the period 1985–94. This is a weighted average for the region.

4 For example, the share in total income of the lowest 20 per cent of households is reported in early sample surveys to have fallen in Côte d'Ivoire (from 1970–75 to 1986), Kenya (from 1969–71 to 1976), the Sudan (from 1964 to 1967–68) and in Zambia (from 1959–61 to 1976). See Idriss Jazairy, Mohiuddin Alamgir and Theresa Panuccio, *The State of World Rural Poverty*, published for the International Fund for Agriculture Development by New York University Press, 1992, Table 5, pp. 402–3. A World Bank study also suggests that in the 1980s inequality increased in Côte d'Ivoire, Ethiopia, Ghana, Nigeria and Tanzania (Lionel Demery, Binayak Sen and Tara Vishwanath, 'Poverty, Inequality and Growth', Washington, DC: World Bank, ESP Discussion Paper Series 70, June 1995). Also see Lionel Demery and Lyn Squire, 'Macroeconomic Adjustment and Poverty in Africa: an Emerging Picture', *World Bank Research Observer*, Vol. 11, No. 1, February 1996.

5 World Bank, *World Development Report 1990*, New York: Oxford University Press, 1990, Table 2.1, p. 29.

6 Jazairy, Alamgir and Panuccio, op. cit., Table 2, p. 387.

7 The World Bank has published three major studies of sub-Saharan Africa in each of which analysis is followed by policy prescription. See World Bank, *Toward Sustained Development in Sub-Saharan Africa: a Joint Program of Action*, Washington, DC, 1984; World Bank, *Sub-Saharan Africa: From Crisis to Sustainable Growth*, Washington, DC, 1989; and World Bank, *A Continent in Transition: Sub-Saharan Africa in the Mid-1990's*, Washington, DC, 1995. Also see World Bank, *Adjustment in Africa: Reforms, Results and the Road Ahead*, New York: Oxford University Press, 1994 for the Bank's assessment of policy reforms in 29 countries. The World Bank tends to blame uneven implimentation of reforms for the failure of structural adjustment rather than the choice of the reform strategy itself. In Ishrat Husain, *Why Do Some Economies Adjust More Successfully Than Others? Lessons From Seven African Countries*, World Bank: Washington, DC, Policy Research Working Paper 1364, October 1994, uneven implementation is attributed to lack of 'domestic ownership' and 'capacity'. The policies themselves, in other words, are assumed to be correct. World Bank and IMF policies, however, have been severely criticized by the Economic Commission for Africa. See ECA, *African Alternative Framework to Structural Adjustment Programmes for Socio-Economic Recovery and Transformation* (AAF-SAP), E/ECA/CM.15/6/Rev 23, Addis Ababa, 1989 and Adebayo Adedeji, *Structural Adjustment for Socio-economic Recovery and Transformation: the African Alternative*, Addis Ababa: United Nations Economic Commission for Africa, 1990.

8  An upper limit on the inflation rate of 20 per cent is of course arbitrary, but there is some evidence that inflation harms growth only after the rate of inflation becomes rather high, namely, above 40 per cent. See Michael Bruno, 'Does Inflation Really Lower Growth?' *Finance and Development*, Vol. 32, No. 3, September 1995.

9  In 1994 gross domestic savings were negative in Rwanda, Burundi, Malawi, Chad and Lesotho.

10  There is evidence that many countries in sub-Saharan Africa did adjust the real exchange rate to cushion the impact of the decline in the external terms of trade on domestic economic activity. (See Michael Hadjimichael, Dhaneshwar Ghura, Martin Mükleisen, Roger Nord and E. Murat Uçer, *Sub-Saharan Africa: Growth, Savings and Investment, 1986–93*, Washington, DC: International Monetary Fund, January 1995). The question remains, however, whether nominal exchange rates were fully adjusted to compensate for inflation.

11  In 1993, official development assistance (ODA) was 10.5 per cent of GNP in sub-Saharan Africa. This was much higher than the proportion in all other developing regions apart from East Asia (excluding China), where it was 19.5 per cent. The average for all developing countries was 1.4 per cent (UNDP, *Human Development Report 1996*, New York: Oxford University Press, 1996, Table 47, p. 212).

12  See Paul Collier, 'The Marginalization of Africa', *International Labour Review*, Vol. 134, Nos. 4–5, 1995 for an attempt to explain the delinking of Africa from the world economy.

13  For example, formal sector wage employment as a percentage of the total labour force declined in Kenya from 18 per cent in 1988 to 16.9 per cent in 1994; in Uganda from 17.2 per cent in 1991 to 12.7 per cent in 1995; in Zambia from 29.4 per cent in 1980 to 18.2 per cent in 1994; and in Zambabwe from 34.1 per cent in 1980 to 25.3 per cent in 1995. (Rolph van der Hoeven, 'Labour Markets and Structural Adjustment', paper presented at a seminar on Policies for Economic Growth and Development in Southern Africa, Harare, Zimbabwe, 1–3 April 1996, Table 12. Also see Willem van der Geest and Ganeshan Wignaraja, *Adjustment, Employment and Labour Market Institutions in Sub-Saharan Africa in the 1990s: a Survey*, Geneva: International Labour Office, Employment Papers 10, 1996.)

14  For example, real earnings in manufacturing in Kenya declined 30.5 per cent from 1987 to 1992 and in Zambia the decline was 23.6 per cent from 1987 to 1991. (Van der Hoeven, op. cit., Table 15.)

15  Vali Jamal and John Weeks, *Africa Misunderstood or Whatever Happened to the Rural–Urban Gap?*, Geneva: International Labour Office, 1988.

16  Vali Jamal, ed., *Structural Adjustment and Rural Labour Markets in Africa*, London: Macmillan, 1995.

17  In the case of internationally mobile resources, however, reallocation certainly is possible. There was a large exodus of human capital from Africa in the form of the emigration to Europe and North America of high-skilled, professional, managerial and technical labour. There was also considerable capital flight. Both these scarce resources could in principle be repatriated under favourable conditions, such as those associated with an investment-led strategy of structural adjustment.

18   The implication of this argument is that in a context of economic decline and a fall in total government expenditure, public expenditure on human capital formation should be protected and hence the proportion of government expenditure devoted to education (and health) actually should rise.

19   See Keith Griffin and Terry McKinley, *Implementing a Human Development Strategy*, London: Macmillan, 1994, Ch. 2.

20   Ingrid Palmer has argued persuasively that the reduction in state-provided health services that has accompanied structural adjustment has increased disproportionately the burden on women since it is they who must now provide substitutes for the lost services. (Ingrid Palmer, 'Public Finance from a Gender Perspective', *World Development*, Vol. 23, No. 11, November 1995.)

21   See the essay on 'Domestic Policies in Developing Countries and their Effects on Employment, Income Inequality and Poverty', in Keith Griffin, *Studies in Globalization and Economic Transitions*, London: Macmillan, 1996.

22   Large inflows of foreign aid can lean in an anti-development direction by (i) reducing real rates of interest, (ii) putting upward pressure on the exchange rate, (iii) increasing consumption at the expense of savings and (iv) distorting the composition of investment. (See the essay on 'Foreign Aid after the Cold War', in Griffin, op.cit.

23   Rolph van der Hoeven recommends 'a moratorium on African debt for the next 10 years…' (Rolph van der Hoeven, 'External Dependence, Structural Adjustment and Development Aid in Sub-Saharan Africa', in Karel Jansen and Rob Vos, eds, *External Finance and Adjustment, Failure and Success in the Developing World*, London: Macmillan, 1996.)

24   For evidence in support of the 'crowding in 'hypothesis see Lance Taylor, *Varieties of Stabilization Experience*, Oxford: Clarendon Press, 1988; Lance Taylor, ed., *The Rocky Road to Reform*, Cambridge: MIT Press, 1993; Helen Shapiro and Lance Taylor, 'The State and Industrial Strategy', *World Development*, Vol. 18, 1990; and implicitly, World Bank, *World Development Report 1994*, New York: Oxford University Press, 1994.

# 8   Domestic Resource Mobilization and Enterprise Development in Sub-Saharan Africa

1   See Chapter 7.

2   See however Chapter 7.

3   Adebayo Olukoshi, *Economic Crisis, Structural Adjustment and the Coping Strategies of Manufacturers in Kano, Nigeria*, UNRISD Discussion Paper 77, September 1996.

4   The table is taken from ibid., Table 9. Calculations are based on 1991 and 1992 field surveys of 100 manufacturing concerns in Kano, Nigeria. Ibid., Table 2 gives the number of firms in each subsection.

5   See Keith Griffin, *Studies in Globalization and Economic Transitions*, London: Macmillan, 1996, Ch. 7.

6   Each figure in Table 8.2 represents the simple average of ODA for the years in question for the particular country concerned. Overall ODA per capita figures are calculated as the simple average for the 38 countries for which

we have data. This method is adopted so as to give each country's adjustment experience equal weight, a sort of 'natural experiment' in adjustment.

7  It must be noted that while these numbers would surely be much smaller were the average weighted by population, we reiterate our commitment to treating each country as a separate experiment in adjustment.

8  See Chapter 7. Note that this estimate for GDP growth has been calculated in much the same way as the previous figures, taking country averages for the 14 years in question and then taking a simple average of the 33 countries where data are available. Also note that while low compared to the rest of the world, this figure should be considered an upper bound on the growth rate for the entire region, as many of the countries for which data are unavailable were racked by political violence, a fact likely to lower their growth rates below the average of the rest of sub-Saharan Africa.

9  World Bank, *World Development Report 1996*, New York: Oxford University Press, 1996. It is worth noting that even if ODA were promoting capital formation at a rapid pace, given the political climate in many donor countries, present prospects for its continued availability let alone increased levels are slim.

10  Keith Griffin and Azizur Rahman Khan, *Globalization and the Developing World*, Geneva: UNRISD, 1992, p. 30.

11  Keith Griffin and Azizur Rahman Khan, eds, *Poverty and Landlessness in Rural Asia*, Geneva: ILO, 1977, Ch. 1, pp. 29–37.

12  The classic statement for mobilizing surplus labour for investment is Ragnar Nurkse, *Problems of Capital Formation in Underdeveloped Countries*, New York: Oxford University Press, 1953.

13  K.N. Ray, D.K. Grover and D.S. Nandlal, 'Investment and Saving Pattern in Irrigated and Unirrigated Zones of Haryana State', *Indian Journal of Agricultural Economics*, October–December 1969.

14  A.S. Kahlon and Harbhajan Singh Bal, *Factors Associated with Farm and Farm Family Investment Pattern in Ludhiana (Punjab) and Hissar (Haryana) Districts: (1966–67 through 1969–70)*, Department of Economics and Sociology, Punjab Agricultural University, Ludhiana, n.d.

15  Allan C. Kelly and Jeffrey G. Williamson, 'Household Saving Behaviour in the Developing Economies: the Indonesian Case', *Economic Development and Cultural Change*, April 1968.

16  Marcia L. Ong, Dale W. Adams and I.J. Singh, 'Voluntary Rural Savings Capacities in Taiwan, 1960 to 1970', Economics and Sociology Occasional Paper No. 175, Ohio State University, n.d.

17  Keith Griffin, *Land Concentration and Rural Poverty*, London: Macmillan, 2nd edn, 1981, Ch. 3.

18  Colin Leys, *Underdevelopment in Kenya: the Political Economy of Neo-Colonialism*, London: Heinemann, 1975, p. 53.

19  For example, see Helen Shapiro and Lance Taylor, 'The State and Industrial Strategy', *World Development*, Vol. 18, No. 6, 1990 and Lance Taylor, 'Stabilization and Adjustment', in United Nations Development Programme Structural Adjustment Advisory Teams for Africa (UNDP/SAATA), *Stabilization and Adjustment*, New York: United Nations Publications, 1991.

20  For evidence of 'crowding in' and the complementarity between public investment in infrastructure and private investment in directly productive

Notes

activities, see for example, David A. Aschaur, 'Is Public Expenditure Productive?', *Journal of Monetary Economics*, Vol. 23, No. 2, March 1989; Ernst R. Berndt and Bengt Hausson, 'Measuring the Contribution of Public Infrastructure Capital in Sweden', *Scandinavian Journal of Economics*, Vol. 94, Supplement 1992; M. Ishaq Nadiri and Theofanis P. Mamuneas, 'The Effects of Public Infrastructure and R&D on the Cost Structure and Performance of U.S. Manufacturing Industries', *Review of Economics and Statistics*, Vol. 76, No. 1, February 1994; and Catherine J. Morrison and Amy Ellen Schwartz, 'State Infrastructure and Productive Performance', *American Economic Review*, Vol. 86, No. 5, December 1996. These studies use data from the United States and Sweden. Given the paucity of infrastructure in sub-Saharan Africa, the complementarity between public and private investment should be stronger there than in developed countries. See World Bank, 'Infrastructure for Development', *World Development Report 1994*, New York: Oxford University Press, 1994.

21  As with earlier calculations, averages are calculated unweighted for each region. See endnote 6.

22  For example, Alice Amsden reports that in 1952 as much as 56 per cent of total industrial production in Taiwan was accounted for by the public sector. Alice Amsden, 'Big Business and Urban Congestion in Taiwan: the Origins of Small Enterprise and Regionally Decentralized Industry (Respectively)', *World Development*, Vol. 19, No. 9, 1991.

23  International Labour Office (ILO), *Employment, Incomes and Equality: a Strategy for Increasing Productive Employment in Kenya*, Geneva: International Labour Office, 1972.

24  International Labour Organization, *African Employment Report*, Addis Ababa, Jobs and Skills Programme for Africa, 1988, as cited in World Bank, *Sub-Saharan Africa: From Crisis to Sustainable Growth*, Washington, DC: The World Bank, 1989.

25  For 'informal' sector designations using size measures, see for example Abid A. Burki and Uzma Afaqi, 'Pakistan's Informal Sector: Review of Evidence and Policy Issues', *Pakistan Journal of Applied Economics*, Vol. XII, No. 1, 1996, and Monica Neitzert, "Human Capital in the Hot Sun', *Economic Development and Cultural Change*, Vol. 45, No. 1, October 1996. For a measure based on individual incomes, see William J. House, Gerrishon K. Ikiara and Dorothy McCormick, 'Urban Self-employment in Kenya: Panacea or Viable Strategy?' *World Development*, Vol. 21, No. 7, 1993.

26  The idea that individuals and firms vary in their degrees of participation in the legal and bureaucratic institutions of society, and that this is ubiquitous across countries and firm size is not new. See, for example, Alejandro Portes, Manuel Castells and Lauren A. Benton, eds, *The Informal Economy: Studies in Advanced and Less Developed Countries*, Baltimore: The Johns Hopkins University Press, 1989. However, most analyses recognize this characteristic only secondarily, and often revert to the 'formal' vs 'informal' dichotomy in the bulk of their analysis.

27  ILO, *African Employment Report*.

28  Victor Tokman, 'Policies for a Heterogeneous Informal Sector in Latin America', *World Development*, Vol. 17, No. 7, 1989, footnote 10.

29  Paul Strassman, 'Home-based Enterprises in Cities of Developing Countries', *Economic Development and Cultural Change*, Vol. 36, No. 1, 1987.

30  For a taste of the broader debate as well as the specifics of informalization see, for example, Victor E. Tokman, *Beyond Regulation: the Informal Economy in Latin America*, Lynne Rienner Publishers, Boulder, 1992; Portes *et al.*, op. cit.; House *et al.*, op. cit.; Kate Meagher, 'Crisis, Informalization and the Urban Informal Sector in Sub-Saharan Africa', *Development and Change*, Vol. 26, 1995. For discussion of flexible specialization see Michael Piore and Charles Sabel, *The Second Industrial Divide: Possibilities for Prosperity*, New York: Basic Books, 1984.

31  See Manuel Castells and Alejandro Portes, 'World Underneath: the Origins, Dynamics, and Effects of the Informal Economy', and Juan Carlos Fortuna and Suzana Prates, 'Informal Sector versus Informalized Labor Relations in Uruguay', in Portes *et al.*, op. cit.

32  Abstracted from the Manufacturers Association of Nigeria (Kano Branch), *Report on the Industrial Situation in Kano, January–October 1984*, pp. 5–12, as cited in Adebayo Olukoshi, September 1996, op. cit. p. 17. Calculations based on Table 8.

33  These recruits, who reported directly to management, came to be known as *angulun maigida* (Hausa for 'the boss's vulture'), ibid., pp. 34–5.

34  Lourdes Benería, 'Subcontracting and Employment Dynamics in Mexico City', in Portes *et al.*, 1989, op. cit.

35  Fortuna and Prates, op. cit.

36  The term 'flexible specialization' has been most associated with the work of Michael Piore and Charles Sabel. See for example, Piore and Sabel, op. cit.

37  United Nations Industrial Development Organization (UNIDO) and United Nations Development Programme (UNDP), *Cyprus Industrial Strategy*, Vol. 1, *Overview and Executive Summary*, New York, United Nations, 1987. For other instances of flexible specialization entering the debate on global restructuring see, for example, Raphael Kaplinsky, 'From Mass Production to Flexible Specialization: a Case Study of Microeconomic Change in a Semi-industrialized Economy', *World Development*, Vol. 22, No. 3, 1994; Burki and Afaqi, op. cit., and Jeffrey James and Ajit Bhalla, 'Flexible Specialization, New Technologies and Future Industrialization in Developing Countries', *Futures*, July/August, 1993.

38  International Fund for Agricultural Development (IFAD), *Kenya: Special Programming/General Identification Mission on Small Scale Enterprises*, Report No. 0204-KE, 2 Vols, Rome: International Fund for Agricultural Development, April 1990, as cited in Ian Livingstone, 'A Reassessment of Kenya's Rural and Urban Informal Sector', *World Development*, Vol. 19, No. 6, 1991.

39  For more on Ghana's Suame Magazine, see the World Bank, op. cit. For Tanzania, see the discussion of the Tanzanian hammer mills in M.S.D. Bagachwa, *Technology Choice in Industry: a Study of Grain-milling Techniques in Tanzania*, Ottawa: IDRC, 1991, as cited in Lynn Krieger Mytelka, 'Rethinking Development', *Futures*, July/August, 1993. For pre-civil war Rwanda, refer to C. Maldonado, 'The Underdogs of the Urban Economy Join Forces – Results of an ILO Programme in Mali, Rwanda and Togo', *International Labour Review*, Vol. 128, No. 1, 1989.

40  This term has been coined by Alice Amsden to distinguish between the industrialization experience of East Asia, Mexico, Brazil and others, as compared to that of Europe and the United States. She argues that the success of the late industrializers crucially depended on their ability to borrow existing technologies and adapt them to local conditions. This often included designing methods of production to conform more closely with domestically available inputs, reverse-engineering and down-scaling, as well as other process innovations. In the discussion that follows, we will draw from Alice H. Amsden, op. cit.; Alice H. Amsden, 'Third World Industrialization: "Global Fordism" or a New Model?', *New Left Review*, No. 182, July–August, 1990; Alice H. Amsden, 'Taiwan in International Perspective', in N.T. Wang, ed., *Taiwan's Enterprise in Global Perspective*, New York: M.E. Sharpe, Inc. 1992; and Alice H. Amsden, *Asia's Next Giant: South Korea and Late Industrialization*, New York: Oxford University Press, 1989.

41  Amsden, 'Big Business and Urban Congestion'.

42  Brian Levy, 'Obstacles to Developing Indigenous Small and Medium Enterprises: an Empirical Assessment', *World Bank Economic Review*, Vol. 7, No. 1, 1993. It must be noted that due to small sample size, 19 observations, care should be taken when drawing conclusions from these results. However, many other surveys support the contention that access to credit is a major constraint to enterprise development.

43  ILO, 'L'économie informelle en Guinée: Analyse et stratégie de développement', Geneva, 1990, as cited in Leila Webster and Peter Fidler, eds, *The Informal Sector and Microfinance Institutions in West Africa*, Washington, DC: The World Bank, 1996.

44  See the Bangladesh Institute of Development Studies and International Food Policy Research Institute, *Development Impact of the Food for Works Program in Bangladesh*, a report prepared for the World Food Program, Washington, DC, 1985, as cited in Atiur Rahman and M. Mahabub-ul Islam, 'The General Performance of the Grameen Bank', in Abu N.M. Wahid, ed., *The Grameen Bank: Poverty Relief in Bangladesh*, Westview Press, Boulder, 1993.

45  See Pierre-Olivier Colleye, 'Mali', as cited in Webster and Fidler, eds, op. cit.

46  See for example J.D. Von Pischke, Dale W. Adams and Gordon Donald, eds, *Rural Financial Markets in Developing Countries*, The World Bank, Washington, DC, 1983, and World Bank, *World Development Report 1989: Financial Systems and Development*, New York: Oxford University Press, 1989.

47  For evidence of credit rationing in the UK, US, Italy and Japan, respectively, see M. Devereux and F. Schiantarelli, 'Investment, Financial Factors, and Cash Flow: Evidence from U.K. Panel Model', in R.G. Hubbard, ed., *Information, Capital Markets and Investment*, University of Chicago Press, 1990; S. Fazzari, G. Hubbard and B. Peterson, 'Financing Constraints and Corporate Investment', *Brookings Papers on Economic Activity*, No. 1, 1988; M. Galeotti, F. Jaramillo and F. Schiantarelli, 'Investment Decisions and the Role of Debt, Liquid Assets and Cash Flow: Evidence from Italian Panel Data', Boston University Working Paper, March 1990; and T. Hoshi, A. Kashyap and D. Scharfstein, 'Corporate Structure and Investment: Evidence from Japanese Panel Data', MIT Sloan School of Management Working Paper, 1988, as cited in Joseph E. Stiglitz and Andrew Weiss, 'Asymmetric

Information in Credit Markets and its Implications for Macro-Economics', *Oxford Economic Papers*, Vol. 44, 1992. For China see, for example, Gershon Feder, Lawrence J. Lau, Justin Y. Lin and Xiaopeng Luo, 'The Nascent Rural Credit Market in China', in Karla Hoff, Avishay Braverman and Joseph E. Stiglitz, *The Economics of Rural Organization*, Oxford University Press, New York, 1993.

48  See Stiglitz and Weiss, op. cit., as well as Joseph Stiglitz and Andrew Weiss, 'Credit Rationing in Markets with Imperfect Information', *American Economic Review*, Vol. 71, No. 3, 1981; Joseph Stiglitz and Andrew Weiss, 'Incentive Effects of Terminations: Applications to the Credit and Labor Markets', *American Economic Review*, Vol. 73, 1983; and Joseph Stiglitz and Andrew Weiss, 'Credit Rationing: a Comment', *American Economic Review*, Vol. 77, No. 3, 1987.

49  See, for example, Irfan Aleem, 'Imperfect Information, Screening, and the Costs of Informal Lending: a Study of a Rural Credit Market in Pakistan', in Hoff, Braverman and Stiglitz, op. cit. and Ammar Siamwalla, Chirmsak Pinthong, Nipon Poapongsakorn, Ploenpit Sasanguan, Prayong Nettayarak, Wanrak Mingmaneenakin and Yuavares Tubpun, 'The Thai Rural Credit System and Elements of a Theory: Public Subsidies, Private Information, and Segmented Markets', in Hoff, Braverman and Stiglitz, op. cit.

50  For a more detailed discussion of the design of various group lending programmes, and the variations on liability that are observed, see Monika Huppi and Gershon Feder, 'The Role of Groups and Credit Cooperatives in Rural Lending', *The World Bank Research Observer*, Vol. 5, No. 2, 1990.

51  See Joseph E. Stiglitz, 'Peer Monitoring and Credit Markets', *World Bank Economic Review*, Vol. 4, 1990.

52  On this point see T. Besley and S. Coate, 'Group Lending, Repayment Incentives and Social Collateral', *Journal of Development Economics*, Vol. 46, No. 1, 1995.

53  Eric Van Tassel, 'Group Lending under Incomplete Information', manuscript, University of California Riverside, 1996.

54  Avishay Braverman and J. Luis Guasch, 'Administrative Failures in Rural Credit Programs', in Hoff, Braverman and Stiglitz, op. cit.

55  Huppi and Feder, op. cit.

56  Ibid.

57  Leila Webster and Peter Fidler, 'Microenterprise Support Programs in West Africa', in Webster and Fidler, op. cit.

58  See Wahid, op. cit., Chapters 2, 5, 10 and 15, from which our account is drawn.

59  An important element of the group structure is that only one member of a household is allowed to join any one group, and relatives are not allowed to form groups with each other.

60  Wahid, op. cit., Chapter 4.

61  These repayment rates are reported as of August 1992, as cited in ibid., Chapter 10.

62  A small subsidy to targeted credit programmes is not necessarily undesirable. First, since formal credit markets do not clear because of imperfect information, a subsidy in the informal credit market may actually increase overall efficiency. Second, targeted credit programmes may generate positive

externalities, e.g. by providing rudimentary management training, by encouraging basic education or by promoting family planning.

63   Ibid., Chapter 5.

64   The following material is drawn from Richard H. Pattern and Jay K. Rosengard, *Progress with Profits: the Development of Rural Banking in Indonesia*, San Francisco: ICS Press, 1991, Chapter 4.

65   Forced savings linked to targeted credit programmes are common. The lender retains, say, 5–10 per cent of the group's (or an individual's) loan as an interest bearing deposit, which is returned to the group (or individual) when the loan is repaid.

66   The long-term loss ratio is defined as the ratio of the total amount overdue to the total amount due.

67   W. Paul Strassman, 'Home-based Enterprises in Cities of Developing Countries', *Economic Development and Cultural Change*, Vol. 36, No. 1, 1987.

68   Samuel Kofi Afrane, 'Job Creation in Residential Areas: a Comparative Study of Public and Private Residential Communities in Kumasi, Ghana', in Mulkh Raj and Peter Nientied, eds, *Housing and Income in Third World Urban Development*, London: Aspect Publishing, 1990.

69   Strassman, op. cit.

70   This case study of Medellin is drawn from Nora Elena Mesa, 'Economic Use of Housing "Pirata" and Invasion "Barrios" Medellin', in Raj and Nientied, eds, op. cit.

71   See Angelo F. Leynes, 'Impact of the Slum Upgrading Programme in Metropolitan Manila on the Housing-based Income Generation Activities', in Raj and Nientied, op. cit.

72   Strassman, op. cit.

73   Ibid.

74   UNCHS (Habitat), *The Global Strategy for Shelter to the Year 2000*, Nairobi, UNCHS, 1990.

75   Strassman, op. cit.

76   Neelima Risbud, 'Housing and Income Generation Policies for the Urban Poor – Linkages and Limitations (A Case Study of Madhya Pradesh)', in Raj and Nientied, eds, op. cit.

77   T.W. Schultz, 'Investment in Human Capital', *American Economic Review*, March 1961.

78   George Psacharopoulos, 'Education and Development: a Review', *World Bank Research Observer*, Vol. 3, No. 1, January 1988.

79   Keith Griffin and Terry McKinley, *Implementing a Human Development Strategy*, London: Macmillan, 1994, Ch. 3.

80   For a study of the impact of education on the urban areas of East Africa, see John Knight and Richard Sabot, 'Educational Policy and Labour Productivity: an Output Accounting Exercise', *Economic Journal*, Vol. 97, No. 385, March 1987.

81   For a study of the rural areas in Latin America, see Daniel Cotlear, 'The Effects of Education on Farm Productivity', in Keith Griffin and John Knight, eds, *Human Development and the International Development Strategy for the 1990s*, London: Macmillan, 1990. Also see Marlaine Lockheed, Dean Jamison and Lawrence Lau, 'Farmer Education and Farm Efficiency: a Survey', *Economic Development and Cultural Change*, October 1980. For a

survey of research on the returns to expenditure on extension services, see Dean Birkhaeuser, Robert Evenson and Gershon Feder, 'The Economic Impact of Agricultural Extension: a Review', *Economic Development and Cultural Change*, Vol. 39, No. 3, April 1991.

82  Douglas Marcouiller, Veronica Ruiz de Castilla and Christopher Woodruff, 'Formal Measures of the Informal-Sector Wage Gap in Mexico, El Salvador and Peru', *Economic Development and Cultural Change*, Vol. 45, No. 2, January 1997.

83  See J. Behrman and N. Birdsall, 'The Quality of Schooling: Quantity Alone May Be Misleading', *American Economic Review*, 1983 and John Oxenham with Jocelyn DeJong and Steven Treagust, 'Improving the Quality of Education in Developing Countries', in Griffin and Knight, eds, op. cit.

84  For details see Griffin and McKinley, op. cit., Ch. 5.

85  See Jacques Gaude and Steve Miller, 'Rural Development and Local Resource Intensity: a Case-Study Approach', in Griffin and Knight, eds, op. cit.

86  UNDP, *Human Development in Bangladesh*, Dhaka: UNDP, 1992, p. 25. On the public works programme in Bangladesh see Raisuddin Ahmed and Mahabub Hossain, *Developmental Impact of Rural Infrastructure in Bangladesh*, Washington, DC: International Food Policy Research Institute, 1990; and 'Food for Work Program', Special Issue of *Bangladesh Development Studies*, Vol. 11, 1983.

87  Thomas Rawski, *Economic Growth and Employment in China*, New York: Oxford University Press, 1979.

88  Sarthi Acharya, *The Maharashtra Employment Guarantee Scheme: A Study of Labour Market Intervention*, New Delhi: ILO, ARTEP, Working Paper, May 1990.

89  The next two paragraphs are taken from Griffin and McKinley, op. cit., p. 75. Slight alterations have been made to the original text.

90  This proposal is taken from Keith Griffin, 'Rural Poverty in Asia: Analysis and Policy Alternatives', in Rizwanul Islam, ed., *Strategies for Alleviating Poverty in Rural Asia*, Dhaka: Bangladesh Institute of Development Studies and Bangkok: ILO, ARTEP, 1985, pp. 63–5.

91  Keith Cowling, 'Reflections on the Privatisation Issue', in Ha-Joon Chang and Peter Nolan, eds, *The Transformation of the Communist Economies*, London: Macmillan, 1995.

92  See Griffin, *Studies in Globalization*, Ch. 7.

93  Keith Griffin, ed., *Poverty and the Transition to a Market Economy in Mongolia*, London: Macmillan, 1995, Ch. 1.

94  For analysis of the experience in Poland, Hungary, Slovakia and the Czech Republic see Yilmaz Akyüz, Detlef Kotte, Andràs Köves and László Szamuely, eds, *Privatization in the Transition Process: Recent Experiences in Eastern Europe*, Geneva: UNCTAD, 1994.

# 9  Structural Adjustment and Macroeconomic Reform in Vietnam

*  Originally published in *Human Systems Management*, Vol. 17, No. 1, 1998.

1  World Bank, *From Plan to Market, World Development Report 1996*, New York: Oxford University Press, 1996.

2  Keith Griffin, 'Foreign Capital, Domestic Savings and Economic Development', *Bulletin of the Oxford University Institute of Economics and Statistics*, Vol. 32, No. 2, May 1970.

3  Government of Vietnam, *Vietnam: A Development Perspective*, document prepared for the Donor Conference, Hanoi, September 1993, p. vii.

# 10   Employment, Poverty and Social Protection in Kazakhstan

*  A shorter version of this chapter was published in the *International Journal of Social Economics*, Vol. 26, 1/2/3, 1999.

1  See Amartya Sen, 'Development as Capability Expansion', in Keith Griffin and John Knight, eds, *Human Development and the International Development Strategy for the 1990s*, London: Macmillan, 1990.

2  Amartya Sen, *Inequality Re-examined*, Cambridge: Harvard University Press, 1992.

3  The human development approach was pioneered by UNDP. The central ideas of the approach and their application to specific development issues are discussed in the annual *Human Development Report*, New York: Oxford University Press, beginning in 1990.

4  See Keith Griffin, ed., *Social Policy and Economic Transformation in Uzbekistan*, Geneva: International Labour Organization, 1996, Ch. 1.

5  For an early statement of the argument see T.W. Schultz, 'Investment in Human Capital', *American Economic Review*, March 1961.

6  For an influential study of the returns on investments in education see George Psacharopoulos, 'Education and Development: a Review', *World Bank Research Observer*, Vol. 3, No. 1, January 1988.

7  This point is emphasized in Amartya Sen, 'What's the Point of a Development Strategy?' London School of Economics, STICERD, DERP No. 3, April 1977.

8  The first three points are made by Amartya Sen, *Employment, Technology and Development*, London: Oxford University Press, 1975. The fourth point is made by Keith Griffin and Terry McKinley, *Implementing a Human Development Strategy*, London: Macmillan, 1994, p. 72.

9  See the *Economic Survey of Europe in 1996–1997*, Geneva and New York: United Nations, Ch. 4, June 1997. Between 1992 and 1996 tax revenue fell from 21.5 to 10.5 per cent of GDP; government expenditure fell from 31.9 to 17.2 per cent of GDP. (Ibid., Table 4.2.2.)

10  See Keith Griffin and Azizur Rahman Khan, 'The Transition to Market Guided Economies: Lessons for Russia and Eastern Europe from the Chinese Experience', in Bernd Magnus and Stephen Cullenberg, eds, *Whither Marxism? Global Crises in International Perspective*, New York and London: Routledge, 1995.

11  UNDP, *Kazakhstan Human Development Report 1996*, Almaty: UNDP, 1996, p. 25.

12  Government of Kazakhstan, Centre for Economic Reforms, *Kazakhstan Economic Trends*, Almaty, May 1997, Table 10.1.

13 UNDP, *Kazakhstan Human Development Report 1996*, p. 20.
14 The decline in government revenue has been a very serious problem because it prevents the government from financing a public investment programme to stimulate growth. Tax reform should therefore be high on the agenda of policy makers.
15 See Griffin and Rahman Khan, op. cit.
16 Keith Griffin, ed., *Economic Reform in Vietnam*, London: Macmillan, 1998 and Chapter 9 above.
17 United Nations, *Economic Survey of Europe in 1996–1997*, Ch. 4.
18 UNDP, *Kazakhstan Human Development Report 1996*, Table 3.1.3, p. 30.
19 UNDP, *Kazakhstan Human Development Report 1997*, Almaty: UNDP, 1997, Appendix Table 1, p. 74.
20 Ibid.
21 UNDP, *Kazakhstan Human Development Report 1996*, Table 3.1.8, p. 31.
22 See Armin Bauer, Niña Boschmann and David Green, *Women and Gender Relations in Kazakhstan*, Manila: Asian Development Bank, 1997, especially Ch. III.
23 See Michael Bruno, 'Inflation, Growth and Monetary Control: Non-linear Lessons for Crisis and Recovery', mimeographed, Washington, DC: World Bank, 1995; also see Michael Bruno, 'Does Inflation Really Lower Growth?', *Finance and Development*, Vol. 32, No. 3, September 1995.
24 World Bank, *From Plan to Market*, *World Development Report 1996*, New York: Oxford University Press, 1996.
25 International Monetary Fund, 'Republic of Kazakhstan: Recent Economic Developments', 4 June 1997, mimeographed, Appendix Table 14, p. 100.
26 For an analysis of the role of foreign investment in Kazakhstan so far see Michael Kaser, *The Economies of Kazakhstan and Uzbekistan*, London: Royal Institute of International Affairs, 1997, Ch. 3.
27 UNDP, *Kazakstan Human Development Report 1997*, p. 5.
28 For a good discussion of demographic policy in other Asian countries, and the ways policies contributed to development, see Asian Development Bank, *Emerging Asia: Changes and Challenges*, Manila: Asian Development Bank, 1997, Ch. 3.
29 See Griffin and McKinley, op. cit., Ch. 5.
30 For greater elaboration see Keith Griffin, 'Poverty: Concepts and Measurement,' in Keith Griffin, ed., *Poverty and the Transition to a Market Economy in Mongolia*, London: Macmillan, 1995.

# 11   Poverty Reduction in China

1 Official Chinese estimates are prepared by the State Statistical Bureau and are available from them.
2 World Bank, *China: Strategies for Reducing Poverty in the 1990s*, Washington, DC, 1992.
3 The independent study is based on two surveys carried out in 1988 and 1995 by an international group of economists in collaboration with the Economics Institute of the Chinese Academy of Social Sciences. The results

of the 1988 survey are reported in Keith Griffin and Zhao Renwei, eds, *The Distribution of Income in China*, London: Macmillan, 1993. The results of the 1995 survey, and a comparison of the two surveys, are reported in Azizur Rahman Khan, *Poverty in China in the Period of Globalization: New Evidence on Trend and Pattern*, Issues in Development Discussion Paper No. 22, International Labour Organization, Geneva, 1998 and in Azizur Rahman Khan and Carl Riskin, *Inequality and Poverty in China in the Age of Globalization*, New York: Oxford University Press, forthcoming.

4   The problems and biases in the official data are discussed in Rahman Khan, op. cit. and in Rahman Khan and Riskin, op. cit. Changes in the incidence of poverty over time are sensitive to the poverty threshold used and the price deflator used to correct for inflation. In the above studies, the rural poverty threshold used is roughly half the rural per capita personal income and the urban poverty threshold is about 40 per cent of the urban per capita personal income.

5   The savings rate declined from 34 per cent of GDP in 1978 to 28 per cent in 1981; it then crept up to 32 per cent of GDP in 1984.

6   The savings rates are based on World Bank data which, in turn, are based on the official estimates of GDP. The level of GDP, however, is probably an underestimate of the true level. This implies that the savings rates quoted probably are somewhat higher than the true rate. Changes in the savings rate over time, however, would not be affected by adjustments in the level of GDP. See Rahman Khan and Riskin, op. cit., for the data and related analysis.

7   See Mark Brenner, 'The Distribution of Wealth in Rural China, 1988–1995, Ph.D. dissertation in progress, University of California, Riverside. For a detailed study of the distribution of land (and other assets) in 1988, see Terry McKinley, *The Distribution of Wealth in Rural China*, Armonk, New York: M.E. Sharpe, 1996.

8   Azizur Rahman Khan, Keith Griffin and Carl Riskin, 'Income Distribution in Urban China during the Period of Economic Reform and Globalization', *American Economic Review*, Vol. 89, No. 2, May 1999.

9   Feng Wang and Xuejin Zuo, 'Inside China's Cities: Institutional Barriers and Opportunities for Urban Migrants', *American Economic Review*, Vol. 89, No. 2, May 1999.

10  In the surveys conducted by the State Statistical Bureau, as well as in our own 1988 and 1995 surveys, the 'floating population' is not included. The sample for all of these surveys is drawn from the population of official urban residents.

11  Martin Ravallion and Jyotsna Jalan, 'China's Lagging Poor Areas', *American Economic Review*, Vol. 89, No. 2, May 1999.

12  This argument is made in Justin Lin, Fang Cai and Zhou Li, 'Social Consequences of Economic Reform in China: an Analysis of Regional Disparity in the Transition Period', unpublished report for UNDP, Beijing, 1997.

13  Ibid.

14  See Rahman Khan and Riskin, op. cit., Chapter 7.

# Index

*Notes*: 1. Page references for **chapters** are in **bold**; 2. Only authors *named* in the text or *quoted* in the Notes are included.

Adelman, I., 68
adjustment, *see* structural adjustment
Africa, 59, 237; culture, 23, 24, 26, 28;
   globalization, 36, 39, 40, 42, 43, 44;
   human development, 55, 59;
   income and growth, 74, 84, 91;
   *see also* sub-Saharan Africa
ageing population, 37, 64, 276
agriculture, *see* rural areas
Ahluwalia, M.S., 68–9
aid, foreign, *see* ODA
Alarcon, D., 10
Albania, 117; demography, 110, 111,
   112, 115; economic performance,
   96, 98, 99, 101, 102, 103, 105, 106;
   state, 136, 137
alcoholism, 114
Alesina, A., 70, 71, 72, 76–8
Algeria, 40
alternative reform strategies in
   transition, 116–27; essential
   reform, 117–20; sequential and
   disequilibrium management, 122–7;
   simultaneous (big bang), 98–9,
   120–2, 125–7, 131
Amsden, A., 312, 314
Angola, 139, 140, 141, 152, 154
Arabs, 25; *see also* Middle East
Argentina, 90, 198
Armenia: demography, 109, 110,
   112, 113, 114, 115; economic
   performance, 96, 97, 99, 100, 102–5
   *passim*; state, 127, 128, 136, 137,
   138
Asian Development Bank, 49, 74–5,
   274
assets: creation and employment,
   223–6; *see also* capital; human
   capital; land; natural capital;
   physical capital

asymmetrical liberalization, 36–8
Australia, 36, 198, 306
authoritarian regimes, 22, 24, 77–8
Azerbaijan, 110; economic
   performance, 96, 97, 99, 100, 102,
   103, 105, 106, 108; state, 127–30
   *passim*, 136, 137, 138

Badan Kredit Kecamatan (BKK) case
   study, 215–16
balance of payments deficit, *see* debt
   crisis
Bangladesh, 3, 12, 44, 63, 209,
   214–15, 224
banks, 50, 100, 117, 243; in
   Kazakhstan case study, 269, 270,
   274; in sub-Saharan Africa, 146–8,
   149, 150, 170, 214, 215, 216
Barro, R., 74
Beijing conference, 62–3
Belarus, 122; demography, 109–15
   *passim*; economic performance,
   96, 97, 99, 102, 103, 105, 106;
   state, 127, 128, 137
Belgium, 45, 198
Benería, L., 204–5
Benin, 164; classification, 140, 141;
   investment and adjustment, 184,
   186, 188, 190, 196; stabilization
   and adjustment, 146, 152
Bertola, G., 77
big bang and transition, 98–9, 120–2,
   125–7, 131
Birdsall, N., 80, 85, 86–7
birth: rate and fertility rate, 5, 86,
   111–12, 262, 265; unattended, 60
Bolivia, 198, 202
Bosnia, 30
Botswana, 164; classification, 139,
   141, 143; investment and

adjustment, 184, 186, 188, 190, 196; labour, 146, 152–3
Bowles, S., 78, 80
Braverman, A., 213
Brazil, 24, 36, 194, 198, 314; income and growth, 85, 86, 90–1
Brenner, M.: on sub-Saharan Africa, 9, **179–234**
Bretton Woods, 63–4, 65
Britain, 3, 35, 47, 113, 306, 314; culture, 16, 22; and sub-Saharan Africa, 194, 227; tax revenue and government expenditure, 198
Bulgaria: demography, 109–13 *passim*, 115; economic performance, 96, 99, 101, 102, 103, 105, 106, 107; state, 128, 137
bureaucracy/public administration, 129; *see also* state
Burkina Faso: classification, 41, 140; investment and adjustment, 184, 186, 188, 190, 196; labour, 164, 166; stabilization and adjustment, 146, 152–3
Burundi, 309; classification, 41, 140; investment and adjustment, 171, 184, 186, 188, 190, 196; labour, 164, 166; stabilization and adjustment, 146, 152–3

Cambodia, 273, 300
Cameroon, 164; classification, 139, 140, 141; investment and adjustment, 184, 186, 188, 190, 196; stabilization and adjustment, 146, 152, 154
Canada, 36, 43, 45, 198, 306
'capabilities', expansion of human, *see* human development
Capability Poverty Measure, 60
Cape Verde, 139, 141, 164, 184, 186
capital, financial: accumulation in Vietnam, 241–4; and income and growth, 76–7; –labour ratio, fall in, 163–5; markets in sub-Saharan Africa, 170; *see also* capital flows; finance; investment; savings
capital flows, international, 41–3, 49; *see also* FDI; IMF; ODA; trade

capital, non-financial, *see* human capital; natural capital; physical capital
capitalism, transition to, *see* transition
capitalist class, *see* capital; wealth
Caribbean, 36, 39, 85, 237
Casanovas, R., 202
case studies of transition, 214–16; *see also* Kazakhstan case study; poverty reduction in China; Vietnam case study
Central African Republic, 164; classification, 140, 141; investment and adjustment, 184, 186, 196; stabilization and adjustment, 146, 152
Central America, 58, 91, 198; globalization, 45, 46, 49; resource mobilization and enterprise development, 194, 204–5
Central Asia, 39, 56, 228–9; culture, 27–9; *see also* transition
Central and Eastern Europe, 5, 38, 40, 229, 237; *see also* transition
Chad, 164, 309; classification, 140, 141; investment and adjustment, 161, 174, 196; stabilization and adjustment, 146, 152
Chernobyl, 44
Chichilnisky, G., 301
children, 55; allowance in Kazakhstan, 276, 279–80; mortality, 57; underweight, 4, 60, 297; *see also* birth; education
Chile, 51, 85, 198, 202
China, 159, 301; case study, *see* poverty reduction in China; culture, human development and economic growth, 22, 23, 25, 26, 28; globalization, 34, 36, 39, 40, 41, 42; human development, 62–3, 65; income and growth, 82, 84, 88; and Kazakhstan compared, 258, 266, 273; resource mobilization and enterprise development, 171, 182, 192, 208, 224, 228; transition, 5–6, 97, 99, 101, 107, 109, 111, 112, 122–32 *passim*, 137, 257; and

China – *continued*
  Vietnam compared, 237–40, 242, 245, 247
choice, increasing range of, *see* freedom; human development
Clarke, G., 70
class, 75, 78, 85; capitalist, *see* capital; wealth; underclass, *see* poverty
Cline, W., 90–1
CMEA (Council for Mutual Economic Assistance), 118, 247, 256, 259
Cold War, end of, 62; *see also* transition
Colombia, 194, 198, 217–18
colonialism, 28, 33, 194
commercialization of state enterprises, 169–70, 177, 227–30
commodity-centred view of development replaced, *see* human development
Commonwealth of Independent States, *see* Soviet Union
communications, 27, 31, 34, 35–6
Comoros, 140, 141, 186
compatibility, incentive, 80
competition, 65, 154–5; needed, 229
comprador capitalism, 238
computers and electronics, 31, 35–6
conflict, war and violence, 28, 31, 62; and globalization, 34, 46, 47–9, 51–2; sub-Saharan Africa, 142, 154–5; and Vietnam case study, 237–8; war crimes tribunals, 2
Congo: classification, 139, 140, 141; investment and adjustment, 161, 171, 186, 188, 190, 196; stabilization and adjustment, 146, 152
contraction, structural adjustment through, 157–8
cooperation, 21, 198, 220; international, 62; *see also* globalization; regional development
Copenhagen Social Summit, 62
corruption, 125
Costa Rica, 46, 58, 198
Côte d'Ivoire, 164, 308; classification, 140, 141; investment and adjustment, 161, 171, 186, 188,

190, 196; stabilization and adjustment, 147, 152
Council for Mutual Economic Assistance, 118, 247, 256, 259
CPM (Capability Poverty Measure), 60
creativity and innovation, 26–7, 29, 31
credit: and case studies, 268–9; and income and growth, 78–9; rationing, 314–15
credit in sub-Saharan Africa, 194, 209–12, 223, 232, 315–16; bank lending rates, 146–8, 150, 215, 216; *see also* debt
crime, 23; smuggling, 2, 43, 109; and transition, 109, 114, 117
Croatia: demography, 110, 112; economic performance, 96, 98, 99, 100, 102, 103, 104, 105; state, 127, 128, 137
Cuba, 85
culture, human development and economic growth, 1–2, **15–32**; globalization and cultural interchange, 27–30, 51–2; growth promoting human development, 18–20; human development promoting growth, 20–2; inequality and growth, 22–4; intrinsic and instrumental values of culture, 30–2; sources of economic growth, 16–18
Cyprus, 205
Czech Republic: demography, 110–15 *passim*; economic performance, 96, 98, 99, 100, 102, 103, 105, 106, 107; state, 128, 131, 134, 135, 137
Czechoslovakia, former, 100, 101, 103

death, *see* mortality
Deaton, A., 71
debt crisis, 40, 144, 171, 310; *see also* credit
Deininger, K., 69, 71–3, 77, 79, 80, 91
delinking, 300
democracy, 21–2, 24, 77; need for, 48
demography: ageing population, 37, 64, 276; and economic collapse, 108–14; Kazakhstan case study, 262, 265; in sub-Saharan Africa, 139–42, 143; and transition, 5, 95–7;

demography – *continued*
  Vietnam case study, 238–40; *see also*
  birth; mortality
dependency ratio, 37
Desai, M., 57
development strategy, *see* case studies;
  human development; strategic
  visions; systemic transformation
diet, *see* nutrition/food
diseases, 28, 168
disequilibrium management, 122–5
Djibouti, 140, 141, 308
domestic financing for investment-led
  adjustment in sub-Saharan Africa:
  private sector, 192–5; public sector,
  195–200
domestic markets creation in
  transition, 117, 129
domestic resources, *see* resource
  mobilization
Drèze, J., 21
drug abuse and trade, 43, 44, 114
'dual price system', 124–5, 247

East Asia, 300, 301, 314; culture, 22,
  23, 25, 26, 28; globalization, 34, 35,
  36, 39, 40, 41, 42, 49, 51; human
  development, 62–3, 65; income and
  growth, 74–5, 78, 79, 82, 83–8; and
  Kazakhstan compared, 258, 266,
  272, 273; resource mobilization and
  enterprise development, 171, 182,
  192, 199, 207–8, 224, 228; and
  structural adjustment, 159, 168;
  tax revenue and government
  expenditure, 198, 199; transition,
  *see under* China; and Vietnam
  compared, 237–40, 242, 245, 247
Eastern Europe, *see* Central and
  Eastern Europe
economic growth, *see* growth
economic performance during
  transition, 97–116; demographic
  consequences of economic collapse,
  108–14; income inequality and
  income poverty, 105–8; output,
  income and growth, 101–5; prices,
  explosion, 98–101; social pathology,
  114–16

economic space and globalization,
  39–42
economic theory and explanations of
  growth and inequality, 78–84
education and training, 3, 23, 40, 54,
  55, 58, 64; in case studies, 246, 265,
  295; and income and growth, 74,
  79–80, 85–7; in sub-Saharan Africa,
  168, 174, 195, 221–3, 233; and
  transition, 130, 138; of women, 80,
  210, 220; *see also* learning
efficiency and equality, 66
El Salvador, 194, 198
empirical evidence on growth and
  inequality, 67–74; human capital,
  distribution of, 73–4; Kuznets
  hypothesis, 66, 67–9, 81, 84;
  Kuznets hypothesis reversed, 69–72;
  land, distribution of, 72–3
employment, *see* labour
English language as *lingua franca*,
  30–1
equality, 66; *see also* inequality
Equatorial Guinea, 140, 141, 164
Eritrea, 140, 141, 308
Estonia: demography, 110, 112–15
  *passim*; economic performance, 95,
  96, 99, 102, 103, 105, 106, 107,
  108; state, 127, 128, 134, 137
Ethiopia, 28, 164, 308; investment
  and adjustment, 184, 186;
  stabilization and adjustment, 147,
  152, 154
ethnic conflict, *see* conflict
ethnicity, *see* race
EU (European Union), 25, 47, 51, 115
Europe, 69, 205, 243, 273, 314;
  culture, 16, 22, 25, 28, 29, 299, 300;
  GDP decline, 306; globalization, 33,
  35, 37, 38, 39, 43, 44, 45, 46, 47,
  51; tax revenue and government
  expenditure, 198; and transition,
  87, 113; *see also* Britain
European Bank for Reconstruction
  and Development, 274
exchange rates, 85, 269–70; and
  sub-Saharan Africa, 148, 150–1,
  309
exports, *see* trade

external sector and structural adjustment in sub-Saharan Africa, 151–4, 159–61, 166

external shocks, 152–4, 257, 259

external sources of financing investment-led adjustment, 120, 121, 183–92

'externalities', 50–1, 130

factor markets, 129–30

'fatal impact', 28

FDI (foreign direct investment), 33, 41, 50, 132; and Kazakhstan case study, 264, 271; and poverty reduction in China, 284, 291–2; and sub-Saharan Africa, 171, 187–92, 229; and Vietnam case study, 244, 248–9

Fields, G., 70

finance: deepening, overcoming barriers to, 212–14; *see also* capital; credit; investment; savings; taxation

financing investment-led adjustment, *see* external sources; internal sources

fiscal inequity in China, ending, 293

food, *see* nutrition

Fortuna, J.C., 205

France, 16, 35, 43, 198, 237–8

'free-rider' problem, 50–1

freedom, 21, 57, 61–2; negative, 252

Gabon, 164; classification, 139, 141; investment and adjustment, 184, 186, 188, 190, 196; stabilization and adjustment, 147, 152–3

Gambia, 140, 141, 147, 152, 164; investment and adjustment, 184, 186, 196; stabilization and adjustment, 147, 152

GDI (gender-related development index), 63

GDP (gross domestic product): and China case study, 282, 283, 289, 320; in HDI, 298; and income and growth, 74; and Kazakhstan case study, 259–60, 261, 264, 266, 269; and resource mobilization and enterprise development in

sub-Saharan Africa, 185, 187, 192, 200, 311; and structural adjustment in sub-Saharan Africa, 139, 141–2, 146–7, 149, 151, 160–1; and transition, 102–3, 127, 136–7, 306; and Vietnam case study, 11, 239–41, 244–6, 248; *see also* GNP

GEM (gender empowerment measure), 63

gender, 61, 62–3, 302; *see also* men; women

genocide, 28

Georgia: demography, 110, 112; economic performance, 96–106 *passim*; state, 136, 137

Germany, 2, 198, 273, 306

Ghana, 206, 308; firm size and mechanization, 9–10; investment and adjustment, 184, 186, 188, 190, 196, 217

Gintis, G., 78, 80

Global Strategy for Shelter, 220

globalization, 2–3, **33–52**, 181, 284; asymmetrical liberalization, 36–8; and cultural interchange, 27–30; and culture and development, 51–2; and economic space, 39–42; governance, global, 46–51; as new phenomenon, 34–6; state, squeeze on, 42–6

GNP (gross national product), 19, 127, 239; decline in importance, 18, 54, 55, 57; and human development, 57, 58, 59; and income and growth, 66–7, 78–80, 85–6; and sub-Saharan Africa, 185, 186–7, 190–1, 195–7, 198–9, 308; *see also* GDP

governance, global, 46–51

government, *see* state

gradual reform, 122–7

Grameen Bank case study, 214–15

Griffin, K., 55–6, 184–91 *passim*

group lending, 212–13

growth, economic, 33, 123; China's poverty reduction strategy, 289–92; and culture, *see* culture; human development promoting, 20–2; and inequality, *see* inequality and

growth, economic – *continued*
   growth; and Kazakhstan case
   study, 229–61, 269–70; and poverty
   reduction in China, 281–3,
   289, 291; promoting human
   development, 18–20; sources
   of, 16–18; state and, 24–7;
   and structural adjustment in
   sub-Saharan Africa, 139–44;
   and transition, *see* economic
   performance; and Vietnam case
   study, 239–47; *see also* structural
   adjustment
GSS (Global Strategy for Shelter), 220
guaranteed employment, 223–6, 233
Guasch, J.L., 213
Guatemala, 194, 198
Guinea, 164; classification, 140, 141;
   investment and adjustment, 184,
   186, 196, 209; stabilization and
   adjustment, 147, 152
Guinea-Bissau: classification, 140,
   141, 143; investment and
   adjustment, 184, 186, 188;
   labour, 163–4; stabilization and
   adjustment, 147, 148, 150, 152


Haiti, 237
ul Haq, Mahbub, 55–6, 61
HBEs (home-based enterprises), 83,
   202–3, 217–20
HDI (Human Development Index),
   57–8, 59–61, 136–8, 297
health care, 3, 19–20, 40, 55, 60, 64;
   in case studies, 246, 276, 295; in
   sub-Saharan Africa, 168, 174, 192,
   195; and transition, 130, 138
heterogeneity of informal sector in
   sub-Saharan Africa, 201–3
Hirschmann, A.O., 306
history, 27, 52
home-based enterprises, *see* HBEs
homicide, 114
homogeneous culture, 29
Hong Kong, 40
housing, 123, 132, 285; in
   sub-Saharan Africa, 202, 217–21,
   232–3; *see also* HBEs

human capital, 3–4, 17, 54; in case
   studies, 241–2, 246, 253–4, 265,
   295; distribution of, 73–4; and
   income and growth, 79, 83, 85; in
   sub-Saharan Africa, 157–8, 168,
   173–4, 192, 195, 221–6, 233;
   and transition, 130, 138; *see also*
   education; health; human
   development; nutrition
human development, 3–4, **53–65**,
   136–7; evolution, 55–6; impact
   63–5; Index (HDI), 57–8, 59–61,
   136–8; institutionalization, 61–3;
   and Kazakhstan case study, 165,
   176, 251–4; measurement, 56–61;
   origins, 53–4; and transition, 137,
   139; *see also* culture; human capital
*Human Development Reports*, 56, 57,
   61–3
Human Freedom Index, 61
Human Poverty Index, 60–1
*Human Resources Development*, 56
human rights, 21
Hungary: alternative reform strategies,
   116; demography, 109–15 *passim*;
   economic performance, 96, 98, 99,
   101, 102, 103, 105, 106, 107; state
   128, 131, 134–5, 137
Huntington, S., 300

Ickowitz, A.: on income and growth,
   4, **66–91**
identity, 31, 45
IFAD (International Fund for
   Agricultural Development), 144,
   205
ILO (International Labour
   Organization), 47, 55, 200, 201, 209
IMF (International Monetary Fund),
   7, 48, 49–50, 63–4, 264
imperialism, 28, 33, 194
import substitution, 154
imports, *see* trade
incentives: compatibility, 80; in
   Kazakhstan, 266–70; and structural
   adjustment in sub-Saharan Africa,
   167–70
income and growth, 4–5, **66–91**;
   country studies, 84–8; and culture,

income and growth – *continued*
16, 18–19; and human
development, 16, 18–19, 56–9, 65;
inequality and income poverty,
105–8; and Kazakhstan case study,
260–2; and output in transition,
101–5; policy implications, 88–91;
and poverty reduction in China,
281–5, 287; in sub-Saharan Africa,
138–41, 154; and transition, 95–7,
101–8, 109; and Vietnam case
study, 237, 238–40; *see also*
empirical evidence; GDP; GNP;
growth; inequality and growth;
poverty; theoretical explanations
India, 273; culture, 27, 28, 29;
globalization, 34, 36, 39, 44, 45;
income and growth, 12, 81, 82, 88;
resource mobilization and enterprise
development, 194, 221, 224, 225
Indonesia, 12; globalization, 44, 49;
resource mobilization and
enterprise development, 192, 194,
215–16; tax revenue and
government expenditure, 198; and
Vietnam compared, 237, 242
industry/industrialization, 83–4, 88,
124, 154, 256; and Vietnam case
study, 240–1, 244; *see also* growth;
small and medium enterprises;
urban areas
inefficiency, 145, 227
inequality, 59; and labour, 37–8; land,
79, 82–3; and politics, 22–3;
removal, *see* human development;
and transition, 105–8, 133; *see also*
poverty
inequality and growth, 22–4, 66–7;
and globalization, 39–42; and
income, *see* Kuznets; *see also*
empirical; income and growth;
theoretical explanations
infant mortality, 57, 262
inflation: and Kazakhstan case study,
256, 259–60, 263; in sub-Saharan
Africa, 144, 145–8, 309; and
transition, 99–100, 117, 127; and
Vietnam case study, 247, 249–50;
*see also* prices

informal sector in sub-Saharan Africa,
108–9, 200–8, 232
infrastructure, 130, 173, 175, 287;
*see also* transport
innovation and creativity, 26–7,
29, 31
instantaneous transition, *see* big bang
institutionalization of human
development, 61–3
institutions, market, creation of, 117
instrumental values of culture, 30–2
interest rates, 148–50, 268–9
internal sources of finance,
*see* domestic financing
International Bank for Environmental
Settlements suggested, 301
International Court of Justice, 2, 48
International Fund for Agricultural
Development, 144, 205
International Labour Organization,
*see* ILO
International Monetary Fund, *see* IMF
intrinsic values of culture, 30–2
investment and investment-led
growth, 76, 290; and culture, 17,
20–1, 23; foreign and official,
*see* FDI; IMF; ODA; and human
development, 20–1; in Kazakhstan,
263–6, 271; and resource
mobilization and enterprise
development, 181–2, 194, 230–2;
and transition, 104–5, 123; and
Vietnam case study, 241–5; *see also*
capital; savings
investment-led structural adjustment
in sub-Saharan Africa, 7–8, 139–78,
180–2, 208–30; commercialization
of state enterprises, 169–70, 177,
227–30; credit access and credit
markets, 209–12; education
and technical training, 221–3;
guaranteed employment
programmes, 223–6; housing as
productive asset, 217–21; *see also*
domestic financing; external
sources; structural adjustment;
targeted credit programmes
Iran, 25, 40, 45
Iraq, 25, 40, 45, 47, 300

Ireland, 44, 198
Islam, 29, 45
Israel, 25
Italy, 35, 198, 306, 314

Jain, S., 69, 70
Japan, 2, 84, 113, 314; globalization, 33, 35, 37, 49, 51; resource mobilization and enterprise development, 207–8; tax revenue and government expenditure, 198
Java, 215–16
'Jiangsu' Model, 132
joint liability, 213
joint ventures, 132, 246
*Journal of Human Development*, 63

Kaldor, N., 81
Kazakhstan, 117; demography, 110, 112, 114, 115; economic performance, 96, 97, 99, 102, 103, 104, 105, 106, 107; state, 129, 130, 131, 136, 137
Kazakhstan case study, 11, **251–80**; development objectives, 251–5; outcome of reform process, 259–63; poverty concepts and lines, 277–80; systemic reform, 255–9; *see also* revised strategy in Kazakhstan
Kenya, 308, 309; classification, 140, 141; firm size and mechanization, 9–10; informal sector, 200, 205–7; investment and adjustment, 171, 184, 186, 190, 196; labour, 163–4; stabilization and adjustment, 147, 152
Khan, A.R.: on China, 12, **281–96**
Knight, J., 55
Kosovo, 2
Kurdistan, 45
Kurds, 25
Kuwait, 40, 59
Kuznets, S., 66, 67–9, 81, 84; criticized, 69–72
Kyrgyzstan: demography, 110, 112, 113; economic performance, 96, 97, 99, 102, 103, 105, 106, 107; state, 127, 128, 136, 137

labour/employment, 19; creation, 55, 62, 265–6, 272–6; flow, *see* migration; and income and growth, 76–7, 87; and inequality, 37–8; and Kazakhstan case study, 254–5, 262, 265–8, 272–4, 275–6; mobility in China, 294–5; and poverty reduction in China, 285–6; and taxation, 43
labour/employment in sub-Saharan Africa, 175, 178; and adjustment through contraction, 163–6; asset creation and, 223–6; guaranteed, 223–6, 233; unproductive, 193
land (*mainly* redistribution and reform), 23, 65; in case studies, 247, 264–5, 271, 284, 291–2; commercialization, 264–5, 271; and income and growth, 72–3, 79, 80, 82–3, 84–5, 87–8, 90–1; rights, 131
language, 30–1
Latin America, 55, 314; culture, 24, 28; globalization, 35, 39, 40, 43, 45, 47; income and growth, 74–5, 78, 84–7 *passim*, 90–1; resource mobilization and enterprise development, 194, 202–5, 217–18, 220; tax revenue and government expenditure, 198–9; transition, 97, 107, 120; *see also* Central America
Latvia, 117; demography, 109, 110, 112–15 *passim*; economic performance, 96, 99, 102, 103, 105, 106, 108; state, 128, 136, 137
law, 2, 29, 48, 49, 258; and transition, 117, 121, 129, 130; *see also* crime
learning, 29, 32; *see also* education
legal system, *see* law
lending: group, 212–13; rates, 146–8, 150, 215, 216; *see also* credit
Lesotho, 164, 309; classification, 140, 141; investment and adjustment, 161, 184, 186, 196; stabilization and adjustment, 147, 152
Levy, B., 209
liberalization, 167; asymmetrical, 36–8; external capital, 120, 121; policy-induced, 35, 51; trade, 117–18, 247–9, 289–90; *see also* democracy; transition

Liberia, 154, 171
life expectancy, 20, 57, 58, 60; and
  case studies, 240, 262, 295; and
  transition, 5, 109–11; *see also*
  mortality
linkages, 207–8; indirect, 19–20
literacy, adult, 57, 58, 60, 246, 295
Lithuania: demography, 109, 110,
  112–15 *passim*; economic
  performance, 96, 99, 102–6 *passim*,
  108; state, 128, 133, 134, 135,
  137
living standards, *see* income; prices;
  purchasing power; quality of life
Livingstone, I., 207
loans, *see* credit; debt

Macedonia, 137; demography, 110,
  112, 113; economic performance,
  96, 99, 100, 102, 103, 105
McKinley, T., 56
macroeconomic reform: policy, 88–9;
  *see also* case studies; resource
  mobilization; structural adjustment;
  transition
Madagascar, 140, 141, 147, 153, 164;
  investment and adjustment, 184,
  186, 188, 190, 196
Maddison, A., 39
Malawi, 309; classification, 140, 141;
  investment and adjustment, 184,
  186, 189, 190, 196; labour, 164;
  stabilization and adjustment, 147,
  148, 153–4
Malaysia, 3, 192, 198, 237, 242
Mali, 140, 141, 147, 153, 164;
  investment and adjustment, 184,
  186, 189, 190, 196, 210
market economy, *see* transition
Marxism, 16
Mauritania, 140, 141, 147, 153, 164;
  investment and adjustment, 184,
  186, 189, 190
Mauritius, 59, 147, 153, 164;
  classification, 139, 140, 141, 143;
  investment and adjustment, 161,
  184, 189, 190, 196
measurement of human development,
  56–61

Mellor, J., 88
men, life expectancy of, 109–11,
  113–15; missing, 113–14
Mexico, 49, 85, 90–1, 198, 204–5,
  314; firm size and mechanization,
  9–10
Middle East, 59, 163, 300; culture, 25,
  26, 28, 29; globalization, 37, 39, 40,
  42, 44, 45, 47
migration, 44; from Africa, 309; and
  Kazakhstan case study, 259, 262;
  and poverty reduction in China,
  285, 286, 294–5; restricted, 36–8
minority groups, 25, 26–7
mobility of labour in China, 294–5
Moldova: demography, 110, 112, 113,
  114; economic performance, 96,
  97, 99, 102–6 *passim*; state, 126,
  137, 138
Mongolia, 56, 134, 136, 228–9;
  transition, 101, 107, 111, 112, 131,
  135, 137
monopolies, 100, 228–9, 258, 271;
  *see also* public sector
Morocco, 59
Morris, M.D., 57
mortality/death rates, 5, 111–12; in
  case studies, 240, 262, 265; infant,
  57, 262; *see also* life expectancy
Mozambique, 163–4, 171;
  classification, 140, 141, 143;
  stabilization and adjustment, 147,
  148, 153–4
multiculturalism, 25–7, 51–2
Myanmar, 300

Namibia, 164; classification, 139, 142;
  investment and adjustment, 161,
  196; stabilization and adjustment,
  147, 153
nationalism and nationality, 30;
  sub-nationalist politics, 3, 42–6;
  *see also* race; state
natural capital and resources, 16, 28,
  89; allocation inefficient, 145; and
  growth, 19–20; and Kazakhstan case
  study, 259, 264
needs, basic human, 55
negative freedom, 252

Nepal, 237
New Zealand, 36, 198
Niger, 164; classification, 140, 142, 143; investment and adjustment, 184, 186, 189, 190, 196; stabilization and adjustment, 147, 153–4
Nigeria, 308; classification, 140, 142; informal sector, 204; investment and adjustment, 161, 185, 186, 189, 191; stabilization and adjustment, 147, 148, 150, 153, 181–2
North Africa, 28, 59, 163; globalization, 39, 40, 42, 44
North Korea, 300
North–South relations, 62; colonialism, 28, 33, 194; *see also* FDI; ODA; trade
nutrition/food, 55; in case studies, 278–9; food-for-work schemes, 224; lack of, 4, 60, 154, 297; production, *see* rural areas; in sub-Saharan Africa, 168, 192, 195

ODA (official development assistance), 7, 49–50, 62; and case studies, 243, 244; and sub-Saharan Africa, 158–9, 171, 183–7, 230, 309, 310–11
OECD (Organization for Economic Cooperation and Development), 70; and resource mobilization and enterprise development, 184–91, 197; tax revenue and government expenditure, 198, 199
official development assistance, *see* ODA
oil, 129, 264, 266, 270
Okun, A., 66, 84
Olukoshi, A., 181–2, 204
open cultures, 29
Organization for Economic Cooperation and Development, *see* OECD
output, *see* growth

Pacific area, 39, 46
Pakistan, 3, 12, 25, 34, 44, 82
Palestinians, 44

Palmer, I., 310
Parker, S., 128
participation, 20–1, 201
pathology, *see* social pathology
Paukert, F., 68–9
peace-keeping forces, 49
pensions, 64, 276
Perotti, R., 71
Persson, T., 69–71, 75–6, 77
Peru, 199, 203, 217, 218, 219, 220
Philippines, 44, 218–19
physical capital, 16–17, 35, 40, 65; and case studies, 241–2; challenged, *see* human development; and income and growth, 82–3, 89–90; in sub-Saharan Africa, 174–5
Physical Quality of Life Index, 57, 58
Pieterse, J., 2
planned economies, *see* authoritarian regimes; transition
pluralism, 25–7, 51–2
Poland, 5, 237; alternative reform strategies, 116, 125; demography, 109, 110, 112–15 *passim*; economic performance, 95, 96, 99–103 *passim*, 105–8 *passim*; state, 128, 130, 131, 134, 137
police, 49
politics: and growth, 75–8; and inequality, 22–3, 75–8; 'of nostalgia', 30; *see also* democracy; sub-nationalist
pollution, 44, 130–1, 259
population, *see* demography
poverty, 85; and human development, 55, 60–1, 62, 63; Human Poverty Index, 60–1; and reform, *see* Kazakhstan; in sub-Saharan Africa, 139, 144, 151, 205, 233; and transition, 101, 105–8, 124, 135–8; *see also* credit
poverty reduction in China, 12, **281–96**; nature and causes of poverty, 281–6; strategy, 286–8; *see also* restructuring
PQLI (Physical Quality of Life Index), 57, 58
Prates, S., 205

prices, 298; and case studies, 247, 249–50; explosion in transition, 98–101; and Kazakhstan case study, 255–7, 259–60, 263, 266–70; in sub-Saharan Africa, 145, 148, 150–1, 166–9, 181; and transition, 95–7, 116, 121, 124–5, 130; *see also* inflation

primary products, *see* physical capital

principal agent problem, 227–8

private sector: in East Asia, 6, 199, 285; and human development, 64; in Kazakhstan, 258, 270–2; in sub-Saharan Africa, 9, 170, 171, 192–5, 231–2; and transition, 116, 118, 131; *see also* informal sector

privatization, *see* public sector privatization

procrastination, 122

profits, 22; of investment in human development, 20–1; in sub-Saharan Africa, 193, 195; tax on, 119

property relations and transition, 116–17, 131–5

Psacharopoulos, G., 74

public goods, 130; *see also* infrastructure; law

public sector/state-owned enterprises (*mainly* investment and expenditure), 3, 64; commercialization of, 7, 169–70, 177, 227–30; deficit, 100, 144; and income and growth, 75, 85–7; and Kazakhstan case study, 253–4, 256–9, 265, 271–4; and poverty reduction in China, 284, 285, 286–95; sale of, 229–30; and transition, 119, 127–30, 138; and Vietnam case study, 245–7

public sector/state-owned enterprises, privatization of, 119–21, 131–4, 257–9; in sub-Saharan Africa, 145, 176–7, 228–9, 234

public sector/state-owned enterprises in sub-Saharan Africa, 9–10, 173, 175–61, 231; domestic financing for investment-led adjustment, 195–200; inefficiency of, 227; privatization, 145, 176–7, 228–9,

234; structural adjustment, 144, 169–70, 173, 175–7

purchasing power parity, 58, 95–7

quality of life, 57, 58

race/ethnicity and racism: and culture, 25, 28, 30; globalization, 42–3, 45, 51; *see also* nationalism

Ram, R., 74

rapid reform, *see* big bang

reallocation, structural adjustment through, 155–7

redistribution, 55, 65; of land, *see under* land

reform, economic, *see* alternative reform; systemic transformation; transition

regional development and groupings, 47, 50; reducing imbalances in China, 292; *see also* CMEA; EU

religion, 29, 30

research and development, 54

resource mobilization and enterprise development in sub-Saharan Africa, 9–11, **179–234**; *see also* domestic financing; external sources; informal sector; investment-led structural adjustment

resources, *see* natural capital

restructuring China's poverty reduction strategy, 288–95; fiscal inequity, ending, 293; and growth, economic, 289–92; households, distributing benefits to, 290–1; labour mobility, 294–5; need for, 289; regional imbalances, reducing, 292; rural economy, growth of, 291–2; targeting improved, 295; urban unemployment, 293–4

Reunion, 142, 147, 308

revenue, 19–20, 127–9; *see also* taxation

revised strategy in Kazakhstan, 263–77; employment creation on public works, 272–4; investment-led growth, 263–6; macroeconomic stabilization, 263; prices and

revised strategy in Kazakhstan –
*continued*
incentives, 266–70; small and
medium private enterprises, 270–2;
social protection and residual
poverty, 275–7
Robinson, S., 68
Rodrik, D., 70, 71, 72, 76–8
Romania: demography, 109–13
*passim*; economic performance, 96,
99, 101, 102, 103, 105, 106; state,
127, 128, 131, 137
Ross, D., 80, 85, 86–7
'rubbing' of cultures, 27–8
rural areas and agriculture, 23, 262;
and China case study, 6, 281–5,
287, 290–2, 293; and income and
growth, 81–3, 85; and resource
mobilization and enterprise
development, 193–4, 222, 224–6;
and structural adjustment in
sub-Saharan Africa, 144, 154–7,
164–6, 169, 170, 173; and
transition, 122, 129; and Vietnam
case study, 6, 240–1, 244, 247, 248
Russian Federation: alternative reform
strategies, 117, 125; demography,
108–15 *passim*; economic
performance, 95, 96, 97, 99–107
*passim*; state, 127, 128, 129, 133–4,
137, 138
Rwanda, 2, 309; classification, 140,
141, 143; informal sector, 206;
investment and adjustment, 185,
186, 189, 191, 196; labour, 164,
166; stabilization and adjustment,
147, 153, 154

Sabot, R., 80, 85, 86–7
'safety net', 64, 158, 183
Saith, A., 69
São Tomé and Principe, 140, 142, 185
savings, 22; and case studies, 244, 266,
290, 320; and income and growth,
4–5, 81–2, 83, 90; in sub-Saharan
Africa, 171–3, 192–5, 214–16, 226,
231, 309, 316; *see also* investment
Schultz, T.W., 54
Schumpeter, J., 299

science, *see* technology and science
Scitovsky, T., 84
Sen, A., 21, 53, 57
Senegal, 59, 164; classification, 139,
140, 142; investment and
adjustment, 185, 186, 191, 196
sequential reform strategies, 122–7
Serbia, 2, 45
services, 35–6, 260; and Vietnam case
study, 240–1, 244
Seychelles, 139, 142
'shock therapy', *see* big bang
shocks, exogenous, 152–4, 257, 259
Sierra Leone, 164; classification, 140,
142; investment and adjustment,
185, 186, 196; stabilization and
adjustment, 147, 148, 150, 153
simultaneous reform strategies,
*see* big bang
Singapore, 3, 22, 40, 51, 198
slavery, 36
Slovakia: demography, 110, 112;
economic performance, 96, 98, 99,
100, 102, 103, 105, 106; state, 131,
137
Slovenia, 137; demography, 110, 112,
113, 114; economic performance,
96, 99, 100, 102–6 *passim*
small countries, 42, 45–6, 139, 142–3,
165; *see also* sub-Saharan Africa
small farms, 23
small and medium enterprises, 23, 65;
and income and growth, 83–4, 88;
in Kazakhstan, 270–2, 273; in
sub-Saharan Africa, 9–10, 170, 172,
175, 205–8, 232; and transition, 6,
118, 122–3
smuggling, 2, 43, 109
social pathology and transition, 5,
114–16; *see also* crime
social policy and social services, 119,
124, 253–4, 275–7; *see also*
education; health; human
development; nutrition
Somalia, 140, 142, 154, 164, 171, 308
South Africa, 36, 164, 171;
classification, 139, 142;
stabilization and adjustment, 147,
153–4

South America, *see* Latin America
South Asia, 4, 63, 273, 297; culture, 25, 27, 28, 29; globalization, 34, 36, 39, 42, 44, 45; income and growth, 74, 75, 81, 82, 84, 88; resource mobilization and enterprise development, 194, 209, 214–15, 217, 219, 221, 224, 225
South-east Asia, 25, 26, 120, 159; delinking, 300; globalization, 40, 43, 44, 46, 47, 49, 51; human development, 56, 58, 60, 64, 65; income and growth, 74–5, 85–6; and Kazakhstan compared, 266, 272; resource mobilization and enterprise development, 171, 182, 192, 194, 215–16; tax revenue and government expenditure, 198, 199; transition, *see under* Vietnam; and Vietnam compared, 237, 242
South Korea: culture, 22, 23, 27; globalization, 40, 49; income and growth, 84, 85–6, 87–8; resource mobilization and enterprise development, 192, 199, 207–8; tax revenue and government expenditure, 198
sovereignty, decline of, 2
Soviet Union, former/Commonwealth of Independent States, 3, 33, 65, 298, 301, 306; alternative reform strategies, 116, 118, 120, 121, 126; demography, 111; economic performance, 95–103 *passim*; globalization, 34, 38, 40, 44, 49; and Kazakhstan, 251, 256–7; Soviet bloc countries, *see* Central and Eastern Europe; state, 127, 132, 138; and Vietnam, 238–40, 243, 247, 248
Spain, 28, 29, 45, 69, 198
Squire, L., 69, 71–3, 77, 79, 80, 91
Sri Lanka, 44, 217, 219
stabilization, 55, 64; in Kazakhstan, 263; in sub-Saharan Africa, 144–51, 180–1; and transition, 122, 129; *see also* structural adjustment
state: and culture, 24–7; -owned enterprises, *see* public sector; squeeze on, globalization and,

42–6; in sub-Saharan Africa, 167–8, 170–8, 233; Westphalian model of, 2, 3; *see also* revenue; taxation
state, role in transition, 127–38; poverty, inequality and human development, 135–8; property relations, 117, 131–5
Stiglitz, J., 78, 211
Strassman, W.P., 202–3, 218, 219, 220
strategic visions, *see* culture; globalization; human development; income and growth
structural adjustment and human development, 55, 64; *see also* stabilization; Vietnam case study
structural adjustment in sub-Saharan Africa, 7–8, **139–78**; external sector, 151–4, 159–61, 166; incentives, 167–70; investment, 145, 149, 151–4, 159, 161–2, 167–8, 170–8; labour and adjustment through contraction, 163–6; purposes, 181–2; stabilization, 144–51; state, role of, 170–8; three alternative paths of, 155–9; *see also* investment-led structural adjustment
sub-nationalist politics, *see under* nationalism
sub-Saharan Africa, 4, 97, 297; globalization, 35, 39, 40, 41–2, 45; income and growth, 74, 84; *see also* resource mobilization; structural adjustment in sub-Saharan Africa
Sudan, 24, 44, 140, 142, 154, 165, 171, 185, 308
suicide, 114–15
sustainability, 59
Swaziland, 139, 142, 165, 185, 186
Sweden, 198, 243, 306
Switzerland, 25, 46, 198
Syria, 25, 45
systemic transformation and economic reform: in Kazakhstan, 255–9; *see also* resource mobilization; structural adjustment; transition

Tabellini, G., 70–1, 75–6, 77
Taft Morris, C., 68

Taiwan, 23, 40; income and growth, 82, 83–4, 87–8; resource mobilization and enterprise development, 199, 208
Tajikistan, 137; demography, 109, 110, 115; economic performance, 12, 96, 97, 99, 100, 102, 103, 105
Tanzania, 165, 308; classification, 141, 142; informal sector, 206; investment and adjustment, 185, 186, 197, 209; stabilization and adjustment, 147, 148, 153
targeted credit programmes in sub-Saharan Africa, 212–16; case studies, 214–16; overcoming barriers to financial deepening, 212–14; policy implications, 216
taxation: and case studies, 247, 275, 285, 293; global, 62; and income and growth, 75, 76; and labour, 43; and migrants, 38; negative income, 50; and structural adjustment in sub-Saharan Africa, 167; and transition, 119, 130
technology and science, 27–9, 31, 35, 290; transfer, 188; *see also* communications; transport
terms of trade, 284; in sub-Saharan Africa, 151–4; *see also* trade
Thailand, 43, 85, 192, 198, 237, 242
theoretical explanations of growth and inequality, 75–84; economic theory, insights from, 78–84; political insights, 75–8
Togo, 165; classification, 141, 142; investment and adjustment, 161, 185, 186, 189, 191, 197; stabilization and adjustment, 147, 153
Tokman, P., 202
tourism, 123
township and village enterprises, 132
trade, international, 33, 35, 41–5, 49, 87; and Kazakhstan case study, 260, 269, 270; liberalization, 117–18, 247–9, 289–90; and poverty reduction in China, 284, 289–90; and sub-Saharan Africa, *see* external sector; tariffs, 51; and Vietnam case study, 245, 247–9

trade unions, 204
'trade-offs', 22–4, 66–7
training, *see* education
transformation, *see* systemic transformation
transition to market-oriented economy, economic policy during, 5–7, **95–138**, 306; sequence of reform, 126–7; seven sets of essential reforms, 117–20; *see also* alternative reform strategies; case studies; economic performance during transition; state, role in transition; structural adjustment
transnational cultures, 25
transport, 27–8, 34, 35
Tritt, G., 128
Turkey, 25, 45
Turkmenistan, 122; demography, 110, 112; economic performance, 96, 97, 99, 102, 103, 105, 106, 107; state, 128, 129, 136, 137
TVES (township and village enterprises), 132

U hypothesis, *see* Kuznets
Uganda, 165, 309; classification, 141, 142; investment and adjustment, 161, 171, 185, 186, 195, 197; stabilization and adjustment, 147, 148, 153
Ukraine, 44, 117; demography, 109–15 *passim*; economic performance, 95, 96, 97, 99–106 *passim*, 108; state, 127, 128, 137, 138
UNCDP (UN Committee for Development Planning), 55–6, 57, 59–63
UNDP (UN Development Programme), 261, 287, 297, 301; and sub-Saharan Africa, 139–41, 185, 205; and transition, 106, 108, 115, 137
unemployment: in China, 293–4, 296; in Kazakhstan, 262; in sub-Saharan Africa, 165, 223–4
United Kingdom, 35, 47, 113

United Nations, 205; Department of Economic and Social Affairs, 102–3; Educational, Scientific and Cultural Organization (UNESCO), 47; Global Strategy for Shelter, 220; and globalization, 47–9, 50; UNICEF, 55, 297; *see also* UNCDP; UNDP
United States, 22, 238, 273, 306, 314; globalization, 35, 36, 37, 38, 41–3, 47–8, 49; tax revenue and government expenditure, 198
urban areas: and Kazakhstan case study, 262; and poverty reduction in China, 281–7, 290, 292, 293–4; in sub-Saharan Africa, 166, 222, 225; and Vietnam case study, 241, 243; *see also* industry
Uruguay, 199, 205
Uruguay round, 35
Uzbekistan, 27–8, 56, 122; demography, 110, 111, 112, 115; economic performance, 96, 97, 99, 102, 103, 105, 106, 108; state, 127, 128, 131, 136, 137

Van der Hoeven, R., 310
Vietnam, 84, 159, 182; globalization, 40, 46; human development, 56, 58, 60, 65; and Kazakhstan compared, 258, 266; structural adjustment, *see* Vietnam case study; transition, 5–6, 99–101, 107, 111, 112, 122–3, 125, 128–9, 131, 132, 137
Vietnam case study, 11, **237–50**; capital accumulation, 241–4; data credibility, 244–6; nature and sequence of reforms, 246–50; structural change, 240–1
violence, *see* conflict
voting behaviour, 75–8

war, *see* conflict
water, safe, 60
wealth, 22; *see also* income
Weiss, A., 78, 211
Westphalian model of state, 2, 3

Williamson, J.G., 86
women: in case studies, 262; conference on, 62–3; credit for, 216, 232; discrimination against, 59; education, 80, 210, 220; illiterate, 60; liberation of, 23–4; in sub-Saharan Africa, 169, 210, 216, 222, 232
Woo, W.T., 128
World Bank: and globalization, 39, 48, 49–50; and human development, 55, 56, 63–4; and Kazakhstan case study, 260, 263–4, 274, 275; and poverty reduction in China, 281, 287, 320; and sub-Saharan Africa, 7, 139–42, 144, 146–7, 152–3, 164–5, 196–9, 307–8; and Vietnam case study, 237, 238, 249
*World Development Indicators*, 64; and transition, 96, 106, 110, 112, 128
*World Development Report*, 56, 238, 260; and sub-Saharan Africa, 140–2, 146–7, 152–3, 164–5, 196–9; and transition, 99, 105–6, 134, 137
WTO (World Trade Organization), 47, 51

Yemen, 28
Yugoslavia, former Republic of, 2, 44, 116, 128; demography, 110, 112; economic performance, 96, 98, 100, 101, 102, 103, 106
Yunus, M., 214

Zaire, 141, 142, 165, 171, 185, 186
Zambia, 165, 308, 309; classification, 141, 142; investment and adjustment, 161, 185, 186, 197, 217, 219; stabilization and adjustment, 147, 148, 150, 153
'Zhejiang Model', 132
Zimbabwe, 165, 309; classification, 139, 141, 142; investment and adjustment, 185, 186, 197; stabilization and adjustment, 147, 148, 153